D1608029

Assessing Democracy in Latin America

Russell H. Fitzgibbon

Assessing Democracy in Latin America

A Tribute to
Russell H. Fitzgibbon

EDITED BY

Philip Kelly

WestviewPress
A Division of HarperCollinsPublishers

Copyright © 1998 by Westview Press, A Division of HarperCollins Publishers, Inc.

Published in 1998 in the United States of America by Westview Press, 5500 Central Avenue, Boulder,
Colorado 80301-2877, and in the United Kingdom by Westview Press, 12 Hid's Copse Road, Cumnor
Hill, Oxford OX2 9JJ

A CIP catalog record is available from the Library of Congress.
ISBN 0-8133-3444-6

The paper used in this publication meets the requirements of the American National Standard for Permanence of Paper for Printed Library Materials Z39.48-1984.

10   9   8   7   6   5   4   3   2   1

Contents

Tribute to
Russell H. Fitzgibbon

Russell H. Fitzgibbon, to whom this book is dedicated, was born in Columbus, Indiana, on June 29, 1902. He died January 8, 1979, in Sun City, Arizona, survived by his wife, Irene, a son, Alan Lee, and a married daughter, Katherine Irene Lilly. In political science, he earned his B.A. degree at Hanover College, his M.A. at Indiana University, and his Ph.D. from the University of Wisconsin. Fitzgibbon joined the UCLA faculty in 1936, rising to the full professor rank in 1948. He chaired his department, was a longtime director of the UCLA Center for Latin American Studies, and held the chairmanship of the Academic Senate's statewide budget committee, one of the most influential faculty committees in the University of California system. From 1964 until his retirement in 1970 he taught at the University of California, Santa Barbara.

His principal books include *Cuba and the United States*; *Uruguay: Portrait of a Democracy*; and *Latin America, Past and Present*. Professor Fitzgibbon was compiler of William Allen White's "Forty Years on Main Street," a collection of the most noteworthy editorials of that Emporia, Kansas, native, and was editor of *Global Politics* and *Constitutions of the Americas*. He held fellowships from the Social Science Research Council, the Doherty Foundation, and the Fulbright organization, and under the auspices of these organizations he studied, taught, and researched in Spain, Italy, Uruguay, and Argentina. In 1956–1957 he served the Western Political Science Association as president.

Beyond these professional statistics, however, Russell Fitzgibbon touched the lives of many. In a personal letter to me, David Myers wrote:

> Fitz cared about his graduate students and went out of his way to give them every opportunity to pursue the career they had chosen. He was intolerant of sloppy scholarship. His criticism was devastating—but never personal. Fitzgibbon did more than any professor in my graduate school career to cure me of any tendency toward unsubstantiated generalizations.

His colleague on the democracy survey, Kenneth F. Johnson, in a June 23, 1997, letter to me, remembered Fitzgibbon as "a shy and retiring person":

> I spent quite a bit of time with him as a graduate student, visited him later on in the hospital in Santa Barbara, and he always came to my guest lectures when he was in

semiretirement in Arizona and he taught part time at ASU. Whenever he invited me I went to see him but it was always in a very formal atmosphere. Not that there was anything cold about him, quite the contrary. What Fitz had was integrity! His word was good. He tried to stay out of office politics at UCLA which were tearing the place apart. Fitz was a good friend, shy, brilliant, reclusive but still able to exude warmth. He guided me through a difficult dissertation process. I have never heard anyone say anything but the very best in reference to Russell Fitzgibbon.

In a *Latin American Research Review (LARR)* "Communications" of 1980, Ken Johnson likewise wrote this moving tribute to Russell Fitzgibbon. I felt it appropriate to reproduce here:

> Many will remember Russell Fitzgibbon as the scholar who pioneered a controversial "measurement of democracy" scheme, one that will be the subject of social science debate well into the future. Others may remember him also as their mentor, the teacher who produced more Latin American specialists, perhaps, than any other scholar of note within political science and related disciplines. He was as towering in his scholarly influence as he was diminutive physically and shy. If you knew Fitz (as some of us called him, affectionately) you would remember his probity above all else, but your list of outstanding character traits would surely include these: a penetrating intellect with a historical bent (of which he was very proud), a compassion for the disadvantaged, his commitment to frugality, his generous giving of himself to the cause of interdisciplinary higher education within the Latin American area studies context, and his dedication to the cause of political democracy and human decency in Latin America. He would have cheered the collapse of the Nicaraguan tyranny, and, at once, been appalled by the human carnage that was paid to accomplish it.
>
> Fitzgibbon had an enormous influence on the way we study Latin America, at least here in the United States. His background included a doctorate from Wisconsin, field service with the Office of Inter-American Affairs during part of World War II, Special Observer status with the OAS during the early 1960s, and long distinguished service thereafter as professor and researcher at UCLA and UCSB. His legion of articles appeared in most of the major political science and interdisciplinary journals in this country and he authored books on Cuban-U.S. relations, Colombia, and Uruguay. His interests and abilities transcended several disciplines, and his legacy, the Image-Index measurement scheme cited above, will continue to stir healthy debate and valuable reflection in academic and policymaking circles. Fitz believed that a "democratic weathervane" was visibly operative throughout Latin America and he devised a method, albeit, and by his own admission, an imperfect one, for reflecting scholarly images of the ongoing patterns of Latin American political change. The most recent of the Image-Index studies appeared, in part, in the Summer 1976 issue of this review; the expansion and further elaboration of Fitzgibbon's work that is now being planned may perpetuate his influence well onto the coming century.
>
> Those of us who trekked the worn steps of Haines Hall to Russell Fitzgibbon's tiny UCLA office will not forget the gentle humanist with his shortly cropped and brilliantly white hair, and his disarming shyness that one came to regard fondly in the course of time. My first encounter with the venerable Fitzgibbon occurred in the spring of 1959, when I made a bus trip from San Diego to Westwood just to see him

and to promote my status as an aspiring graduate student. Fitz generously arranged to see me on a Saturday morning and promptly, but gently, chided me for having written "greatful" in my letter requesting an interview. That was our first meeting.

Nearly twenty years later, on the occasion of our last meeting, in February 1977 at Arizona State, Fitz chided me again, still gently, over my being too tough on the Latin Americans for what he had just heard me describe in my presentation as their chronic governmental ineptitude and corruption. I had recently returned from living amidst the final throes of the second (or third?) Perón era. Fitzgibbon always had a warm heart, and urged me to follow him along that charitable path. If there was even an ounce of good left in something, even in Perón, he was disposed to seek it out; and for that I had to admire him.

But what impressed me even more at our last meeting was that Fitzgibbon, then in visibly poor health, had driven alone through the Phoenix traffic to hear me speak. Such loyalty to his graduates was another trait that all of us who knew him and bene-fitted from his teaching will not forget. Fitz stayed with us; yet few of us would say that we ever really knew him well at the personal level. And therein lay much of his charisma and charm, one's captivation by his elusive, fleeting glimpse of a smile when he bent a furrowed brow toward you and listened intently to your statement of belief or dilemma. Fitz then debated silently, and using few but well-measured words, he shared with you his own doubts, hopes, and wisdom.

Russell Fitzgibbon leaves us a rich heritage of optimistic compassion, professional integrity, and a magnificent corpus of scholarly works, all of which he married com-fortably with a cautious dose of healthy cynicism. His legacy is a formidable standard of excellence by which to judge ourselves, and academia worldwide will be much the better because Fitz was here. For those of us who felt we knew him he will always re-main the shy, frail, but powerful humanist, who sought to persuade others to em-brace a positive faith as he did, and who seemed always to view his professional man-date as a sacred trust.

We appreciate the permission granted by the *LARR* publishers to reprint this Communication, originally published in *LARR* 15, no. 2 (1980):219–220.

Preface

In journeys about Asunción as an international observer of the 1989 Paraguayan presidential and congressional elections, I remember having fascinating discussions with other team members about what factors might bring democracy to Latin America. Some suggested greater expenditures on education. Others viewed economic and social development to be the most vital to good government. I cited the importance of progressive leadership. A few pessimistic souls predicted a continuation of dictatorship, or cycles of dictatorship and democracy, based upon a culture and environment in the south that prevents an open and effective representative government.

What seems to have prevailed among us at the time was the consensus that democracy is multicausal and multidimensional, stemming from and a result of many sources under variegated conditions. That conclusion became, indeed, a format for this book, the insight that we could not force the concept and the practice of democracy to fit a narrow model of analysis.

The recent experience among our neighbors shows that since the early 1980s most of Latin America clearly is in transition toward various forms of democratic government. In fact, among the twenty original republics, only Cuba remains autocratic, although democracy in some other states may be precarious. Why this transition? We could posit such ingredients as generational cycles; reaction against military corporatism; the ending of the Cold War; maturing social, economic, and political systems; the emergence of a democratic culture; a new educated cadre of leaders; and an assortment of other factors.

Reflecting an interest in the explanation, the inspiration for this book comes from the surveys taken over a fifty-year period concerning democracy in Latin America. In 1945 UCLA Professor Russell Fitzgibbon asked a panel of ten North American Latin Americanist scholars to rank the original twenty Latin American countries according to various criteria that define democracy. His panelists were reassembled in 1950, and others have participated in the survey every fifth year since. This year's project, with ninety-six scholars involved, marks the fiftieth year of the Fitzgibbon study; a total of eleven democracy rankings have by now been tabulated. The tables in Chapter 1 show these rankings.

Although our focus is upon a broad view of Latin American democracy more than upon the Fitzgibbon surveys themselves, the chapters have been volunteered by distinguished writers from among the recent survey panelists, and we are using the fifty years' worth of data as a comparative benchmark for our analyses of what factors might be responsible for democracy. I will introduce the topic of democracy in the first chapter, giving the background of the Fitzgibbon survey as well as certain statistical calculations that isolate pertinent variables associated with the ordinal democracy rankings of the twenty Latin American states. Four general chapters follow, likewise providing descriptions and analyses of democracy, and the next fifteen chapters report on democratic conditions in specific regions and countries: Mexico, Central America as a whole, Costa Rica, Nicaragua, the English-speaking Caribbean, Cuba, Haiti, the Dominican Republic, Venezuela, Ecuador, Peru, Chile, Uruguay, Argentina, Paraguay, Bolivia, and Brazil.

As recognized scholars, all of the authors have published extensively on the topics they have chosen for this edition. In the University of Kansas library alone, I located 119 books authored by the twenty-one contributors. Several have led Latin American studies centers, others have served in governmental and private consulting agencies, and many have held positions of leadership in national and regional Latin Americanist scholarly associations.

I asked the authors to recount progress toward democracy from their own research perspectives, paying special attention to recent happenings in Latin America and generalizing about causes for democracy where appropriate. Otherwise, no set chapter format was demanded. Accordingly, each author set his or her own course. I felt this approach encouraged the sort of spontaneity and flexibility most suitable to an understanding of the many contrasting processes of democracy and, above all, to a tribute most suited to Russell H. Fitzgibbon.

Philip Kelly

Part One

Special Topics in Addressing Democracy in Latin America

Philip Kelly, in the initial pages of Chapter 1, "Measuring Democracy in Latin America: The Fitzgibbon Index," sketches the evolution of the democracy survey, the instrument itself, and the several changes attempted by Fitzgibbon, Ken Johnson, and himself. He debates next the panel method itself for assessing democracy, asking how accurate scholars' images are—and whether other data sources are an improvement. Table 1.1 shows democracy standings for the eleven individual Fitzgibbon polls (1945 through 1995). Table 1.2 sums the eleven polls and provides a cumulative ranking of democracy among the twenty Latin American republics, showing Costa Rica and Uruguay holding the highest positions, Paraguay and Haiti the lowest. In a later portion of the chapter, Kelly locates two variables, daily newspaper circulation per capita and tractors per hectare, that appear to correlate strongly to democracy rankings in Latin America.

How relevant are political parties to the process of democratization in Latin America? John D. Martz addresses this question in Chapter 2, "Studying the Ebb and Flow of Political Parties in the Quest for Democracy." Noting comparisons amongst the Fitzgibbon country rankings and criteria since 1945 that reflect the dynamics of national politics, Martz sees a gradual strengthening of parties through the 1980s until the present decade, when a "deconstruction" tendency has set in, caused by weakened ideologies and doctrines, by closed and rigid party organizations, and by inattentive leadership and apathetic publics. He calls for a "rediscovery of those elements and characteristics by means of which the parties may play the important role [in supporting democracy] that they themselves have identified."

In Chapter 3, "Social Democracy in Latin America," Robert L. Peterson first outlines the slow evolution of Latin American social democracy after World War II, its ties to the Socialist International and to European social democratic (SD) parties, and the resistance to social democracy from the United States. Other forces also retarded SD expansion, primarily the weakness of capitalism in Latin America and, to a lesser extent, the noncooperation of Communists (although Peterson contests this latter assertion). Nonetheless, the author predicts the eventual rise of social democracy, reflective of its vital and necessary role of "restructur[ing] and stabiliz[ing] democracy in Latin America," as lower-class and worker political actors and broadly based popular alliances begin to integrate themselves more assertively in a new era of Latin American politics.

In Chapter 4, "Democracy and the Environment in Latin America," Kathryn Hochstetler and Stephen Mumme argue that democracy has not guaranteed successful results for any contemporary group that aims to construct new policy. Rather, the rules of political access and participation are merely equalized. Hence, implementation of environmental protections into law has been mixed and has proven to be as successful within authoritarian regimes in Latin America as within democratic regimes. In fact, these authors conclude that "barring the deepening and strengthening of democratic institutions, today's environmentalists are apt to place their bets on society instead of the state as they strive to advance environmental protection nationally and regionally."

The final chapter of this first part, that of Martin Needler, "Assessing Democracy Then and Now: A Personal Memoir," poses the question: Can democracy be continuously measured over a fifty-year span when the Latin American political and economic setting has shifted so dramatically? Needler begins by equating democracy with "development," but he then presents his conclusion that violence and other disruptions during transitions to higher levels of development could well indicate progress toward democracy and, in turn, bring outcomes that parallel U.S. interests in the region. This latter convergence in reality occurred in the foreign policies of the Bush and subsequent administrations. But democracy operates differently now than during the 1960s and 1970s (the period underlying Fitzgibbon's original survey design), for instance, in the advent of massive campaign monies that "could induce democratic electorates to vote against their own interests" and in the growth of capitalistic "conglomerates without national identity, perpetually downsizing their workforces and being intermittently looted by financial speculators." Consequently, Needler completes his argument by rejecting the Fitzgibbon survey itself for being outdated; for, he asks, how can democracy be measured amid "the porous boundaries between constitutional rulers, fabulously wealthy capitalists, and drug-dealing gangsters?"

Chapter One

Measuring Democracy in Latin America: The Fitzgibbon Index

PHILIP KELLY

In 1945 Professor Russell Fitzgibbon, a UCLA political scientist, asked a panel of ten distinguished U.S. scholars to rank the twenty Latin American republics according to a set of criteria that he felt would measure the extent of democracy in each of the countries. Fitzgibbon added brief "paragraphs of analysis and explanation [to supplement] each of the criteria in order that the semantic reactions of those being polled might be as nearly uniform as possible" (1951:518). He selected these fifteen standards for defining and assessing democracy:

1. An education level sufficient to give the political processes some substance and vitality
2. A fairly adequate standard of living
3. A sense of internal unity and national cohesion
4. A belief by a people in their individual political dignity and maturity
5. An absence of foreign domination
6. Freedom of press, speech, assembly, radio, and so on
7. Free elections; honestly counted votes
8. Freedom of party organization; genuine and effective party opposition in the legislature; legislative scrutiny of the executive branch
9. An independent judiciary; respect for its decisions
10. A public awareness of the collection and expenditure of governmental funds
11. An intelligent attitude toward social legislation; the vitality of such legislation as applied

12. Civilian supremacy over the military
13. A reasonable freedom of political life from the impact of ecclesiastical controls
14. An attitude toward and development of technical and scientific government administration
15. An intelligent and sympathetic administration of whatever local self-government prevails

Panelists rated the republics separately according to each of the criteria, and the poll results were tallied later with different weights assigned to the various measures. Kenneth Johnson and I, who directed the later polls, eliminated this weighting variance in the 1980 survey and in subsequent surveys, giving equal emphasis to all of the criteria.

Fitzgibbon replicated his canvass at regular five-year intervals through 1970, adding more panelists than his original ten but maintaining the original fifteen criteria (Fitzgibbon 1967, 1956a, 1956b). Kenneth Johnson became associated with the project in 1960 (Fitzgibbon and Johnson 1961), and he assumed sole authorship for the 1975 and 1980 polls after Fitzgibbon's retirement (Johnson 1982, 1976). As the present director of the project, I assisted Johnson in 1985 (Johnson and Kelly 1986) and administered the instrument alone for the two most recent evaluations, those of 1991[1] and 1995. In total, eleven democracy surveys, taken every five years and all adhering to Fitzgibbon's original format, have been conducted since 1945. (See Table 1.1 for ordinal rankings of the eleven surveys.) Ninety-six panelists responded to the 1995 survey.

Although the panel approach is not an impeccable indicator of comparative democracy levels among states, it does have the advantage of utilizing a group of distinguished area specialists for measuring Latin American democracy, making biases or mistakes in individual evaluations less significant. Other data sources, such as voter turnout, for example, or number of elections, as well as social and economic variables, may be no more dependable in studying trends in democracy than the collective and continuous ratings of scholars. The tabulation's longevity and repetition also add to its strength. Two primary disadvantages of the survey method lie in the probable inability of most panelists to accurately assess all of the criteria for all of the countries and in the possibility of the indicators themselves not reliably reflecting the processes of democracy. I will have more comment on these points later.

Over the years, Fitzgibbon, Johnson, and I made a variety of attempts to improve the survey; most were tried only once and not kept. Fitzgibbon added a "provision for indicating self-assessment as to the respondent's familiarity with both [Latin American] states and [the fifteen] criteria" (1967:155). Dropping this technique from later investigations, he lamented: "Perhaps there are deductions to be made from such [familiarity] distribution[s] but the author shies away in timidity from making them" (159).

TABLE 1.1 Fitzgibbon-Johnson Index: Specialists' View of Democracy in Latin America, 1945–1995

Country	Rank											Totals
	1945	1950	1955	1960	1965	1970	1975	1980	1985	1991	1995	
Argentina	5	8	8	4	6	7	5	11	3	5	4	7
Bolivia	18	17	15	16	17	18	17	18	16	14	14	18
Brazil	11	5	5	7	8	10	9	12	9	6	6	8
Chile	3	2	3	3	3	2	11	14	14	4	3	4
Colombia	4	6	6	6	7	6	4	4	5	8	7	5
Costa Rica	2	3	2	2	1	1	1	1	1	1	1	1
Cuba	6	4	7	15	18	13	7	6	10	12	16	9
Dominican Republic	19	19	19	18	14	14	13	8	13	11	13	15
Ecuador	14	9	10	10	12	9	14	9	11	9	9	11
El Salvador	13	14	11	12	11	8	10	16	17	19	17	13
Guatemala	12	10	14	13	13	13	15	17	19	18	19	16
Haiti	16	18	17	19	20	20	20	20	20	20	20	20
Honduras	17	15	12	14	15	16	16	15	15	17	18	17
Mexico	7	7	4	5	4	5	3	3	6	7	8	3
Nicaragua	15	16	18	17	16	17	18	7	12	10	11	14
Panama	8	11	9	11	10	11	12	10	9	15	10	12
Paraguay	20	20	20	20	19	19	19	19	18	16	15	19
Peru	10	13	16	9	9	11	8	5	8	13	12	10
Uruguay	1	1	1	1	1	3	6	13	4	3	2	2
Venezuela	9	12	13	8	5	4	2	2	2	2	5	6

In one instance, Fitzgibbon tested for possible correlations between certain social, cultural, economic, demographic, and political variables and the democracy
rankings of his 1960 and 1965 surveys (1967:159–164). But he could not raise significant statistical relationships. Fitzgibbon observed a "bunching" tendency, with
many states not moving far from their original rank positions throughout the extended survey period (1967:165–166). Johnson and Kelly encountered these clus-
terings as well.

As an additional scale, Johnson culled five "select criteria" from the fifteen
(1976:131–132) that he felt might more directly indicate a political side of
democracy, that is, freedom of press, speech, radio, and so on (the sixth of the criteria listed earlier); free elections (seventh); freedom of political organization
(eighth); an independent judiciary (ninth); and the degree of civilian supremacy
over the armed forces (twelfth). Since this extension correlated highly with the
complete scale, Kelly dropped this approach in 1991. Johnson and Miles Williams
established a "Power Index" that drew upon panelists' responses to questions relative to the impact of certain groups within the Latin American political milieu
(1978:37–47). Likewise, Johnson and Kelly in the 1985 poll added an "Attitudinal
Profile of [panel] Respondents" that never saw publication. Neither the Power Index nor the Attitudinal Profile were carried over to later surveys.

Evaluation of the Fitzgibbon Survey

The strength of the Fitzgibbon survey of Latin American democracy, with its life
span of fifty years, derives first from its longevity. Few other quantitative projects
in academia can boast of this half-century perspective. Consequently we indeed
possess ample data to test possible democratic trends and causes; to study the impact of social, economic, demographic, and other variables on democracy since
the 1940s; and to isolate the particular forces most influencing constitutional regularity within the various republics.

Another contribution of Fitzgibbon's approach comes from its panel-of-ex-
perts technique. We solicit data from the collective mind of leading scholars, a
technique that for the most part provides a reflection of political conditions in
Latin America. "Specialists are likely to introduce desirable nuances and bal-
ances," asserted Fitzgibbon, "which are impossible in the use of cold statistical information, even of the most accurate sort" (1967:135). Trusting other statistics,
for example, on "civilian rule," "voter turnout," "political maturity," "disorder,"
and the like could prove at least as difficult in definition and in reliability of collection.

In addition, we have in Fitzgibbon the built-in advantage of both a conceptual
definition of democracy, rendered in his fifteen criteria, and a feasible opera-
tionalization process, provided in his panel approach. The data that result have
the value of being quantifiable, in both ordinal and interval levels of measurement, so that statistical testing can be utilized. Finally, the whole procedure pos-

sesses a dynamic quality, staying open to adjustment and likewise remaining available for replication by others.

To be sure, there are also drawbacks in the survey. Do the panel experts in fact exhibit clear enough insights into the true character of Latin American politics and government? Can they all show close familiarity, for instance, with the Haitian court system, the Bolivian mode of government administration, and the like? Most students of Latin American democracy cannot possibly keep attentive to all events in the south, nor do our panelists. Instead, they must rely upon common images, some of them certainly imperfect, having originated in the North American media or in memories of past Fitzgibbon surveys. Furthermore, because a large percentage of panelists have classified themselves as "liberal" (as seen in the 1985 Johnson-Kelly Attitudinal Profile), certain governments, for example, in Cuba and Nicaragua, may rank higher on the scale and others lower as a reflection of scholars' biases. We admit to these deficiencies; yet we respect the survey approach and readily accept its data as reflective of general democracy comparisons among Latin American states.

Further, rarely does one see recent mention of the Fitzgibbon polls in the extant literature on democracy and Latin American politics. Nor do the polls seem to have influenced public policy or to have contributed to scholarship about democracy itself, despite the fact that the survey panelists, recognized scholars in the field themselves, have regularly participated in the project.

Nonetheless, for the next survey, in the year 2000, the panelists and I will probably update the survey instrument. We may eliminate certain of the rating criteria, among these, for example, the fifth, "An absence of foreign domination," and the thirteenth, "A reasonable freedom of political life from the impact of ecclesiastical controls." Other criteria may be altered and new ones may be added. The larger Caribbean countries might be included and the process for selecting panelists changed. Fortunately, the dynamic quality of the Fitzgibbon method allows for this flexibility.

Analysis of the Survey

Table 1.2 shows the cumulative democracy standings for the eleven Fitzgibbon surveys in Table 1.1 when the ordinal positions of each country are summed and the totals ranked.[2]

Costa Rica ranks first, having scored first since the 1965 poll. Uruguay stands some way below in second place. A clustering arises among the next five republics, only seven points separating Mexico from Argentina. Cuba and Peru match each other's positions, as do Panama and Ecuador, and a bunching appears among Nicaragua, the Dominican Republic, and Guatemala. Paraguay and Haiti occupy in the lowest positions of the survey.

Shifts in rank positions among the Latin American states for the eleven surveys, similar to Fitzgibbon's earlier bunching phenomena, showed countries consis-

TABLE 1.2   Cumulative Democracy Rankings, 1945–1995

1. Costa Rica (16)	11. Ecuador (116)*
2. Uruguay (36)	12. Panama (116)*
3. Mexico (59)	13. El Salvador (148)
4. Chile (62)	14. Nicaragua (157)
5. Colombia (63)	15. Dominnican Republic (161)
6. Venezuela (64)	16. Guatemala (163)
7. Argentina (66)	17. Honduras (170)
8. Brazil (88)	18. Bolivia (180)
9. Cuba (114)*	19. Paraguay (205)
10. Peru (114)*	20. Haiti (220)

*Rank ties broken by summations of raw scores for all years except 1970.

tently positioned on the democracy spectrum over the years. For my testing of variance as shown in Table 1.3, I have used the measures of range, or the difference between highest and lowest rankings, and standard deviation, or the extent of spread of republics from their mean average position on the scale.

Based on the extent of variation from poll to poll, three groupings of countries appear in the table. A first group, with lower ranges and standard deviation scores, includes Costa Rica, Paraguay, Bolivia, Colombia, Haiti, Mexico, Honduras, and Ecuador. All of these except Ecuador rated either among the four highest on the scale or among the four lowest. With the exceptions of Bolivia and Colombia, none experienced major revolutions or prolonged domestic turmoil that could translate to major shifts in position from survey to survey. In the cases of Bolivia and Colombia, political disruptions came soon after Fitzgibbon initiated his surveys, and both nations restored their own brands of stability soon after the mid–1950s.

A second group contains four republics, Guatemala, Argentina, Brazil, and Panama, which hold a middle position on the democracy standings between seventh and sixteenth position. Reflective of moderate variation, these nations weathered alternating periods of stable regimes and political change.

The final group, Cuba, Peru, Chile, Uruguay, Venezuela, Nicaragua, the Dominican Republic, and El Salvador, represents the highest level of shifting. All suffered major transformations during the survey years, when democracies alternated with dictatorships and revolutions replaced subjugation. The status of each, frequently changing, ranged from second (Uruguay) to fourteenth (Nicaragua) and fifteenth (the Dominican Republic).

Changes in democratic images by panelists seem to reflect governmental and political transitions within the respective countries. Costa Rica, Colombia, Mexico, Ecuador, Bolivia, Paraguay, and Haiti continued in much the same stance throughout the fifty years, whereas Cuba, Peru, Chile, Uruguay, Nicaragua, Venezuela, El Salvador, and the Dominican Republic underwent significant political transformations. For evaluating democracy in Latin America, it appears that

TABLE 1.3 Country Variations in Rank Orders from All of the Surveys

Country	Highest Rank	Lowest Rank	Average Position	Range	Standard Deviation
Costa Rica (1)	1	3	1.5	2	2.2
Uruguay (2)	1	13	3.3	12	11.4
Mexico (3)	3	8	5.4	5	4.0
Chile (4)	2	14	5.6	12	15.2
Colombia (5)	4	8	5.7	4	4.3
Venezuela (6)	3	13	5.8	11	12.9
Argentina (7)	3	11	6.0	8	7.3
Brazil (8)	5	12	8.8	7	7.6
Cuba (9)	4	18	13.0	14	17.3
Peru (10)	5	16	10.4	11	9.6
Ecuador (11)	9	14	10.5	5	6.2
Panama (12)	8	15	10.5	7	5.9
El Salvador (13)	8	19	13.5	11	10.9
Nicaragua (14)	7	18	14.3	11	11.7
Dominican Republic (15)	8	19	14.6	11	11.6
Guatemala (16)	10	19	14.8	9	9.6
Honduras (17)	12	18	15.5	6	5.2
Bolivia (18)	14	18	16.4	4	4.7
Paraguay (19)	15	20	18.6	5	5.3
Haiti (20)	16	20	19.1	4	4.6

the panelists' survey decisions and the historical events of Latin America tended roughly to agree.

I assembled an array of forty variables[3] to test for possible statistical linkages between the democracy positions of Table 1.2 and certain national traits of the twenty Latin American republics. Enlisting the Spearman rho coefficient as a preliminary barometer of associational strength, I found that these variables revealed very high bivariate correlations with the democracy rankings:

- telephones per capita *.82*
- urbanization *.80*
- electrical energy consumption per capita *.80*
- general energy consumption per capita *.78*
- physical quality-of-life index *.77*
- daily newspaper circulation per capita *.76*
- tractors per hectare *.74*
- public education expenditures per capita *.73*
- gross national product per capita *.73*

All nine variables indicate a strong positive correspondence between democracy and socioeconomic status. On a per capita basis, countries exhibiting more telephones, higher electrical energy and general energy consumption, greater daily newspaper circulation, higher public education expenditures, and a higher gross national product appeared consistently more democratic. Likewise, urban states with higher literacy and life expectancy and lower infant mortality rates ranked higher on the democracy scale.

To carry these comparisons further, I grouped all nine of the variables together within a stepwise regression procedure in order to assay a more concise prediction of democracy. This technique possesses the advantages of controlling for spuriousness and of reducing the number of variables for simpler utilization. From this endeavor, an R^2 score of .84 arose, consisting of the two variables, *daily newspaper circulation per capita* and *tractors per hectare*. Consequently, these two variables accounted for 84 percent of the variance among the nine traits in forecasting democracy in Latin American. Democracy seems to be present wherever substantial per capita newspaper circulation and strongly mechanized or tractor-oriented agriculture exist.

At first glance, the appropriateness of both indicators, newspaper circulation and tractor usage, seems to be justified. The first shows social maturity and political openness, the second urbanization and agricultural reform. Still, for more certain explanations we probably need further probing into both variables; we probably need to ask, for example, what sorts of newspapers were surveyed and how peasants were compensated for the agrarian development. This, however, is beyond the scope of this chapter.

Other variables appeared less relevant to democracy. Racial homogeneity, population density and growth rates, size of territory and population—all demographic traits—showed minimal correlation. Military variables likewise showed no special linkage to constitutionalism. With the exception of public education expenditures per capita, as noted earlier, other educational traits did not sway democracy ratings. As in Fitzgibbon's findings (1967:161), political variables, too, did not correlate strongly with the democracy rankings.

Conclusions

The Fitzgibbon panel technique offers a unique study of democracy in Latin America, its findings contributing, we feel, to an understanding of the political processes in the region since the middle 1940s. My analyses of the cumulative surveys seem to indicate that democracy is amenable to being measured through the personal images and references of specialists and that democracy appears to be associated with certain of the social and economic qualities of Latin American nations.

If, in fact, democracy, for whatever reason, connects closely to higher levels of newspaper circulation and to agrarian mechanization, then could not this correlation offer insight into policy directions for citizens and government administrators? Leaders both within and outside of the United States who favor democracy and its political benefits would profitably heed and support this point.

Notes

1. I missed 1990 because of my teaching and researching in Paraguay as a Fulbright scholar. Kenneth Johnson encouraged me to resume the surveys upon my return despite the one-year lag.

2. I summed ordinal figures instead of interval figures because of the subjective nature of both democracy and the Fitzgibbon panel method. The ordinal fit seemed to me more appropriate. In addition, I could not locate interval figures for the 1970 index.

3. Most variables come from Kurian 1979. Although a newer edition of this book exists, I chose the first edition because it approximated the midpoint of the total survey period.

Bibliography

Fitzgibbon, Russell H. 1967. Measuring political change in Latin America. *Journal of Politics* 29:129–166.

_____. 1956a. A statistical evaluation of Latin-American democracy. *Western Political Science Quarterly* 9:607–619.

_____. 1956b. How democratic is Latin America? *Inter-American Economic Affairs* 9:65–77.

_____. 1951. Measurement of Latin-American political phenomena: A statistical experiment. *American Political Science Review* 45:517–523.

Fitzgibbon, Russell H., and Kenneth F. Johnson. 1961. Measurement of Latin American political change. *American Political Science Review* 55:515–526.

Johnson, Kenneth F. l982. 1980 image-index survey of Latin American political democracy. *Latin American Research Review* 19:193–201.

_____. 1976. Scholarly images of Latin American political democracy in 1975. *Latin American Research Review* 11:129–140.

Johnson, Kenneth F., and Philip L. Kelly. 1986. Political democracy in Latin America 1985: Partial results of the image-index survey. *LASA Forum* 16:19–22.

Johnson, Kenneth F., and Miles W. Williams. 1978. *Democracy, Power, and Intervention in Latin American Political Life: A Study of Scholarly Images.* Tempe: Center for Latin American Studies, Arizona State University, Special Studies no. 17.

Kurian, George Thomas. 1979. *The Book of World Rankings.* New York: Facts on File.

Chapter Two

Studying the Ebb and Flow of Political Parties in the Quest for Democracy

JOHN D. MARTZ

During the half-century since Russell H. Fitzgibbon undertook his first reputational survey of democracy in Latin America, dramatic and far-reaching changes have occurred in the region's politics. Much the same is true of political parties. At times they have been relegated to a position of negligible importance, if not virtual irrelevance for the interplay of politics in the region. On other occasions they have been in the forefront of both informal and institutional efforts to build and to nourish an enduring condition of democratic rule. Certainly there has been an ebb and flow across the years, as my chapter title suggests. In a similar fashion, the reports of those social scientists participating in the Fitzgibbon undertaking have shown shifting perceptions of the parties and the degree of influence they have exercised. Their assessments of the extent of party-related democratization have also varied over time, as might be expected, and the rankings of the individual nations have also fluctuated. Though none of this is startling on the face of things, there is ample justification for a broad reconsideration as the twenty-first century approaches. As my contribution to an overview that at the same time does homage to the pioneering research by Fitzgibbon—some of which extends well beyond his effort to measure dimensions of Latin American political change over time—let me raise and assess some basic aspects of the parties.

My intention is not to offer an all-encompassing theoretical or analytic treatment in a few pages. Such an effort dictates a book-length effort, one that would necessarily incorporate the study of such crucial elements as doctrine and ideology, organization and structure, leadership, candidate selection, and policymaking. Furthermore, attention would unavoidably be devoted to the symbiotic relationship of the parties with the patterns forged through historical-cultural perceptions of legitimacy, the boundaries established by constitutionalism, the constraints of electoral regulation, and a host of additional forces.

Consequently this modest chapter will focus on two particular issues: The first, derived from qualitative studies of the recent and contemporary periods, will range across the nations in commenting on the state of political parties across the five decades, with particular attention to those countries receiving the most positive democratic evaluations by respondents to the survey. The second will look more closely at the two criteria most applicable to the parties: free party organization and free elections. Fitzgibbon conceived of the former as based upon "genuine and effective party opposition in a legislative arena that permits scrutiny and/or challenge of the executive branch of government." Free and popular elections quite simply meant "impartial rules impartially applied, no voter intimidation, and honest voting procedures."[1]

The totality of resultant findings will be more than purely intuitive, drawing as they will on Fitzgibbon's empirical evidence. The data he gathered, although by no means fully testable and subject to mathematical verification, at the same time should reflect prevailing scholarly opinion about the evolving state of democracy and the relative significance of political parties. For the sake of taxonomic convenience and of imposing a degree of order to my discussion, I will proceed in chronological fashion. Logically opening the review with the initial surveys, I will first consider the 1945–1960 period, years of relatively marginal party activity in much of the region.

Four separate attempts to measure democracy and political change were undertaken during this time span. During the next two decades Latin America experienced basic and drastic shifts from predominantly democratic systems to the era of bureaucratic authoritarianism and then back, with a resuscitation of civilian rule and constitutional legitimacy. The third period, running from the close of the 1970s and the opening of the 1980s to the present, enjoyed a recrudescence of democratic government, spurred on and stimulated in no small part by a host of competitive modernizing parties bearing a conjunction of characteristics much different from those observed during the earlier, more traditionalist era. By way of conclusion, I will venture into speculative territory by projecting and anticipating some of the impending challenges to political parties and their linkage to the entire process of democratization that is presently so widely articulated in the literature. Throughout this intellectual voyage, I will be guided by the course of actual events as well as by the perceptions and evaluations of the respondents to Russell Fitzgibbon's successive inquiries.

The Initial Surveys (1945–1960)

As World War II drew to a close, historical circumstances paved the way for a movement toward democracy, at least in formal institutional terms. This raised the possibility that Latin American political parties might be about to assume a heightened role. If so, it would indicate a shift in degree and kind, for up until 1945 only a limited number of nations possessed anything resembling a truly meaningful history or presence of political parties. Furthermore, those parties were with few exceptions eminently traditionalist organizations that largely eschewed mass membership, were less than sympathetic to extensive civic participation, and lacked systematic political doctrine or ideology. The leadership most often came from the upper echelons of society, and even where electoral systems permitted extensive suffrage the influence of the middle and popular sectors was relatively slight. Thus even those nations perceived in the 1945 Fitzgibbon survey as being most democratic were not particularly notable with regard to our two analytic categories: free party organization and free elections. Both the raw scores and the adjusted scores agreed on the ordering of countries according to the norms established for the study of democracy and trends over time. Uruguay led the way, followed in order by Costa Rica, Chile, Colombia, and Argentina. However, even in these five the party systems were often both unsettled and unhealthy.

Uruguay and Chile were the major exceptions. The former was marked by the biparty hegemony of Colorados and Blancos within a system dating from the ideas and influence of José Batlle y Ordoñez early in the century. However, the peculiarities of the electoral system distorted the position of the parties, while the Colorados stood undefeated at the polls for decades. The Chilean parties, because of the durability of the Radicals, the Conservatives, and the Liberals, along with the vocal participation of the Socialists and the Communists in a quasi-parliamentary setting, came closer than the parties of any other Latin American nation in constituting a major force in the promotion of democracy.

The remaining members of the "top five" in 1945 differed in important ways. In Costa Rica, the second-ranking democracy, the role of the military had admittedly been diminished, and periodic elections supported the notion of governmental legitimacy. Yet the contests were largely between representatives of rival groupings of the socioeconomic elite. The highest tier of leadership was sparse, as suggested by the multiple presidencies of such figures as Cleto González Víquez and Ricardo Jiménez Oreamuno. Only in 1940, with the election of Rafael Calderón Guardia, did the oligarchic rule of the coffee barons begin to diminish. However, there were no political parties per se in the country. This contrasted with the Colombian situation, where Conservatives and Liberals traced their origins back to 1848–1849. Nevertheless, both were elitist-dominated groups in which the nation's socioeconomic leadership vied with one another for power and tended to see politics as a zero-sum game. The Conservatives had monopolized power from the early 1900s until the 1930s, when hegemonic control shifted to the Liberals. Elections were controlled by those in power rather than reflecting a true popular choice, and by the mid-1940s the entire system was showing deterioration, which exploded with the unprecedented riots and demonstrations of the *bogotazo* in April 1948. The fifth-ranked country in 1945, Argentina, was emerging from more than a decade of Conservative rule, followed by military intervention and the initial appearance on the national scene of Colonel Juan Domingo Perón.

Even if the 1945 rankings of democratic nations were seemingly inconsistent with the primitive condition of most party systems, this is not necessarily a gross misjudgment on the part of the survey respondents. Rather, it reflects the prevailing political reality along two basic dimensions. For one thing, democracy as broadly defined and understood at that time was neither deep-seated nor fully appreciated in the region, a fact that had in fact been underlined in the survey. Of the fifteen variables, free elections ranked ninth and free party organization tenth. Clearly, neither was viewed as among the most critical for the evolution and implantation of meaningful democracy in Latin America, at least as perceived by North American eyes. It is also worth noting that only ten individuals participated in the 1945 evaluation and that only two had a particular interest in the study of parties.[2] The survey was also distributed prior to the immediate postwar period, when a host of military dictators and strongmen were ousted as the winds of democracy blew across the hemisphere after the defeat of the Axis powers and with the touting of the "four freedoms" of the Allied war effort.

At the same time, interpretative claims of postwar democratization, upon reflection, were exaggerated. The examples were not numerous and by no means proved to be durable. For example, in Venezuela there was a brief period of strong reformist party-based rule from 1945–1948, but in 1948 this so-called *trienio* gave way to a full decade of military dictatorship. In Peru the same three years saw the first meaningful entry to electoral office in years by the American Popular Revolutionary Alliance (APRA)—although the party was prohibited from competing for the presidency—but the party was closed down by military intervention in 1948. Colombia was meantime slipping further toward one-party hegemonic dictatorship in the wake of the *bogotazo;* Peronism in Argentina was daily more authoritarian and oppressive; and only in Brazil was civilian-elected government on the upswing, after the 1945 removal of Getulio Vargas.

The overall record, then, was not particularly encouraging, and this was confirmed by the 1950 survey. The ranking of democratic countries again had Uruguay first, followed in order by Chile, Costa Rica, Cuba, and Brazil. Costa Rica's short-lived but hard-fought civil war doubtless explained its drop from second. Cuba, which in 1945 had been sixth, rose as its competitive democratic system was maintained. Argentina understandably dropped from the top five, while the seeming stabilization of civilian rule and party competition in Brazil carried it from eleventh in 1945 to fifth in 1950.[3] The experts also downgraded even further the variables relating to parties: free party organization fell from tenth to fourteenth of fifteen, while free elections went from ninth to fifteenth and last in the 1950 survey.

Over the next decade the perceptions of Fitzgibbon's experienced observers were not significantly altered. In 1955 the overall positioning vis-à-vis democracy was Uruguay, Costa Rica, Chile, Mexico, and Brazil. The appearance of Mexico, ranked seventh in both 1945 and 1950, is surprising, but it moved into the top five because Cuba moved lower: Cuba suffered in the rankings as a result of the Batista dictatorship, which replaced the island's competitive party system in 1952. The 1955 assessment was based on the views of an expanded number of respondents—now doubled to twenty—of whom five had substantial interest in political parties.[4]

Five years later the country ranking was once again headed by Uruguay, followed in order by Costa Rica, Chile, Argentina, and Mexico. Colombia was sixth and Brazil seventh. The recovery of Argentina presumably responded to the 1955 ouster of Perón. Mexico remained an anomaly; otherwise there is no need for further explanation. More important, however, the party-related variables had risen in the eyes of the respondents. Thus free party organization rose from fourteenth in 1950 and 1955 to seventh in 1960; free elections in turn moved up from fifteenth (and last) in 1950 and twelfth in 1955 to fifth in 1960. The domination of authoritarianism during much of the 1950s in Latin America gradually gave way, although the expanding family of Fitzgibbon respondents was less alert to developments than it might have been. Whereas the 1955 survey had included twenty participants, by 1960 the number had grown to forty, some ten of whom had concentrated their research interest on the parties.[5]

The Middle Years (1960–1980)

The decade of the 1960s was at first regarded as marking the successful advent to Latin America of true democracy, accompanied by the powerful stimulus of modern political parties.[6] Tad Szulc of the *New York Times* had argued in a widely read work that the historical era of the dictator was passing in favor of civilian democratic government (Szulc 1959). He presented biographical treatments of a host of recently departed strongmen, such as Fulgencio Batista of Cuba, Marcos Pérez Jiménez in Venezuela, Colombia's Gustavo Rojas Pinilla, Manuel Odría in Peru, and of course Juan Domingo Perón. Others who left power as victims of assassin's bullets were Rafael Leonidas Trujillo of the Dominican Republic and Nicaragua's Anastasio Somoza García. Yet there were asymmetries as well as systemic complications in a number of cases. Perón had fallen in 1955, to be followed by years of endemic instability and periodic military intervention in Argentine politics; Odría of Peru had voluntarily left power in 1956 after completing his regular six-year constitutional term and would soon return as the head of the major political party; Batista's departure heralded the Marxist dictatorship of Fidel Castro, although, to be sure, only a few observers anticipated this outcome at the time; Trujillo's assassination was followed by several years of turmoil, civil strife, and, in 1965, the direct intervention of over 20,000 U.S. troops; and the legacy of Somoza was inherited and continued by members of his family, through his sons Luis and the younger Anastasio, until the historic fall of the dynasty in 1979.

The advent of the 1960s, then, did not usher in as sweeping a change from dictatorship to democracy as many observers suggested. At the same time, it is obviously true that a number of longtime authoritarian political players had left the field of action. Furthermore, one could readily recognize and identify the continuing emergence of political party systems and the parties themselves, which were either coming into being nationally or were being transformed from traditional to modern status. Certainly this was true of those social democratic movements taking shape and in several cases winning national power, such as the Partido Liberación Nacional (PLN) in Costa Rica, Acción Democrática in Venezuela, the Partido Revolucionario Dominicano in the Dominican Republic, and Honduras's Partido Liberal. In Bolivia the Movimiento Nacionalista Revolucionario extended the domination it had seized in 1952 until its founder Víctor Paz Estenssoro was overthrown, along with an internally factionalized party, in November 1964. Peru's APRA, and its internationally recognized caudillo Víctor Raúl Haya de la Torre, who was denied apparent electoral victory by the military in 1962, would remain marginalized for two more decades in the most recent episode of its long and tortuous history. Hemispheric Christian Democratic movements were also on the rise, and before the close of the 1960s they would win electoral victories and assume power in Chile and Venezuela. They also gained a modicum of influence in Peru, while in El Salvador they moved against enduring oligarchic rule under the guidance of José Napoleon Duarte, although they did not achieve until the 1980s.

The Fitzgibbon survey of 1965 was at least moderately responsive to such changes in the field. Uruguay as always was identified as most democratic, although this time being tied by Costa Rica (they were listed as 1 $\frac{1}{2}$ in the published rankings). The latter had long since put behind it the civil strife of 1948, and José Figueres with the PLN bestrode the nation's political scene (although his party lost power in 1958 as the consequence of an internal split, and after returning in 1962 it was to be defeated again in 1966). Chile, where Eduardo Frei had become Latin America's first Christian Democratic president in 1964 by defeating a Marxist coalition while the traditional parties continued to dissolve, retained the third position that it had occupied from 1955 on. Mexico, which had been fifth in 1960, returned to its 1955 position of fourth. More interesting, Venezuela, which had been ranked twelfth and thirteenth during the dictatorial years of the 1950s before rising to eighth place in 1960, entered the top five. Presumably its post-1958 stabilization, notwithstanding Trujillo-inspired rightist military threats and a major Marxist insurrection, along with the competitive vigor of its newly shaped party system, encouraged respondents to register this positive evaluation. As to the fifteen specific criteria, free party organization retained its 1960 ranking of seventh. Freedom of speech, which had been fifth, was joined in a tie by the criterion of social legislation (which in 1955 and 1960 had been respectively fourth, then eighth).[8]

By the 1970s the survey, at this point written up by Kenneth F. Johnson, who had previously worked with and sometimes coauthored articles with Fitzgibbon, was pulling together no fewer than eighty participants to register the scholarly image of political democracy in Latin America. The 1975 rankings, affected by the interventionist onslaught of so-called bureaucratic-authoritarian forces—which were felt across the Americas but which were most controversially and oppressively antidemocratic in Uruguay, Argentina, and Chile—proved less than insensitive. Both Uruguay and Chile left the top five; Uruguay dropped to number six and Chile to eleven in the 1975 index. Costa Rica predictably assumed first place, followed by Venezuela. The remainder were, in order, Mexico, Colombia, and Argentina. Five years later Costa Rica was against first, Venezuela second, Mexico third, and Colombia fourth. Argentina, given the post-Peronist chaos and the military return to power, was only eleventh, whereas Peru moved from eighth in 1975 to fifth in 1980. Its return to the constitutional path with the election of Fernando Belaúnde Terry, more than a decade after he had been bodily removed from the presidency by the armed forces, may have been influential, although the ranking nonetheless seems at least mildly puzzling.

In any event, given the conditions of the nations in question, along with broader hemispheric patterns, it cannot be denied that the period was one of flux in which a number of new or revivified forces were impinging upon political systems and the quest for democracy. The 1980 data also documented the experts' growing conviction that the parties were becoming a fundamental base on which democracy might be erected. Indeed, some of the individual rankings were less predictable than might have been foreseen. For free party organization, Venezuela had vaulted into first place, closely followed in the raw scores by Costa Rica. The remainder of the top five included in order Colombia, Peru, and the Dominican Republic. The experts recorded a similar opinion in terms of free elections; Costa Rica narrowly led Venezuela, followed in order by Colombia, Peru, and the Dominican Republic. The two leaders were natural, given the competitive character of civilian party politics in each. Costa Rica and Venezuela had both evolved a dominant two-party system, although the latter in particular also displayed a number of minor parties. Regularized elections had occurred without interruption in Costa Rica since 1953 and in Venezuela since 1958. The ranking for Colombia was also eminently understandable, with the traditional hegemony of the Liberals and Conservatives as deeply rooted as ever following the transition away from the all-inclusive two-party monopoly mandated for sixteen years through the power-sharing Frente Nacional arrangement that dated from 1958.

The listings of both Peru and the Dominican Republic were surprising. In the former, as mentioned above, the withdrawal of the military after a dozen years in power came only in 1980. The process had first produced elections for a constituent assembly, after which the drafting of a new constitution led to the competition that returned Fernando Belaúnde to the presidency. At that time the APRA could truly be classified as a modern, well-organized party—notwithstanding internal repercussions following the death of Haya de la Torre, who had founded, shaped, and decisively guided the party for some six decades. The APRA's competitors, including Belaúnde's Acción Popular, were still attempting to organize into entities that were more than mere electoral conglomerates. As for the Dominican Republic, electoral stability of a sort had set in; for specialists participating in the 1980 exercise, the positive assessment could be rationalized by the 1978 defeat of Joaquín Balaguer at the polls. To be fair, there was no way of anticipating that as late as 1996 Balaguer would be occupying the presidency and powerfully influencing electoral politics when he was about to turn ninety years of age. However, the configuration of political parties in 1980 was weakly articulated, and Balaguer only reluctantly accepted his defeat and stepped aside under severe pressure from both Jimmy Carter in Washington and Carlos Andrés Pérez in Venezuela.

The justification for including Peru and the Dominican Republic in the top five, then, must be seen in negative terms as a commentary on the weakness of political democracy at the close of the 1970s. Such old standbys as Chile and Uruguay, not to mention Argentina and Brazil, still just missed positive assessments because of their continuing bureaucratic authoritarianism. That respondents were hard pressed in composing their rankings for party organization and free elections is seen by the fact that after the top five in 1980, the next two countries on each of the two lists of criteria were Ecuador and Mexico. Yet we recall that Ecuador had only returned to constitutional government at the close of the 1970s in a diffuse and disorganized multiparty competition in which the outgoing military exercised firm veto power over candidates of whom it disapproved. As for Mexico, the long official domination of the Partido Revolucionario Institucional (PRI)was a simple continuation of conditions that had prevailed for many years. All of this confirmed the decline of political parties and the dilution or elimination of free electoral competition during the heyday of bureaucratic authoritarianism in the hemisphere. This was inevitably destined to change, although the extent of the transition was unimagined as Latin America entered the two final decades of the twentieth century.[9]

The Renaissance of Political Parties (1980–)

The unparalleled transition toward democratic government, at least in formal and legalistic fashion, had begun when the Ecuadoran military withdrew from power and returned to their barracks in 1978.[10] Within two years the Peruvians had followed suit, and events followed a similar path across the Americas. By the close of the 1980s civilian government had been restored in Argentina, Brazil, Chile, and Uruguay. The trend toward at least a modicum of formalistic, electorally based democratization would appear in Central America, most notably El Salvador and Guatemala. Not even Paraguay was immune, as the seemingly indestructible personalist rule of General Alfredo Stroessner disintegrated and disappeared with his ouster in February 1989. In Haiti the book on the Duvalier dynasty was closed out in 1986 when "Baby Doc" (Jean-Claude Duvalier) fled to Paris, although Haiti was and remains far removed from true democracy, let alone party competition. At the risk of overstating the significance and profundity of the movement toward democracy across the hemisphere—something about which too many scholars prematurely voiced rash and ill-informed overgeneralizations[11]—the political context was one in which political parties were encouraged to flex their organizational muscle and to accept unqualified responsibility for the course of events in their respective nations. All of this was reflected in the three most recent surveys.

Of these, the images produced in 1985 are indicative of the shifting hemispheric patterns of political democracy. The overall assessment of Latin American democracy by country found Costa Rica and Venezuela once again in the lead. Argentina placed third, presumably based on the rapidity with which civilian rule was reestablished under the Radicals and Raúl Alfonsín. Uruguay followed as fourth, with Colombia completing the top five. Peru had fallen back to eighth while Mexico stood sixth. The rankings for our particular criteria are revealing and are largely consistent with an intuitive analysis of the political state of events in Latin America at that point. Regarding party organization, Venezuela was first and Costa Rica second. The next three were Colombia, Argentina, and Peru. Once again it was the placement of Peru that might seem questionable. It was followed by Mexico and then by a redemocratized Uruguay. One must ask whether party organization in Peru, where its history had been negligible except for the APRA, could compete with the reestablished Uruguayan pattern. Be that as it may, the ranking for free elections was perhaps less subject to debate. Venezuela and Costa Rica were once more in the vanguard; this time the *ticos* (that is, Costa Ricans) were first. Third was Argentina, closely followed by Colombia and then by Peru, which in 1985 experienced its second successive free election in history.

By the time of the 1991 survey, the presence of democratizing elements was even more evident to the respondents. Overall assessments by nation were familiar; once more, Costa Rica and Venezuela occupied the two leading positions. Uruguay moved up from fourth to third, while Argentina slipped from third to fifth. Chile, with General Augusto Pinochet at last out of the presidency, was restored to its pre-1973 image in vaulting from fourteenth to fourth. The 1991 data also showed the highest scores on party organization for Costa Rica, followed by Venezuela. Argentina apparently impressed the panelists with its transition from Alfonsín and the Radicals to Carlos Menem and the Peronists, thus coming in third. Next came the newly democratized Chileans in fourth place, and Colombia completed the top five. Uruguay was very close behind the Colombians. The 1991 findings, however, in a sense represented a midway point for summarization of the post-1980 pattern of expert responses. The 1995 findings, the most recent, merit a closer look in considering the parameters of contemporary Latin American democracy. They mirror a number of qualitative changes that occurred during the interim following the 1991 survey.

Several of these changes are directly relevant to this inquiry. First and foremost was the deterioration of Venezuela's parties, one of several critical manifestations of that nation's profound political and socioeconomic crisis. Two failed military uprisings in 1992 helped to undermine President Carlos Andrés Pérez, who was subsequently forced to resign from office in May of the following year. Constitutional provisions were maintained through an interim presidency, after which former president Rafael Caldera won in national elections in December and was inaugurated in January 1994. Although the political system and the parties themselves have survived to the moment of writing, both have been sorely taxed. The first is moving forward haltingly in the face of many years of socioeconomic travail and mismanagement by the state, while the increasingly fragmented party system is limping toward scheduled elections in December 1998. Elsewhere in the hemisphere Peru's Alberto Fujimori had succeeded in winning election to a second term and had returned to the state of constitutionality that he had earlier defied during his *autogolpe* (a self-administered nonconstitutional takeover by the sitting head of state) and suspension of the country's previous charter. The renewed competition among the parties, although consistent with democratic practices, did not mask the fact that, aside from Fujimori's own shifting alliance of political forces, there were no politically significant or effectively organized parties in Peru.

Elsewhere the changes were more gradual. Colombia maintained its democratic status while adjusting to the new Constitution of 1991. However, the ceaseless internal war against guerrilla insurgents, along with the violence revolving about the drug industry, inevitably colored external perceptions. This was further aggravated by the swirl of charges that President Ernesto Samper had received drug money to finance his successful 1994 electoral campaign. After more than a year of constant charges and countercharges, Samper was found innocent by the lower house of Congress, which was dominated by members of his own Liberal Party. This did not assure his survival in office, but whatever else might transpire, the scholarly image of Colombia could only be damaged for the time being. Rampant scandal and corruption in other nations was a factor in qualitative judgments. Brazil saw its youngest president in history, Fernando Collor de Mello, impeached in 1992 on charges of corruption. In Ecuador, Sixto Durán Ballen ended his term under a cloud of suspicion, while his vice president, Alberto Dahik, fled the country to avoid charges of corruption and theft of government funds. The spreading hemispheric preoccupation with official misdeeds also registered in Mexico, stimulated by the unsolved mystery surrounding the 1994 assassination of Donaldo Colosio, the PRI's presidential candidate and presumed victor in approaching elections. Later charges of graft and influence peddling reached the brother of outgoing president Carlos Salinas de Gortari, who himself was later the target of public suspicion.

While this is not the place for a rundown of current political events across the Americas, it is useful to recall some of the preceding circumstances when reporting on the opinions of the panelists. According to the 1995 responses, democracy in Latin America was still most fully realized in Costa Rica, and Uruguay—which had been the leader throughout the years from 1945 through 1965—was second.

Venezuela, which had ranked second from 1975 through 1991, dropped to fifth as a result of the circumstances already mentioned. Chile moved up from fourth to third, and Argentina from fifth to fourth. Beyond the top five nations, it might be added that Brazil, Colombia, and Mexico were respectively sixth, seventh, and eighth. When we turn one final time to the criterion of party organization, none other than Costa Rica is at the top of the list. Chile ranked second and Uruguay third, while Venezuela had fallen to fourth and Argentina was fifth. Beyond that, Colombia placed sixth, Brazil was seventh, and post-Sandinista Nicaragua appeared as eighth. Other interesting results included Mexico's placement as only tenth, while the Fujimori-dominated Peru was far down the scale as number seventeen. Only Guatemala, Haiti, and Cuba were lower.

A few additional remarks may be in order. In actual point of fact Costa Rica's consistently high ranking for party organization masked the fact that the nation had been long dominated by a single party, the PLN. Although frequently opposed and sometimes defeated by a variety of temporary electoral alliances, the PLN's organizational strength and doctrinal policy overshadowed national politics until the eventual emergence of Rafael Angel Calderon Fournier. The son of a former president, he successfully built a second coherent party as the Partido de Unidad Social Christiano (PUSC), and after an electoral loss in 1986 he won the presidency in 1990. With Chile, the old traditions of civilian, party-based competition were being reasserted as the long dictatorial interlude slipped further into the background, notwithstanding the survival of General Pinochet as commander in chief of the armed forces. The passing of generations was also dramatized by the election of the son of former president and Christian Democratic Party founder Eduardo Frei; this had been paralleled by Costa Rica's 1994 election of the son of the PLN's storied José Figueres. Uruguay's standing in the survey suggested a return to preauthoritarian political patterns, further invigorated by the presence of major party forces to contest with the Colorados and Blancos. At the same time it was appropriate that Venezuela had dropped in the rankings, although its position in fourth place may well have been higher than circumstances justified. For Argentina, in rounding out the top five for 1995, its ranking bespoke the party competition that had come to incorporate electorally significant forces beyond those of the Peronists and Radicals. There were also serious internal conflicts, even as President Menem moved into his second term.

The Future of Political Parties

The collective wisdom and cumulative assessments of participants in the Fitzgibbon-Johnson Index can be expected to provide current and topical insight into the Latin American question for political democracy. This will inevitably include consideration of the political parties, both in organizational and electoral terms. For the moment, until the next round of questioning in the year 2000, we must briefly undertake a more qualitative review. In doing so, it becomes difficult to avoid the fact that Latin American political parties are presently in a state of decline, or at least are confronting challenges to their existence and even relevance. It is at least arguable that the parties have been undergoing a process of deconstruction. For the purposes of a general perspective, consider three areas critical to the political parties: doctrine and ideology; organization and structure; and leadership selection. Although these do not exhaust all the facets of political parties, they help to explain the relative failures of recent years in many countries, along with the challenges to be met if a reconstruction of representative, participatory, mass-based parties has a realistic chance of success.

Political ideology and doctrine have progressively declined. This is in part a function of the collapse of international communism and the end of the Cold War. Although Marxist parties and movements have survived in Latin America, their role, at least for the present, is secondary at best. As for intellectual appeal, they are dogged by the necessity of explaining the events in the Soviet Union and eastern Europe before seeking a persuasive rationalization for the Americas. At the same time, while Social Democratic and Christian Democratic movements are by no means dead, they find less need for ideological justification or self-defense than had been true previously. Furthermore, many of their philosophical commitments and policy recommendations have been swept aside by both internal and external forces. The hasty and often poorly organized retreat from statism in the face of economic crises and international demands for neoliberal policies, privatization, and a shrinking of the state have further vitiated the relevance and validity of party ideology. As a result, organizational energies have been devoted principally to the seeking of partisan electoral advantage.

Although the general subordination of doctrinal to practical political considerations has underlined a desensitizing of ideology and a shifting of priorities, parties have also been suffering from errors of omission and commission regarding organization and structure. They have either fragmented over doctrinal or personalist rivalries—nothing new, to be sure—or they have become bureaucratized to the extent of deadening any internal vigor and vitality. The inevitable expansion of party machinery has provided splendid examples of democratic centralism in operation, wherein a small handful of party elites essentially decides the course of the party. Roberto Michels's iron law of oligarchy has set in with a vengeance. Internal party democratization has virtually disappeared in many cases, as oligarchic control has exercised unchallenged dominion over the rank and file. This naturally spills over into the area of leadership selection. Party elites defend their own perquisites of power and influence by attempting to dictate the choice of candidates, electoral policies, and the like. Loyalists are properly rewarded, and party apparatchiks prevail. All of the preceding predictably provokes public alienation and encourages electoral deconstruction in the 1990s. Cynicism toward politics and a withdrawal of interest from public affairs has spread.

These developments have also contributed to an erosion, albeit unconscious, of institutional legitimacy. Such events as Venezuela's deadly *caracazo* (a widespread and spontaneous urban riot in Caracas) in 1989, in which unanticipated popular protest led to violence and looting that cost hundreds of lives and the loss of millions of dollars, may well be repeated elsewhere—and as was true in Venezuela, beyond the reach and without the knowledge of the political parties. Party electorates are also fragmented, accompanied by the fact that the leadership itself is often cavalierly unaware of the decline of the parties in the eyes of the public. Abstention becomes ever more pronounced, and civic participation in politics is virtually nil. All of this suggests that the search for party reconstruction in itself is vitally important for the support and promotion of democracy in Latin America. Many of the problems are relatively easy to understand and to approach; however, remedies are far more difficult to identify. The character of contemporary needs are less likely to be understood, let alone implemented. Nevertheless, today Latin America must undertake a search for reconstruction—for a rediscovery of those elements and characteristics by means of which the parties may play the important role that they themselves have identified. If indeed, as we would insist, democratization of the political parties is a fundamental requirement for the survival and strengthening of the political systems themselves, then far greater research and investigation lies ahead.

Notes

1. These are an abbreviated version of Fitzgibbon's original and more detailed statements of criteria, as reported by Professor Philip Kelly.

2. These two were Austin F. Macdonald and Russell H. Fitzgibbon himself.

3. Once again there were ten respondents. Macdonald and Fitzgibbon were joined by George I. Blanksten as an additional panelist with interest and expertise on the subject of political parties.

4. Among those respondents studying political parties who joined Blanksten, Fitzgibbon, and Macdonald were Harry Kantor, Robert E. Scott, and Philip B. Taylor Jr.

5. By the time of the 1960 survey, the forty participants included at least ten with party-related concerns. Those joining for the first time were Robert J. Alexander, Frank R. Brandenburg, Federico G. Gil, and Kalman H. Silvert.

6. My own assessment illustrated the dominant attitude in the scholarship of the day; see Martz 1964.

8. Fifty respondents participated in the 1965 survey. Those with particular interests in political parties who had not previously been invited into the pool of experts included Ronald H. Chilcote, John D. Martz, and Martin C. Needler.

9. The panel of respondents has grown through the years, effectively vitiating any conceivable misgivings about the extent and representativeness of its participants. By 1980 the panel had become so extensive that its listing required a full page in *Latin American Research Review*. That particular report includes Kenneth F. Johnson's (1982) commentary about political change and democracy in the hemisphere at the close of the 1970s.

10. I surveyed some of the more relevant historical trends while raising issues about recent and contemporary "democratization" in Martz 1955:357–387.

11. My own lamentations about the faddishness of scholars who follow their hearts rather than their heads with intuitive rushes to judgment about systemic changes are by no means unique. Among my more impatient expressions of dismay and of specific criticism are the series of reviews appearing periodically in *Studies in Comparative International Development*. For a recent extended essay that, for better or worse, conveys some of my intellectual and theoretical misgivings, see Martz 1996.

Bibliography

Johnson, Kenneth F. 1982. The 1980 image-index survey of Latin American political democracy. *Latin American Research Review* 17:193–201.

Martz, John D. 1996. Economic challenges and the study of democratization. *Studies in Comparative International Development* 31:96–120.

_____. 1964. Dilemmas in the study of Latin American political parties. *The Journal of Politics* 26:509–531.

Martz, John D., ed. 1955. *United States Policy in Latin America: A Decade of Crisis and Challenge*. Lincoln and London: University of Nebraska Press.

Szulc, Tad. 1959. *Twilight of the Tyrants*. New York: Henry Holt.

Chapter Three

Social Democracy in Latin America

ROBERT L. PETERSON

The relevance of any type of alternative to the neoliberal authority structures of Latin America may be easily questioned. The history of the past forty years in the region has centered on, first, militarism and development, and second, capitalism, austerity, and liberal democratic procedures. How could an ideological posture and sociopolitical doctrine like social democracy be of any significance today?

Social democracy contains a strong critique of today's political and economic currents in Latin America. It rejects the premise that economic development is achieved either through nationalization of the means of production or state abdication of responsibility for the welfare of its citizens. Capitalism, in and of itself, is neither rational nor just. If Latin American governments wish to deal successfully with their growing problems of poverty and income disparities while remaining attractive to private investors and promoting economic efficiency, then they can realize a functional type of socialism while the ownership of productive resources remains in private hands (Przeworski 1993:835). Moreover, social democracy is not alien to the region. However, it only forms a minor theme in Latin American history.

The purpose of this chapter is not to advocate social democracy as a panacea for Latin America's social, economic, and political ills. It will, however, consider social democracy more seriously, and in more depth, than is typical in treatments of democracy and social development in Latin America.

The Evolution of Social Democracy in Latin America

Social democracy is a relative newcomer to the Latin American political scene. It must be noted that the successful establishment of democracy of any sort was retarded in Latin America following World War II and was the result of a number of domestic and international factors. Internally, populism was spreading across the region, setting the stage for military dictatorship a decade or so later. Regionally, the United States actively worked against the creation or stabilization of popular regimes in Latin America:

> The United States assisted the recovery of democracy in Europe, but in 1965 it invaded the Dominican Republic, and in the early 1970s . . . destabilized Chilean and Uruguayan democracies. The United States traded with China and the former Soviet Union, whereas Cuba suffered from a criminal commercial embargo for decades. . . . Franco's Spain was supported by U.S. diplomacy, yet Nicaraguan elections were not good enough when the Sandinistas triumphed, although they were fine when Chamorro was elected. Berlin was protected, yet Guatemala, the Dominican Republic, Grenada, and Panama were invaded. (Boron 1995:153)

Relatively little research has been conducted on the ties or relations that have been established between European social democratic movements and their Latin American counterparts, but these contacts have been expanding and increasing in significance. In the 1960s, as the welfare state was expanding and broadening its social scope in Europe, the West German Social Democratic Party (SPD) began reaching out to Latin America, developing contacts in a number of countries. The Friedrich Ebert Foundation established the Latin American Center for Social Research in Santiago in 1966 and eventually set up offices in most Latin American countries. The foundation has been particularly useful for German bilateral efforts in the region (Vellinga 1993:5–6).

In 1976 Venezuela hosted a meeting that brought together the leading European social democrats of the time. Hosted by Carlos Andrés Pérez in Caracas, the objective of the conference was to condemn human rights violations by Latin American military regimes, and it involved a large number and variety of Latin American parties and groups. The meeting did more than concentrate on the human rights situation, however. It provided for a large number of subsequent conferences, discussions, statements, and symposia. For the most part these activities were held in Latin America and brought the participation of European social democratic parties (Vellinga 1993:6).

The Socialist International (SI) was founded in 1951. Its predecessor, the Second International, had remained Eurocentric both in membership and social theory until dissolved shortly after the beginning of World War II. It was only in 1947 that Robert Alexander, a U.S. socialist, emphasized to his European counterparts the necessity of including Latin America in future internationals:

> The Socialist Parties need the aid of the European Socialist Parties, but they feel that the Europeans also need the participation of extra-European elements in SI gatherings, and specifically they need the participation of the Latin American Socialists, who now constitute one of the strongest groups of socialist movements anywhere in the world, and with perhaps more future than many of those in the Old World. (Alexander 1947–1948:24, quoted in Whitehead 1986:26)

The Latin American section of the SI was not organized, however, until 1951 with the establishment of a Latin American Secretariat in Montevideo. The first conference of the Latin American section took place the next year and brought together Acción Democrática of Venezuela, the Partido Liberación Nacional of Costa Rica, the Partido Radical of Chile, the Jamaican People's National Party, and the People's National Movement of Trinidad-Tobago (Vellinga 1993:5). This initial foray into the western hemisphere was to be cut short in 1959, however, with the rise of Fidel Castro and his Twenty-Sixth of July Movement in Cuba, a development that was to split the Latin American Left. Combined with factors singular to European politics at the time, the aftermath of the Cuban Revolution greatly reduced the activities and significance of the SI (Whitehead 1986:27–28).

The SI attempted a comeback in the 1970s. European leaders, particularly Willy Brandt, with financing from the West German SPD, pushed for an augmented organization with significantly increased endeavors outside of Europe, most especially in Latin America (Whitehead 1986:29). Menno Vellinga points out that the interest in Latin America was encouraged by the ideological direction of the North-South debate on the economic relations between Western nations (1993:7). Again, however, events were to subvert this renewed interest in Latin America. The civil wars and guerrilla struggles in Central America, most notably the establishment of the Sandinista regime in Nicaragua at the end of the decade, produced ideological and policy discords within the SI (Whitehead 1986:29–30).

SI interest and support of social democracy in Latin America was not totally thwarted. The SI held its Seventeenth Congress in Lima in 1986, the first time such a meeting had been held in Latin America, and the members of the SI Committee for Latin America and the Caribbean (SICLAC) continue to convene regularly. At its March 1996 meeting in Santo Domingo, for example, SICLAC reaffirmed its commitment to work for improved democratic methods and structures, for economic alternatives to neoliberalism, and for political programs to combat poverty and reduce inequalities and the like. The SI now regularly monitors Latin American elections and counts ten Latin American political parties as Full Member Parties, seven Latin American parties as Consultative Parties, and two Latin American parties as Observer Parties.

The SI has often found itself at odds with the United States over the definition and implementation of democracy in Latin America. U.S. foreign policy makers have pressured individual European SI leaders and attempted to bring about dissension within the organization itself (Whitehead 1986:30). U.S. hegemony in the western hemisphere, therefore, has certainly limited the effectiveness of the SI.

Rejection of Social Democracy in Latin America

Howard Wiarda has stated that

> the current consensus in development theory may be termed neoclassical. It emerges from the experience of the last thirty years . . . and not from theory. It suggests that

development is markedly faster and more sustainable if fundamental reliance is placed on markets for the allocation of goods and services, and not on some all powerful government. . . . Socialism has been shown to be woefully inefficient and not conducive to development, and so have the excessively statist economies of Latin America. (Wiarda 1993:139)

These remarks need not be construed as an attack on social democracy, since social democratic governments have edged closer to classical liberalism in recent years (Lipset 1991:198), but they do sound a warning for facile applications of this variety of political and economic relationships to Latin America.

Robert Kaufman offers a detailed and specific set of criticisms. He notes that, in general, social democratic movements have accepted the various parameters on state action demanded by the rules of a market economy. Within these limitations, these movements "provide more or less humane models of legitimation" in which union-based political parties provide legislative majorities at the same time that corporatist arrangements among big labor and big business negotiate social policy with the state bureaucracy (Kaufman 1986:103). Can these arrangements be carried over to Latin America?

Kaufman argues that several structural and historical barriers prevent the realization of social democracy in the region. First, the industrial working class is relatively small and economically powerless, "the outgrowth of 'dependent capitalist' industrialization" (Kaufman 1986:103). Second, and more important, social democratic regimes require the active support of Communist Parties: "Whereas no social-democratic movement that excludes Communists is likely to be elected, no elected government that includes them is likely to last very long" (Kaufman 1986:104).

Kaufman might be excused for this last argument on the grounds that no one foresaw the dissolution of the Communist regimes in eastern Europe and the Soviet Union and the devastating effects that these developments would have on Communist Parties around the world: "Not only members and sympathizers of the minority orthodox Communist parties but also members of the majority of other leftist parties and organizations have suddenly found themselves in a devastated political space in which references to the utopias that had inspired their actions during the last six or seven decades have completely lost credibility" (Cavarozzi 1993:153).

Kaufman, however, cannot be absolved in this manner. The assertion that there is a necessary political relation between social democrats and Communists is erroneous. The recent experience of eastern Europe bears eloquent testimony on this matter:

Many SD [social democratic] parties had been forced to join fronts organized by the communists, and it was difficult for them to live this down. They also were weakened by transition politics in that the communist parties did not disappear but achieved respectability through participation in the electoral process, scoring a goodly number of votes in the early elections. With changed names (usually including the socialist, and only in the single case of the Czech Republic, the communist tag), with no

chance of recovering the monopoly of power that they once held, freed from the association with a Soviet bogey, and still endowed with the organizational skills that
have been so characteristic of communist parties, the parties bid fair, in at least two
cases—the Hungarian and the Slovak—to grow into the social democratic space
which others are having such difficulty in filling (Waller 1994:57).

Actually, the short history of social democracy in Latin America does not show
any significant roadblocks being thrown up by entrenched Communist interests
or traditional leftist schisms in the region. The good fortune of the SI in Latin
America in the 1970s was in no small part the result of a favorable reception on
the part of the Latin American Left (Evers 1993:25–26). By this time the postures
of the region's Communist Parties or factions were irrelevant.

A more serious obstacle to social democracy in Latin America is discussed by
Paul Cammack, who points to the relative lack of capitalist structures and
processes in the region. At best capitalism has only begun to mature. The Latin
American bourgeoisie does not behave as it should in the social and political arenas. Capitalist hegemony and a simultaneous obligation to social and economic
redistribution though a myriad of reforms is only a very remote possibility: "The
fact is that in Latin America today there is a widespread perception, supported by
the daily reality of the lives of the majority as well as by abundant statistical evidence, that only a minority gains from capitalism and that it defends its privileges
with selfish intransigence" (Cammack 1993:98).

If Cammack's objection is combined with Kaufman's assertion that the Latin
American proletariat is small and powerless, then the argument is that the lack of
capitalist development in Latin America is responsible for the frailty of social
democracy, which is dependent upon capitalist institutionalization and maturity.

The point is extended by the critique made by Stephen Haggard and Robert
Kaufman. In a social democracy the capitalists obtain and maintain political primacy and stabilize the socioeconomic order in exchange for welfare state policies,
dominant center-left political parties, and the participation of labor and other
working-class or peasant groups in the formation and implementation of social
and economic policies:

> Compared to center-right systems and possibly even to the two-party model, inclu-
> sionary features of the social-democratic outcome would provide it with a relatively
> strong base of legitimacy and support. Precisely because of their identification with
> the left, moreover, social-democratic governments might be in a better position to
> moderate wage and welfare demands emanating from their core constituency. (Hag-
> gard and Kaufman 1994:84)

Latin America lacks the social and political conditions necessary for the emergence of social democracy. As noted, the working class is lacking in coherence and
organization. Even with an organized labor base, questions and difficulties arise
over the integration of labor with other popular organizations, groups that are

concerned with gender issues, environmental issues, agricultural issues, and the like and whose goals may conflict with those of organized labor. Further, to extend the critique, it implies a reconciliation of the Left with military and business elites (Haggard and Kaufman 1994:85). Application of a social democratic model to Latin America is problematic because conservative Latin American countries have historically had the capability to assimilate, frequently superficially, new theoretical mores and institutions while maintaining an undisturbed elitist-authoritarian structural and behavioral core (Wiarda 1992a:19).

This last concern may be put less theoretically and, at the same time, may be extended to the entire process of democratization in Latin America. A close examination of the region today reveals a number of disturbing trends that threaten the democratic gains of the last two decades or so. First, present-day governments have generally failed to better the economic and social conditions of their populations. In a number of countries, living standards, which deteriorated badly in the 1980s, have yet to catch up with what they were two decades ago. Countries such as Argentina and Chile are improving economically and have many positive growth indicators, but others, Brazil and Mexico for instance, have developed a great many economic problems. Cuba, Guatemala, Haiti, Honduras, and Nicaragua have actually experienced negative growth (Klepak 1995:4). Moreover, whatever might be said about traditional measures of economic and social development must be contrasted with the type of improvement being implemented:

> Economic dislocation, caused often by structural adjustment policies and reactions to globalization, is rampant, with its resulting and increasing under-employment and unemployment. Virtually all economists agree that the gap between the rich and poor is widening rapidly and dangerously, and that the much-touted trickle-down effect of economic change is often showing itself painfully reluctant to appear. (Klepak 1995:4)

If growing public and private corruption, the immense increase in crime, and a surge in the drug and arms trade are added to these problems, then the prospects for democracy of any type in Latin America become much bleaker than is often assumed (Klepak 1995:4–5).

The Case for Social Democracy in Latin America

The arguments that can be raised against social democracy are much more numerous and extensive than the favorable arguments that I will raise later. Given the general rejection of social democracy in Latin America—at least its feasibility, if not its desirability—can a case be made for its relevance and its suitability for Latin America? If this question appears naive, remember that it was only a decade and a half ago that some Latin American scholars were despairing over any type of democracy ever reappearing in the region. Perhaps, to begin the argument, scholars are doing much the same in regard to social democracy today.

James Cockcroft has defined and conceptualized what he calls the "new politics" in Latin America. The term refers to the political patterns that have evolved with the implementation of democratic procedures and popular participation in politics and that are the strongest in the eight most industrialized countries of the region—Brazil, Mexico, Argentina, Colombia, Venezuela, Chile, Uruguay, and Peru:

> The impetus for Latin America's politics gradually shifted from the military officers' clubs, the foreign embassies and corporate offices, the salons of the ruling elite families, and the old political class, to the streets and homes of so-called average citizens. During the long night, the new politics emerged as a bottom-up challenge to military national security states and/or civilian bureaucratic authoritarian or corporativist states dominated by one or two political parties. (Cockcroft 1996:30–31).

What are these patterns, and what is their significance for social democracy in Latin America?

The first feature of the new politics has involved the replacement or restructuring of the politics of the past. Here Cockcroft refers to such phenomena as the transformation of Peronism in Argentina or the rejuvenation of the Aprista Party in Peru (Cockcroft 1996:32).

Second, the new politics was idealistic and strongly committed to democracy. This commitment was underscored by a third characteristic, namely the formation of broadly based popular alliances during the military dictatorships of the 1960s and 1970s. These alliances incorporated a wide variety of previously conflicting political parties and groups (Cockcroft 1996:33).

The development of cooperative political fronts was accompanied by the advent of the urban poor as important political participants. With the emergence of lower-class political actors, the new politics was characterized by new and more militant labor movements and the mobilization of women, particularly lower-class women. Feminism was instrumental in promoting human rights and in demanding basic social reforms. In fact, women have become increasingly assertive, active, and able to assume leadership roles in both governmental (Cockcroft 1996:34–35) and nongovernmental organizations:

> The perspectives of women on democracy are important. As a majority of the population and de facto heads of household for many families, women have become a social force to be reckoned with. Historically marginalized from both formal electoral politics and from vertically integrated interest aggregations, women are now at the forefront of the movement to amplify the boundaries of social, economic and political space. (Saint-Germain and Landolt 1994:3)

The new politics in Latin America has allowed repressed indigenous populations to reassert themselves in new and dramatic ways, has brought about a revival in peasant movements, and has awakened young people to the possibilities of genuine political change.

An early feature of the new politics was the advent of reformist and nationalist portions of the military, whose attempts at reform were usually blocked by conservative sociopolitical elements. These efforts, however, can be viewed as simply part of an experimentation with new approaches to the economy, society, and politics in individual Latin American countries (Cockcroft 1996:36).

Cockcroft's analysis is valuable for a number of reasons. First, it serves as a reminder that conditions are not static in Latin America and that ideologically driven accounts of political and socioeconomic phenomena are often limited by the static nature of their own assumptions.

Second, the analysis forces us to focus on factors and groups that are often relegated to a secondary role in political inquiries and on the rapidly growing significance of these groups in the region. In other words, Cockcroft insists that we deal with concrete organizations and identifiable movements. This avoids the all-too-easy reliance on more abstract entities such as "the bourgeoisie" or "the proletariat." It is ironic that those who employ these Marxist categories sometimes have accused those advocating social democracy of adopting an exclusively Eurocentric approach to Latin America (Torres-Rivas 1993:240).

Third, Cockcroft's analysis forces us to reconsider the nature of contemporary democracy in Latin America. To put the matter bluntly, it is difficult to see how the implementation of procedural democracies in Latin America can cope with the rise of these new or augmented political forces. Relying on formal reforms without paying serious attention to the legitimate needs of the great majority of the population will only bring democracy into disrepute. Much of the population of Latin America lacks secure access to even such basic necessities of life as food, education, employment, housing, and health: "The social reality of Latin America and the Caribbean cries out for social reforms, without which it will be very difficult to assure the consolidation of democratic reconstruction and its formal advances in a continent that, in recent decades, daily lived the experience of authoritarian political culture" (Lozano 1994:60).

Atilio Boron is even more emphatic on this point, stating that democratic reform cannot be divorced from the "insoluble injustice of capitalism." The struggle for democracy in Latin America today must focus on the "popular classes" who "are the fundamental social forces that can democratize the state" and who "may offer a progressive and civilized solution to the political crisis that affects capitalism" (Boron 1995:27).

The argument, therefore, is that social democracy, or some variant of it, is necessary to restructure and stabilize democracy in Latin America. It should be remembered that social democratic programs provide for a redistribution of wealth and resources and have represented an essential and legitimate alternative to the neoliberal, market-determined economic and political programs of Europe for a considerable period of time. Indeed, it can be argued that the social democratic agenda has worked so well in western Europe that it has become a victim of its own success (Vellinga 1993:10).

Wiarda reminds us that in Latin America the good society

> is ordinarily pictured as one where each individual is rooted and secure in his station, where representation is determined by status or function and not as a result of certain "inalienable" rights of citizenship, and where decision-making is based upon a number of well-integrated corporate elites, all of whom agree on certain primary values, accept the operating "rules of the game" and are harmonized and coordinated into an organic whole. The various elites . . . are connected directly and vertically to the central authority rather than having their interests channeled through a variety of secondary groups, or organized horizontally and impersonally across group boundaries. The state, in turn, is expected—even required—to exercise firm but paternalistic authority over this whole national "family." (1992b:228)

Latin American corporatism has received few positive reviews and has been viewed as developing from the same sources as western European corporatism without having been circumscribed by the growth of liberal democratic procedures and institutions. The argument is overdrawn. Certainly the worst excesses of corporatism were revealed in the fascist regimes of Germany and Italy in the 1930s and 1940s. In Latin America, even though there was a fear during World War II that fascist sympathies would lead to totalitarianism, corporatism remained authoritarian. Because of this, native corporatism may play a positive role in attempts to solidify democracy in Latin America. Baohui Zhang has asserted that, unlike totalitarian regimes that emphasize the control mechanisms of corporatism at the expense of representation, corporatist authoritarian governments have a greater chance of making successful planned transitions to democracy:

> Elitist in nature, such pacts usually restrict the scope of direct mass participation during the transition state and so lessen the fears of authoritarian elites and their incentives to reverse the transition process. These pacts usually pertain, at least in the initial stages, to the rule-making aspect of democracy rather than broader socioeconomic democratization. In a word, they are most likely to result in new regimes that only meet the minimum procedural requirements of democracy. As a result, old authoritarian elites have less to fear from such democratic regimes and may believe that they can still exercise great influence under the new rules of the game. (1994:110–111)

This is about as far as the argument can be pushed. Both the desirability and feasibility of social democracy in Latin America can be asserted and defended as intellectual positions, but the actual establishment of this type of democracy is dependent upon the outcome of processes whose outlines are only beginning to be understood. Still, as Wiarda has asked: "Can it be, heretical though it seems in the United States, that the Latin American nations with their organic, unitary, and patrimonialist conception of the proper ordering of state and society will in the long run prove to have coped better with the wrenching crises of modernization than the United States with its secular, divisive, fragmented interest group pluralism?" (Wiarda 1992a:20).

Bibliography

Alexander, Robert J. 1947–1948. Socialism in Latin America. *Socialist World* 1 (December 1947–February 1948):20–24; quoted in Whitehead 1986:26.

Boron, Atilio A. 1995. *State, Capitalism, and Democracy in Latin America*. Boulder: Lynne Rienner.

Cammack, Paul. 1993. Latin American social democracy in British perspective. In *Social Democracy in Latin America: Prospects for Change* (Menno Vellinga, ed.), 82–102. Boulder: Westview Press.

Cavarozzi, Marcelo. 1993. The left in South America: Politics as the only option. In *Social Democracy in Latin America: Prospects for Change* (Menno Vellinga, ed.), 146–162. Boulder: Westview Press.

Cockcroft, James D. 1996. *Latin America: History, Politics, and U.S. Policy*. 2nd ed. Chicago: Nelson-Hall.

Evers, Tilman. 1993. European social democracy in Latin America: The early history with emphasis on the role of Germany. In *Social Democracy in Latin America: Prospects for Change* (Menno Vellinga, ed.), 23–60. Boulder: Westview Press.

Haggard, Stephen, and Robert Kaufman. 1994. Democratic institutions, economic policy, and performance in Latin America. In *Redefining the State in Latin America* (Colin I. Bradford Jr., ed.), 69–90. Paris: OECD.

Kaufman, Robert R. 1986. Liberalization and democratization in South America: Perspectives from the 1970s. In *Transitions from Authoritarian Rule: Comparative Perspectives* (Guillermo O'Donnell, Philippe C. Schmitter, and Laurence Whitehead, eds.), 85–107. Baltimore: Johns Hopkins University Press.

Klepak, H. P. 1995. Far from a sure thing: Prospects for democracy in Latin America. Canadian Security Intelligence Service, Commentary no. 61 (September 1995).

Lipset, Seymour Martin. 1991. No third way: A comparative perspective on the left. In *The Crisis of Leninism and the Decline of the Left* (Daniel Chirot, ed.), 183–232. Seattle: University of Washington Press.

Lozano, Lucretia. 1994. Adjustment of democracy in Latin America. In *Latin America Faces the Twenty-First Century: Reconstructing a Social Justice Agenda* (Susanne Jonas and Edward J. McCaughan, eds.), 51–62. Boulder: Westview Press.

Przeworski, Adam. 1993. Socialism and social democracy. In *The Oxford Companion to Politics of the World* (Joel Krieger, et al., eds.), 832–839. New York: Oxford University Press.

Saint-Germain, Michelle A., and Laura K. Landolt. 1994. Women and democratization in Central America. Paper prepared for delivery at the 1994 World Congress of the International Political Science Association.

Torres-Rivas, Edelberto. 1993. Personalities, ideologies, and circumstances: Social democracy in Central America. In *Social Democracy in Latin America: Prospects for Change* (Menno Vellinga, ed.), 240–251. Boulder: Westview Press.

Vellinga, Menno. 1993. The internationalization of politics and local response: Social democracy in Latin America. In *Social Democracy in Latin America: Prospects for Change* (Menno Vellinga, ed.), 3–22. Boulder: Westview Press.

Waller, Michael. 1994. Groups, politics, and political change in eastern Europe from 1977. In *Democratization in Eastern Europe: Domestic and International Perspectives* (Geoffrey Pridham and Tatu Vanhanen, eds.), 38–62. London and New York: Routledge.

Whitehead, Laurence. 1986. International aspects of democratization. In *Transitions from Authoritarian Rule: Comparative Perspectives* (Guillermo O'Donnell, Philippe C. Schmitter, and Laurence Whitehead, eds.), 3–46. Baltimore: John Hopkins University Press.

Wiarda, Howard J. 1993. *Introduction to Comparative Politics: Concepts and Processes.* Belmont, California: Wadsworth.

_____. 1992a. Introduction: Social change, political development, and the Latin American tradition. In *Politics and Social Change in Latin America* (Howard J. Wiarda, ed.), 1–24. Boulder: Westview Press.

_____. 1992b. Law and political development in Latin America: Toward a framework for analysis. In *Politics and Social Change in Latin America* (Howard J. Wiarda, ed.), 211–238. Boulder: Westview Press.

Zhang, Baohui. 1994. Corporatism, totalitarianism, and transitions to democracy. *Comparative Political Studies* 27, no. 1:108–136.

Chapter Four

Democracy and the Environment in Latin America

KATHRYN HOCHSTETLER AND
STEPHEN MUMME

Democracy's paradox, if we accept a strict Shumpeterian construction, is that it empowers the good and the bad equally. Taken strictly as a system of rules for electoral contestation, it has no normative purpose beyond guaranteeing eligible participants equal procedural treatment in constituting representative government. An empty vessel, its rules extend the same privileges to the entire pool of eligible voters and legal contenders for political power. Democratization, as both an end and a process, may thus cut in opposite directions where substantive policy is concerned.

This "paradox" is certainly evident in the case of Latin America's emerging environmentalism. Latin America's democratic transition in the 1980s overlaps the development of regional environmentalism and the emergence of many new social movements in general. Democratization has given environmentalism a degree of legitimacy and a political presence heretofore absent in the region's politics. Reforms have ushered in greater political participation, which, in turn, is manifested in a growing number of policies and investments aimed at environmental protection.

Latin American states' receptiveness to environmental concerns is hardly one-sided, however. One of democratization's puzzles is that where formal transitions have taken place, new social actors have sometimes been sidelined in the phase of democratic consolidation (Hipsher 1996; Navarro 1994). As political parties and civilian bureaucrats returned to center stage, they replaced not only military actors but also many of the independent organizations of civil society. Environmental groups are vulnerable since their policy area is highly technical and regulatory, requiring substantial commitments of expertise and financial resources. This plays into the hands of skilled elites and against the capacity of local public and grassroots organizations to effectively participate in the crafting of environmental policy (Fiorino 1996). Considering the indiscriminate nature of democratic empowerment, it is hardly surprising that environmental reformers have met resistance within these institutional apertures. The Brazilian justice minister recently justified altering the procedures for demarcating indigenous land, noting that "the decree needs to address the rights of all citizens, including those who wish to promote industrial projects in Brazil and not just indigenous groups" (Tension mounts between natural resources projects and citizen rights 1995:8).

The problematic of environmental reform in the region is further complicated in its north-south dimensions. The emergence of environmental concern can scarcely be separated from the long-standing and vigorous debate on regional (and national) development policy. Indeed, much of the debate on "sustainable development" before and after the Brundtland Report and the 1992 Rio Conference has been forged with reference to the Latin American situation. Throughout the region, environmental discourse is contextualized in debates on the merits of urban versus rural and market-driven versus state-led approaches to environmental improvement and on a cost-benefit calculus of alternative policies.

In the following pages, we discuss some of the most important dilemmas confronting environmentalism, dilemmas that arise from the region's democratization. In the first section we identify the principal problems associated with emergent environmentalism in the region. In the second section we look at the development of environmental movements in Mexico and Brazil to better understand the challenges of environmental mobilization in these national contexts. As our cases show, democratization and political transitions are processes that are not limited to the moments of formal military-civilian transition, nor are they unilinearly progressive for the environmental issue area.

Emergent Environmentalism: Patterns and Challenges

Latin America is host to some of the world's most compelling environmental issues. Problems range from the destruction of Amazonia and its trove of biodiversity to the social and epidemiological ailments of Latin America's megacities. The choice of Rio de Janeiro as the site for the most recent UN environmental conference was appropriate, for Rio symbolizes well Latin America's urban explosion. Many of the difficulties facing contemporary environmentalism in Latin America are rooted in the region's emergence as a center of rapidly industrializing economies with highly urbanized societies. Environmentalism as a new social movement is certainly related to growing public appreciation of the social and environmental costs of uneven rapid development and the need to conserve national resources.

Translating environmental concern into political action is problematic, however, and the process is shaped by the larger system of state-society relations. Many of the problems associated with environmental mobilization in Latin America are traceable to the persistence of various structural constraints that restrict civic involvement in the crafting and execution of state policies. This pattern of restricted liberalization should be understood as an element of Latin American political development that both precedes and follows the military interregnums and authoritarian phases associated with the politics of particular countries. The contemporary restoration of civilian government in various democratic forms has often been only partial, accompanied by formal limitations on civic expression and association or by reversions to earlier clientelist and corporatist patterns in state affairs. A cardinal feature of restricted liberalization is the noninclusionary character of policy formation, that is, the domination of policy decisions by a limited number of policy elites, administrative technocrats, or privileged social actors without widespread opportunities for public participation in crafting government decisions. The actuality of participation is seldom neutral. Political claims that challenge dominant economic models—as environmental agendas may do—often are not welcome.

Beyond these general patterns, each of the Latin American countries has its own patterns of restrictions. One virtue of the Fitzgibbon rankings is that they are based on a composite ranking of multiple political institutions judged separately. This approach captures the unevenness of political liberalization and the restrictions still evident in at least some, but different, institutions in all of Latin America's new democracies. Such patterns are important factors shaping the possibilities for environmental mobilization in the region.

Throughout Latin America, the adoption of explicitly environmental legislation after the UN Conference on the Human Environment (held in Stockholm in 1972) is largely associated with the efforts of small groups of government technocrats or professional groups working with government officials and international environmental organizations as these sought to advance environmental protection in specific countries. Though variations are found, environmental concern was largely confined to government and internationalist circles; few significant, mass-based environmental groups emerged. The 1970s, of course, are associated in various countries with repressive military interventions or a deepening of authoritarian controls, factors that certainly limited the prospects for social movements and interest groups in the region. The technical nature of such issues coupled with low levels of public awareness about them contributed to the domination of the issue area by specialists and government insiders. Environmental policy thus remained heavily formalist, much of it simply a relabeling of older health and natural resources statutes.

The emergence of popular, environmentally oriented political groups coincides with the period of political liberalization and restoration of civilian government in the 1980s. Such mobilization is also a function of several intersecting forces, in-

cluding growing pollution in large urban areas, the international publicity surrounding notorious cases of environmental depredation and problems of global
concern, organizational opportunities arising from new information technologies, and government and international nongovernmental organization sponsorship. In certain cases, Mexico, for instance, the mobilization of environmental
groups was actively supported by the state, both in response to emerging social
demands and as an effort to shape the character of the groups. A similar observation is made in the case of Guatemala's environmental movement (Berger
1997:113).

These new environmental groups manifested a range of aims, members, and
resources. For the most part, Latin America's emergent environmental groups
could be characterized as urban, made up of members of the socioeconomic middle strata, multipurpose rather than single issue, relatively small in individual
numbers (not including national networks of associations), and poorly funded.
By the end of the 1980s, however, such volunteer groups were joined in virtually
every country by a handful of more specialized and professional environmental
organizations and foundations, most of which relied heavily on international
funding for national conservation projects. Moreover, many groups interested in
rural development—ranging from grassroots *campesino* or peasant organizations
and indigenous groups to organizations of rural professionals—have since
learned to appropriate environmental themes. Though most groups subscribed to
the emerging international consensus on the desirability of "sustainable development," they differed markedly as to preferred modes of implementation, reflecting the broader range of views in Latin America's development debate. (An excellent example of these cleavages is seen in the case of Chilean environmentalism;
see Silva 1996–1997.) This ideological diversity has led to significant competition
among environmental groups, creating new challenges for cooperation.

By the early 1990s one could argue that Latin America's environmental groups
had at least formally made a significant imprint on the policy structure of Latin
American governments. One measure of their accomplishment is simply the visibility of environmental functions in national government. Whereas in 1980 few
governments had designated a cabinet-level environmental ministry, by 1994 at
least six of twenty-three countries had such a ministry, with another six designat-
ing a cabinet-level agency for natural resources management (Mumme and Korzetz 1997). Most governments had adopted some form of environmental legislation and had entrusted a least a subministerial agency or agencies with its
administration. Another measure of accomplishment is the proliferation of
groups themselves. By the end of the 1980s, for instance, Brazil could tally at least
900 environmental organizations, and Mexico nearly that many by some counts
(Mumme and Korzetz 1997). Still another measure is the pervasiveness of environmental concerns in the political platforms and agendas of political parties.
Though the evidence is sketchy, it is certainly true that environmental considerations were appearing with increased frequency in party platforms; a handful of

green parties had appeared in the region by 1990. Yet another measure of the power of environmental ideas is the increasing practice of social groups recasting traditional political claims in environmental rhetoric to gain more media, public, and governmental attention (Fuks 1995).

Even so, Latin American environmental groups face significant obstacles in shaping national policy agendas. The enduring constraints of a clientelist or corporatist character, weak judicial and administrative systems, and electoral impediments potentially limit the influence of environmental groups. The persistence of inadequate public awareness of environmental issues continues to challenge reformist social movements. Lingering cultures of nonparticipation, a legacy of authoritarian regimes, also limit popular mobilization. Other transitional factors, such as the decisive tilt of Latin America's liberalizing regimes toward export-oriented development and the relaxation of protectionist policies, have further stressed environmental groups' capacity to defend their values in national policy arenas. To better understand the range of challenges confronting Latin America's new environmentalism, we turn now to look at social movements in two countries, Mexico and Brazil, which offer important insights into the problems of environmental mobilization in liberalizing regimes.

Environmental Mobilization in Mexico and Brazil

Mexico

Proximate to the United States and one of Latin America's leading industrializers, Mexico's environmental predicament has attracted considerable international attention. That Mexico has paid a profound price for its industrial development can hardly be doubted. Mexico City is an international metaphor for urban degradation. Wanton petroleum development, oil spills, the despoliation of rural areas and landscapes, massive deforestation and threats to its rich trove of biodiversity, and numerous public health problems form the lore of Mexico's contemporary environmental crisis (Mumme 1991). Paradoxically, Mexico is also one of the most advanced countries in Latin American in the articulation of environmental policy, a process accelerated by economic liberalization and trade integration in the 1990s. Mexico thus affords an exceptional opportunity to look at some of the paradoxes, contradictions, and challenges confronting Latin American environmentalism.

Mexico, of course, is one Latin American country that avoided outright military intervention or a sharp swing toward authoritarianism during Latin America's postpopulist authoritarian phase. On the other hand, Mexico's limited authoritarian, predominantly one-party political system did move toward political liberalization in the late 1970s, a process that overlaps liberalizing trends elsewhere in the Americas and that continues to unfold.

Within this general political context, the emergence of Mexican environmentalism follows the Latin American trajectory described earlier. Host to one of the preparatory meetings before the Stockholm 1972 conference, Mexico was one of the first Latin American countries to establish an environmental bureau and to draft environmental statutes for air and water quality in the early 1970s. Throughout the 1970s, however, policy remained dominated by a tiny cadre of government planners in the Health Ministry. Worsening environmental conditions, particularly in Mexico City, contributed in the early 1980s to the formation of Mexico's first broadly based environmental organizations and to a modest government response to localized problems in Mexico City and along the U.S.-Mexican border, a process that resulted in Mexico's first comprehensive environmental law. Electoral reforms in 1978 that opened up the party spectrum provided additional opportunities for placing environmental concerns on the public agenda. Seizing on an emerging national issue, Miguel de la Madrid's administration, 1982–1988, created an environmental ministry in 1983 and undertook to mobilize national environmental concern, courting established groups and virtually creating others. A 1988 reform strengthened national environmental law. By then, the environment had insinuated its way into party platforms, a green party had emerged, and national media were touting environmental issues, modestly affecting the 1988 presidential campaign (Mumme, Bath, and Assetto 1988).

In sum, at the level of civil society the de la Madrid reforms helped diffuse and legitimize national environmental concern. Unfortunately, Mexico's debt crisis crippled investment in environmental measures. The environmental ministry, wedded to urban development, proved a bastion of political patronage. Worsening conditions in Mexico City and high-visibility problems like the 1985 earthquake and the Laguna Verde nuclear plant policy fiasco tainted the government's environmental record.

Carlos Salinas de Gortari, de la Madrid's successor, significantly upgraded the priority accorded environmental measures, focusing on high-visibility problems like Mexico City's chronic air pollution and the pollution of Mexico's rivers. The Salinas administration aggressively sought out multilateral and foreign financing for its environmental programs after 1988. Stung by U.S. criticisms following from Mexico's bid for the North American Free Trade Agreement (NAFTA), the Salinas administration sharply stepped up regulatory action, amplified the standards in force, scrapped the environmental ministry and transferred its functions to a powerful Ministry of Social Development, and completed a process of drafting state environmental laws to supplement national legislation. For his efforts Salinas won the Green Nobel in 1992, United Earth's prize for international environmental achievement.

Though these developments put Mexico in the forefront of Latin American nations in the environmental issue area, the legitimation of environmental concern as social policy and the strong insertion of the state in this issue area had mixed effects on Mexico's environmental movement. On the positive side, legitimation accelerated group formation and gave many environmental groups a degree of public visibility they would not otherwise have had. By 1990 at least three nationwide associations of environmentalists were active, the PEM (the Mexican Ecology Party), the Pacto, and the Alianza Ecologista. Other less-formal associations were also active. An elite group, the Grupo de Cien, made up of leading artists and intellectuals, worked to draw national and international attention to Mexico's problems and, at the very least, could generate sufficient notoriety to embarrass the Mexican regime. Without these combined pressures it is doubtful that the government would have taken the remedial measures it did or moved as fast to do so. On the negative side, environmental organizations found themselves highly dependent on the Mexican state, with limited internal leverage in policy matters. Government patronage in the form of subsidies, sponsorship, or simply consultation became important for a number of environmental organizations. Some leading environmentalists were recruited directly into government administrative positions. These trends clearly demonstrated the potential for government co-optation, influence, and even control of environmentalists' agendas within the political sphere (Demmers and Hogenboom 1992:72–76).

In the electoral-legislative arena, for instance, much of the focus of political liberalization in the 1980s and 1990s was on electoral improvements advancing party competition and congressional representation of minority parties. For environmental organizations, electoral reform was certainly valuable, but the benefits were less tangible. At the rhetorical level, environmentalists benefited from the general adoption of environmental themes in most party platforms. However, they continued to have only modest influence in party organizations. Environmental values remained clearly subordinate to other political concerns. Of the mainstream parties, no particular party emerged as a champion of environmental concerns, though it is fair to say that leading parties, the government's Institutional Revolutionary Party (PRI), the conservative National Action Party (PAN), and the leftist Revolutionary Democratic Party (PRD), varied by degrees in their favored approaches to addressing environmental concerns. If the PRI's ability to point to concrete government projects and actions is discounted, then virtually all party platforms remained vague in their articulation of concrete priorities and policy measures. At this level, then, environment could well be construed more as symbolic than as practical politics.

The emergence of Mexico's lone green party, PEM, was clearly an outcome of the new electoral rules encouraging the formation of minor parties. Formed in advance of the 1988 presidential elections, PEM was from the outset plagued by controversy: Many environmentalists resisted the idea of a separate party; others saw its founder, a former PRI congressman, as bent on dividing the environmental movement. Lacking representation in the national congress, it has had little effect on national policy. Though PEM enjoys a coterie of enthusiastic supporters in Mexico City it has little national presence and, at best, affords a protest vote to a segment of the voting public interested in environmental issues (Mumme 1991).

The ability to affect government programs and policies through the bureaucratic process has been a good deal more important to environmentalists than has electoral contestation. Official elevation of environmental concern is evident at this level in the establishment of new environmental institutions, the elaboration of regulatory statutes and international agreements, and the development of new programs for environmental protection. It is here that the Mexican government has been most active, garnering international credit for its environmental initiatives.

As seen above, the development of the environmental ministry and a complex of environmental programs in the 1980s stimulated social mobilization on environmental issues. From the perspective of environmental organizations, however, the strategic opportunities afforded them often carry substantial costs in terms of accessing and allocating scarce resources, agenda distortion, intragroup conflict, and other difficulties arising from Mexico's one-party, centralist political institutions (Pezzoli 1995:31). On the resources side, for instance, few Mexican environmental groups have the financial resources or means to systematically follow environmental policy developments; the drafting and implementation of such policy is spread across nearly a dozen federal ministries. The problem is compounded by a sexenial system of public administration—in which terms of elected office holders are limited to six years—that invites frequent changes in agency structure and statute law, compounding the costs of accessing and influencing government officials. Since 1983, for instance, the nomenclature, personnel, and structure of the national environmental ministry has changed three times. Such administrative flux gives public officials a de facto advantage in mastering the rules of the game.

Government policy dominance also poses a substantial risk to environmental groups of agenda distortion. Government fora are a preferred mechanism of eliciting the participation and support of environmental groups in government programs. Such fora receive media attention and tend to set the agenda of public concern. They also provide government officials with a means of favoring certain groups over others, and subtly function as a means of enlisting support for predetermined initiatives. Participation in fora is problematic for groups who desire an uncompromised public image but who need to cultivate bureaucratic support to advance their own goals (Umlas 1996).

In general, strategic choices on participation or support for government activities are a common source of stress among and within groups, even groups that operate on a hierarchical basis. It is here that ideological differences within and between environmental groups come into play. In Mexico political liberalization has meant market liberalization, and a significant number of environmental groups are suspicious of market approaches to environmental protection. Since 1988 government programs in forestry, water resources, hazardous waste management, air pollution, and other areas are increasingly predicated on market solutions and decentralized administrative processes (Pezzoli 1995:31). Because the environmental community has not been a major player in crafting such policies, decisions to participate in or to endorse such government initiatives are potentially divisive within and among groups.

In sum, environmental administration in Mexico presents environmentalists with numerous challenges in mobilizing resources, sustaining their goals, and

maintaining the support of their members. One of the very practical consequences of these challenges is the marked tendency among Mexican groups to try
to minimize reliance on formal procedures and bureaucratic mechanisms as
means for achieving their goals (Pezzoli 1995:31).

In the judicial area the elaboration of a new body of statutes, standards, and
regulatory measures over the past decade has accentuated the need to improve
public compliance with the new environmental regime. Mexico's poor record of
compliance with environmental regulations became a major issue in the NAFTA
debate, compelling the government to step up the pace of official enforcement actions after 1992.

Mexico's heightened emphasis on environmental enforcement has drawn international praise. Even so, most enforcement has relied on voluntary compliance
mechanisms. Judicial enforcement, the imposition of sanctions, remains sporadic. In this atmosphere environmental groups remain relatively powerless to do
more than petition for government action or to draw attention to flagrant abuses
through the media. Though the elaboration of new statutes and regulatory rules
provides environmentalists with more bases than ever from which to employ litigation to force regulatory action, such avenues are rarely employed. Ironically, the
Mexican judicial process is far more likely to be used by industry to avoid or delay
government sanctions than by environmentalists. The reasons are various, ranging from the limited resources of environmental organizations to formal and informal procedures that protract the judicial process and complicate the use of litigation to achieve policy aims. In the absence of litigation, environmentalists
remain dependent on government agencies to act on their behalf, reinforcing the
pattern of petitionary politics, negotiated solutions, and bureaucratic domination
of the policy process.

Finally, recent political liberalization in Mexico has stressed federal decentralization—the greater involvement of states and *municipios* in policy development
and implementation. The environmental area has been a significant focal point of
such initiatives. Given Mexico's tradition of administrative centralism, however,
such reforms may be criticized as "formalist" in the absence of systemic decentralization that would empower subnational governments. Such change has been
painfully slow in coming. States and municipalities remain poor stepsisters in the
process of delivering environmental values, hampered by budget scarcity, dependence on federal agencies, and the endemic patronage features of the one-party
system. For environmental groups, policy decentralization simply amplifies their
costs of utilizing government to achieve policy objectives.

Brazil

Like Mexico, Brazil faces a full spectrum of environmental issues, from those typical of industrialized countries to those that plague impoverished preindustrial
ones. Over the last three decades Brazil's environmental challenges have regularly
commanded international attention. In the 1970s the military government's eco-

nomic miracle showed its uglier side in cities like Cubatão, renowned as one of the most polluted cities in the world; in the 1980s attention turned to the rapid and accelerating destruction of Brazil's Amazon rain forest; in the 1990s, conversely, Brazil received international credit for its performance as host of the UN Conference on Environment and Development.

The two major UN conferences on the environment, in Stockholm in 1972 and in Brazil itself in 1992, provide striking signposts of the transformation of environmental attitudes in Brazil. At Stockholm the Brazilian delegation stridently questioned the relevance of environmental concerns for developing countries. Although the Brazilian government's position was not unusual for a poor country then, it fit especially well with the specific concerns of Brazil's military government. First, the military government, as an undemocratic regime that could not claim procedural legitimacy, drew its primary rationale and legitimacy from its economic performance. The military's economic model featured grandiose projects of state-led industrialization, many of which claimed an international comparative advantage based on either Brazil's abundant natural resources or on the lower costs of production without environmental safeguards. Second, the military's prominent security focus spotlighted a national vulnerability in Brazil's unmarked continental boundaries, which had prompted unprecedented efforts to populate and conquer the Amazon rain forest starting in the 1960s.

By the 1992 conference the civilian government was taking a very different stance. Secretary of the Environment José Lutzenberger, a pioneer of the environmental movement, articulated a strongly pro-environment stance as Brazil's international environmental ambassador. His criticisms of the Brazilian government's environmental record led to his being fired shortly before the conference, leaving the foreign affairs ministry, Itamaraty, to define Brazil's participation in the conference itself. Itamaraty presented Brazil as a judicious but supportive host of a major international environmental conference. Both positions, in any case, explicitly rejected the antagonistic attitude taken by the military government at the earlier conference.

In fact, the Brazilian government actively campaigned to host the 1992 conference in order to gain international recognition of its new stance. Although policies and implementation did not always match the rhetoric, as we will see, there is no question that Brazilian environmental politics changed dramatically between 1972 and 1992. Like the political transition itself, however, the transformation of environmental politics proceeded in fits and starts. The military government did provide some significant and early openings to the environmental agenda and pro-environmental actors; the new civilian governments have closed some of those early channels while partially opening others. After a brief discussion of environmental mobilization under the military, we look at three political domains to understand the impact of democratization on the environment in Brazil: party and electoral politics, the national environmental bureaucracy, and the new role of the military. Such small, routine features of national political organization—

and the role of new social actors within them—reveal more about the consequences of political change than do the events and policies that grab international
headlines.

The representatives of Brazil's military government who trumpeted their disdain for environmental considerations at Stockholm were already out of date
even within Brazil. In 1971 Lutzenberger and others in southern Brazil had
formed one of Brazil's first activist conservation groups, Agapan. Over the next
decade groups from many parts of Brazil also mobilized themselves to take on
new environmental challenges. These groups found a muffled echo in new national environmental institutions, notably the Special Secretariat of the Environment (SEMA), which began with a tiny staff and budget in 1973 to combat pollution and to create ecological reserves (Guimarães 1991). Despite the official
condemnation of environmentalism, the new environmental actors found significant political openings. The military government's technocratic orientation provided an opening to the first generation of Brazilian environmentalists who had
strong ties to academic communities. Individual environmentalists regularly went
to Brasília to testify and to provide information to the military government,
drawing on their status as scientific experts. Environmentalists also benefited
from the military government's underestimation of environmentalism as a serious political issue in the 1970s. Compared to the new militance of the unions or
to the upsurge of political opposition after the 1974 elections, mobilizations for
trees and clean air seemed comparatively innocuous to the military. Consequently
the early environmental movement's ranks were greatly increased by opponents
of the military, who found environmentalism a relatively safe way to express their
opposition. One of the broadest environmental mobilizations ever in Brazil came
in 1979, when a coalition of opposition parties, unions, housewives, lawyers, and
students joined environmentalists to protest a new military plan for harvesting
trees in the Amazon. In turn, environmentalists grew more politicized and joined
the broad antimilitary coalition as it turned to more specifically political mobilizations, mobilizations for amnesty, for direct presidential elections, and for a
new constitution.

The peculiarities of the long, military-controlled transition in Brazil brought
important changes in the early 1980s, even though the military retained power
until 1985. In 1981 the military government thoroughly reorganized the national
environmental bureaucracy, coordinating dispersed activities and even including
environmentalists on a new executive council. The 1982 congressional and local
elections marked a new openness in party and electoral politics. In these first
more-competitive elections, three environmental candidates were elected to state
and local offices, heralding a new kind of political participation for environmentalists. By the time the military vacated the government, the many political
changes seemed to broadly favor democratic consolidation and new social actors
like environmental movements. National policy decisions would be made by
elected leaders and representatives, who should be more responsive to their con-

stituents than the military had been. The new rules reestablished basic political rights to mobilize and express opinions, both through the electoral and party systems and outside them.

Nonetheless, environmental movements in Brazil share certain democratization dilemmas with many other new social movements all over Latin America. First, part of the strength of new social movements in the waning days of authoritarianism came from specific organizational characteristics. Unlike traditional political and economic groups, new social movements had no headquarters to raid, no hierarchical leaders to jail or co-opt, and so on. Their tendency to pop up and disappear readily made the new social movements a kind of nimble "guerrilla" opponent to the more ponderous military governments. Compared to other social actors, social movements were thus unusually well adapted to authoritarianism, which provides few regularized channels of access for nonmilitary actors. Democratic consolidation, in contrast, is often defined by general acceptance of institutionalized rules and procedures for political participation. These rules provide plenty of access for nonmilitary actors but favor more permanent forms of social organization like political parties, elected bodies, and other institutionalized avenues of political participation. The special, if temporary, legitimacy that comes to these institutions from the contrast with the outgoing military government also induces many of the former militants to self-censor activities that might destabilize the new democracies. The growth and persistence of social movements and noninstitutional protest in established democracies shows that this self-censorship is not permanent. Many social movements are already reviving in Latin America as dissatisfaction with the limits of democratization increases (Hipsher 1996). But in the short-term politics of the transition, some decline in social movement visibility is therefore likely as earlier activists learn new rules or gather the resources for other kinds of political participation.

Second, much of the success of new social movements' activities in the waning years of the military regimes can be credited to their participation in extraordinarily cohesive opposition coalitions. In Brazil a complex alliance between elite actors—the bar association, the Catholic church hierarchy, the political opposition, and others—and middle-class groups like academics, environmentalists, and scores of unions, neighborhood groups, and other popular organizations was cemented by all participants' opposition to the military (Alves 1985). Members of all these groups mobilized jointly on whatever issues allowed them to express their shared opposition. With their common goal achieved by the military-civilian transition, each of these groups now pursues its own specific agenda in the new civilian order. Individually, they lack the resources and influence of the collective mobilizations. The 1979 Amazon mobilizations, for example, maintained organizational units in eighteen states and the federal district for nearly two years by drawing on the full array of opposition forces. Environmentalists alone were unable to re-create such geographic breadth until the UN Conference mobilizations a decade later, and even then it was done by recreating a cross-sectoral coalition.

Finally, as discussed in the introduction, liberalization is always restricted in practice or by design. This may be temporary, since political elites need to learn new rules and procedures for incorporating popular participation. The postmilitary elite may also have more enduring reasons to restrict the scope of the new democracies, however, either as part of formal and informal pacts made with the outgoing regime or, more perniciously, in the service of their own political and economic interests.

Within these general challenges that democratization poses for new social movements, especially at the moment of transition, there are still new and meaningful opportunities for participation. In comparison to other social movements in Brazil and elsewhere, Brazilian environmentalists have been relatively successful at seizing such new opportunities, although they have also faced significant roadblocks. During the 1980s they tried several different electoral strategies that brought some legislative successes. They have been less successful at penetrating the national environmental bureaucracy, which is itself very weak. Throughout their efforts they have been repeatedly stymied by the economic crisis of the state and by continuing military control of key policy areas.

Brazil's military regime was unusual in allowing political parties and elections to continue throughout its rule. At first political activity was closely controlled by the military, but over the long transition process the armed forces gradually liberalized. By the time of the 1979 party reforms and general amnesty, many social actors saw significant participatory possibilities in this arena. A further round of reforms in 1985 removed more restrictions to party formation, provided free television and radio time to political parties, and set up rules for a Constituent Assembly. In this liberalized context. Brazilian environmentalists pursued a number of electoral strategies, with mixed success.

Three environmentalists were elected to state and local offices in 1982 with the support of local environmentalists. Each of them was instrumental in presenting important environmental legislation, although each eventually had conflicts with environmentalists as well. Their experiences show two classic dilemmas that party politics poses for environmentalists: First, competition among political parties can become conflict among environmentalists, and second, electoral and legislative politics may call for compromises where the environmental agenda does not. Such dilemmas also appeared at the national level for environmental congressman Fábio Feldmann, who was the only environmentalist elected from a national "Green List" of environmentalist candidates in 1986. Feldmann was the crucial actor who coordinated the mobilization for a chapter on the environment in the 1988 constitution, even championing controversial positions like eliminating Brazil's nuclear program. Nonetheless, he barely made São Paulo's 1990 Green List because of many environmentalists' concern that he was now more of a political actor than an environmental one. A perusal of environmental legislation at all governmental levels shows that, except for a few high-profile presidential initiatives, it is the environmentalists-turned-politicians who have proposed and pushed much of Brazil's now-extensive environmental protections. In this way democratization has clearly moved the environmental agenda forward.

The role of organized environmentalists in this process is less clear. They have mobilized in support of some of the more important pieces of legislation, including the environmental chapter. But in electing environmentalists to office, their broadest national mobilizations—the 1986 Green List campaign and the Green Party—have been less successful. Only Feldmann was elected from the approximately twenty national candidates on the Green List. The Green Party has foundered in the face of party registration requirements and barely exists as an organization, although its charismatic founder, Fernando Gabeira, was elected to the national Chamber of Deputies after several unsuccessful campaigns. Environmentalists' electoral strategy since the Green Party was first collectively discussed in 1985 has been to support individual environmentalist candidates regardless of party, and they have had some success at state and local levels, especially in the south and southeast, where they are strongest.

One larger dilemma for Brazilian environmentalists is that passing legislation no longer seems like an adequate political strategy. The weak and undemocratic nature of Brazil's other national institutions make good legislation irrelevant in too many cases. Both the judicial system and the environmental bureaucracies are too weak or underfunded to use the new legislative and judicial tools. The problems of the national environmental bureaucracy can be summed up in large part by simply stating its changing bureaucratic position. Since 1985, there have been major reorganizations every two years on average, many of which substantially reclassified environmental issues—and all by executive decree. The simple fact of constant reformulation leaves those both inside and outside the agencies confused about who is supposed to do what how. Accountability, rare in any Brazilian ministry, is impossible. It is no wonder that environmentalists have tended to ignore the national environmental agencies. Transition is certainly taking place, but democratization is far from a synonym for transition in this case.

In addition to reorganization, environmental bureaucracies have also suffered from the government's fiscal crisis. While Lutzenberger was environmental secretary in 1991, for example, 90 percent of his budget was frozen for four months. Similar problems exist for state-level bureaucracies. When Feldmann became São Paulo's secretary of the environment in 1995, one of his first challenges was to absorb budget cuts of 30 percent. In line with the current emphasis on downsizing the state, some officials have suggested privatizing part of the agencies' land or responsibilities, a move with potentially negative environmental consequences.

The issue of reduced funding underlines the fact that much of the policy formulation and legislation affecting the environment is not about the environment per se. Narrowly focused on aims like promoting economic growth or national security, such bills may have greater environmental impact than environmentally explicit legislation. Export promotion and budget rescissions to satisfy international creditors have clearly had negative consequences for environmental quality.

President José Sarney cited both economic and security considerations for his environmental nationalism on developing the Amazon, and even the more conciliatory governments since have failed to decisively halt deforestation. In an additional measure with historic reverberations, air pollution levels in Cubatão have returned to their 1984, pre–pollution control, levels. Economic policymaking under Brazil's civilian government thus resembles military patterns in both its process and its content. If anything, the rolling back of government control over the industrialization process opens new avenues for environmental degradation.

Finally, the military retains important controls over key environmental policy implementation. It is the Secretariat of Strategic Affairs (SAE, created from the military government's intelligence service, the Secretariat for National Intelligence [SNI]) that is responsible for the economic and ecological zoning of the country and for nuclear policy. The Aeronautics Ministry oversees Amazon security and environmental surveillance. One author has suggested that the Amazon is being used as a safety valve for controlling military dissatisfaction: "It was the remoteness of the northern Amazon frontier from the national ecumene and the relative unimportance to national well-being that now made it an ideal place to give vent to geopolitical thinking and thus to serve as a sink for military energies that might otherwise go into political misadventures" (Foresta 1992:129).

Any continued military role outside of its traditional one of external security raises questions about the completeness of the democratic transition and reduces the opportunity for citizen participation. And military administration of the Amazon, considering its record, augers poorly for environmental progress.

In the context of all of these steps forward and backward in democratization and environmental protection, many Brazilian environmentalists find themselves disillusioned about the prospects for the environmental agenda in civilian politics. One of their responses has been to turn to other sectors of civil society. In preparations for hosting a nongovernmental conference parallel to 1992's conference of governments, Brazilian environmentalists put together a cross-sectoral coalition with other social movements and nongovernmental organizations that looked remarkably similar to the antimilitary coalition. At the conference itself, they tried to create similar ties to civil groups worldwide, arguing that only citizens, in the end, could ensure environmental, social, and political progress. To many, the most promising path to democratization lies more outside governments than within them. The next edition of this book can evaluate this claim.

Conclusion

As our cases reveal, Latin America's contemporary social movements confront serious challenges. The opportunities of restricted liberalization are often offset by enduring political constraints or the restructuring of economic and political power. One of the principal lessons to be taken from this study is that, barring the deepening and strengthening of democratic institutions, today's environmentalists are apt to place their bets on society instead of the state as they strive to advance environmental protection nationally and regionally.

Bibliography

Alves, Maria Helene Moreira. 1985. *State and Opposition in Military Brazil*. Austin: University of Texas Press.

Berger, Susan A. 1997. Environmentalism in Guatemala: When fish have ears. *Latin American Research Review* 32:99–116.

Demmers, Jolle, and Barbara Hogenboom. 1992. *Popular Organization and Party Dominance: The Political Role of Environmental NGOs in Mexico*. Amsterdam: University of Amsterdam.

Fiorino, Daniel J. 1996. Environmental policy and the participation gap. In *Democracy and the Environment* (William M. Lafferty and James Meadowcraft, eds.), 194–212. Cheltenham, UK: Edward Elgar.

Foresta, Ronald. 1992. Amazonia and the politics of geopolitics. *Geographical Review* 82:128–142.

Fuks, Mario. 1995. Environment-related litigation in Rio de Janeiro: shaping frames for a new social problem. Paper presented at 1995 Conference of the Latin American Studies Association, Washington, DC.

Garcia, Flávio. 1987. O pacote florestal que Ameaça a Amazonia. *Pau Brazil* 16:27–40.

Guimarães, Roberto. 1991. *The Ecopolitics of Development in the Third World: Politics and Environment in Brazil*. Boulder: Lynne Rienner.

Hipsher, Patricia. 1996. Democratization and the decline of urban social movements in Chile and Spain. *Comparative Politics* 28:273–297.

Hochstetler, Kathryn. 1995. Social movements in institutional politics: Organizing about the environment in Brazil and Venezuela. Unpublished manuscript.

Hurrell, Andrew. 1992. Brazil and the international politics of Amazonian deforestation. In *The International Politics of the Environment* (A[ndrew] Hurrell and B. Kingsbury, eds.), 398–429. Oxford: Clarendon Press.

Keck, Margaret. 1995. Social equity and environmental politics in Brazil: Lessons from the rubber tappers of Acre. *Comparative Politics* 27:408–424.

Lamounier, Bolivar. 1989. *Partidos e Utopias: O Brasil no Limiar dos Anos 90*. São Paulo: Edições Loyola.

Mainwaring, Scott. 1991. Politicians, parties, and electoral systems: Brazil in comparative perspective. *Comparative Politics* 24:21–43.

Mumme, Stephen. 1991. Clearing the air: Environmental reform in Mexico. *Environment* 330 (December):1–30.

Mumme, Steven P., C. Richard Bath, and Valerie J. Assetto. 1988. Political development and environmental policy in Mexico. *Latin American Research Review* 23:7–34.

Mumme, Steven P., and Edward Korzetz. 1997. Democratization, politics, and environmental reform in Latin America. In *The Politics of Latin American Environmental Policy in International Perspective* (Gordon MacDonald, Daniel Nielsen, and Marc Stern, eds.), 40–59. Boulder: Westview Press.

Navarro, Zander. 1994. Democracy, citizenship, and representation: Rural social movements in southern Brazil, 1978–1990. *Bulletin of Latin American Research* 13:129–154.

Pádua, José Augusto, ed. 1987. *Ecologia e Política no Brasil.* Rio de Janeiro: Editora Espaço e Tempo and IUPERJ.

Pezzoli, Keith. 1995. The political ecology of human settlements: Mexico City in comparative perspective. Paper presented to the 1995 meeting of the Latin American Studies Association, Washington, D.C.

Silva, Eduardo. 1996–1997. Democracy, market economics, and environmental policy in Chile. *Journal of Inter-American Studies and World Affairs* 38:1–33.

Stepan, Alfred, ed. 1989. *Democratizing Brazil: Problems of Transition and Consolidation.* New York: Oxford University Press.

Tension mounts between natural resources projects and citizen rights. 1995. *Environment Watch: Latin America* (June):8.

Umlas, Elizabeth. 1996. Environmental non-governmental networks: The Mexican case in theory and practice. Ph.D. diss., Yale University.

Vieira, Paula, and Eduardo Viola. 1994. Del preservacionismo al desarrollo sustentable: Un reto para el movimiento ambiental de Brasil. In *Retos para el Desarrollo y la Democracia: Movimientos Ambientales en América Latina y Europa* (M. P. García-Guadilla and J. Blauert, eds.), 105–121. Caracas: Fundación Friedrich Ebert de México and Editorial Nueva Sociedad.

Chapter Five

Assessing Democracy Then and Now: A Personal Memoir

MARTIN NEEDLER

I have shared—and indeed share now—the two beliefs that underlie Russell Fitzgibbon's surveys of the democratic charter of the Latin American countries: that degree of democracy is central to the evaluation of Latin American regimes and that political science should become as quantitative as possible—or, in view of the kind of articles that find their way into the political science journals today, let me amend that to read "as quantitative as reasonable."

Of course, there were several major problems with Fitzgibbon's method, as we all know: The dimensions of democracy that he specified, although reasonable, were subjective; they were not reliably independent of each other; the weights he assigned them, equal or not, were arbitrary; and the people he polled, no matter how knowledgeable some of them might have been, were in no position to make detailed quantifiable judgments on all dimensions for all of the twenty countries that were included in the survey. Despite that, the final rankings he came out with seemed intuitively to be pretty accurate because, I believe, the methodological weaknesses of the survey tended to cancel each other out. That is, because the people polled had no particular knowledge, for example, of the autonomy of local government in Honduras or the quality of the judicial system in Bolivia, they tended to reply in terms of their feelings about the state of democracy in Honduras or Bolivia as a whole, in a phenomenon that I believe pollsters call "response set." The quantitative apparatus may have impressed the unsophisticated or casual reader, but what Fitzgibbon was ending up with, in effect, was the central tendency in a sample of subjective estimates for each country.

Unfortunately, the technical shortcomings of the method made it easier for the apologists for Latin American dictatorships and military regimes to scoff at the concern most of us have for the fate of democracy in the region as naive or ethnocentric, which it certainly is not.

Beyond Ethnocentricity

There were indeed naive and ethnocentric elements in the stone-age political science of the postwar era, though. Fitzgibbon's appreciation that there are educational and economic dimensions to the realization of democracy marked a substantial advance over the legalism and formalism present in much commentary on the region.[1] (Most of academic commentary in public administration seems still to be in that stage, as does the technical assistance in public administration offered by U.S. agencies to the governments of Latin America.)

Mainstream political science, embarrassed by the apparent sentimentality or tendentiousness of using democracy as the central concept, tried "Westernization" and "modernization" and finally settled on "development." We still had democracy in mind when writing about development, however, and most commentators let a fuzzy and idealized version of U.S. institutions and practices stand in for any sort of rigorous conception of what a democratic or "developed" polity would look like.

Of course, there were honorable exceptions to those tendencies. Charles W. Anderson's *Politics and Economic Change in Latin America: The Governing of Restless Nations* (1967) was a sophisticated exploration of the relation between politics and economic development in Central America and received most votes in a survey that asked which was the most important book that had been published on Latin American politics (Kenski 1974).

To Define Political Development

As I puzzled over the question of political development in the early 1960s, it seemed to me that it contained inherently paradoxical elements. Trying not to be subjective or ethnocentric, I defined political development as the increasing actualization of the political ideals the society sets for itself, for example, in the increasing approximation in practice to the norms outlined in a political constitution. A developing polity would then be one in which a constitution, originally embodying a set of goals very imperfectly realized in practice—which was a commonplace in commentary about Latin American institutions—would increasingly be reflected in reality. Political practice would increasingly conform to constitutional norms, for example, with a decreasing incidence of interruptions of constitutional continuity by military seizures of power, with greater respect for the results of elections, and the like.

Development in that sense could occur in any era. A state whose formal belief system and whose constitution was that of oligarchy or patriarchy could "develop" into a more perfect oligarchy or patriarchy. In a democratic era, then, development had to mean the increasing actualization of effective, active popular participation in political life. Under the circumstances generally prevailing in Latin America at the time, however, it was likely that increasing democratic participation would take the form of strikes and demonstrations that would intimidate elites into yielding a portion of their control, as the lesser of the evils available to them. Seen in this light, violence might be under some circumstances and at some times a sign of lack of development, and in other forms and at other times an indication that development was taking place.

In keeping with the spirit of the time, and certainly with the ethos of the University of Michigan, where I taught from 1960 to 1965, I sought quantitative tests for these hypotheses. Trying to avoid subjectivity, my own and that of others, I developed an index of constitutional practice that consisted of the number of years that had been spent under a legally elected, constitutionally functioning government. My index of participation was the proportion of the total population voting. Today we may have refined our sense of what a genuinely free and fair election is too much not to be uneasy about giving the actual elections that take place so central a role in theory, though it is hard to see what else one can do.

Political development, understood as a *combination* of the scores on the constitutionality and participation indices, I found to correlate with economic development.[2] Now this was a statistical correlation in which there were outlying cases that were by themselves anomalous. The chief of these was Argentina, highly developed on the social and economic indicators but nowhere in terms of democratic practice. (As the joke had it: "Of course Argentina is a developed country. During the last *coup* all the tanks stopped for the red lights.") In Venezuela the economic indicators got ahead of the political ones during the early 1960s, but the political indicators caught up, vindicating the theory. In Costa Rica, similarly but conversely, the economic indicators caught up to the political ones.

Whereas political development correlated positively with economic development, the two political scores—constitutionality and participation—were in inverse relation to each other. I accounted for this finding by hypothesizing that if a society was more hierarchic, political development expressed itself peacefully in greater fidelity to constitutional norms, whereas if the society was more egalitarian, political development expressed itself in greater mass participation. The more hierarchic societies I identified as those with a traditionally repressed Indian component.

Development as Subversion

Theory on these matters was elaborated with one eye on the construction of U.S. policy toward the underdeveloped world in general. Cambridge, Massachusetts, was the center of such thinking in the 1960s, where Samuel P. Huntington and Myron Weiner chaired a joint Harvard-MIT faculty seminar on political development. I was at the fringes of this activity, having been one of the first to use the term "political development" (Needler 1961). I had been graduate assistant to Huntington in 1957 and 1958 in his course on U.S. defense policy; he became interested in political development after I left Harvard in 1959, and I began sending him papers I was presenting at meetings. Our thinking on these questions proved to be parallel in many respects, and he invited me back to Harvard as a research associate of the Center for International Affairs for the academic year 1965–1966. There I participated in the joint Harvard-MIT seminar, in which virtually all of the luminaries working on political development at the time participated.[3]

However, Huntington and I went on to draw rather different conclusions from the insight we shared that constitutional stability stood in opposition to the requirements of democratic participation in developing societies during a certain period in their history. Huntington tended to draw elitist conclusions that favored the maintenance of order over revolutionary violence. Continuing along that line, he made some unfortunate observations during the time of the Vietnam War. With respect to Latin America, subsequently, he came to take too seriously Howard Wiarda's overemphasis on "cultural" factors in accounting for undemocratic practice in Latin America, an approach that tends to minimize exploitation and class conflict and to whitewash U.S. policy. Huntington has since followed this line of thought even further, as can be seen in his article "The Clash of Cultures" (1993), which compounds various misunderstandings[4] in ideological statements that seem chiefly valuable for giving the Pentagon a now very badly needed rationale on which to hang its budget requests.

My intellectual evolution was different. From the same insight, that manifestations of political development might appear subversive of a constitutional order, I drew different conclusions. Rather than identifying the interest of the United States as being on the side of the conservative forces in the world, I argued that the aim of ostensibly subversive movements was actually no more than democratic government and the higher standards of living that could in fact be promoted by free trade and a free-market economy. Taking a long-range view, accordingly, the movement toward democratic participation in Latin America should be seen as entirely consistent with the basic interests of the United States, both political and economic. Democratic governments in Latin America would naturally sympathize with the United States, and Latin American economies more developed in an egalitarian direction would be the best partners for the U.S. economy (Needler 1972).

My personal views were in fact rather more radical than this formulation implies, but I believed it was unrealistic to expect the government of the United States to pursue policies that could not clearly be understood as being in the interest of the United States and of its dominant economic forces. My pragmatism was rewarded by the partly gratifying and partly mortifying spectacle of seeing what appeared to be the views I expressed during the 1960s and 1970s reappear as the rationale for the Latin American policies of the Bush administration. Actually, Bush-era officials such as Bernard Aronson deserve great credit for extricating the

United States from the disasters of Reagan's Central American policies, helping Oscar Arias to earn his Nobel Peace Prize.

Democratization and the World Economy

To appreciate the mixed message conveyed by the Bush administration's support for democracy in the region is to indicate the limitations of even the more sophisticated approaches to the problem of Latin American democracy of the 1960s and 1970s. We knew enough to distinguish between having elections and not having elections and between fair elections and clearly fraudulent ones. We were not then prepared for the extent to which money, in the form of campaign contributions to legislators, expenditures on pollsters and public relations geniuses, and dominance of the mass media by reactionary buccaneers, could induce democratic electorates to vote against their own interests (and not only in Latin America). And we had no inkling that the free-market economies of the end of the twentieth century would be not the Scandinavian-style mixed economies that seemed then to be the wave of the future but, instead, the playgrounds of today's continuously reconfigured conglomerates without national identity, perpetually downsizing their workforces and being intermittently looted by financial speculators.

Perhaps the more important point in assessing the democratic character of any of the regimes in present-day Latin America is how much difference it makes that a government represent the majority of the people when the freedom of action of that government is so thoroughly circumscribed by the implacable imperatives of the world economic and financial system in the era of the triumph of capitalism.

Much as in physics Newton's billiard-ball universe gave way to a quantum universe of quivering packets of energy, the ground has disappeared from under the old certainties in thinking about Latin American politics.

The Mexican Example

I do not wish to convey the impression that making judgments about degree of democracy in the 1950s and 1960s was a simple matter. There were certainly problems then in assessing democratic performance. For example, how was one to strike a balance arithmetically between Mexico's formal democracy and the reality of its peculiar one-party system?

Trying to assess the degree of democracy that should be assigned to Mexico presented unique problems. Challenges to the ruling Institutional Revolutionary Party (PRI) were so feeble that those searching for possible evolutionary routes to democracy found them more plausibly within the ruling party itself, in the competition among the various sectors of the party (Padgett 1966) and even in the possibility that the sectors would break away from the party and form individual parties of their own (Scott 1964). I used to tour polling places during Mexico's presidential elections in the 1960s and 1970s. In urban areas, the prescribed rules were followed literally, but in rural areas it was rare to find poll watchers from the opposition parties because those parties simply had no presence outside a handful of cities. Skeptics unfamiliar with Mexico assumed that opposition parties were prevented from functioning and that opposition ballots were thrown out. Although this happened on occasion, it was more common for the PRI to encourage opposition party activity in order to give elections a more plausible look.

As far as votes for the opposition were concerned, no reliable national opinion polling existed, so it was not possible to compare votes as reported with opinions expressed. However, some very simple extrapolations of the opinion data reported by Gabriel Almond and Sidney Verba in their *Civic Culture* (1965) suggested that votes recorded for the National Action Party (PAN) in the 1952 election apparently reflected the distribution of opinion accurately (Needler 1971).

Today it is universally assumed that Mexican electoral authorities manipulate the vote result. This is clearly the case in state elections, and it is highly probable that more subtle fine-tuning of the results takes place at the national level. Yet, as Miguel Basáñez has pointed out,[5] in 1994 the national results, at least, seemed to mirror those opinions collected in the polls with the soundest sampling methodology. Alan Knight has advanced the intriguing suggestion,[6] perhaps partly in jest, that the opinion polls give the ruling party's election manipulators an idea of the range in which they can fix electoral results and still have them appear plausible.

In any case, how can one characterize Mexico today, with a much more competitive party system and a livelier opposition in the legislature and the media, but with political power ebbing and flowing across the porous boundaries between constitutional rulers, fabulously wealthy capitalists, and drug-dealing gangsters? When Phil Kelly asks me now to respond to the democracy survey, I tell him I am retired.

Notes

1. For example, William P. Tucker's (1957) completely formalistic description of Mexico in his book *The Mexican Government Today*.

2. These ideas were laid out in my book *Political Development in Latin America: Instability, Violence, and Evolutionary Change* (1968). It was rated a distant second to Anderson's book in the Kenski survey.

3. I remember remarking to Michael Hudson that if a bomb dropped on the room in which we met it would mean the end of the study of political development.

4. For example, Japan is apparently sometimes "Confucian," sometimes "Western"; significant conflicts that do not fit the model—in northern Ireland or southern Africa—are passed over in silence; obvious class conflicts (for example, even popular dissatisfaction with International Monetary Fund–mandated austerity programs) are presented as clashes between cultural outlooks; and, most important, the point is missed that Islamic extremism is overwhelmingly concerned not with international politics but with lax observance of religious injunctions about dress and behavior within Muslim societies themselves (see Esposito 1995). There is no reason why U.S. strategic doctrine, and the level and type of armament it attempts to justify, should find any sustenance here.

5. At a conference sponsored by the UT Center for Mexican Studies in Austin in September 1994.

6. At the same conference.

Bibliography

Almond, Gabriel, and Sidney Verba. 1965. *The Civic Culture*, abridged ed. Boston: Little Brown.

Anderson, Charles W. 1967. *Politics and Economic Change in Latin America: The Governing of Restless Nations*. Princeton: Van Nostrand.

Esposito, John L. 1995. *The Islamic Threat: Myth or Reality?* New York: Oxford University Press.

Huntington, Samuel P. 1993. The clash of cultures. *Foreign Affairs* 72:22–49.

Kenski, Henry C. 1974. *Teaching Latin American Politics at American Universities: A Survey.* Tucson, Ariz.: Institute of Government Research.

Needler, Martin C. 1972. *The United States and the Latin American Revolution.* Boston: Allyn and Bacon.

_____. 1971. *Politics and Society in Mexico.* Albuquerque: University of New Mexico Press.

_____. 1968. *Political Development in Latin America: Instability, Violence, and Evolutionary Change.* New York: Random House.

_____. 1961. The political development of Mexico. *American Political Science Review* 55:308–312.

Padgett, Leon Vincent. 1966. *The Mexican Government System.* Boston: Houghton Mifflin.

Scott, Robert E. 1964. *Mexican Government in Transition*, rev. ed. Urbana: University of Illinois Press.

Tucker, William P. 1957. *The Mexican Government Today.* Minneapolis: University of Minnesota Press.

Part Two

Assessing Democracy in Mexico and Middle America

A "paradox of authoritarianism and democracy" conditions politics in Mexico, according to Guy Poitras, author of our first chapter of Part Two, "Mexico's Problematic Transition to Democracy." The *practice* of politics is authoritarian; the *promise* or potential is democratic. What is key to democratization is a consolidation of a democratic consensus where the political rules of competition become accepted by all participants. To Poitras, such has not yet occurred. But his description of forces fostering and arresting democratic consolidation allow the reader the opportunity to evaluate current trends and predict future possibilities.

Chapter 7, "Province Versus the Center: Democratizing Mexico's Political Culture," also examines democracy in Mexico, this time from the perspective of a national political culture coalescing sufficiently to support democratic reforms in government, a coalescing that Roderic Ai Camp finds has not appeared. He argues that "Mexicans are not yet in agreement on how these structural problems can be solved, nor on the best techniques for citizens themselves to articulate their demands and replace governing authorities." Hence higher democratic performance must await a greater unity of national political culture.

"Democracy has not come to Central America," writes Thomas M. Leonard in Chapter 8, "The Quest for Central American Democracy Since 1945," although the "old order" of traditional elites and the military is being seriously challenged at present by middle and lower-sector groups. Giving us a fifty-year overview of political and economic conditions in Panama, Honduras, Guatemala, Costa Rica, and El Salvador, Leonard describes substantial violence against the "established order" throughout most of the region during the 1980s, but order returning after the oligarchy had been rescued by the armed forces, precluding a deeper establishment of democracy that might have benefited more sectors of society.

Why Costa Rica measures so much more highly in democracy than does its neighbor, Nicaragua, is the focus of Chapter 9, "Elections and Democracy in Central America: The Cases of Costa Rica and Nicaragua," by Charles L. Stansifer. Despite their "common language and religious and cultural inheritance, their close historical linkages, and their proximity to each other," Stansifer sees, for example, in Costa Rica, compared to Nicaragua, fewer class and racial antagonisms, minimal international interference, less desire for a military, fewer authoritarian colonial inheritances, and other such differences that apparently have created the variation in democratic evolutions.

Planned and directed labor and other disturbances in Britain's Caribbean colonies during the Great Depression years triggered "revolutionary" changes, states W. Marvin Will in Chapter 10, "Institutional Development, Democratization, and Independence in the Anglophone Caribbean." These disturbances caused a racial shift in political elites, followed by greater development of democratic institutions and eventual national independence for the English-speaking countries of Middle America.

In Chapter 11, "Passion and Democracy in Cuba," Damián J. Fernández predicts the rise of an "uncivil society" post-Castro Cuba, one not based on liberal democratic tenets but on the resurfacing of traditional Cuban traits: corporatism, clientelism, informalism, nonrationality, and idealism. In particular, a "politics of passion" and "the politics of affection are likely to be detrimental to democracy and civility," retarding pragmatism and stability. These conditions may persist for some time until the disruptions of the post-Castro transition calm.

Democracy in Haiti, concludes Richard L. Millett in Chapter 12, "Haitian Democracy: Oxymoron or Emerging Reality?" is "by no means without hope. And hope, not optimism, is perhaps as much as can be reasonably expected when trying to discern the future of democracy in Haiti." In his initial pages, Millett outlines reasons for the country's abysmal democratic record; he then outlines the trends he sees either toward or away from constitutionalism since former President Aristide's return from exile in 1994. He finally evaluates the conditions necessary for maintaining this decade's progress, including economic improvement, international support, and competent Haitian political leadership.

Howard J. Wiarda believes Latin America possesses a "vast problem of ungovernability" and a general ambivalence toward democracy and that there is hence a need for strong, even at times authoritarian, leadership as a stabilizer to democracy. In Chapter 13, "The Dilemmas of Democracy in the Dominican Republic: A Paradigm for *All* of Latin America?" he illustrates this point by examining the long and successful political career of Joaquín Balaguer, who personified a stabilizing mix between authority and democracy and who was able to administer the nation effectively within a transition between dictatorship and "facade" democracy. Wiarda also calls for a democracy scale other than Fitzgibbon's, one that would measure stages of governing that exist between authoritarian and democratic systems.

Chapter Six

Mexico's Problematic Transition to Democracy

GUY POITRAS

At the heart of Mexican politics lies the paradox of authoritarianism and democracy, which must be resolved if Mexico is to become a more democratic country. Extending this argument further, important factors are at work to make it easier to conceive of a more democratic Mexico in the years to come, but there are also potent factors emerging from the unresolved paradox of Mexican politics that give us cause to be skeptical about a meaningful consolidation of democracy in Mexico for the near future. Until and unless the paradox between authoritarian practice and democratic promise is resolved, a more democratic future must remain problematic.

The factors promoting a genuine democratic transition and those that could arrest it emerge out of the unique hybrid that is Mexican politics. The impressive stability of Mexican politics is unmatched by other Latin American countries; but this stability has also delayed for many years the onset of liberal democracy (Knight 1992:141). Even after numerous episodes of political reform, Mexicans imagine more than they live democracy (Meyer 1991a).

The paradox of Mexican politics has yielded a charming array of terms to capture its hybrid character. At one time, "one-party democracy" was in vogue. More recently, Mexico has been typecast as a "semi-democracy" (Levy 1989:462), a "partial democracy" (Cornelius, Gentleman, and Smith 1989:41), an "exclusive democracy" (Brachet-Marquez 1994:19–20), and a "selective democracy" (Cothran 1994:231). For his part, President Carlos Salinas de Gortari (1988–1994) spoke of "democracy within reason" (Centeno 1994:217).

The other way to perceive Mexican politics is to stress the authoritarian side of the coin. Mexico is a "perfect dictatorship" (Vargas Llosa in Reding 1991) or simply "presidentialism" (Reding 1991). Others sought to juxtapose these contradictions by referring to "technocratic populism" (Teichman 1988:142), "hybrid, semi-authoritarianism" (Cornelius and Craig 1991:121), "inclusionary authoritarianism" (Brachet-Marquez 1994:25), "reconfigured authoritarianism" (Poitras and Robertson 1994:29), and "electoral bureaucratic authoritarianism" (Centeno 1994:32).

The Democracy Conundrum

So what, then, is meant by democracy? This perennial issue in political theory cannot be resolved here. However, since Mexico aspires to join North America politically and economically, we will rely upon conventional ideas drawn from liberal democratic theory as well as from ideas about the social conditions of democracy.

The 1980s and 1990s witnessed a third wave of democratization in Latin America. Four decades earlier, Russell Fitzgibbon sought to gauge the state of democracy in Latin America. Using fifteen criteria, experts were asked to rate twenty countries at regular intervals. How did Mexico fare? It did reasonably well for that era and compared to its neighbors. Mexico scored relatively well in the rankings on several criteria: civilian supremacy over the military, regular elections, lack of ecclesiastical dominance, internal unity, and political maturity (Fitzgibbon 1951:522; 1956:74; Johnson 1975:134). These traditional and rather formal criteria of democracy actually said as much about Mexico's unique brand of political stability as it did about its democratic credentials.

However, reassessing Mexico at the end of the century could lead to a less sanguine conclusion. The world has changed politically much faster than has Mexico since the midpoint of the century. Consequently Mexico's experience with democracy in the late twentieth century is indeterminate. Three criteria for liberal democracy can be used to gauge Mexican democracy: (1) regular, free, and fair elections of representatives, with universal and equal suffrage; (2) the responsibility of the state apparatus to the elected parliament, and (3) freedom of expression and association as well as protection of individual rights (Rueschemeyer, Stephens, and Stephens 1992:43). Judging Mexico against the three criteria yields a more critical appraisal of Mexican democracy.

Elections are held regularly in Mexico, just as they were when Fitzgibbon began his survey of democracy in 1945. Yet after decades of elections, only one party, the government's Institutional Revolutionary Party (PRI), has ever won control of the national government. Elections are sometimes dirty and usually unfair contests between one party with most of the advantages and the opposition parties with very few. It is still big news if the opposition parties in Mexico win an election—any election.

The second criterion also does not shed a very favorable light on Mexican democracy. Democracy requires a strong role for a representative legislature. However, the Mexican president—not the legislature—is the mainspring of the state. The bicameral Congress was once not much more than a rubber stamp. Recently it has risen to the level of a debating society, as was demonstrated during the approval of the North American Free Trade Agreement (NAFTA) legislation in late 1993 (Poitras and Robertson 1994:13).

How a democracy treats its people, and particularly how it treats the opposition, is also critical. Although Mexicans do not live in a police state and can exercise many civil and human rights without undue fear, the government's arbitrary power tempts unscrupulous leaders from time to time to use this power against anyone who opposes them. Contemporary Mexico has a decidedly mixed record on civil and human rights (Barry 1992:63–70).

Democracy is more than process and institutions. In its broader sense, democracy has social and economic dimensions, too. Mexico has undergone remarkable economic modernization since Fitzgibbon began his work. The economy grew for three decades and developed manufacturing and service sectors. Mexicans increasingly worked as wage earners in cities rather than for a subsistence in the countryside. Incomes generally rose from the 1940s until the 1970s, although wealth did not usually trickle down to the poorest. Today Mexicans are more educated and more mobile than ever before, and they must find their way in a complex, urban society that is increasingly more modern and challenging. In other words, the Mexican state succeeded in advancing modernization. By fostering economic and social modernization, the government created a society that is too complex to govern from one center. Economic and social change outpaced political change.

Transition and Consolidation

Democratization has two stages: transition and consolidation. Both are vital if Mexico is to become a less centralized and authoritarian system. Both stages of democratization are necessary to eliminate the central paradox of its political system. This would be the most far-reaching political change since the Revolution almost 100 years ago.

Given its unique blend of juxtaposed tendencies, Mexico embodies both democratic and antidemocratic features. For Mexico to move farther along the road toward democracy it must consolidate the democratic elements of political change and mute and gradually discard the authoritarian features.

The democratic transition is often about elections. Given Mexico's electoral history, the transition could start with electoral reform, but by no means may it end there. The transition would have to broaden into other areas. The democratization of Mexico would include fair and competitive elections, but it would also embrace comprehensive change: a decentralized state, a more even balance between presidential and other institutional power, transparency of government operations, the curtailment of government corruption, a democratic culture, judicial reform, the rule of law, a reformed (or dismembered) PRI, a more competitive party system, a more prosperous economy, and a more egalitarian society.

Transition must be followed by the consolidation of democracy if democracy is to take root. To transform Mexican politics by consolidating democracy requires a consensus about "rules and codes of political conduct and the worth of political in-stitutions" (Burton, Gunther, and Higley 1992:4). There has to be spontaneous, self-interested compliance of the elites and major players with these rules of conduct, re-gardless of any specific election results or policy outcomes (Przeworski 1991:26).

Forces for Democratization

Social and economic change, policy reform, the state, political culture, interna-tional factors, group representation, the party system, and the presidency are in-dispensable forces for democratizing Mexican politics.

Social and economic change in Mexico has made it much more difficult to erect statist barriers and to secure state autonomy. Economic pressures and ill-ad-vised policies during the 1970s and early 1980s forced many authoritarian states into crisis. Debt, unemployment, impoverishment, and inequality called into question the protectionism and state intervention in the economy carried out by authoritarian governments in Mexico and in Latin America. Unable to borrow any more, deeply indebted states had to manage the crises from the social and economic spheres by adjusting their ways of doing things. The "lost decade" drove a stake through the heart of authoritarian orthodoxies.

Struggling to alleviate social and economic reversals, the Mexican government embarked upon a major course correction. It jettisoned its historic commitment to populist and statist policies and, instead, launched a recovery and liberalization pro-gram that probably changed economic policy forever. Economic reform was offered as the balm necessary to soothe deep wounds. Unable to guarantee a social safety net any longer, the government itself was questioned. Economic reform and liberal-ization became the new orthodoxy for correcting the missteps of the statist past.

Neoliberal reforms of the economy called for deregulation and privatization and the end to protectionism and statism. Banking, finance, and trade, as well as most corners of the national economy, felt this new direction. Subsidies to busi-nesses and consumers were curtailed. Even privately owned highways were built to link some major cities. Economic reform meant less state intervention and less state power. To President Salinas, this is what was meant by democracy (Camp 1993b). But a smaller state did not bring democracy per se. As seen by the neolib-eral elite, the state's role was to spur economic growth rather than to embrace democracy. A market economy was the top priority. Years or even decades later, a democracy might finally emerge from economic reform, but it was not the real priority of this new agenda.

The influence of the United States on Mexican democracy is muted at best. Historically the United States was more interested in stability than democracy in Mexico, but when the crisis of the 1980s led to potential upheaval the United States favored some political liberalization. However, by 1988 the United States had come to the conclusion that it was better to have the PRI in power again than to have a leftist party led by Cuauhtémoc Cárdenas gain control (Meyer 1991b).

Historical Mexican sensitivity about U.S. intervention and its collaboration on NAFTA gave little reason for the United States to press a democratic agenda (Paternostro 1995). Still, integrating Mexico into North America over the long run will raise issues of democracy for both the United States and Mexico, whether or not either side is willing to confront this eventuality.

The political culture also began to change as well. Mexicans began to expect rather than just imagine a future with greater democracy. The government and the presidency in particular were questioned by large numbers of Mexicans as never before (Camp 1993a:150). Trust, efficacy, aspirations, and expectations began to change among many Mexicans. Their skepticism about leaders and institutions notwithstanding, Mexicans want a gradual political liberalization with a more prominent role for the opposition (Camp 1993a:72). Growing expectations may have a long term effect on the chances for democratization.

Another way to advance democracy is through representation. The traditional model of representation was corporatism. Since the 1930s the state and the PRI incorporated the labor, peasant, and popular sectors into a system of top-down representation. The state organized these sectors and provided them with some benefits. The price of inclusion was subordination to the ruling elites or to their junior partners in charge of the sector organizations, especially labor bosses.

This system of group representation is now in an advanced state of entropy. In 1991 the PRI combined the labor and peasant sectors. Corporatist representation in the state and the PRI is being downplayed in favor of individual and territorial principles of representation. The growth of independent unions, cooperatives, and other groups outside the old system is a further reminder of how things are beginning to change. The most important new allies of the government—large business interests—are for the most part outside the corporatist system. Governmental control of group representation is not as dominant as it was even two decades ago. At the same time, some groups who were on the fringe for many years have been brought into the political mainstream. For example, the Salinas administration revised the Mexican Constitution to give the clergy and the church greater political rights.

Single-party dominance has changed as well. The Liberal Democratic Party in Japan and the Kuomintang Party in Taiwan cannot match the PRI's uninterrupted control of government at the national level. The PRI's ability to win big—and especially to win the presidency without fail—is legendary. But it is clearly on the wane. It used to be that these victories were absurdly lopsided. For example, López Mateos (1958–1964) won the presidency for the PRI by about 90 percent of the votes, and his controversial successor, Díaz Ordaz (1964–1970), won by almost as impressive a margin (Cothran 1994:93).

Memories of such victories are fading. In more recent contests the PRI has had to struggle just to gain an absolute majority (50 percent + 1 vote) for the presidency, the key to all national political power in Mexico. For a time during the 1994 campaign it even seemed possible that the PRI might have to settle for a plurality of votes. The 1988 election vote totals (fraudulent as they clearly were) showed that the percentage for the PRI candidate was virtually the same as in 1994. In both elections, the PRI could only convince one out of two voters to cast ballots for its presidential candidate. For those who still recall the era of PRI-ista hegemony, this indeed is significant. Electoral reform in 1990, 1993, and 1994 made further concessions in favor of more honest, transparent, and balanced contests at the polling booths.

The emerging party system in Mexico could likewise be critical for the democratic transition. The opposition parties, never very strong, have perhaps gained from intra-PRI infighting. In fact, the Revolutionary Democratic Party (PRD) exists due to the 1987 divorce between the left populists (that is, Múñoz Ledo, Cárdenas) who bolted from the PRI and the neoliberal technocrats (or *técnicos*) who have controlled the presidency since then. But the opposition party that has done the best is the conservative National Action Party (PAN). Its electoral prowess has improved even as the PRI's economic platform has come to reflect much of what PAN has stood for since it was founded in 1939.

The major opposition parties have done reasonably well compared to prior decades. In 1988 the government's use of fraud was intended to give the PRI the simple majority for the presidency that it did not actually achieve at the ballot box, but the opposition probably did not win a plurality or a majority of the votes in any event. Since then, gains for the opposition have been minor. The two major opposition parties were not able to make significant inroads on the vote margin for the presidency in 1994 compared to 1988. They simply changed positions for second and third place in the voting, with the PAN becoming the second largest party in terms of votes. Their success at the local and state levels is more impressive. For example, the PAN has demonstrated real electoral strength in many cities, the Federal District, and in the states of Baja California Norte, Guanajuato, and Chihuahua. Half of all Mexicans claim to be independents, and half also want more representation of the opposition parties in the government (Camp 1993a:67,69).

The irony of Mexican democratization is that presidential initiative may be indispensable for its success. Ernesto Zedillo Ponce de Leon (1994–2000) mentioned early in his *sexenio*, or six-year term, the possibility of ending the PRI's privileged relationship with the state (Bailey 1994). This has long been a clear and unfair advantage that neutralizes the efforts of the opposition on election day. No one can predict if this step, if actually taken, would democratize or destroy the PRI.

Another change could involve the president's relations with the PRI. Zedillo has pledged not to dictate to the party machine on basic issues such as candidate nomination. If a promise kept, this "unilateral disarmament" of the president's role in party affairs could have immense repercussions for reform within the party and even for the fate of the party itself (Bailey 1994). Self-restraint on arbitrary presidentialism could have far-reaching but unknown consequences for democratization. Extending electoral reform that really levels the playing field would further democratize Mexican politics. Ironically, presidential autonomy can also aid democratization in a country like Mexico. Though liberal democracy would eventually liquidate old-style presidentialism, a strong president can use his power to ensure that local elections are honestly tallied, as Salinas himself did on occasion.

Social, economic, and political changes have altered but not transformed the climate necessary for fostering genuine democratization. In managing the political and economic crisis of the last two decades, Mexican politics has become less statist, corporatist, and authoritarian. But what stands in the way of its becoming more liberal, democratic, and pluralistic?

Forces Arresting Democratization

In Mexico, less authoritarian rule does not necessarily mean a great deal more democracy. What is more, transforming society and the economy are important foundations for political change, but they do not preordain what kind of change will eventually emerge. Given the Mexican paradox, the same political forces that have fostered political reform in this unique system may also arrest democratization as well.

Although social and economic changes have undercut the old system, Mexican society and the economy continue to embody antidemocratic tendencies. The lost decade reduced incomes by 30 percent. Government policy removed much of the social safety net for many. Although conventional democratic theory has claimed that a strong middle class is necessary for democracy, the middle sector of Mexico is more insecure than it has been for decades.

Despite its revolutionary ideals, Mexico has always endured a severe gap between the rich and the poor. A more liberal economy has so far done nothing to alleviate this and may have even exacerbated it. The "lost decade" of the 1980s, the economic reforms of Salinas, and the financial crisis of 1994–1995 have left important scars on the people and punctured their confidence in the government. They have also suffered from declining incomes; the 80 percent of the poorest Mexicans can least afford such staggering reversals of fortune. In 1994 there were twenty-four Mexican billionaires, up from just two billionaires not so long ago. These two dozen Mexicans control $44.1 billion, exceeding the income of the poorest 40 percent of Mexican households (Broad and Cavanaugh 1995–1996:27). Things became worse for most Mexicans by the mid-1990s; this is hardly a promising note upon which to herald the onset of democracy.

As important as societal transformation and economic crisis are for the long-term prospects of democracy, the more immediate transition toward democracy is at the mercy of political forces.

This is very problematic as well. The basic problem is the sincerity and willingness of the ruling elite to place its own immediate self-interest below what is necessarily required for a democratic set of rules about how power should be contested. The ruling elite has hesitated to embrace a consensus with the opposition founded on the premise that its own interests are identical to the interests of a democracy or even compatible with the rules of a democratic game.

In a country like Mexico, the state is vital to democratization. Under Salinas the state became smaller, but it still retains its centralized, mostly closed character (Centeno 1994:171). The state adopted the neoliberal economic agenda, but it did not abandon its basic operating principles. Salinas strengthened his hold on the state and gained greater support for or acquiescence to its new agenda. The state was under the control of the neoliberal *técnicos*. The rise of a "technocratic state" or "new political class" under the Salinas stewardship gave a strong indication that that administration jealously monopolized its great power to make policy with little or no consultation with a large segment of civil society. The new state did not reflect civil society. Rather, it attempted to mold, persuade, and control it (Centeno 1994:30).

The technocratic state conducted a pragmatic, neoliberal counterrevolution during the Salinas *sexenio*. It sought—and largely achieved—political stability, economic reform, and popular support for bearing the costs of this reform (Centeno 1994:39). To do this meant deferred democracy if not actually less democracy. The apostles of this technocratic state embraced a method for thinking about the sources of knowledge, policy, and power that allowed little effective voice for their "irrational" critics, especially on the left. Centralization in the neoliberal strongholds within the government, cohesiveness among the new technocratic elite, and the hegemony of a single, exclusionary policy paradigm left no room for anything more than a partial commitment to democracy "restrained by reason" (Centeno 1994:40–41). Concentration of power rather than significant power sharing was the operating motif of the neoliberal state. Whereas a strong president may be necessary to put Mexico on the road to democracy, a strong president with no such intentions or a well-intentioned but weak president can frustrate the transition and consolidation of democracy. Adam Smith was the economic hero of the technocratic state, but its political icon was clearly not Thomas Jefferson.

Even a presidentially centered and relatively autonomous technocratic elite must have allies. The Mexican state engaged in a balancing act between its economic brethren in the private sector and its political minions in the old corporatist structure. In this way it was able to play a reformist game without dismantling the Mexican state. Business was courted and embraced under the rubric of neoliberal reform; labor was divided and conquered (Morris 1995:111). Business elites became the senior, unofficial partners of a reconfigured coalition (Poitras and Robertson 1994:14–18). The state diluted corporatism and therefore devalued the power of those of its traditional supporters who objected to the new economic agenda. But it did tie itself directly through President Salinas to the people in local communities through Solidarity, a program for direct assistance for development projects. New methods of state control and local initiatives allowed the state to connect directly to the people without conceding much to corporatist organizations and without forsaking a great deal of its historic manipulation over some elements of civil society.

The PRI and the state reinforced their symbiotic bond by accommodating and resisting pressures from the opposition. To the ruling elite, democracy was less a matter of greater popular involvement and a fairer representation of the opposition than it was a matter of *concertación,* or coalition, among powerful groups with its emphasis on solidarity and harmony under governmental tutelage (Centeno 1994:220; Brachet-Marquez 1994:33). Salinas was able to use the classic prerogatives of the state to shore up the alliance of neoliberal *técnicos* and traditional politicos in the PRI, on the one hand, and to undercut and divide the right-left opposition through economic reforms, political opening, and church-state reforms, on the other (Morris 1995:111). In this way meaningful concessions on democracy were delayed.

The opposition is certainly a factor in democratization, but it was not much stronger a decade or so after the 1988 political crisis. Salinas's concern for economic reform diminished his willingness to pursue genuine electoral reform with the same ardor. The 1990, 1993, and 1994 electoral reforms did little to level the playing field, and there is still no unified opposition party able to compete with the PRI head-to-head for the presidency and throughout the country. The PAN remains a regional party with national aspirations; the PRD on the left has been marginalized and divided. The absence of a responsible and coherent party on the left tilts the party system away from popular forces (Cornelius 1994:61). Given differences over economic policy and constituency, the opposition is unlikely to coalesce against the electoral strength of the PRI.

The opposition remains a second-class member of the Mexican party system. The government's resources put at the disposal of the PRI makes relatively honest but unfair elections a very real possibility for the future. Campaign spending limits are so high that the PRI has an overwhelming advantage (Cornelius 1994:57). Therefore the 1994—rather than the 1988—election could well be the template for party competition at the century's end. Low credibility, contested results, and low citizen confidence in elections still cloud the prospects for democratization.

If the Salinas *sexenio* is any indication, the opposition in general may not have an easy time of it either. Salinas showed very little tolerance for opposing views within civil society and in the media (Golden 1993:A9). Pressure from above was put on the media to squelch candid criticism. Radio and television, the most important sources of political information, remained in the PRI's hip pocket. Violence against PRD supporters bordered on a political purge.

The PRI's fate could also determine a good deal of Mexico's experience with democratization. So far its role has been pivotal yet equivocal. Its popular image, competitive advantage, and intraparty conflict all raise doubts about its democratizing credentials for the immediate future. If the democratic transition is to move forward, then the voters' traditional fixation on one party—the PRI—must change as well. Voter attitudes toward the PRI remain very important for explaining voter behavior. In the 1988 and the 1991 national elections, voters' perceptions of the prospects and future of the PRI and their past party preferences (for or against the PRI) went a long way toward explaining voting patterns (Domínguez and McCann 1995:34). Despite the refusal of voters to lend overwhelming support to the PRI as they once had done, their stand on the PRI remains the key to understanding their voting. Mexican voters are not very issue oriented, nor do they use economic expectations or even rely very much upon class differences to decide on how they will vote (Mercado Gasca and Zuckerman Behar 1994:22). This may allow the PRI to hold on to power longer than it would otherwise.

The PRI's place within the party system is more ambiguous than it has been for decades. It is weakened but remains formidable. While unable to sustain hegemony at the ballot box in all local and state elections, the PRI holds tenaciously on to the biggest prize: the presidency and the national state apparatus. Pluralism with some competition here and there is possible in different states like Chihuahua, Baja California Norte, and Guanajuato, but competitive contests for the big prize will be steadfastly resisted beyond the end of the century. The dominant party appears to be desperate enough to hold on to national power by virtually any means at its disposal. For its part, the opposition is gradually building up its strength by nibbling at the margins of political power.

What internal reform of the PRI might mean for democratization is hard to foresee. The unsteady alliance of *técnicos* and populists will require constant maintenance. More disturbing is that the assassinations in 1994, drugs, corruption, fratricide, and patronage hang heavily over the PRI's credibility. This may erode public confidence even further, but it could also steel PRI resistance to concessions for greater openness. A besieged PRI and a divided opposition may raise the specter of change, but that is certainly no guarantee of democracy.

Corruption, criminality, and cover-up suggest that Mexican politics at the top continues to permit leaders to remain above the law. This is corrosive of democratization in general and of judicial reform in particular. The lurid revelations since the end of the Salinas *sexenio* confirm the worst fears about the system's corruptibility, but the fact that this has come out in public provides limited consolation to those who wish to find a silver lining. Past presidents now openly criticize each other, but open bickering and crisis management are not the same as democratization. It is a popular saying in Mexico that corruption is not part of the system; rather, it is the system. Besieged and corrupt, the PRI-government elite plays a "reformist game" rather than a democratic one, a game in which the government manages reform from above to prevent rather than trigger fundamental change from below (Morris 1995:192; 1992).

Waiting for the Millennium

Genuine democratization would end the basic paradox of Mexican politics. If presidentialism, centralization, secrecy, single-party dominance, an enfeebled op-

position, a subservient legislature, and capricious and arbitrary rule are to become quaint relics of the twentieth century, then Mexican politics will have to
evolve a good deal during the twenty-first century. Something else could happen,
though. For one thing, Mexico could muddle along, doing more of the same but
very gradually becoming less of what it once was without moving unambiguously
toward a fully consolidated democracy. Continuity with the past would prolong
the paradox. For another, a political earthquake several times greater than Chiapas could shake Mexico. Both stability and democracy could be threatened if such
an unlikely event were to occur.

If change does come, the paradox of Mexican politics will not be resolved fully
any time soon. Much depends on the president and the PRI. A fair and competitive election for the presidency that leads to a stable transfer of power from one
party to another would allow Mexico to travel down the road toward democratic
consolidation.

As Mexico emerges slowly from its 1990s crisis, the prospects for democracy remain murky. Depending on one's perspective, the glass is partially full or partially
empty, and it may remain that way well into the third millennium. To become
more democratic, Mexican politics must be more competitive, pluralistic, law-
abiding, and open. To be a consolidated democracy, a consensus must evolve in
which democratic rules about fairly contested elections must be put above the
narrow, partisan self-interest of the players. Accepting democratic rules of the
game about how politics is waged across the board as well as in the voting booth is
the defining feature of a democratic consolidation in Mexico. If, on the other
hand, arbitrary power and the reformist game are used to manage the next crisis,
the paradox could prove to be as durable as Mexican politics has so far proven to
be unique. Mexico will have matured politically if and when stability is equated
not with PRI rule but, rather, with rule of law and the democratic process. As the
century comes to an end, the forces for democratization struggle inconclusively
against those delaying it. That is why Mexico's democratic transition is problematic. For now, Mexicans have the freedom to imagine a democracy, but it may be a
distant time during the next millennium before they can actually live in one.

Bibliography

Bailey, John. 1994. Mexico's moment. *New York Times* (November 30):A17.
Barry, Tom. 1992. *Mexico: A Country Guide.* Albuquerque, N.M.: Inter-American Hemi-
  spheric Education Resource Center.
Brachet-Marquez, Viviane. 1994. *The Dynamics of Domination: State, Class, and Social Re-
  form in Mexico, 1910–1990.* Pittsburgh: University of Pittsburgh Press.
Broad, Robin, and John Cavanaugh. 1995–1996. Don't neglect the impoverished south.
  Foreign Policy 101:18–35.
Burton, Michael, Richard Gunther, and John Higley. 1992. Introduction: Elite transforma-
  tion and democratic regimes. In *Elites and Democratic Consolidation in Latin America*

and Southern Europe (John Higley and Richard Gunther, eds.), 1–37. Cambridge: Cambridge University Press.

Camp, Roderic Ai. 1993a. *Politics in Mexico*. New York: Oxford University Press.

———. 1993b. Political modernization in Mexico: Through a looking glass. In *The Evolution of the Mexican Political System* (Jaime E. Rodriguez, ed.), 245–262. Wilmington, Del.: Scholastic Resources Books.

Centeno, Miguel Angel. 1994. *Democracy Within Reason: Technocratic Revolution in Mexico*. University Park: Pennsylvania State University Press.

Cornelius, Wayne. 1994. Mexico's delayed democracy. *Foreign Policy* 95:53–71.

Cornelius, Wayne, and Ann L. Craig. 1991. *The Mexican Political System in Transition*. San Diego: Center for U.S.-Mexican Studies, University of California at San Diego.

Cornelius, Wayne, Judith Gentleman, and Peter H. Smith. 1989. Overview: The dynamics of political change in Mexico. In *Mexico's Alternative Political Futures* (Wayne Cornelius, Judith Gentleman, and Peter H. Smith, eds.), 1–51. San Diego: Center for U.S.-Mexican American Studies, University of California at San Diego.

Cothran, Dan A. 1994. *Political Stability and Democracy in Mexico: The "Perfect Dictatorship."* Westport, Conn.: Praeger.

Domínguez, Jorge I., and James A. McCann. 1995. Shaping Mexico's electoral arena: The construction of partisan cleavages in the 1988 and 1991 national elections. *American Political Science Review* 89:34–48.

Fitzgibbon, Russell H. 1956. How democratic is Latin America? *Inter-American Economic Affairs* 9:65–77.

———. 1951. Measurement of Latin American political phenomena: A statistical experiment. *American Political Science Review* 45:517–523.

Golden, Tim. 1993. Despite new laws, Mexican leader's allies are accused of muzzling critics. *New York Times* (October 7):A9.

Johnson, Kenneth F. 1975. Scholarly images of Latin American political democracy in 1975. *Latin American Research Review* 11:129–140.

Knight, Alan. 1992. Mexico's elite settlement: Conjuncture and consequences. In *Elite and Democratic Consolidation in Latin America and Southern Europe* (John Higley and Richard Gunther, eds.), 113–145. Cambridge: Cambridge University Press.

Levy, Daniel. 1989. Mexico: Sustained civilian rule without democracy. In *Democracy in Developing Countries: Latin America* (Larry Diamond, Juan J. Linz, and Seymour Martin Lipset, eds.), 459–497. Boulder: Lynne Rienner.

Mercado Gasca, Lauro, and Leo Zuckerman Behar. 1994. La encuesta a la Salida de las Casillas: Un vencedor más del 21 de Agosto. *Nexos* (September):20–26.

Meyer, Lorenzo. 1991a. La democracia, solo un horizonte. *Excelsior* (August 14):A1, A23.

———. 1991b. Mexico: The exception and the rule. In *Exporting Democracy: The United States and Latin America* (Abraham F. Lowenthal, ed.), 93–110. Baltimore: Johns Hopkins University Press.

Morris, Stephen. 1995. *Political Reformism in Mexico: An Overview of Contemporary Mexican Politics*. Boulder: Lynne Rienner.

———. 1992. Political reformism in Mexico: Salinas at the brink. *Journal of Inter-American Studies and World Affairs* 34:27–58.

Paternostro, Silvana. 1995. Mexico as a narco-democracy. *World Policy Journal* 12:41–47.

Poitras, Guy, and Raymond Robertson. 1994. The politics of NAFTA in Mexico. *Journal of Inter-American Studies and World Affairs* 36: 1–34.

Przeworski, Adam. 1991. *Democracy and the Market: Political and Economic Reforms in Eastern Europe and Latin America*. Cambridge: Cambridge University Press.

Reding, Andrew. 1991. Mexico: The crumbling of the "perfect dictatorship." *World Policy Journal* 8:255–288.

Rueschemeyer, Dietrich, Evelyne H. Stephens, and John D. Stephens. 1992. *Capitalist Development and Democracy*. Chicago: University of Chicago Press.

Teichman, Judith. 1988. *Politics in Mexico*. Boston: Allen and Unwin.

Chapter Seven

Province Versus the Center: Democratizing Mexico's Political Culture

RODERIC AI CAMP

Mexico has labored under many legal, historical, and structural consequences that have affected intergovernmental relations and the distribution of political power on the local, state, and national levels. The 1917 Constitution gives much stronger powers to the executive branch, not only in relation to other branches but, equally important, in relation to the distribution of powers between local and national government. Among the most important of these powers, measured by practical economic and political consequences, is the power to tax.[1] Today federal government levies account for more than 85 percent of tax revenues, much of it distributed back to state and local authorities.[2] The national executive branch, by controlling the legislative chambers, may remove and replace governors, who in turn exercise, if necessary, similar powers over mayors (Camp 1994).

Political control by the center has generated considerable resentment toward Mexico City from the provinces. This resentment translated into secessionist movements in the nineteenth century, as provinces fought to maintain their identity and autonomy. Perhaps the most notable of these struggles took place in Yucatán (Reed 1964). Strong regional resentments were the seedbed of considerable discontent at the end of the century, contributing heavily to the precursor movements to the 1910 Revolution (Young 1992). In fact the principle of municipal autonomy per se was highlighted in the movement of Pascual Orozco (Meyer 1967:63). The provinces' nonconformity with the center's political direction and domination produced two important consequences in the postrevolutionary period.

The first of these consequences was the generation of a series of local and regional political organizations, many of which were influential on those levels but rarely exercised political power beyond local or regional boundaries. The National Revolutionary Party's establishment in 1928–1929 was based in large part on the aggregation of many of these organizations (Garrido 1982:41). Nevertheless, pockets of opposition continued to oppose the postrevolutionary leadership's increasing centralization of power and the symbolization of that unification: a national government party, the Institutional Revolutionary Party (PRI). These dissenting voices have always provided the historical basis for voter opposition in Mexico, a pattern already well established in electoral behavior by the 1940s (Camp 1991:97).

A second consequence is the development of political pressures similar to pressures also found in the United States, where the federal government used its political leverage to eliminate or modify those local political traditions seen as standing in the way of national, progressive political trends. In the Mexican case, local leaders, or caciques, and the practices they represented were judged as obstacles to "national modernization." Mexico's problems might be seen as somewhat analogous to what some historians view as southern governors' obstinacy in enforcing voter rights and eliminating local segregation practices in the United States.

Mexico's pattern, however, can be viewed in a different light. Mexico's central government successfully removed or hampered many local and regional figures, in many cases improving political conditions. But because the same leadership group has remained in control since the 1930s, it typically replaced local authorities with national representatives, whose abuse of power and authoritarian control, supported by the center, made relief equally difficult to obtain (Rodríguez O. 1993; Sánchez Gutiérrez 1993). Thus homogenization and centralization of power in the hands of the Mexican presidency, unshared with any other national competitor, renewed strong opposition precisely at local and state levels (Philip 1992; Schmidt 1991).

National governments are not always initiators of progressive political trends; often, in fact, they oppose or inhibit such patterns. For example, in his recent account of electoral laws and patterns in the central state of Puebla, José Alarcón Hernández demonstrates that Puebla, like many other Mexican states, was well ahead of the federal government on the issue of feminine suffrage. Women voted in state elections long before they were given a similar opportunity in the 1950s at the national level (Morton 1962). On the other hand, Mexico introduced a proportional representation system in the national legislative branch in the early 1960s, allocating more seats to opposition parties. This national concept did not reach Puebla until the late 1970s (Hernández 1993).

It is evident that historical precedents and structural impediments built into Mexican constitutional laws and practice established certain boundaries for intergovernmental relations. Nevertheless, a cultural component, both a by-product of and an explanation for more-institutionalized patterns, also contributes to these structural developments.

It is a difficult task to measure the impact of Mexican political attitudes toward intergovernmental relations, given the available data. This topic has never been a focus of public opinion surveys (Basáñez 1987:181–184). Surveys focusing on local or regional politics are also rare (a major exception to this is the detailed study of Jalapa using survey data and field research; see Fagen and Tuohy 1972). Our exploration is necessarily incomplete, a partial view of the potential impact of an analysis of data on regional differences in political knowledge and attitudes and on perceptions of local, state, and national decisionmakers and governmental performance (the most comprehensive survey of empirical cultural studies is Craig and Cornelius 1980:325–393).

Political Interest, Importance, and Awareness

If we control for regional origins and for urban and rural residence and break down Mexican responses on the basis of political knowledge, interest, and participation, we can discover some interesting differences that may suggest future characteristics about intergovernmental relations.

In the early 1960s, compared to the United States, England, and several European countries, Mexicans demonstrated a fairly low level of knowledge about, but considerable interest in, politics (Almond and Verba 1965:58, 66). In the 1990s, despite the conflictual nature of elections of 1985, the increasing scope of the opposition, and the involvement of the U.S. media, Mexicans did not consider politics to be of great importance in their lives. Generally speaking, only 40 percent of all Mexicans thought politics to be significant. In contrast, more than 70 percent found religion and time important. Not surprisingly, even higher percentages considered their families and jobs important. As might be expected, women were less taken with the value of politics than men.

On a regional basis, however, the importance of politics to Mexicans varies. Politically speaking, prior to 1995 the most competitive elections in Mexico were those in the north and in the extended Mexico City metropolitan zone. This level of competition has been true for some time, especially since 1982. Mexico can be divided into four large regions: the north, a highly-developed, well-educated, politicized region, 64 percent urban, many of whose states border the United States; the south, Mexico's poorest, least-educated, mostly rural (62 percent), and heavily indigenous region; the center, including many traditionally important states, representing the mainstream of Mexico's development, containing a population that is 45 percent urban; and the Federal District, the metropolitan, cosmopolitan, industrialized, 93-percent urban political center.

Mexico City and the northern residents are most interested in politics, measured by its importance to their daily lives. These two regions, although often at political loggerheads with each other, share many political characteristics. Their level of sophistication produces an interest in politics conducive to increased political competition. The importance of politics to residents of these two regions is

TABLE 7.1   Mexicans' Interest in Politics by Region: How Often Is Politics Discussed?

Region	Frequently	Occasionally	Never	Don't Know
North	19%	53%	25%	3%
Center	13%	58%	26%	8%
South	11%	63%	24%	2%
Federal District	18%	54%	27%	1%

Source: World Values Survey. 1990. Institute for Social Research, University of Michigan. Under the direction of Ronald Inglehart.

not significantly above the norm for all Mexicans, but it is consistently higher. The lack of difference in political interest among regional groups is also supported by responses separated according to urban and rural residence. They demonstrate no differences between those Mexicans living in cities of less than 50,000 people compared to those of 50,000 and higher.

Although assessing the importance of politics offers an insight into the personal philosophy of the respondent, asking them to report the frequency with which they discuss politics is a more significant measure of their actual interest. As can be seen in the data presented in Table 7.1, a majority of Mexicans, typically about three-quarters, discuss politics. But among those who *discuss it frequently*, nearly twice as many do so in the north and in Mexico City as in the south. It is impossible to determine whether Mexicans' interest in politics has increased electoral competitiveness in these regions or whether electoral competitiveness has exaggerated their interest. It is fair to conclude, however, that interest and activity are interrelated.

The frequency with which Mexicans discuss politics varies considerably with the size of their community compared to the region in which they reside. Typically, the larger the community, the greater the interest in discussing politics. For example, as the data in Table 7.2 suggest, especially if the communities are collapsed into several broad categories, 72 percent of all Mexicans discuss politics frequently or occasionally, but only about half of all Mexicans do so in smaller communities, notably villages with fewer than 2,000 residents, or small towns of between 5,000–10,000 people. If local residents' political activism, measured only by the simple act of voting, is linked to political interests, the likelihood of changing political authorities, and intergovernmental relations, is much smaller.

The reason rural communities show less interest in politics is probably associated with their levels of education and with political knowledge. Other studies have demonstrated a strong correlation between higher levels of education, political cognition, and political interest. For example, most Mexicans read a newspaper, a major source of political news, but fewer read national newspapers. Rural Mexicans are much less likely to read any newspaper, let alone a national paper, which is illustrated by the fact that 73 percent of urban residents read national media, compared to only 54 percent of the rural population. On the other hand, 23 percent of rural residents read a local paper compared to only 13 percent of urban Mexicans.[3]

TABLE 7.2   Mexicans' Interest in Politics by Community Size: How Often Is Politics Discussed?

Region	Frequently	Occasionally	Never	Don't Know
1–2,000	14%	33%	43%	10%
2,000–5,000	16%	51%	33%	0
5,000–10,000	7%	37%	48%	8%
10,000–20,000	14%	49%	35%	2%
20,000–50,000	3%	61%	30%	6%
50,000–100,000	8%	79%	11%	2%
100,000–500,000	14%	56%	25%	5%
500,000+	19%	56%	24%	1%

Source: World Values Survey. 1990. Institute for Social Research, University of Michigan. Under the Direction of Ronald Inglehart. Courtesy of Miguel Basáñez.

One of the common ways to measure an individual's interest in electoral politics is to ask them about their sympathies for a political party. The majority of Mexicans, more than half, do not identify with any political party. Of those who willingly expressed sympathy for a political party, nearly a fourth identified PRI; 11 percent named the National Action Party (PAN), the party with the greatest success in winning local and state gubernatorial and mayoralty offices from PRI; and 4 percent named all other parties. Although most Mexicans do not strongly identify with any political party, they do believe that political participation, including voting, should increase in the 1990s. Nearly half of all Mexicans considered it to be the second most important issue in this decade.

Participation involves more than voting. Voting, legally required (but not enforced) in Mexico, is the most common and passive form of political involvement. Other forms of participation, especially since 1989, often determine decisionmaking style and process and relations between national, local and state authorities. The least risky political behavior beyond that of voting is the petition. The percentage of people willing to involve themselves in a petitioning process not only reflects their degree of activism but also suggests the size of the potential pool of participants who might associate themselves with incipient interest groups.

The percentage of Mexicans who have actually involved themselves in the petitioning process is quite sizable. Indeed, nearly one out of three Mexicans claim to have actually signed a political petition. Another 40 percent suggest they would be willing to sign a petition if the issue interested them. Petitioning seems to be most common to residents of the capital, where 40 percent have actually engaged in this activity. Given the number of interest groups operating in Mexico City, especially since the 1985 earthquake, it is not surprising that capital residents are more sophisticated (Annis 1991:100). This kind of procedure for articulating demands is not nearly as well developed in rural sections such as the south, where only half as many, 20 percent, have actually tried such an approach.

The data on urban-rural responses confirm the suspicion that Mexico's most rural region, the south, has the least experience with this type of process. In fact, data on responses by size of community make clear that a cutoff point for a community's population determines the level of political sophistication, at least involving the petitioning process. For example, although we have noted that 70 percent of all Mexicans have signed, or would be willing to sign, a political petition, in the smallest communities, those under 10,000, figures range from a low of 33 percent, less than half the national average, to a high of only 57 percent, still well below the average national figure. Once communities reach 10,000 residents or higher, little distinction exists in their responses to the petition process.

Internationally, an increase in conventional political participation has occurred. If we use Ronald Inglehart's definition of "conventional" as discussing politics frequently, having a strong interest in politics, and having signed a political petition, the following patterns are apparent over the last decade. As Table 7.3 suggests, Mexico is not an exception to patterns in the western hemisphere. As Inglehart argues, the change is dramatic. Although only half as many Mexicans as Canadians and North Americans have signed petitions, the percentage of those having done so increased 127 percent since 1980. In general, therefore, the pace with which Mexicans are emulating their Western peers, involving themselves more deeply in political activities, is quickening.

Although younger people are more interested in politics, participating more actively in conventional forms other than voting, they vote less and express greater independence from parties. In Mexico pressure for political change will probably come from the north and Mexico City. For example, only a small percentage of Mexicans, 6 percent nationally, have participated in a boycott. In Mexico City and the north, these figures are 9 and 7 percent respectively. In both the south and the center, only 3 percent count boycotts among their political experiences. Although the figures are small, the differences by region are large, sometimes more than double. The events in Chiapas beginning January 1994, reflect participation to an extreme, and may, in the medium term, raise both the level of consciousness and participation in the south, the region in which Chiapas is located. Immediately following these events, by mid-1994, hundreds of groups with similar demands and frustrations began demonstrations throughout Mexico.

Typically the more activist political behavior is increasingly becoming identified with urban, developed Mexico's political culture, whereas rural, traditional states have yet to socialize their residents to these new, more flamboyant techniques. Rural residents' participation corresponds to figures for the south and center, only 3 percent. In fact, of those sampled in villages of fewer than 2,000, no one had signed a petition. It is quite likely, however, that no such petitions have been circulated. This is not to say that since 1990, when survey data was made available, states located in the other two regions, such as Michoacán, Yucatán, or Chiapas, have not accentuated other forms of political participation. Indeed, each of these states, as a single entity, might score higher on these responses than Mexico City.

TABLE 7.3   Patterns of Conventional Participation in Mexico, Canada, and the United States

Countries	% Ranking on Conventional Participation		
	1981	1990	% Change
United States	41	50	22
Canada	38	53	39
Mexico	11	25	127

Source: Adapted from Ronald Inglehart, Neil Nevitte, and Miguel Basáñez. 1994. *Convergencia en Norteamérica.* Mexico: Siglo XXI.

One of the techniques that has been widely used in Michoacán to force recognition of opposition victories, or alleged victories, on the local level is occupying public offices and demonstrating against political authorities. Widespread demonstrations against government authorities, both authorized and unauthorized, produced a notable consequence for intergovernmental relations on the state level. Beginning with the 1991 gubernatorial elections in San Luis Potosí and Guanajuato, where opposition parties claimed extensive fraud, the executive branch, specifically the president, began a pattern of intervention to resolve provincial political disputes. This led to a consistent pattern in which all parties, including the government-controlled PRI, looked to the president to determine the outcome of state elections. Presidential intervention legitimized political demonstrations.[4] Interestingly, however, Mexicans themselves did not agree on whether national intervention supported democracy (14 percent) or weakened government (17 percent) (*Excélsior* 1993:10A). By fall 1993 the government realized that it would be forced to intervene in each successive gubernatorial race when competition was most heated. President Carlos Salinas de Gortari suddenly reversed his strategy in Tamaulipas, once again taking a hard line against the opposition and permitting fraudulent elections to stand. Ernesto Zedillo's record on this is mixed. On the one hand, he persuaded the PRI victor in Chiapas to resign, and tried unsuccessfully to do the same in the highly disputed and fraudulent elections in Tabasco. He has allowed the Yucatán election results of 1995 to stand, prompting legal action from the opposition.

Demonstrations have, however, become an acceptable tool in Mexican political life. As of 1990 one out of five Mexicans had participated in an authorized demonstration. Rural Mexicans, again in communities with fewer than 10,000 people, with some exceptions, were much less involved in such activities or willing to use them. Demonstrations, common for years in U.S. politics, are most popular along the Mexican border, drawing the attention of the North American media.

Mexicans, as is true of North Americans, are less willing to join unauthorized demonstrations. Such a commitment, of course, suggests a high level of political involvement and interest. About 7 percent of all Mexicans have participated in illegal demonstrations, a figure that is higher still in the capital and the north and

lower in the south. The figures in the south can again be explained by the dispro-
portionate percentage of rural communities. The figures for the north are owing
to the fact that it includes border states, and those north of Mexico City, such as
Guanajuato and San Luis Potosí, where gubernatorial elections have been highly
contested, producing national intervention.

In Michoacán members of the Revolutionary Democratic Party (PRD) occupied key buildings in certain municipalities, the same technique widely used in
Guerrero, one of Mexico's poorer, rural states, and in more localized situations in
Oaxaca. This, of course, is also a technique used by the Zapatista Army of National Liberation in indigenous, rural locales in Chiapas. Typically, rural Mexicans
(those residing in communities of less than 10,000 population) are not yet avid
advocates of this political approach. Fewer than 2 percent have ever joined their
peers in a sit-down strike. Among the political techniques measured in the World
Values Survey (1990), this is the most radical, involving considerable personal
risks. Again, the north ranks highest in this category, although the percentages are
quite small since the national average is less than 5 percent.

The north ranks ahead of the Federal District in producing Mexicans who
demonstrate and occupy buildings because its residents share a more activist culture and it provides substantially more opportunities than the capital for physically occupying specific buildings. Until 1997, when they elected their own mayor,
capital residents did not have any local executive authorities directly responsible
to, and elected by, them. When they decide to occupy a building, it generally
means taking on a federal rather than a municipal or state office, a more formidable task that may be somewhat more inhibiting to Mexicans than invading the local town hall.

Attitudes Toward Change

Mexico is undergoing an extraordinary period of internal change and adjustment, not so much from the presidency, which gets the media's attention, but
from the citizenry. Whatever the attitudes of individual Mexicans toward their institutions' legitimacy, local and national, and the prestige of decisionmaking by
level of government, broader attitudes toward change determine a willingness to
put new parties in power and to demand structural change involving national or
local power sharing.

A first step in permitting changing patterns in intergovernmental relations is
the election of opposition party candidates to executive posts. Despite severe criticism of PRI, in 1994 a third of all Mexicans were not yet willing to concede that
PAN or PRD had the ability to govern. In fact, only 43 percent of Mexicans believed these parties were capable of governing (*Excélsior* 1993:10A).

Very little variation exists in attitudes toward the pace of political reform in
Mexico on a regional basis. When asked if they believe political change is occurring too quickly, most Mexicans reply negatively. Capital city residents disagree

most strongly. Two out of five opposed this interpretation, compared to only one-third of most Mexican respondents. Those favoring stronger or radical political reforms number about a third of the population. The south, as might be expected, in spite of its severe economic and social problems, scores slightly lower, and the Federal District, with a much faster rate of economic growth and development, responds somewhat higher, but not substantially so. In fact, on the basis of level of urbanization, the responses are inconsistent, in some cases much lower than the national norm for smaller communities and in others, higher.

It has been clearly demonstrated from an analysis of the 1988 presidential elections that those who perceived their economic fortunes to be in decline voted in large numbers for the opposition candidacy of Cuauhtémoc Cárdenas, but it is not clear that the most traditional and less-educated sectors of society drew a strong link between government policy and leadership, on the one hand, and economic crisis on the other (Domínguez and McCann 1995). This conclusion is reinforced again by the fact that the south scores lowest on support for a faster pace of change. Although the majority here favor faster change, they do so in percentages smaller than those found in any other region. It has always been the case that the higher the level of development, regardless of how measured (education, urbanization, income, institutional density, and so on), the greater the percentages of votes cast for the opposition (Ames 1970:153–167; Camp 1993:252–253). Higher opposition support introduces the potential for changing the structural pattern of national-local government relations.[5]

Since regional origins do not suggest wide variance in Mexicans' evaluations of the pace of change, it is worth examining how they see themselves in the larger context of the nation-state. Mexico, like all other Third World countries, has fought in the twentieth century to strengthen its sense of national identity. It has successfully accomplished this task. Not only is the degree of regional pride a measure of resistance against nationalism, but it also provides a stronger indication of local autonomy and regional independence. Mexicans were asked to indicate with which of the following geographic groups they would primarily and secondarily identify: city, region, country, or world.

As regions, all chose their own place of residence as their primary source of geographic identity, although Mexico was a close second in two of the regions, and tied for first choice in the center region. The south most strongly identified with its local place of residence, with 45 percent selecting hometown over larger geographic identities. This response is not surprising given its rural, less-sophisticated, and less-educated population. On the basis of community size, most also chose their own town and region as their first and second choices, although Mexico followed hometown as a first choice. Residents of towns of between 2,000 and 50,000 most strongly identified with their local community. Residents of the smallest communities selected their own village as a second choice, while residents of major metropolitan centers, over 500,000, moved beyond regional identities, selecting Mexico as their second geographic priority.

Attitudes Toward Decisionmaking

The layered system of Mexican national-state-local decisionmaking structures could be altered by a change in the fiscal system, by increasing the role of the legislative process, and by changing attitudes toward citizen participation in policymaking. Mexico has operated under a semi-authoritarian, one-party system for more than six decades. One of the ways to test citizen receptivity to changing this system is to pose questions concerning the openness of decisionmaking and the lines of authority.

When Mexicans were asked if the government decisionmaking should be more open to the average citizen, half of all Mexicans agreed completely, and another third agreed somewhat. Only a minuscule 5 percent were satisfied with citizen access to decisionmaking as presently structured.

On a regional basis, little variation exists in the support for opening up governmental decisionmaking. In the Federal District, where demands for self-government are on the increase and the desire for a local legislative system with real authority is hotly debated, support is strongest, reaching an extraordinary 88 percent. In fact, in 1993 81 percent of respondents in the Federal District believed their "mayor" should be elected rather than appointed by the president (*Excélsior* 1993:10A). In all other regions, support hovers around 80 percent for open decisionmaking, so again, this is a universal pattern. The only regional differences in this response is that in both Mexico City and in the center, support is deeper among those who are in complete agreement with the statement.

When Mexicans are confronted with more-precise questions about the structure of decisionmaking, in particular, questions about those alterations that directly affect intergovernmental relations, we can obtain a clearer understanding of how they perceive federal-state relations. A 1987 national survey using different regional categories asked respondents to respond to four specific statements about centralization: "National programs should receive attention before regional programs"; "Federal government objectives have had a high cost for the provinces"; "State governors should accept federal executive decisions even when they are not best for his state": and "Centralism has contributed to the country's development."

Generally speaking, the majority of Mexicans believe that they should focus on local problems before attending to national issues. Nearly half of all Mexicans agree with the premise that federal government objectives have been costly to their states. When asked whether they thought centralization contributed to Mexico's development, of those who expressed an opinion, two-thirds said no. For each of these statements regional differences were slight, but they suggest that Mexicans are strongly interested in the concept of state autonomy and in giving preference to local problems and authorities over national issues and structures. The most precise statement dealing with the distribution of decisionmaking authority—whether state governors should accept federal decisions—produces the strongest regional variation. The north responds differently from the center, south, and west. All regions strongly disagree with federal supremacy in decision-making, but the north, at 64 percent, does so most firmly.

Not only do their attitudes about the centralized structure of decisionmaking suggest the potential for changing intergovernmental relations, but so do attitudes toward authority figures themselves. Recent studies demonstrate that Mexicans, critical of the way decisions are made, give more positive evaluations to their national executives compared to their state and local executives. In 1988, when the Mexican presidency was at its lowest ebb, only 26 percent of all Mexicans ranked the president as good, compared to 35 percent for governors and 31 percent for mayors (*Encuesta Nacional de Proceso Electoral* 1988; data courtesy of Miguel Basáñez). Just two years later, after President Salinas, the most popular chief executive in recent decades (until December 1994) had been in office a year and a half, the figures were reversed. Although support for mayors and governors remained approximately the same, at 27 and 29 percent respectively, positive views of the president had increased dramatically, almost doubling to 44 percent. In their evaluation of national leadership, rural and urban residents make little distinction. However, in their evaluation of local and state leadership, community size is significant. Rural residents give their mayors and governors more positive ratings, at 35 and 37 percent respectively (*Encuesta Nacional de Opinión Pública Iglesia-estado* 1990).

When Mexicans are asked to distinguish between their leadership and the government's daily operations, their evaluations are surprisingly positive, considering Mexico's overall economic and political situation. In 1983, just after Miguel de la Madrid was elected and the Mexican government entered into a severe economic austerity phase, respondents, divided by state of residence, were asked to evaluate government functions by level. In the first place, their overall evaluations were more positive than negative. They favored state and federal performance or local efforts. The fact that city governments have the fewest resources to implement government policy, although their representatives are the most likely to deal with the average Mexican, may help explain this response. It also may be explained by the fact that the most disliked government representatives, the police, typically are city employees.

If residents of those four states giving the *lowest* positive evaluation of government performance are selected, a certain pattern among states, and a possible linkage among levels of government performance, is evident. Mexicans who evaluated government performance least positively, in two out of four cases, were from the same states, Morelos and Chiapas, regardless of level assessed. Morelos is just south of Mexico City, the home of Zapatism during and after the 1910 Revolution. It gave the PAN and PRD a majority of votes in the 1988 elections, suggesting that their disillusionment with government extended back some time. Chiapas, generally supportive of PRI prior to 1994, given weak opposition party grassroots developments in the state, is one of Mexico's poorest, most rural, and

TABLE 7.4   Mexicans' Perceptions of Government Functions

Level of Government	Percentage Ranking Performance as					
	Very Good	Good	OK	Bad	Very Bad	Didn't Know/ Didn't Answer
City	7	29	40	12	4	8
San Luis Potosí	4	16				
Morelos	2	16				
Guerrero	4	19				
State	10	35	36	9	3	7
Baja California	4	23				
Chiapas	8	21				
Federal District	4	27				
Morelos	6	28				
Federal	8	34	35	10	4	9
Morelos	4	28				
Federal District	6	25				
Chiapas	9	22				
Baja California	3	24				

Source: Encuesta Nacional de Partidos. 1983. Mori Company of Mexico. Courtesy of Miguel Basáñez.

most heavily indigenous states. It has been frequently cited by international organizations for its level of human rights abuses.[6] This finding anticipated by more than a decade the levels of frustration with, and low levels of support for, government authorities prior to the uprising. Baja California and the Federal District, both of which had strong representation from PAN and in 1988 from the antecedents of the PRD, voted overwhelmingly for opposition parties. San Luis Potosí, which boasts the strongest, oldest local civic action organization in Mexico, has been denouncing electoral fraud and corruption since the 1950s.[7]

The data in Table 7.4 also suggest that when perceptions of local authorities' performance are less favorable, they can be translated into similar evaluations of national performance. In Mexico the linkage between evaluations of governmental performance by level might be associated with the facts that in the past all levels were controlled by the same party and that national authorities determine funding levels for local and state governments.

If we move beyond general evaluations of government performance to more specific cases involving the individual citizen, positive ratings tend to decline. For example, in 1988 Mexicans were asked how their personal requests or complaints were handled by the government, without specifying level of authorities. Only 26 percent described their personal experience as good or very good. A slightly larger number, 29 percent, found their experience satisfactory, and 24 percent evaluated it as bad (*Encuestra Nacional de Opinión Pública Sobre el Proceso Electoral de 1988* 1988; data courtesy of Miguel Basáñez). Does a relationship exist between how individuals generally perceive government performance and their own experience? One would expect so, especially if someone has had an unsatisfactory experience. The data bear this out. Of the four states whose residents report the least positive experience dealing personally with the government, three, Chiapas, the Federal District, and Morelos, are those evaluating government performance more critically than their peers.

Finally, an indirect means for attacking the supremacy of the executive branch, but on the national level, is through the legislative branch. Mexico has never been able to strengthen the legislative branch because the president controls his party's congressional nominees, and the government party dominates single-member districts. These constituency relationships are nonexistent because members of Congress cannot repeat consecutively in office and Congress does not initiate legislation (Camp 1994:17–36). Mexicans clearly perceive this lack of representation, since 76 percent think their congressperson represents them badly, whereas only a mere 10 percent give their representative positive marks (*Encuesta Nacional del Proceso Electoral* 1988).

Conclusion

All societies have more than one level of political culture. One culture exists among the governing elite. It affects their behavior and helps determine their political values. Another culture exists among the citizenry, a mass political culture of national scope. Still another culture can be found, more pronounced in societies that do not yet have a fully developed sense of nationalism, at the local or regional level. In Mexico, however, despite the presence of strong, local historical traditions and many different indigenous cultures, there exists a national political culture subscribed to by most Mexicans.

Decentralization and a change in intergovernmental relations is likely to come about only when the Mexican mass political culture supports a change in political party and is willing to sustain the results at the ballot box through whatever means necessary. Many Mexicans are interested in politics, but not enough Mexicans yet are sufficiently interested, nor have a degree of commitment, to change Mexico's political environment, an outstanding feature of which is national executive supremacy over state and local governments. On a regional basis, change in the mass political culture, having potential influence for intergovernmental relations, is occurring more rapidly in some regions rather than others.

Generally speaking, regardless of the variable discussed, Mexicans residing in the north are more interested in politics, discuss politics more frequently, and participate at higher levels in various forms of political behavior. This pattern has several significant implications, especially since responses in the south, with characteristics different from those of the north, tend to be quite disparate.

Higher levels of political interest, activism, and sophistication are associated with higher levels of economic development, education, and urbanization. In turn these regional environments are most conducive to promoting the development of alternative political views, sympathy for political parties not in power, and opposition to the governing party and its style of decisionmaking. One of the most strongly held beliefs among all Mexicans is that decisionmaking is inaccessible and that local and state policymaking should be more autonomous and less under the thumb of national authorities.

Ironically, regions that would benefit most from such political changes structurally and electorally give it the least support, primarily because they do not have sufficient levels of the necessary civic characteristics conducive to such attitudes. There appears to be a strong linkage between environmental conditions—economic development, access to education, urbanization, and so on—and increased interest and participation in politics. It cannot be concluded that one necessarily produces the other, but it is likely that the growth of favorable environmental conditions in Mexico encourages opposition strength, which in turn affects demonstrative citizen interest and participation.

Changing intergovernmental relations in the poorer, rural regions may continue to be slowed by the fact that Mexicans residing there, Chiapas to the contrary, are not as willing to explore and implement more-radical political techniques against government abuses, techniques such as boycotts and illegal demonstrations, which are more readily used by their urban or more economically developed regional counterparts. Though the symbolic impact of Chiapas greatly reinforces an activist posture, repeated surveys suggest that Mexicans are sympathetic to their goals but strongly oppose their means, specifically violence. A national, voluntary referendum urged the Zapatistas to transform themselves into a political party. The north, as Edward Williams suggests, although increasingly antagonistic toward Mexico City, has served as a model for economic change elsewhere in the republic, including the capital (1990:322–323). In this sense, the successes of the north, and its political as well as economic attitudes, can be incorporated into the mainstream of Mexican culture generally.

The north may have been propelled to these more extreme or progressive political positions by its proximity to the United States, making it an exceptional region. It is evident that its culture is strongly influenced by its northern neighbor. Nevertheless, other individual states, none of which are in the north, including Chiapas, Morelos, San Luis Potosí, and of course the Federal District, are also in the forefront of changing views on government relations, decisionmaking, and performance. Each of these entities acts as a catalyst for change in the growing context of democratizing Mexican political culture.

Culture provides a stage on which the theater of Mexican politics can be played. Cultural variables seem to indicate that criticisms of Mexican politics, including centralization of power, are universal. On the other hand, culture also suggests that Mexicans are not yet in agreement on how these structural problems can be solved, nor on the best techniques for citizens themselves to articulate their demands and replace governing authorities.

Notes

1. As William P. Tucker noted more than forty years ago in his classic work *The Mexican Government Today:* "Centralization of tax power has been growing steadily through the years, mainly through specific reforms to the Constitution. Appropriation of important tax fields by the central government has often been accompanied by granting states 'participation' in the yield; but the result has been a decrease in state and local autonomy" (1957:160). In 1930 the federal government controlled 69 percent of tax revenues compared to 23 percent and 8 percent for state and local authorities. In 1991 the figures were 81, 16, and 3 percent respectively.

2. See Wayne Cornelius's and Ann Craig's statement that "the consequences of political centralism are dramatically evident in Mexico today. Each successive layer of government is substantially weaker, less autonomous, and more impoverished than the levels above it. . . . The average municipal government depends on the federal and state governments for about 80 percent of its income; only 20 percent comes from local sources" (1988:16).

3. *Encuesta nacional de opinión pública iglesia-estado.* April 20–29, 1990, courtesy of Miguel Basáñez. Among urban residents, 7 percent read *Excélsior*, 7 percent *La Jornada*, and 1 percent *El Financiero*. Rural respondents read those papers at 4 percent, 0 percent, and 0 percent, respectively.

4. The Indian government found itself in a similar situation in its postindependence era. Under the British, they widely used civil disobedience to protest government policy, legitimizing it as their major political tool. When this generation of Indian leadership came to power, they could hardly disallow their own techniques as acceptable tools of political participation. Thus the opposition took over these techniques, using them against the Congress Party, until they too became an acceptable part of the political scene.

5. Peter Ward and Vicky Rodríguez enumerate the differences between PAN-ista and PRI-ista administrations in Chihuahua, but they also conclude that PAN has not been very sophisticated politically, thus impeding their ability to give such administrative changes permanence (1992:112ff.).

6. In testimony before the Senate Subcommittees on Human Rights, Ellen Lutz, director of Human Rights Watch, stated: "Rural violence is an unabating problem in Mexico. It occurs in the context of long-standing disputes over land as well as frustrations by peasants and members of Indian communities over the inadequacies of Mexico's land reform program. The Mexican government responds as though the violence were a necessary by-product of land-related tensions in the countryside" (Lutz 1990:78). Chiapas is cited specifically in Americas Watch Report on Mexico, under rural violence, which concludes that "violent evictions of peasant families are commonplace in Chiapas" (Americas Watch Report on Mexico 1990:59).

7. This movement, which is called Navismo and which developed around the late Salvador Nava, is described in detail by Robert Bezdek (1995).

Bibliography

Almond, Gabriel, and Sidney Verba. 1965. *The Civic Culture.* Boston: Little, Brown.

Americas Watch Report on Mexico. 1990. *Human Rights in Mexico: A Policy of Impunity.* New York: Human Rights Watch.

Ames, Barry. 1970. Bases of support for Mexico's dominant party. *American Political Science Review* 64:153–167.

Annis, Sheldon. 1991. Giving voice to the poor. *Foreign Policy* 84:93–106.

Basáñez, Miguel. 1987. Elections and political culture in Mexico. In *Mexican Politics in Transition* (Judith Gentleman, ed.), 181–184. Boulder: Westview Press.

Bezdek, Robert. 1995. Democratic changes in an authoritarian system: *Navismo* and opposition development in San Luis Potosí. In *Opposition Government in Mexico: Past Experiences and Future Opportunities* (Peter Ward and Victoria Rodríguez, eds.), 33–50. Albuquerque: University of New Mexico Press.

Camp, Roderic Ai. 1994. Mexico's legislature, missing the democratic lockstep. In *Legislatures and Democratic Transformation in Latin America* (David Close, ed.), 17–36. Boulder: Lynne Rienner.

_____. 1993. Political modernization in Mexico, through a looking glass. In *The Evolution of the Mexican Political System* (Jaime E. Rodríguez O., ed.), 245–262. Wilmington, Del.: Scholarly Resources.

_____. 1991. Mexico's 1988 elections: A turning point for its political development and foreign relations. In *Sucesion Presidencial: The 1988 Mexican Presidential Election* (Edgar W. Butler and Jorge A. Bustamante, eds.), 95–114. Boulder: Westview Press.

Cornelius, Wayne, and Ann Craig. 1988. *Politics in Mexico: An Introduction and Overview.* La Jolla, Calif.: Center for U.S.–Mexican Studies, University of California, San Diego.

Craig, Ann, and Wayne Cornelius. 1980. Political culture in Mexico: Continuities and revisionist interpretations. In *The Civic Culture Revisited* (Gabriel Almond and Sidney Verba, eds.), 325–393. Boston: Little, Brown.

Domínguez, Jorge I., and James McCann. 1995. Shaping Mexico's electoral arena: The construction of partisan cleavages in the 1988 and 1991 national elections. *American Political Science Review* 89:34–48.

Encuesta Nacional de Opinión Pública Iglesia-estado. 1990. April 20–29. Data gathered by the Mori Company, a private polling company of Mexico, courtesy of Miguel Basáñez.

Encuesta Nacional de Opinión Pública Sobre el Proceso Electoral de 1988. 1988. May–June. Data gathered by the Mori Company, a private polling company of Mexico, courtesy of Miguel Basáñez.

Encuesta Nacional de Partidos. 1983. Data gathered by the Mori Company, a private polling company of Mexico, courtesy of Miguel Basáñez.

Encuesta Nacional de Proceso Electoral. 1988. July. Data gathered by the Mori Company, a private polling company of Mexico, courtesy of Miguel Basáñez.

Excélsior. 1993. February 27:10A.

Fagen, Richard R., and William S. Tuohy. 1972. *Politics and Privilege in a Mexican City.* Stanford: Stanford University Press.

Garrido, Luis. 1982. *El Partido de la Revolución Institucionalizada: La formación del nuevo estado en México (1928–1945).* Mexico: Siglo XXI.

Hernández, José Alarcón. 1993. *Las Normas del Poder.* Mexico: Porrúa.

Inglehart, Ronald, Neil Nevitte, and Miguel Basáñez. 1994. *Convergencia en Norteamérica.* Mexico: Siglo XXI.

Lutz, Ellen. 1990. Current Developments in Mexico. Hearing before the Subcommittees on Human Rights and International Organizations and on Western Hemisphere Affairs, Committee on Foreign Affairs, House of Representatives. September 12.78.

Meyer, Michael C. 1967. *Mexican Rebel: Pascual Orozco and the Mexican Revolution, 1910–1915.* Lincoln: University of Nebraska Press.

Morton, Ward. 1962. *Women Suffrage in Mexico.* Gainesville: University of Florida Press.

Philip, George. 1992. *The Presidency in Mexican Politics*. New York: St. Martin's.

Reed, Nelson. 1964. *The Caste War of Yucatán*. Stanford: Stanford University Press.

Rodríguez O., Jaime E. 1993. *The Evolution of the Mexican Political System*. Wilmington, Del.: Scholarly Resources.

Sánchez Gutiérrez, Arturo. 1993. La política en el México rural de los años cincuenta. In *The Evolution of the Mexican Political System* (Jaime E. Rodríguez O., ed.), 215–244. Wilmington, Del.: Scholarly Resources.

Schmidt, Samuel. 1991. *The Deterioration of the Mexican Presidency: The Years of Luis Echeverría*. Tucson: University of Arizona Press.

Tucker, William P. 1957. *The Mexican Government Today*. Minneapolis: University of Minnesota Press.

U.S. Senate. 1990. Current developments in Mexico. Committee on Foreign Affairs, Subcommittees on Human Rights and International Organizations, and on Western Hemisphere Affairs. September 12.

Ward, Peter, and Victoria Rodríguez. 1992. *Policy-making, Politics, and Urban Governance in Chihuahua*. Austin: U.S.–Mexican Studies Program, LBJ School of Public Affairs.

Williams, Edward J. 1990. The resurgent north and contemporary Mexican regionalism. *Mexican Studies* 6:299–324.

World Values Survey. 1990. Data gathered by the Institute for Social Research, University of Michigan, under the direction of Ronald Inglehart.

Young, Eric Van. 1992. *Mexico's Regions, Comparative History and Development*. La Jolla, Calif.: Center for U.S.–Mexican Studies.

Chapter Eight

The Quest for Central American Democracy Since 1945

THOMAS M. LEONARD

The Central American isthmus includes six nations of Spanish heritage, from Mexico's southern border to the northern border of Colombia on the continent of South America.[1] Despite the divergence of their populations and the lack of effective cooperation among them, the six republics share many political characteristics. Historically Central America's political history illustrates the dominance of the landed elite with support from the military. After World War II this characterization began to change. With the exception of Costa Rica, which disbanded its military, the armed forces' role altered from one of defending the elite to that of a self-serving institution; the middle sector pressured for constitutional government; and lower socioeconomic groups sought improvement in their standard of living.

In this chapter three time periods are used to analyze the region's political dynamics since the end of World War II: (1) 1944–1959, during which the "generation of rising expectations" momentarily challenged the established order; (2) 1960–1979, during which the established order used force to resist the challenge to its privileged position; and (3) 1980 to the present, during which the isthmus experienced a violent upheaval, U.S. intervention, and an alleged return to democracy.

For the purposes of this essay, democracy is defined to include free and open elections, followed by a peaceful transfer of political power from one government to another and an effort by the government in power to reach out to the nation's various social sectors.

First Challenges to the Established Order: 1944–1959

The popular image of Central America near the end of World War II portrayed a region ruled by dictators, propped up by the military and serving the interests of the landed elite. The image was correct save for the Costa Rican and Panamanian experiences. In each of the other four republics a landed aristocracy, with all the trappings of political power and social prestige, could be traced to the Spanish colonial period, and it governed in its own self-interest until the 1930s. At that time dictators Maximiliano Hernández Martínez, Jorge Ubico, Tiburcio Carías, and Anastasio Somoza García took over the presidential palaces in San Salvador, Guatemala City, Tegucigalpa, and Managua.

Though Costa Rica did not experience a strong armed dictatorship, it too had been governed by the landed elite. Since the 1880s, with two exceptions, the presidential sash changed hands at regular intervals following elections, an experience that identified Costa Rica as "democratic." Still, one could question whether Costa Rica's middle and lower sectors were represented in and served by the system. In Panama, elite groups, whose roots could also be traced to the Spanish colonial period, governed from the time of Panama's independence in 1903 until 1931. In Panama, power and prestige rested with either the interior landed elites or those commercial interests that serviced the isthmian transit route. In both countries the portents of political change preceded 1944.

Near the end of World War II groups representing the middle sector and the working classes emerged in El Salvador, Guatemala, Honduras, and Nicaragua to demand constitutional government and the broadening of the base of economic opportunity. Momentary success was followed by a return to the established order.

The oligarchic-military clique in El Salvador first came under attack in 1932 when Augustín Farabundo Martí attempted to overthrow the established order with a peasant-led revolution. It failed, and the subsequent *matanza* massacre left an estimated 30,000 people dead. It also brought to the presidency Maximiliano Hernández Martínez and strengthened the relationship between the landed coffee-growing oligarchs and the military.

Hernández Martínez ruled until 1944 without regard to constitutional niceties, but when he sought to extend his presidency for another term, middle-sector protest for democracy plunged the nation into a series of general strikes and violence. Hernández Martínez fled the country in May 1944. The success of the middle sector was short-lived. After a five-month flirtation with implementing democracy, the military again seized power and arranged the presidential election of General Salvador Castaneda Castro in January 1945. For the next decade and a half, a series of army officers were "elected" president without regard for the principles of representative government. The landowners aligned themselves with the military officers and cajoled and bribed them into protecting their status. The middle sector again became a political nonentity. Though two of the officers, Major Oscar Osorio and Lieutenant Colonel José Lemus, initiated "restrained" social legislation—a housing program, legalization of labor unions, a social security program, completion of the Lempa River hydroelectric plant, and improved port facilities at Acajutla—there was no improvement in the standard of living of the Salvadoran masses.

The second challenge to oligarchic rule at the end of World War II came in Guatemala. There Jorge Ubico had captured the presidency in the uncontested 1931 election and thereafter extended his presidency through constitutional manipulation. As in El Salvador, the Guatemalan coffee barons along with the United Fruit Company benefited from dictatorial rule. The catalyst for change was Ubico's dismissal of a medical school dean, which led to student protests that quickly escalated into a general strike and mass demonstrations to demand a return to democracy. Ubico left the country in July 1944. The new forces, led by the middle sector, set in motion a democratic and social reform movement that lasted until 1954.

In 1945 an idealistic university professor, Juan José Arévalo, was elected president and instituted a policy of "Spiritual Socialism," which translated into such legislative programs as labor and rent-control laws, a social security system, educational reform, and a program of industrialization, all of which sought to benefit the working and lower classes at the expense of the landowners and foreign businesses. Arévalo also included many local communists in his administration. The combination of reform and communists was an anathema to the landed oligarchy, the military, and the church and frightened off many of Arévalo's middle-sector supporters. Arévalo was followed by Jacobo Arbenz Guzman, who won the 1950 presidential election. Arbenz accelerated the reforms, starting with the confiscation and distribution of idle United Fruit Company land. This alarmed the Eisenhower administration, which viewed land distribution as a communist policy. To eliminate the "Red menace" the Central Intelligence Agency (CIA) sponsored an invasion of Guatemala and restored the pre-1944 political order, with military generals sitting in the presidential palace.

In Nicaragua Anastasio Somoza García ruled with an iron fist and the support of the National Guard from 1936 to 1956. Opposition to him came from elite groups. These groups were no less authoritarian; they were merely anti-Somoza. Throughout his tenure Somoza dominated the national economy at the expense of the agricultural and commercial elite, which gave them reason to support political change. In 1944 middle-sector pressure and a split in the Liberal Party prompted Somoza to withdraw a proposed constitutional amendment that would have permitted his reelection in 1947, but he retained sufficient influence to ensure the election of seventy-two-year-old Leonardo Argüello. When Argüello attempted to remove Somoza as head of the National Guard, Somoza forced Argüello's resignation and the acceptance of his own uncle, Victor Ramón y Reyes, as president. Somoza regained the presidency by election in 1950 and governed until his assassination in 1956. The elder Somoza was succeeded by his son Luis who, like his father, relied on the support of the National Guard to secure the presidency.

The Honduran dictatorship of Tiburcio Carías dated to 1933, and during his tenure political opponents were incarcerated or exiled. Carías also restricted freedom of the press, speech, and radio. Although some labor and social legislation had been passed, it was not enforced. Despite vociferous opposition from exiles abroad, Carías was firmly entrenched, with a military that served his purpose. Influenced by events elsewhere on the isthmus in 1944, the Honduran middle sector challenged Carías, but compared to the protest in neighboring Guatemala, El Salvador, and Nicaragua, the Honduran experience was relatively mild. Carías successfully weathered the storm to the satisfaction of the elites and foreign investors, particularly the United and Standard Fruit Companies. In October 1948 Carías's handpicked successor, Juan Manuel Gálvez, won the presidential election unchallenged. The change in leadership, however, set Honduran politics in a new direction. Two new political groups soon came forward, labor and the military, each seeking to have the political system serve its own interests.

Pressure for change in Costa Rica came in the 1930s with Manual Mora and his founding of the Communist Party. The support of his workers was crucial to the 1940 presidential election of Rafael Calderón Guardia and to his social legislation program between 1940 and 1944.

Just prior to the 1944 presidential contest, Mora struck a deal with Teodoro Picado, the candidate of the National Republican Party. In return for promises of political support, Mora gained Picado's assurances that he would accelerate economic and social reforms. Picado won the election, the most fraudulent in Costa Rica's history. Although Mora had delivered on his promise, Picado could not deliver on his promises because the traditional parties controlled the unicameral legislature and resisted any further social change.

Tensions increased as the 1948 presidential contest neared. The opposition coalesced around the National Union Party and selected journalist Otilio Ulate as its candidate to challenge Rafael Calderón Guardia of the National Republican Party. Despite Calderón's social legislation and the continued support of Manuel Mora, Ulate won the presidential elections in February 1949, but the National Electoral Board refused to certify the results. The political stalemate led to a brief civil war in which José Figueres challenged the Calderón-Mora group. Figueres's Social Democratic Party was made up largely of middle-sector businessmen and students who favored not only constitutional government but also social welfare programs. After the dust settled, Figueres ruled through a junta for eighteen months, during which Mora's Communist Party was purged and a socialist constitution completed. With the completion of constitutional reform in 1949, Ulate returned to the presidential palace to complete his term. To many observers, including U.S. Ambassador Nathaniel P. Davis, democracy had returned to Costa Rica.

More significant for the long term was the election of Figueres as president in 1953. His election and those subsequent have been considered expressions of the popular will. Figueres accelerated government-sponsored reforms in public works, health care, education, housing, and social services, which contributed to Costa Rica being described as the "Switzerland of Central America."

In Panama, the construction and opening of the canal brought new factions into the republic's political spectrum—middle-sector intellectuals and professionals, foreigners who owned many of the commercial establishments in Panama that served the canal, and the West Indian workers and their descendants who built and maintained the canal. The middle sector entered the political process in 1931 and was largely responsible for the 1936 treaty revision that brought benefits to Panama without affecting U.S. vital interests. But it was Arnulfo Arias's one-year presidency (1940–1941) that set in motion nationalistic forces that drastically changed the character of Panamanian politics. Arias's policies not only infuriated the traditional elite but also the nonnative Panamanian business groups, students who demanded greater democracy, and West Indian workers who were affected by employment within the Canal Zone. From 1941 until 1952, as the elite rotated the presidency among themselves, the dynamics of the newer groups threatened the existing political order.

Equally significant was the emergence of Panama's National Police as a political force. It suppressed the violence that marred the 1948 presidential campaign and that which followed the election of Domingo Díaz Arosemena when Arias's Panameñistas demonstrated against the fraudulent election results. When Arosemena died in office in July 1948, the police chief, Colonel José Antonio Remón, found himself kingmaker. Remón had supervised the development of the police force in accordance with the 1936 treaty and had by the end of World War II turned it into a quasi-military force directed by a group of like-minded officers. In the tense political atmosphere of 1949, Remón permitted the popular Arias to be elected president on his promise not to interfere with the police, but when he did, he was quickly removed from office.

Remón seized the moment. He resigned from the National Police and successfully ran for the presidency in 1952. New electoral laws denied Arias's Panameñistas from participating. Remón's program reflected the five-party coalition that he assembled to win the election: the Coalición Nacional Patriótica (CPN). Though Remón revised the tax code to cut the government deficit and turned to agro-industrial enterprises to cut dependence on the canal, he also expanded health care and education. Remón came to resemble Nicaraguan strongman Anastasio Somoza by outlawing all "radical" groups, taking a hard line against organized labor, imposing press censorship, and weakening the court system. The National Police came to resemble Nicaragua's National Guard. Remón's assassination in 1956 has never been explained, but it shattered his coalition and paved the way for a return to traditional elite rule until 1968.

Violence in the Political Arena: 1960–1979

The overthrow of Cuban dictator Fulgencio Batista in 1959 by Fidel Castro signaled a threat to the oligarchic rule in Latin America. In Central America the established order, except in Costa Rica, faced increased violence. In Nicaragua and Panama the old order collapsed.

On the far north of the Central American isthmus, the overthrow of the Arbenz regime in 1954 produced two long-term consequences. First, with the exception of the coffee baron César Mendez Montenegro, who was elected president in 1966 but governed with the military's approval, a string of seven military men administered Guatemala from 1954 to 1982 without regard for the principles of democratic government. Second, the quest for political democracy and social change did not abate with Arbenz's ouster in 1954. The two converged to produce a violence-laden society.

An unsuccessful intramilitary revolt in November 1960 proved to be a turning point in Guatemala's postwar history. Led by Marcos Aurelio Yon Sosa, survivors of the revolt formed the Thirteenth of November Revolutionary Movement (MR–13), a Marxist group that lasted for a decade. A second guerrilla group, the Rebel Armed Forces (FAC), was founded by Luis A. Turcio Lima and collaborated with the outlawed and underground Communist Party. With support from university students and leftist army elements, these guerrilla groups contributed to the nation's insecurity throughout the 1960s, which in turn caused the establishment of right-wing terrorist groups: The White Hand and An Eye for An Eye. With U.S. assistance the Guatemalan government checked but did not suppress the insurgents, further contributing to the violence. Beginning with President Colonel Carlos Arana in 1970, the government launched a systematic campaign of terror that took some 15,000 lives over the next ten years. In 1981 Amnesty International proclaimed that anyone who opposed the government or was thought to oppose the government was systematically seized, tortured, and murdered. Guatemala was not a representative government by any stretch of the imagination.

As violence prevented change in Guatemala, it forced change in Nicaragua and El Salvador. In Nicaragua, Luis Somoza, who succeeded his father to the presidency, served one term, choosing not to seek reelection in 1963. Still, he and his brother Anastasio selected René Shick as the next Liberal Party candidate, and he won the 1963 election because the Conservative Party refused to participate and because the Somozas' refused to permit Organization of American States (OAS) supervision of the election. With opposition leaders jailed on election day in 1967, Anastasio Somoza won the presidency. Mounting opposition forced Somoza to postpone the scheduled 1971 elections until 1974 and to install an interim junta in May 1972, a move that did not conceal that Somoza was the real authority.

Between 1945 and 1972 the concentration of enormous wealth and political power by the Somoza family contributed to the formation of several opposition groups and to an atmosphere filled with threats and violence. The Somozas responded with repression. Government brutality and further loss of civil rights increased with each episode. Upper-class opposition included the traditional Conservative Party, whose leadership came from several families who traced their origins to the nineteenth century. After 1950 this group's most visible spokesman was Pedro Joaquín Chamorro, editor of the opposition newspaper *La Prensa*. After 1950 younger Conservatives, disillusioned with their elders' cooperation with Somoza, formed the Popular Christian Democratic Movement (MPDC). This group eventually took control of the party and nominated Fernando Agüerro for the presidency in 1963 and 1967, but they deserted the party when Agüerro agreed to the 1972 junta. A second upper-class opposition group rallied around the Dissident Liberals, a group that originated at the start of the 1944 crisis. Like the Conservatives, the leaders of this group traced their antecedents to the nineteenth century. Both groups represented the traditional "outs" wanting "in."

Middle-sector groups rallied around the Independent Liberal Party (PLI), which also evolved from the 1944 crisis. Though it supported opposition candidates to the Somozas, the PLI was more effective in organizing political groups, the most significant being the Democratic Youth Front (FYD), which mobilized high school and university students starting in 1946. A second middle-sector group, the Nicaraguan Social Christian Party (PSCN), organized in 1948, did not become significant until after 1963, when it collected the MPDC members who had deserted the Conservative Party. The PSCN won two congressional seats in 1967, and many observers suggested that it offered the best hope for the future. During the same time period, many middle-sector unions appeared in urban areas—teachers, women, and white collar workers. Prior to 1972 the peasant was not represented in Nicaragua's political arena. The Communist Party was outlawed, and the Socialists made little effort to appeal to the peasants. In fact, by blind allegiance the peasants remained loyal to the party of their employers—Liberal and Conservative.

In this situation the Sandinista National Liberation Front (FSLN) emerged. Its origins can be traced to the late 1940s, but between 1961 and 1967 the small band of Sandinistas robbed banks to satisfy their financial needs and carried out a few raids; however, in any confrontation they were always defeated by Somoza's National Guard. Between 1967 and 1970, the FSLN improved its organization and appealed to the peasants. While their terrorism and bank robberies kept them in the public eye, the FSLN was not a formidable force as the 1960s came to a close.

The catalyst for change in Nicaragua came with a devastating earthquake that in December 1972 destroyed half of Managua and killed an estimated 10,000 people. In the aftermath, Somoza brushed aside the junta and took personal control of the relief efforts, again marked by personal graft and corruption. He silenced opposition by a series of laws and decrees and prepared to resume the presidency via elections in 1974. As the opposition intensified, so did the violence. Somoza declared a state of siege and permitted the National Guard to brutally attack northern rural villages suspected of being FSLN strongholds. Somoza's actions prompted the middle-sector opposition to coalesce under the Democratic Liberation Union (UDEL). Following the killing of Pedro Joaquín Chamorro in January 1978, the UDEL successfully pulled off a nationwide general strike, and then it joined with the Sandinistas, the Nicaraguan Democratic Movement (a broadly based business and professional group), and the Conservative and Christian Democratic Parties. Uprisings in Masaya, Léon, and Diramba and strikes by teachers, industrial workers, and hospital employees demonstrated the breadth of opposition to the Somoza regime. Somoza continued to resist until July 19, 1979, when he was forced to leave the country and left behind a bankrupt economy.

In El Salvador, the basis for a potential violent confrontation continued to build during the 1960s. Throughout the decade the middle sector maintained its pressure for peaceful political change. At the same time the socioeconomic conditions continued to deteriorate for the lower sectors. Unemployment skyrocketed thanks to the increased use of technology in agriculture and industry. In the late 1960s a plethora of political groups surfaced. The Christian Democratic Party (PDC), which dated to 1961, drew support from urban workers and poor to an extent previously unknown. José Napoleon Duarte became their leading spokesman. A second group, the National Revolutionary Movement (MNR), affiliated with the Socialist International, also appeared in the 1960s. Like its leader, Guillermo Ungo, the party continued to exhibit an abstract image and therefore did not register significant political growth among its followers, mostly workers in large industrial enterprises. A third party was the National Democratic Union (UDC), a splinter group of the official National Conciliation Party (PCN) consisting of mostly of younger army officers. The PDC, MNR, and UDC formed the National Opposition Union (UNO) to nominate Duarte for the presidency in 1972. Duarte's claim to victory was cut short by the military when it forced a stop to the vote counting and exiled Duarte to Venezuela. The military then installed PCN candidate Colonel Arturo Armando Molina as president. The scene was repeated in 1977 when the UNO nominated Ernesto Claramount to run against Carlos Humberto Romero. Romero won amid signs of obvious corruption and voter intimidation, and Claramount was exiled to Costa Rica.

Other political actors also came forward. At first the Catholic church was the most significant. Imbued with liberation theology and subsequently led by the reform-minded Archbishop Oscar Romero, the church sought to organize the poor into action. For its efforts the clergy came under military persecution, culminating in Romero's assassination while saying mass in March 1980. Also during the 1970s several popular front organizations emerged, each with Marxist leanings, including the United Popular Action Front (FAPU), the Popular Revolutionary Bloc (BRP) and the 28th of February Popular League (LP–28). Subsequently an umbrella organization, the Farabundo Martí National Liberation Front, became the most significant. It absorbed a variety of revolutionary groups committed to the violent overthrow of the government. And as in Nicaragua the violence escalated throughout the 1970s as the guerrilla groups increased their attacks on the oligarchy and the government utilized the Nationalist Democratic Organization (ORDEN), a group that included army reservists and retired security officers.

By mid-1979 the country appeared to be on the brink of civil war. The fear of armed conflict, coupled with the fall of Somoza, prompted a group of younger officers to orchestrate a coup d'état in October 1979. In the infighting that followed, a new military junta was formed in early 1980 that included José Napoleon Duarte. The new junta initiated a land reform program that spring, which the oligarchy resisted as a threat to their position and the guerrilla groups denounced as a hoax. Nondemocratic El Salvador appeared to be poised for self-destruction.

In Honduras, Carías's successor, Juan Manuel Gálvez, is credited with limited government and political and social reform, but these were not enough to offset pressure from the lower groups, which culminated with the violent banana worker's strike in 1954. The strike affected Honduras's two political parties. For eighteen years following the strike, the Liberal Party (PLH) became the representative of the lower socioeconomic groups, while increasingly the National Party (PHN) became the representative of the traditional elite groups. The struggle between them provided the military with the opportunity to become a major participant in the political arena.

With the election to the presidency of Ramón Vidella Morales in 1957, the Liberals also gained control of the national Congress, and over the next six years they initiated labor legislation, a social security program, and an Agrarian Reform Law. Although Vidella Morales lived under constant threat of conspiracy, his establishment of a Civil Guard to countervail the national army proved to be his and the party's undoing. Air Force Colonel Oswaldo López Arellano brought down the Liberals in 1963. López then formed an alliance with the National Party so that he, now General López, was elected president in 1965 and the Nationals controlled the Congress. Because of the family relationships between the military leadership and the traditional elites, it was predictable that the days of social and political activism had ended. The Liberals were exiled and their legislation repealed or ignored. At the same time, the National-controlled Congress increased funding for the military, which began to take on its own self-serving identity.

But López could not return the nation to its past. Newly emerged commercial and industrial classes, particularly in the more dynamic northern city of San Pedro Sula, sought entry into the political process and the implementation of government economic policies more favorable to their participation in the world economy. At the same time agriculture became more commercial and mechanized, placing pressure not only on the demand for land but also upon the peasants who resided there. The upshot of these conflicting interests culminated in the 1969 "Soccer War" between Honduras and El Salvador and prompted the coming together of the two political parties in the 1971 national unity plan whereby the two would share administrative power and act together to solve national problems. The agreement did not last long. The National Party won the presidency and control of Congress in 1971, but President Ramón Ernesto Cruz, not a decisive leader, did not seek to cooperate with the Liberals. The political tenseness that ensued prompted General López to engineer yet another coup in December 1972 and set in motion a decade of direct military rule. The military proved to be less reformist and believed that political and social peace were necessary to attract foreign capital for economic development. Under the military's leadership, officers came to occupy bureaucratic and decisionmaking posts, but their policies did not advance the economy.

By the end of the 1970s, in a stagnant economy, the pressures for a return to civilian government intensified. The traditional Liberal and National Parties called for a return to constitutional rule, which they had always dominated. New groups, the Innovation and Unity Party (PINU) and the Christian Democrats (PDCH), sought legal recognition and open and honest elections, in which they saw their best chance for success. By the decade's end Honduras appeared to be grasping for a solution to its political stagnation.

In Costa Rica, from the election of Figueres in 1953 through that of Luis Alberto Monge in 1982, elections had been free expressions of the popular will. Figueres accelerated government-sponsored reforms in public works, health care, education, housing, and social services. Since then presidents continued the process with varying degrees of emphasis, and the economy continued to expand and diversify. The middle sector's opportunities also expanded with technocratic positions in government and the private sector. The improved living standards of all classes could be measured by job diversification, a high literacy rate, improved housing, and fewer infectious diseases. In a region of political turmoil, Costa Rica appeared to be a functioning democracy. Still, the system was fragile and threatened.

Despite diversification, the economy remained dependent upon the profits from the exportation of coffee, bananas, meat, and sugar. Given the impact of the oil shocks in the 1970s, the income from these exports was not sufficient to pay for the social programs. The nation's foreign and public debt accelerated, and the resultant inflation contributed to demands for increased wages at a time when the world's lending agencies were making austerity a prerequisite for the government to receive credits to alleviate the debt. By 1980 the socioeconomic conditions in Costa Rica had worsened sufficiently to threaten its democratic government and force the nation to potentially face the same dangers that tormented its northern neighbors.

The pressures for change continued in Panama throughout the 1960s. Middle-sector elements demanded constitutional government. Small businessmen wanted a greater share of the canal's economic activity; educated Panamanians sought access to higher-paying canal jobs. Both groups desired improved living standards. The West Indian labor groups demanded job protection and increased wages, which infuriated the Panamanian laborers who stood to lose out. And, as always, ownership of the Panama Canal was seen by all as the solution to their individual problems. From 1956 to 1964 the Panamanian government, with assistance from the United States, sought to address many of the social disparities, but it could not offset the ever worsening economy. These frustrations were responsible for the 1964 riots and the election of Arnulfo Arias in 1968. But as in the past, Arias attempted to act on his own and curtail the military's political influence. On October 11, 1968, eleven days after his inauguration and for the third time in his political career, Arias was ousted from the presidency. In the aftermath, Omar

Torrijos emerged as undisputed commander in chief of the National Guard and subsequently head of state.

Torrijos consolidated his power by brutally suppressing the opposition, utilizing the National Guard's Intelligence Unit to identify his enemies, encouraging guard officers to profit from their government positions, and promoting officers frequently. To gain popular support for the guard he initiated civic action programs. The Torrijos regime can be divided into three time periods: During the first, 1968 to 1972, Torrijos ruled through decree after abolishing political parties and stripping the National Assembly and presidency of authority. He sought to develop a mix of domestic and foreign policies that would secure his position. In the second time period, 1972 to 1976, he institutionalized his previous actions. For example, article 277 of the 1972 Constitution designated Torrijos as the "Maximum Leader" of the revolution and granted him extraordinary powers that permitted him to appoint almost all government officials. An assembly of Corregimientos replaced the defunct National Assembly. The new assembly consisted of 505 delegates elected from districts that could be traced to colonial times. This act denied the business and commercial elites influence over government policymaking. In the final phase, 1976 to 1980, the economy worsened and the national debt markedly increased, which prompted the rewriting of the Constitution in 1978. The new document denied Torrijos many of his powers and led to the appointment of Aristides Royas as civilian president, the establishment of the Democratic Revolutionary Party (PRD), and the scheduling of elections for 1984.

Torrijos's decline came about despite the 1977 Panama Canal treaties, which satisfied the long-standing nationalistic desire to remove the U.S. presence from the country, but his loss of popularity illustrated the failure of the regime to satisfy the demands of the various socioeconomic sectors, a failure that contributed to their wish for greater participation in government at a time when National Guard officers had become policymakers and attached themselves to the national economy.

A Final Challenge to the Old Order? 1980 to the Present

In the 1980s political turmoil erupted across the isthmus as the old order failed to accommodate the middle sector's demand for constitutional government or the lower sector's socioeconomic needs. The turmoil also resulted in U.S. intervention in the region as the Reagan administration interpreted events on the isthmus as an extension of international communism rather than as developments indigenous to the region. Washington preferred the old order.

In Managua the revolutionary Sandinista government announced its intention to create a "New Nicaragua," meaning a reconstructed national economy and a society with reduced class inequality and an improved standard of living, increased economic opportunity for the lower classes, and the establishment of a democracy. Rather than a liberal, representative constitutional government, the

Sandinistas intended a more corporatist type of government, with elections post-poned until the establishment of national institutions capable of defending the revolution. But faced with economic isolation and U.S.-funded military opposi-tion, the FSLN leadership split, and many leaders deserted the cause, including Edén Pastora, Violetta Chamorro, and Alfonso Robelo, leaving only the Marxist faction in charge of the FSLN. In an effort to legitimize its position the FSLN moved elections up to 1984, but the major opposition parties refused to partici-pate. The six minor groups were no match for the Sandinistas, who swept to vic-tory that November and sent Daniel Ortega to the presidency. Despite the politi-cal victory, the Sandinistas did not enjoy support from the entire population and were confronted with a worsening economic crisis, including shortages of many consumer essentials.

The fracturing of the Sandinista front came at the same time that the Farabundo Martí Liberation Front (FMLN) launched its so-called final offensive in El Salvador and at the same time that Ronald Reagan entered the White House. Although the offensive failed, the incoming administration in Washington viewed the FMLN as an extension of events in Nicaragua, and both countries were seen by Washington as controlled by the Soviet Union through its Cuban proxy. To prevent El Salvador from succumbing to international communism and to ward off the eventual threat of communism to the entire isthmus, the Reagan adminis-tration determined to maintain the old order in El Salvador and to restore it in Nicaragua, primarily by military means. At first the CIA supported a clandestine war against the Sandinistas via its support of the contras, those former Somocis-tas who left Nicaragua after the FSLN took power. From camp bases in Honduras and Costa Rica the contra forces took the fighting into the heart of the country. By 1983 the contra war was public knowledge and the subject of much debate in the United States. The United States committed military advisers and material as-sistance to El Salvador. Honduras became an armed camp as it became the focal point for U.S. military assistance to the contras and a training ground for Sal-vadoran military. As conditions worsened in El Salvador and Nicaragua, Costa Rica received thousands of refugees fleeing the violence, and in the process the generous Costa Rican social safety network system was severely strained. Only Guatemala refused to be drawn into the fracas.

To legitimize its intervention in El Salvador, the United States engineered two elections, for a constituent assembly in 1982 and a presidential election that ended up in a runoff in May 1984. Although the Christian Democrats captured a majority of the seats in the first election, the party confronted a majority of right-wing groups in the assembly, the most important being the Nationalist Republi-can Alliance (ARENA). Duarte captured the presidency from ARENA candidate Roberto D'Aubisson in the runoff election in March 1985. The FMLN refused to participate in the electoral process. Nor did the electoral process bring peace to El Salvador. Rather, the war escalated, the economy worsened, human rights atroci-ties increased, and Duarte became increasingly dependent upon the military. The army's murder of six prominent Jesuit clergymen in November 1989 revealed how dreadful the Salvadoran situation really was. In this atmosphere, ARENA candidate Alfredo Cristiani captured the presidency that same year. No one could claim that democracy had been restored in the country.

In Honduras, where the economy had stagnated by the time the crucial events of 1979 played out, all political factions accepted the U.S. nudge toward democratization as an alternative to violent political change. Transition toward civilian government began with the April 1980 election of a constituent assembly. The centrist Liberal Party captured thirty-five seats and the conservative National Party thirty-three. When Liberal Party candidate Roberto Suazo Córdoba won the November 1981 presidential election, many observers claimed that Honduras had become a democratic state. On the other hand, critics maintained that armed forces commander Brigadier General Gustavo Alvarez Martínez was the real power. Alvarez ruled the military with an iron fist, isolating the contenders for his post, which led to a barracks coup in December 1984. Alvarez was replaced by Air Force general Walter López, but the change did not signal any change in the military's role in politics.

The 1984 elections were held amid a carnival atmosphere that had been preceded by infighting among both the National and Liberal Parties and an effort by Suazo Cordoba to extend his term, while PINU and the PDCH remained unimportant fringe parties. Amid corruption charges and under a complicated vote-counting system, José Azcona became president, but his Liberal Party did not control the congress, meaning that any attempt to initiate new programs would meet with failure. His administration was marked by cronyism and the selection of incompetent personal friends as administrators. In 1989 the National Party candidate, Rafael Leonardo Callejas, won the presidential contest, and his party gained control of the national legislature, municipalities, and departmental administrations. The election, Honduras's fourth since 1980, was a rejection of the backsliding and mismanagement of the economy. Throughout this period of political turmoil and ever worsening economic conditions, the military remained an independent institution, choosing its leaders without civilian consent and benefiting from U.S. military assistance. After nine years, the United States could not claim that it had succeeded in nudging Honduras into democracy.

The Reagan administration's efforts to bring Guatemala and Costa Rica into its isthmian policy met with less success, but for different reasons. Plagued with a repressive military government and a widening disparity in living standards between rich and poor, Guatemala seemed a likely place for a guerrilla insurrection. In 1982 the Army chief of staff, General Efraín Rios Montt, engineered a coup and immediately ordered an end to violence in urban areas but not in the countryside, violence that took an estimated 2,600 lives in 1983 and sent countless indigenous people into Mexico. Montt attracted other opponents. The landowning upper class opposed his "homesteading" plans for the rural poor and a tax reform program. The middle sector became disenchanted with Montt's failure to move toward constitutional government. These factors prompted General Oscar Humberto Mejía Victores, a rightist supported by the landowners, to oust Montt. The old oligarchic alliance again controlled the government. In an effort to provide credibility to his regime, Mejía Victores decreed elections for a constituent assembly in July 1984. Twenty-three parties entered the race, but only two coalitions were of significance: the moderate group composed of the Christian Democratic Party and the Union of the National Center and the rightist coalition of the National Liberation Movement and the Nationalistic Authentic Central. As a result of the elections, each received twenty seats in the assembly and the remainder were divided up between the other parties. Christian Democrat Vinicio Cerezo was allowed to win the 1985 presidential election, but he was still subject to numerous restrictions on his power by the military. By his own estimate, he entered office with 30 percent of the power, and he made it clear that he would not interfere in internal military affairs and that the defense minister would be selected by the military. The weakness of Cerezo's administration could be measured by the continued rumors of coup attempts against him.

Before Somoza's fall, Costa Rica was an ardent supporter of the Sandinista cause. Afterward, it became a haven for political exiles from the north, served as a ferrying point for the shipment of arms to anti-Sandinista forces within Nicaragua, became the training center and headquarters for Edén Pastora following his desertion from the Sandinista government in Managua, and experienced confrontations along its common border with Nicaragua. With its economy and social security programs strained, Costa Rica became dependent upon foreign assistance. President Rodrigo Carazo (1978–1982) refused U.S. assistance because an acceptance of such funds meant he would be forced to join the fight against the Sandinistas, but his successor Luis Alberto Monge (1982–1986) did not. He assented to the professionalization of his civil guard to deal with increased violence and the construction of roads capable of handling heavy military equipment and an airstrip capable of handling military aircraft. U.S. assistance, however, did not restore the country's economic health; in fact conditions worsened. Some political analysts cautioned that Costa Rica's democracy might crack. Into this vortex stepped president-elect Oscar Arias.

Almost immediately after taking office in 1987 Arias initiated a peace process to end the decade-long regional conflict. Each government saw its own survival in the Arias peace plan. For Costa Rica, an end to the crisis would halt the stream of immigrants, which in turn would alleviate the pressure upon the national welfare system and reduce the potential for being drawn into the quagmire. Guatemala's President Cerezo saw a regional peace as an opportunity to curtail the political presence of the military in his country because the threat of insurrection would be decreased. Honduras viewed the peace treaty as a means of reducing the possibility of Nicaraguan vengeance should the United States abandon the contras. For the Sandinistas, an end to the contra war meant a solidification of their position in Managua. And in El Salvador the Arias peace plan meant an end to outside military support for the FMLN guerrillas. Finally, at Tela, Honduras, in August 1989 the heads of state of these five Central American republics signed a peace accord that promised further democratization in each of their countries.

While the regional crisis was playing out in the northern five republics, Panama's political arena became equally tense. When Torrijos stepped down as "Maximum Leader" in 1978, he continually distanced himself from government and the guard. Whatever his intentions, they came to an abrupt end on July 31, 1981, when he died in a plane crash. Though it may truly have been an accident, every Panamanian has a conspiracy theory. In the end, however, Torrijos intensified the strained relations between Panama's key political sectors. The oligarchy wanted restoration of its position and power. The poor wished to maintain, if not improve, their standard of living. The National Guard wanted to ensure its place in the nation's future. But a power struggle within the guard led to its leadership by Manuel Noriega. His triumph resulted in changing the military's name to the Panamanian Defense Forces (PDF), and Noriega used them as a personal tool to dictate politics throughout the 1980s.

As the 1984 election approached, Noriega's power became apparent. He offered the PRD nomination to Fernando Manfredo, an ally of the late Torrijos. But when Manfredo wanted to run unopposed, placing him in a position to challenge Noriega, the offer was withdrawn and presented instead to Nicolás Ardito Barletta. When Barletta took over the presidency he inherited an economy in a tailspin, and to deal with it he cut back on government spending and dismissed some 15,000 government workers, froze wages, and raised taxes. The austerity measures ignited widespread protest, which the PDF brutally suppressed. Barletta was forced to resign and was replaced by Vice President Arturo Delvalle, who continued the austerity measures, further fanning the flames of protest. By 1986 a cross-section of Panamanians not only wanted a restoration of democracy but also questioned the wisdom of taking over the canal. They came to recognize that a U.S. withdrawal would cost many jobs and its financial contribution to the local economy. Even within the PDF there were signs of fracture as promotions became more difficult to obtain. Still Noriega refused to budge, but his circle of supporters became ever smaller.

Yet Noriega's opponents remained disorganized until plans were made for the 1989 presidential elections. Then the Civil Opposition Democratic Alliance (ADOC) nominated for the presidency Guillermo Endara an ally of Arnulfo Arias. His vice presidential running mates were Ricardo Arias Calderón, head of the Christian Democratic Party, and Billy Ford, head of the National Liberal Republican Movement. Noriega's eight-party coalition, dominated by PRD, nominated Carlos Duque, owner of the Transit S. A. Company, long considered a front for PDF-owned operations.

The May 7 elections were marred by fraud, voter intimidation, and violence. Still, exit polls indicated that Endara was the winner. When the National Electoral Board announced that Duque had won, violence erupted, including the beating of

Endara and Ford by Noriega thugs, which was witnessed on worldwide television. Noriega was forced to cancel the election results, but he retained his influence. He named Francisco Rodriguez provisional president, created a new national legislature, and announced that he would consider holding another election in six months. But the internal opposition alone could not oust the strongman. They soon found an ally in the United States, whose decade-long sanctions against Noriega had failed to dislodge him but did increase his determination to stay the course. He boldly and openly challenged the United States to action. The opportunity to remove him came in mid-December 1989. Two days after naming himself "Maximum Leader," PDF forces detained and harassed a U.S. Navy lieutenant and his wife. The incident provided President George Bush the opportunity to invade Panama to restore democracy and whisk Noriega off to Miami, where he was wanted on federal drug charges.

Panama's path to democracy began on December 27, 1989, seven days after the U.S. invasion, when the Electoral Tribunal validated the May 7 election results. Endara assumed the presidency and the ADOC coalition controlled the national legislature. The PDF was disbanded. He inherited an economy in shambles and a government in bankruptcy. Despite assistance from the United States and the International Monetary Fund (IMF), the economy continued to worsen and the disparity of living standards between rich and poor widened. Corruption and nepotism characterized the administration. Many members of the middle sector openly questioned the wisdom of the U.S. pullout and the turning over of the canal to the republic.

As the 1990s opened, it appeared that democracy had come to Central America. If democracy means only free and open elections, Central America has met the criterion. But if democracy includes the establishment of governments that represent all sectors of society, the six republics have not met the criteria of a democratic government.

Two elections in February 1990 set the tone. In Costa Rica, where the constitution prohibited Oscar Arias from running again, his National Liberation Party (PLN) nominated Carlos Manuel Castillo to run against the Social Christian Unity Party (PUSC) candidate Rafael Calderón Guardia, the son of the former president. The campaign focused not on issues but on personalities and the fact that the PLN had captured four of the last five elections. Calderón, who won the election, began the privatization of state-owned industries and a curtailment of government expenditures in the social services area. During his presidency the nation was also racked by a loss of income due to a drastic decline in prices for the chief exports, coffee and bananas. The government debt soared, and inflation drastically increased. To deal with these issues Calderón was forced to institute austerity measures in order to receive financial support from the world's lending institutions. As a result inflation decreased from an annual rate of 25 percent in 1991 to 9.2 percent in 1993 while unemployment remained the same, at about 4 percent. But the trade deficit and public sector deficit continued to soar. One might expect that these would became the issues of the 1994 presidential campaign between PLN candidate José Maria Figueres, son of José Figueres Ferrar, the founder of Costa Rican democracy, and Miguel Angel Rodríguez (the PUSC candidate), a wealthy entrepreneur who promised to continue the government's austerity program. But they did not, as the candidates resorted to mudslinging.

Figueres won the election but has been unable to deliver on his package of improved social benefits. Under pressure from the World Bank and IMF, Figueres succumbed to their demands for continued austerity: the selling of state-owned industries, including the National Liquor Factory; the firing of an estimated 8,000 government workers; and curtailment of government expenditures in such time-honored social programs as education and health. He shut down the unprofitable national railway. The legislature approved an increase from 10 percent to 15 percent in the national sales tax and increases in contributions by teachers to the retirement system. All of this spawned discontent by the end of 1995 and into early 1996 as Costa Rica experienced strikes, demonstrations, and kidnappings, the last usually only occurring in its neighbors to the north. Many analysts began to question whether the system that had served Costa Rica so well for fifty years could continue to operate in the world's new economic conditions.

In Nicaragua the Sandinistas delivered on their promise to hold elections. In fact they appeared confident of victory, having successfully withstood U.S. pressures for nearly a decade.

But they failed to understand that the costs of the war were attributed to them: rampant inflation, stagnant wages, shortages of basic food items. A centrist-right thirteen-party coalition headed by Violetta Chamorro, wife of the slain Pedro Joaquín Chamorro, won the presidency but not control of the national legislature. The euphoria of a triumphant democracy was short-lived. For five years, the economy continued to deteriorate, the foreign debt soared as the price for major exports declined, and the government could not deliver basic services. Demands for austerity measures as a prelude to international banking assistance further exacerbated the social costs of economic reforms. In the political field, the Sandinistas remained a nemesis, blocking legislation in congress and leading workers strikes. Under the strain, the UNO began to split. The FSLN also split into moderate and traditional hard-line factions. Chamorro was slow to remove General Humberto Ortega as commander of the national army, still largely Sandinista. The contras who returned home were slow to receive land settlements, and the question of returning properties confiscated during the Sandinista period remained a contentious issue. For an eighteen-month period in 1993 and 1994 a quorum in the national legislature was a rarity, and the country subsequently operated under two constitutions. Nicaragua was not a functioning democracy.

In 1995 the focus shifted to the scheduled 1996 elections. In this atmosphere the legislature passed a new constitution to replace that written in 1987 by the Sandinistas. Though the new document expanded congressional authority at the expense of the president, its electoral reforms were more important for the moment. It stipulated that blood relatives of a sitting executive could not seek the presidency, a direct slap at Chamorro's son-in-law and chief of staff, Antonio Lacayo. Furthermore, to avoid a runoff election the successful candidate needed to garner at least 45 percent of the popular vote, and there were also provisos for the spending of government-supplied campaign funds and the limiting of outside aid to technical assistance and training. If this was not difficult enough, twenty-seven political parties surfaced during the 1990s, and by early 1996 several had named candidates for the presidency. Several Sandinistas and former Sandinistas came forward. Former head of state Daniel Ortega headed the Sandinista Party; ex-FSLN member Sergio Ramírez of the Sandinista Renovation Movement, which favors a more centrist position, declared for the presidency; and former FSLN dissident Edén Pastora returned from Costa Rica to lead the Democratic Action Movement. Two Chamorro allies also entered the race: former vice president Virgilio Godoy, who favored greater government intervention in the economy for the Liberal Independent Party; and Chamorro's son-in-law Antonio Lacayo became the candidate for the newly formed Nation Project while at the same time he challenged the new constitution's provision forbidding him from running. Arnold Alemán, the popular anti-Sandinista, former mayor of Managua, and relative of the late Anastasio Somoza, was the choice of the Liberal Alliance. Miriam Argüello, a National Assembly deputy, represented the Popular Conservative Alliance. Nicaragua appeared to be in political disarray.

Salvadoran President Cristiani devoted the first half of his administration to negotiating a peace settlement with the FMLN under the aegis of UN Secretary General Javier Pérez de Cueller. Cristiani was motivated to end the conflict by the loss of U.S. assistance, a massive trade imbalance, and ARENA's loss of its political grip in the March 1991 congressional elections. In December an agreement was concluded ending a decade-long civil war that took an estimated 75,000 Salvadoran lives and to which the United States had committed over $4 billion. Armando Calderón Sol, the ARENA candidate in the March 1993 presidential elections, was forced into a runoff against a three-party leftist coalition: Democratic Convergence (CD), the MNR, and the FMLN. Calderón Sol captured the runoff election in May with 62 percent of the vote, but ARENA did not have a grip on the legislature, where it captured thirty-nine seats, the FMLN twenty-two, the Christian Democratic Party eighteen, and minor parties six. Though the runoff was relatively scandal free, the general election was charged with corruption and fraud on behalf of Calderón Sol.

Both presidents resorted to neoliberal economic policies—government austerity, tax increases, and so on—in order to meet the demands of international lending institutions to receive financial support for the war-torn economy. By 1995 the impact of economic reform on the poor and failed land policy contributed to strikes and demonstrations. War issues also remained unsettled. The government was slow in resettling former FMLN guerrilla fighters and in settling peasant land claim issues. According to the Peace Accords, the Army and the Treasury Police were to be drastically reduced in size and a National Civil Police force created. Although the size of the military had been reduced, many of the men found themselves with positions in the new police force or government agencies. In fact, by the end of 1995 the budget for the Salvadoran military had been increased. Human rights issues drew the greatest attention. A United Nations–sponsored investigation found that active and retired military officers were responsible for many of the killings during the ten-year civil war, including the murders of Archbishop Romero and the six Jesuit priests in 1989. Only under pressure did Cristiani begin to act, and even then only after issuing a general amnesty for all those responsible for the atrocities. In El Salvador the elite remain in control of politics and the military is still a potent political force.

In Guatemala the Cerezo presidency proved to be a failure. Military commanders remained feudal lords over the territories they administered without fear of civilian reprisal. Violence and human rights violations increased. Cerezo's efforts to raise the minimum wage and rework the tax code fell before the oligarchs; this failure, coupled with continued inflation, only lowered the standard of living for the majority of Guatemalans. Most of the nation approached the 1990 presidential election with a sense of hopelessness. Other than a peaceful transfer of power from one civilian to another, the electorate expected no changes in their own lives. In fact the differences were slight between Jorge Carpio Nicolle, a wealthy publisher and founder of the National Center Union, and Jorge Antonio Serrano, a right-wing businessman and evangelist disciple of General Efraín Rios Montt. But six months into his administration, Serrano sought to consolidate his own power by dissolving congress and suspending the constitution, an action that prompted a call for his ouster by businessmen, Indian leaders, unionists, university rectors, and newspaper editors. The military responded, ousting Serrano and replacing him with a known human rights activist, Ramiro de León Carpio. He immediately struck at the military by forcing the retirement of the defense minister, General José Domingo García Samayoa, and transferring several other commanders for their support of Serrano in the previous political turmoil. Next Carpio initiated a campaign against the thieving congressmen and successfully engineered voter approval of forty-three constitutional reforms on January 30, 1994, including the dismissal of congress, the dissolution of the Supreme Court with a new group to be selected by the legislature to be elected in August 1994, and the reduction of the presidential term to five years from six. The congressional elections turned out to be a success for the right-wing Guatemalan Republican Front (FRG), which captured thirty-two seats, and the National Advancement Party (PAN), which captured twenty-four. The remaining twenty-four seats went to four other parties. General Rios Montt became congressional president. The hopelessness of the Guatemalan electorate was registered in both elections: only 30 percent of those eligible to vote did so. During the same time period political assassinations continued and fighting again erupted between guerrillas and the Army.

The country then prepared for the presidential elections in November 1995, and until the Supreme Court ruled against him, Rios Montt sought the FRG nomination. He was not eligible to run because the constitution forbade anyone to do so who had been part of military coup—as Rios Montt had been in 1982. Twenty-seven parties eventually were formed, and alliances among them were common. The November election forced a runoff but produced some interesting results: Alvaro Arzú of the right-wing PAN came in in first place with 35 percent of the vote; Alfonso Portillo of the FRG took second with 22 percent of the vote; Fernando Andrede of the National Alliance (AN) finished third with 13 percent of the vote, and Jorge González del Valle of the New Democratic Front (FDNG) received 7 percent. The FDNG formed in October was the first leftist party in fifty years to participate in a general election. The party was a coalition of indigenous, student, peasant, labor, and human rights groups; it favors agrarian reform and equal rights for the indigenous peoples, who make up about 48 percent of the 10.6 million Guatemalans. Arzú captured the runoff election in January 1996 with 52 percent of the vote, but again absenteeism was the real winner: 63 percent of the eligible voters did not cast ballots. A month into his presidency, Arzú purged several generals who were linked to drug trafficking, car thefts, and human rights abuses, but he showed no signs of taking on the military as an institution. In the meantime, the country continued to be plagued by guerrilla war, human rights violations, a high crime rate, and lower living standards for the middle and lower sectors.

In Honduras, Rafael Callejas commenced his presidency in 1990 amid spiraling inflation and a growing shortage of gasoline, medicine, and foodstuffs. Other signs of economic weakness included a drop in the per capita income from $750 per year in 1980 to $520 in 1990. The public debt was 90 percent of the gross domestic product (GDP) and the foreign debt approached $3.3 billion. Callejas attacked the problems in neoliberal fashion: through the sale of state-owned enterprises, tax increases, devaluation of the lempira, public employee layoffs, and higher fuel and public service charges (water, telephone, and sewer increased 100 percent and electricity 50 percent). The international reaction was positive, as international lending institutions became more willing to advance additional credits, but the middle and lower sectors, hit hardest by the reforms, were not and took to the streets in demonstrations and strikes. In the countryside more land was being converted into cattle fields to increase beef production for export, at a time when the national food supply was critically low. The cattle lands also displaced peasant workers, further straining relations between them and the landowners. The economic crisis was largely responsible for the election of Liberal Party candidate Roberto Reina over the National Party candidate Oswaldo Ramos Soto in the November 1993 elections. The party platforms did not differ much, but the electorate, wearied of the economic reforms, accepted Reina's promises to stop the hemorrhaging.

Initially Reina placed government attention on social issues, but a continued drought further slashed agricultural productivity and threatened to shut down the nation's hydroelectric supply. The electric shortages became so acute that the government bought supplies from Mexico and Panama. Both factors contributed to continued rampant inflation, which reached 28 percent in 1994 and 30 percent in 1995. The future dimmed in mid-1995 when Chiquita Brands International suspended further investments in the country at a time when earnings from banana exports had deceased. Urban and rural groups continued to protest, and in early 1996 worker's unions demanded a 100 percent pay increase—this at a time when 70 percent of the population lived below the poverty line, when unemployment had reached 60 percent, and the vital minimum income for a worker was $180 per month, $100 more than earned. The potential for political upheaval remained.

Both presidents Callejas and Reina came to challenge the military as an institution. Its professionalization dated to the 1950s, and it benefited handsomely from the U.S. military commitment to the region in the 1980s. It acted independently of civilian authority and had come to dominate various government agencies like the National Civil Police and the Treasury Police, which had been responsible for human rights violations, assassinations, and torture during the 1980s, as well as the immigration, merchant marine, and civil aviation offices. Its court system was also independent to civilian oversight. The military's Bank of the Armed Forces (BANFA), its credit card service (PREVICARD), insurance business (PREVIA), and ownership of the national telephone system HONDUTEL were among the most profitable in the country and provided supplemental income for the officers. Determined to limit, if not stop, the pervasive military presence in the country, Callejas cut the military budget 10 percent on the grounds that national security was not currently threatened. But when the abolishment of national conscription was introduced into the legislature, the military issued threats and the bill was withdrawn. Two months after his inauguration in 1993, President Reina continued the assault. He successfully transferred the police force from military control and privatized HONDUTEL, disbanded the Army's Secret Police (DNI), and moved the military's customs responsibilities to civilian control. He also persuaded congress to abolish obligatory military service, effectively reducing the size of the military. In January 1996 when the military chose General Mario Hung Pacheco as its new commander in chief of the armed forces, Reina announced that he would be the last. Beginning in 1999 the defense minister will be a civilian elected official. The final blow to the military came with the Supreme Court ruling that denied a 1981 amnesty law applied to the military, paving the way for army officers to stand trial for crimes committed against civilians.

In Panama, Endara inherited an economy in shambles. The GDP had declined by 25 percent since 1988, inflation was rampant, unemployment was at 25 percent, and an estimated 48 percent of the population lived below the poverty level. Like others on the isthmus, Endara accepted IMF prescriptions to cut government expenditures in order to receive financial assistance, in addition to the aid provided by the United States. Free-market economic practices were also put into effect. As a result, by 1993 Panama showed all the signs of recovery: The GDP was the highest in Central America; unemployment had been cut in half; private investment and consumption as well as tourism all registered gains. Yet there were problems: Poverty and stagnant wages plagued the middle and lower sectors;

many of the residents from the El Chorillo and San Miguelito slums, the areas most damaged in the 1989 invasion, remained temporary residents at the Rio Hato Air Base; and the anticipated pullout of U.S. personnel from Panama heightened middle-sector fears about job loss. Although the PDF had been dismantled, the administration's image as incompetent, corrupt, and filled with nepotism did not auger well. Money laundering and drug trafficking continued.

As the nation prepared for the May 8, 1994, elections, sixteen political parties were organized, of which two were considered the most significant. Ernesto Pérez Balladares, a forty-seven-year-old millionaire businessman, was nominated by the old PDF party, the PRD. The other candidate was Ruben Darío Carles, nominated by the National Republican Liberal Movement (MOLINERA). A former comptroller general, Carles described himself as a neoliberal, which meant that he favored the continued use of foreign capital in the economy. The campaign was devoid of issues and resorted to mudslinging and personal attacks. Balladares captured the presidency with 33 percent of the vote. Analysts interpreted the election as a rejection of Endara's failure to alleviate joblessness and other social ills that afflicted Panama despite its soaring economic growth.

Balladares faced the same issues, and since his inauguration the economic situation has deteriorated. The economic boom that followed the ouster of Noriega in 1989 slowed. Unemployment crept upward. In an effort to attract foreign industry to the republic, Balladares steered a revision of the labor code through congress in August 1995; the revision effectively weakened labor's bargaining position. The legislation caused violent demonstrations in Panama City. Six months later the administration engineered another revision of the code that limited labor's right to strike in order to placate Taiwanese textile manufacturers who wanted to establish plants in the old canal zone. As the Americans began to depart, the impact on the Panamanian economy began to take hold. Efforts to find uses for the now-vacant U.S. properties brought forth many ideas but little action. Democracy may have been restored to Panama, but the government has not met the needs of all social sectors.

Conclusion

Based upon the definition of democracy given at the beginning of this chapter, democracy has not come to Central America. Fifty years ago the oligarchy was in power, and with the possible exception of Costa Rica, it has returned to power in the 1990s. And, as fifty years ago, the oligarchy does not represent the interests of all social sectors.

During the intervening period the experiences of the nations have varied, but they shared several common characteristics. In the first time period, 1944 to 1949, the challenge to the old order in El Salvador, Honduras, and Nicaragua came from elite and middle-sector groups outside the power structure established by dictators Maximiliano Hernández Martínez, Tiburcio Carías, and Anastasio Somoza. In Costa Rica, Guatemala, and Panama the reform effort included an appeal to the lower sectors.

From 1960 to 1979 the challenge to the established order came largely from forces representing the lower socioeconomic sectors. To secure their position against the threat, the oligarchs increasingly relied upon the military to suppress the opposition. In the process the military, as an institution, emerged as the final arbiter of national politics in all the countries save Costa Rica. In fact, Costa Rica had abolished its military, and its government policies fulfilled the definition of democracy provided at the outset of this chapter.

In the 1980s violent conflict dominated the isthmian political arena, again with the exception of Costa Rica. In El Salvador, Guatemala, and Honduras the old order struggled to maintain its position. In Nicaragua and Panama dictators struggled against the forces of change, and such forces proved successful in Nicaragua. A case can be made that the Sandinistas did not meet the definition of democracy after ousting Somoza from power, but they were engaged in a violent struggle with the representatives of the old order. Panama's military dictator, Manuel Noriega, acted like a madman as he struggled against all social sectors to remain in power. Costa Rica faced the threat of being engulfed by the conflict that raged across the isthmus.

When the strife ended in 1990 and the electoral process was restored, the new governments faced similar problems, beginning with the political role of the military. The elite-military alliance returned in El Salvador and Guatemala. The civilian government of Honduras has so far successfully challenged the military's political influence. The elite–middle-sector government in Nicaragua not only fractured but also faced the continued presence of the Sandinistas, who retained control of the military and labor unions and also opposed all policies of the new government. Only in Panama was the military institution destroyed. The decade of conflict also left the isthmian economies in shambles, but the policies pursued by the new governments only worsened the standard of living for the middle and lower sectors. This has resulted in public demonstrations, sometimes violent, and voter apathy. These events suggest that democracy is not a functioning institution across the isthmus.

Yet in Central America's long struggle to obtain democracy there has been much progress since 1945. At first middle-sector groups entered the political arena in their quest for constitutional government. Subsequently the lower socioeconomic groups also entered in their quest for an improved standard of living. Today and into the future, the middle and lower sectors are forces that must be contended with by the guardians of the old order, the elite and the military.

Notes

1. Geographically Belize is also a Central American nation. A former British colony that achieved independence in 1981, its political dynamics are more closely linked to other former British possessions in the Caribbean basin region and therefore the country is not included in this essay.

Bibliography

A Decade of War: El Salvador Confronts the Future. 1994. London: Monthly Review Press for the Transnational Institute, The Netherlands.

Amnesty International. 1988. *Honduras: Civilian Authority, Military Power, and Human Rights Violations in the 1980s.* London: Amnesty International.

Collazos, Sharon Phillips. 1991. *Labor and Politics in Panama: The Torrijos Years.* Boulder: Westview Press.

Falcoff, Mark. 1993. *Searching for Panama: The U.S.-Panama Relationship and Democratization.* Washington, D.C.: Center for Strategic and International Studies.

Goodman, Louis W., William M. LeoGrande, and Johanna Mendelson Forman, eds. 1990. *Political Parties and Democracy in Central America.* Boulder: Westview.

Honey, Martha. 1994. *Hostile Acts: U.S. Policy in Costa Rica in the 1980s.* Gainesville: University of Florida Press.

La crisis política constitucional de Guatemala: Del golpe de Jorge Serrano a la presidencia constitucional de Ramiro de Leon Carpio. 1993. Guatemala: INCEP.

The 1990 Elections in Nicaragua and Their Aftermath. 1992. Lanham, MD: Littlefield.

Ropp, Steve C., and James A. Morris. 1984. *Crisis and Adaptation.* Albuquerque: University of New Mexico Press.

Schulz, Donald E., and Deborah Sundloff Schulz. 1994. *The United States, Honduras, and the Crisis in Central America.* Boulder: Westview Press.

Schwartz, Stephen. 1992. *A Strange Silence: The Emergence of Democracy in Nicaragua.* San Francisco: ICS Press.

Scranton, Margaret E. 1991. *The Noriega Years: U.S.-Panamanian Relations, 1980–1991.* Boulder: Westview.

Seligson, Mitchell A., and John A. Booth. 1995. *Elections and Democracy in Central America: Revisited.* Chapel Hill: University of North Carolina Press.

Trudeau, Robert. 1993. *Guatemalan Politics: The People's Struggle for Democracy.* Boulder: Lynne Rienner.

The United Nations and El Salvador, 1990–1995. 1995. New York: United Nations Department of Public Information.

Winson, Anthony. 1989. *Coffee and Democracy in Costa Rica.* New York: St. Martin's.

Chapter Nine

Elections and Democracy in Central America: The Cases of Costa Rica and Nicaragua

CHARLES L. STANSIFER

I am not the first to attempt to compare Nicaragua and Costa Rica. Many others familiar with Central America have been tempted to explain the contrasting political development of the two neighboring countries. Indeed, few literate Central Americans do not have an opinion on this subject. Salvador Mendieta, a Nicaraguan writer and politician of the early twentieth century, was one of the more outspoken. In his three-volume *La enfermedad de Centro América* he makes reflective, comparative comments on five Central American countries (Honduras, Guatemala, Nicaragua, El Salvador, and Costa Rica) with a view both toward promoting democracy and toward restoring the Central American confederation. Like many Nicaraguans, Mendieta was critical of the Nicaraguan political system and admired the Costa Rican. Among his numerous suggestions for a better, more democratic Central America is an elaborate proposal for a National Elections Council based, it would seem, on Costa Rican electoral procedures of the 1920s (Mendieta 1934:vol. 3, 639–651).

Relatively few students, however, have made a systematic effort to compare the political systems of Nicaragua and Costa Rica. Among the few political scientists to undertake such a comparison is James Busey (1958:627–659), who approximately forty years ago compared the dictatorial tradition of Nicaragua with the democratic political system of Costa Rica. His was a practical study, unblemished by broad theoretical considerations but seriously handicapped, as he recognized, by the dearth of scholarly studies of either country. Nevertheless, despite its deficiencies, his study deserves recognition as one of the first comparative studies of the political systems of two Latin American countries.

Understanding today of the political systems of Nicaragua and Costa Rica is at a much higher level than before owing to the virtual explosion of intellectual curiosity about Central America in the last two decades. But comparative analyses are still lacking. Three recent comparisons should be mentioned. One is a University of Kansas thesis in Latin American Studies by Gary Blackford (1992), who undertakes a comparison of the electoral systems of Nicaragua and Costa Rica. Another is a detailed, systematic comparison of the Catholic church in the two countries that has drawn scholarly attention to its author, Philip Williams (1989), a historian. The third, a sophisticated study of mass political culture in Mexico, Costa Rica, and Nicaragua, challenges the application of democratic European and U.S. models to Latin America but gives little attention to historical and geographical factors (Booth and Seligson 1994). My study is to some extent inspired by Mendieta and Busey, who first drew the problem to my attention, and its structure owes a good deal to Williams's comparative analysis. Blackford's thesis has also been helpful in providing details of the two electoral systems as they have evolved since the 1920s.

Measurement of the degree of democracy is difficult, controversial, and not very satisfying to theoreticians of democracy. Nevertheless, we do have a useful yardstick of Latin American democracy in the Fitzgibbon-Johnson-Kelly index. Every five years since 1945 Latin American experts in the United States have been asked to rank the Latin American countries along a continuum of most democratic to least democratic. In addition they have been asked to assess the conditions favoring or not favoring democracy, such as freedom of expression, regular elections, military or church interference, and the like. However varied the definitions of democracy the experts have been applying to their answers and whatever other limitations this reputational study may have, the results are still striking and should stimulate thoughtful analysis. Since 1965 Costa Rica has consistently been given first place in this survey and in earlier years ranked second three times and third once. Nicaragua, on the other hand, usually occupies a spot third, fourth, or fifth from last. Its highest ranking occurred in 1980, when it ranked seventh; in 1985 it ranked twelfth.[1] In the last two polls Nicaragua ranked tenth and eleventh.

Despite their common cultural backgrounds and their close historical interrelations, Costa Rica and Nicaragua are at opposite ends of the democratic continuum. Why? Considering their common language and religious and cultural inheritance, their close historical linkages, and their proximity to each other, what factors took one country in one political direction and the other in another? From the perspective of the history of democracy in the five republics of Central America, Nicaragua and Costa Rica offer the greatest contrast and therefore the most daunting analytical challenge.[2] A better understanding of this remarkable similarity-dissimilarity will perhaps lead to a clearer understanding of the origins of democracy.

Readers are entitled, at this point, to a definition of a concept as murky and oft-abused as democracy. Schmitter and Karl's definition (1991:76), because of its simplicity and directness, is a good place to begin. According to them: "Modern political democracy is a system of governance in which rulers are held accountable for their actions in the public realm by citizens, acting indirectly through the competition and cooperation of their elected representatives." I would add three points to this definition for the purpose of this chapter, points that deal with elections as well as democracy. First, the accountability of the system depends upon periodic elections in which the candidates freely present their views and whose results are honored by those in power. Second, in general the higher the level of popular participation the more democratic is the system. Third, a political system within a nation is in constant flux, sometimes approaching the nation's democratic goals and sometimes falling short depending on a multitude of factors.[3] This definition avoids the equation of democracy with certain goals such as the promotion of equity and social justice; it recognizes the importance of process and gives partial validity to the classical argument that true democracy can only be government by the people.

The focus of this study is, then, on political democracy rather than on social or economic democracy. Specifically, it is an attempt to explain the factors responsible for the differing trajectories of the political systems in the neighboring countries of Nicaragua and Costa Rica. Though the spotlight is on the political system this approach does not exclude, of course, consideration of the impact of social, economic, cultural, and geographical factors on the political system. As a historical essay this chapter's aim is not to provide a comprehensive narrative history of the two states but, rather, to single out causal factors, to highlight key episodes or individuals, and to explain critical transition points in the history of the two countries.

A brief glimpse at colonial Central American history is helpful because, if nothing else, it demonstrates that the contrast between the two countries is not of recent vintage. Both Nicaragua and Costa Rica were provinces of the Captaincy General of Guatemala in the colonial period. Because they were both conquered and settled from Panama, in contrast to the four other provinces of the Captaincy General (Chiapas, Guatemala, El Salvador, and Honduras), which were settled from Mexico, and because of the distances to Guatemala City, seat of the Captaincy General, they were viewed as isolated colonial outposts. Nicaragua was organized as a *gobernación* first, in 1527, with Pedrarias Dávila as governor. Costa Rica's establishment as a *gobernación* did not occur until nearly fifty years later, after an expedition from Nicaragua finally succeeded in establishing a settlement in the central valley of Costa Rica.

Neither Nicaragua nor Costa Rica promised power, riches, or strategic advantage. They were both at the tail end of political administration, which originated in Spain and passed through Mexico City and Guatemala City before reaching León (Nicaragua's colonial capital) and Cartago (Costa Rica's colonial capital).

Both were lightly populated. Costa Rica had no more than 60,000 inhabitants at the time of independence in 1821, and Nicaragua no more than 175,000. The absence of large numbers of sedentary Indians in both Nicaragua and Costa Rica, especially Costa Rica, limited the development of landed estates. Mineral wealth was of minimal importance in Nicaragua and of virtually no importance in Costa Rica. Compared to El Salvador and Guatemala both Nicaragua and Costa Rica were too poor to attract the attention of European migrants. In colonial times neither Nicaragua nor Costa Rica offered the mother country a transisthmian crossing comparable to Panama's.

Nonetheless, contrast was already evident. Cacao and indigo cultivation had succeeded as money crops in Nicaragua but not in Costa Rica. A larger Indian population in Nicaragua was one advantage for Nicaraguan cacao and indigo planters, who used the *encomienda* and *hacienda* systems to benefit from Indian labor. In Nicaragua the city of Granada on Lake Nicaragua developed as a commercial center for the cacao trade and as an entrepôt, connecting to the Caribbean commercial zone via the San Juan River. It was far enough inland to enjoy relative security from Indian and pirate attack. Because of the needs of Guatemala and El Salvador, Nicaragua's cattle industry sprang up on the Pacific side. Realejo was a minor port and shipbuilding center on the Pacific shore. León, the capital, was also the seat of a bishopric, and because Spanish authorities mistakenly expected Nicaragua to expand, they built a cathedral in León comparable in size to those in Lima and Bogotá. Clerics gathered there in greater numbers than anywhere else in Nicaragua or Costa Rica. Nicaragua's superiority as a cultural leader was further enhanced when a university was established in León in 1811. It was Central America's second university; the first had been established in Guatemala 150 years previously. For all of these reasons Spanish authorities gave more importance to Nicaragua than Costa Rica and placed responsibility for military defense of the southern district of the Captaincy General on Nicaragua rather than Costa Rica. An additional motivation for congregating military forces in Nicaragua was the substantial indigenous population allied to the British on the distant Caribbean or Miskito shore of Nicaragua. No such indigenous enclave existed in Costa Rica.

Nicaragua was, in short, a remote backwater throughout the colonial period, but one that nevertheless derived modest profit and prestige from its Indian population, the strength of the Catholic church, its university, its proximity to Guatemala, its access to the Caribbean, and its military responsibilities.

Costa Rica, in comparison, was settled later, was more economically disadvantaged, and was so unattractive to Spain's enemies that it needed no special military defenses. By the time Costa Rica was being colonized, in the 1560s, the *encomienda* system had already been modified, leaving fewer opportunities for colonists to control Indians and large quantities of land. Although early Spanish settlers of Costa Rica, who came from Nicaragua, attempted to establish cacao plantations, they were only moderately successful. The best cacao areas in Costa

Rica were on the Caribbean coast, far from the central valley where colonists preferred to live. On the coast they were vulnerable to raids from seafaring Indians and pirates. In addition high tariffs, problems of transportation, and the absence of a dependable labor supply helped to prevent the establishment of a *hacienda* economy like those established in Nicaragua and other Spanish provinces in the Americas.

No other economic opportunity emerged in Costa Rica in the colonial period to draw entrepreneurs. Costa Rica was too far away to ship cattle to Guatemala, although a small mule trade with Panama developed to supply animals for the treasure caravans across the isthmus. No precious metals were discovered in sufficient quantity to attract settlers to Costa Rica, despite its name. Except for a brief tobacco prosperity in the 1780s Costa Rica passed through the entire colonial period without a major international commercial crop. Mining was also insignificant in comparison to Nicaragua, Honduras, and Guatemala (McLeod 1973).

Unlike Nicaragua, Costa Rica had no ready transport access to the Caribbean and no port on either the Caribbean or Pacific shore. Administratively, economically, militarily, religiously, and intellectually Costa Rica was dependent on adjacent Nicaragua first and remote Guatemala second.

The outlines of social and economic contrast were already evident. Cacao and indigo plantations and cattle ranches with their Indian workers meant that the two-class system common to most regions in Spain's American empire was entrenched in Nicaragua in the colonial period. Granada, in Nicaragua, had a small aristocratic class based on the cacao trade and commerce. León, as an agricultural center, as the home of a clerical establishment, and after 1811 as the seat of a university, also developed social divisions (Coronel Urtecho 1962:42–43). The vast majority of Costa Rica's inhabitants were small-scale, primarily subsistence, farmers. The capital, Cartago, gave shelter to the small governing class, but to be governor of Costa Rica meant neither wealth nor prestige in colonial Central America (Estrada Molina 1965). The Catholic church in Costa Rica, without a bishop and with few Indians to convert, was weaker than in Nicaragua.

Independence from Spain and subsequently from Mexico in the 1820s seemed to accentuate existing differences. Proximity to Guatemala City helped to draw Nicaraguan cities into the independence struggle, but Costa Rica remained aloof. León and Granada, freed of Spanish control, took opposite stands on the issue of annexation to Mexico, accentuating their already heated rivalry. Cartago, like León, favored the Mexican connection but was quickly defeated by superior forces from San José (Sáenz Carbonell 1985:152–158). When, in 1822, Guatemala issued a call for delegates from all over Central America to discuss the region's destiny, León and Granada were represented but no Costa Rican attended (Vega Carballo 1981:36–57). When Central Americans united in a confederation in 1824 Costa Rica reluctantly participated and was one of the earliest to withdraw a decade later.

By 1838 the two countries had separated from the confederation and embarked on independent paths. Nicaragua immediately experienced a demoralizing descent into economically destructive violence that lasted for some twenty-five years. It was characterized by bitter ideological, family, and regional rivalry between the two virtual city-states: León, headquarters of the Liberal Party, and Granada, headquarters of the Conservative Party. The rivalry was climaxed by the disastrous Liberal invitation to William Walker and his band of filibusterers to join the local political contest. Walker's assumption of the presidency in 1857 plunged Central America into war and further embittered Nicaraguan politics. Although he was executed in 1860 his name lives on in Nicaragua in infamy. To Conservatives, Liberals bore the indelible stain of treason for their mistake. Long memories of the Liberal Party–Walker alliance helps to explain Conservative dominance of Nicaraguan politics for virtually the remainder of the nineteenth century.

Finally, in 1893, Liberals returned to power and immediately promulgated a Liberal constitution and carried out sweeping Liberal reforms, including breaking up church-owned properties and promoting coffee production for export. At the same time they used the power of office to enrich themselves and punish their enemies, the Conservatives. For sixteen years the Liberals went through the motions of elections, which always returned the Liberal dictator José Santos Zelaya to power. His end came in 1909 after he antagonized the United States in various ways. Perhaps his greatest strategic mistake was to oppose Washington's demand for extraterritoriality in connection with canal zone negotiations. This led to Washington's preference for Panama and concerns about Zelaya's unsettling influence in Central America (Stansifer 1977:468–485). A Conservative rebellion against Zelaya gave the United States an opportunity to assist militarily in removing him from office. Now the Conservatives, from the Liberal perspective, had become *vendepatrias,* or traitors, by inviting U.S. intervention.

U.S. marines arrived in Nicaragua in 1912 in order to keep the Conservatives, probably the minority party at this time, in power against an active Liberal rebellion. Conservatives proceeded to undo previous Liberal measures, punish Liberal adherents, and monopolize the spoils of office in the usual manner. Like the Liberals they held regular elections every four years. Marine supervision of these elections, conducted while U.S. and Nicaraguan military forces attempted to capture Augusto César Sandino, the one prominent Nicaraguan political figure who refused to accept the U.S. presence, provided a facade of legitimacy to Conservative dominance. However, at the end of the occupation period—in 1932—the Liberals, now finally acceptable to the United States, won a decisive electoral victory (Vargas 1989; Dodd 1992:85–98). The marines, unable to capture Sandino, retired to the United States, and the United States adopted a policy of nonintervention. Anastasio Somoza García, who had been groomed as head of the National Guard, promptly turned the guard into a partisan instrument of a Liberal Party dictatorship, which he ruled personally until his assassination in 1956.

Although both Liberals and Conservatives in Nicaragua regularly expressed their faith in democracy, they obviously were unable to craft a democratic system of government. By the end of the nineteenth century, Liberals had taken steps to weaken the church and widen the suffrage, but they shelved progressive electoral reforms apparently out of a belief that only they could carry out the progressive economic reforms that they thought the country needed. Part of the problem was the temptation for both party groups to gain power for their own benefit and exploit the illiterate masses. The key factor in their failure appears to be the profound distrust and antagonism between the two principal cities, León and Granada.[4] This bifurcation was an unusual circumstance in Latin American nations, which even today are characterized by primate cities. León and Granada were roughly equal in size and wealth and equally zealous about their preferred ideologies. Family loyalties compounded regional division. Occasional collaboration with foreigners intensified feelings. Not even the surprising agreement to make Managua the compromise capital in 1858 dimmed the ardent competition. In Nicaragua, unlike most Latin American countries, the Liberal-Conservative dichotomy persisted until the mid-twentieth century. The legacy was not necessarily a propensity to dictatorship, as many observers would have it, but a deeply ingrained habit of bitterly partisan politics.

An additional factor beyond the capacity of Nicaraguan leaders to control discouraged democracy from taking root. I refer to the important connection between Nicaragua's geographical circumstance and its political evolution. Engineers believed in the nineteenth century that Nicaragua was the most likely route for a transisthmian canal. Possibilities of transisthmian transportation facilities attracted the attention of the great powers, especially Great Britain and the United States, and their involvement tended to embitter Nicaraguan politics. Even in the twentieth century, after the decision had been made to build the canal in Panama, the threat (largely imagined) of an alternate, rival canal in Nicaragua helped to explain U.S. interference in Nicaraguan politics. Charges of treason and collaboration with foreign foes, which are the consequence of such interference, are not a good basis for a consociational relationship between political factions.[5]

Costa Rica's constitutions and evolving political system in the first few years following independence were not unlike Nicaragua's. Elections were irregular, and coups and dictatorships were not unknown. The differences were more basic: They were social, economic, demographic, and geographical. In the early nineteenth century Costa Rica faced a less-pronounced division of social classes, greater equality of income, fewer racial and ethnic divisions, and greater isolation than Nicaragua. The burden of the colonial tradition, which writers on democracy and economic development in Latin America have given so much weight, was lighter in Costa Rica than in Nicaragua. Costa Rica is not a country steeped in colonial tradition; it is a creature of the nineteenth century.

In recent years scholars have begun to question the cherished truths of traditional Costa Rican egalitarianism. Samuel Z. Stone, Elizabeth Fonseca, Mitchell Seligson, Lowell Gudmundson, and others have demonstrated that Costa Rica had large landowners and an oligarchy at the time of independence (Stone 1975;

Fonseca 1984; Gudmundson 1986; Seligson 1980). Nevertheless, the punctured legend still stands. Costa Rica entered independence with fewer large estates, a smaller oligarchy, a weaker clerical establishment, and a more equitable distribution of land than Nicaragua. These circumstances allowed Costa Rica to ease into national independence without the political strife and caudillismo that plagued its neighbors. In terms of the absence of sharp class division and the absence of intense political conflict, Costa Rica was poised to become a democratic society.

Economically, Costa Rica's unusual transformation from poverty to relative prosperity revolves around coffee. Costa Rica's governors eagerly embraced coffee production in the early nineteenth century, but it was not a matter of conversion of old *latifundia* into new ones, as few old ones existed. The market for coffee in Europe only gradually expanded in those years, and labor in Costa Rica was scarce, resulting in a slow creation of new, medium-sized coffee estates in the vicinity of San José and Heredia (Echeverría Morales 1972; Hall 1985:74–75). Without indigenous labor, proprietors cultivated small or medium-sized estates with family labor. Coffee enabled San José to wrest political power from Cartago, which had a weak economic base, and permitted Costa Rica to emerge, gradually, from colonial backwardness and isolation to a burgeoning coffee-based prosperity in the nineteenth century. Coffee also, it must be admitted, accentuated class division.

The best coffee lands were found in the volcanic soils of the Central valley, which sheltered a cluster of Costa Rica's principal towns: Cartago, San José, Alajuela, and Heredia. As geographers West and Augelli (1989:439) put it: "Better than any other Middle American country, Costa Rica displays a single-cluster distribution of population." Few people lived outside the central valley so there were, in effect, no regional divisions. Costa Ricans were a homogeneous population living in close proximity. As coffee cultivation expanded, the population moved to the edges of the valley and then beyond. Unlike most Latin American countries, which experienced population migration from outlying areas to the core, Costa Rica experienced an outward movement from the central valley. Although the political effects of this phenomenon are not easily evaluated, it would appear that this fostered central valley political dominance and deterred regionalism. People who migrated beyond the central valley maintained close family and economic ties in the valley. Costa Rican politics in the nineteenth century had no sharp regional divisions, as did Nicaragua's, and was not characterized by bitter partisanship.

There are other important distinguishing formative factors in Costa Rica's historical geography of the nineteenth century. Without danger of Indian uprisings or foreign invasion there was little need for military expenditures. Unlike the other four Central American republics, whose interconnectedness regularly drew political and military factions across borders, Costa Rica remained aloof, apart. Panama, to the south, was an insignificant province of Colombia and constituted no threat. Costa Rica's central volcanic chain offered an additional, indirect protection. The great powers that thirsted for control of isthmian transportation directed their attention to Honduras, Nicaragua, and Panama and gave mountainous Guatemala and Costa Rica little or no consideration. Absence of Indians, isolation, and poor transisthmian transportation potential allowed Costa Rica to develop its own destiny with little interference and with little need for a standing army.[6] Owing to the scarcity of Indians and the lack of a bishop the Catholic church in Costa Rica was less of a divisive political factor than the church in Nicaragua. In the late nineteenth century, when both countries were going through a secularization process, it was easier in Costa Rica than in Nicaragua to channel revenues into education rather than into the military.

This leads us to the Costa Rican election of 1889, which is generally considered the first genuinely free election in Central American history. It was in the previous two decades that coffee prosperity and the benevolent, positivist, authoritarian rule of President Tomás Guardia had enabled Costa Rica to begin to build a secularized state, an educational establishment, and a *civilista* mentality (Fischel 1987). The election of 1889 marked the end of authoritarianism and the beginning of the so-called Liberal Republic. In view of the limited suffrage and the absence of a secret ballot we should not claim too much for this particular election. Literacy and property qualifications also prevailed. But if the degree of democracy is judged by free and fair elections, which seems an appropriate measure for the late nineteenth century, the election of 1889 deserves special recognition. There was a choice and a freedom of expression, the votes were counted correctly, and the victorious out-party candidate took office (Pinaud 1979). In 1989, in commemoration of the election, President Oscar Arias dedicated a new San José plaza as "The Plaza of Democracy."

The Liberal Republic lasted until 1948. Within that period elections occurred regularly (with one exception) and the electoral system of Costa Rica was improved and molded to Costa Rican standards. Presidents governed wisely and for the benefit, largely, of the coffee interests. The arrival of the United Fruit Company after 1900 created a powerful economic enclave and, along with the construction of the Northern Pacific Railroad, brought in black West Indian workers, but neither the company nor the black workers appeared to affect the evolution of the Costa Rican political system. Respected leaders like Cleto González Víquez (president 1906–1910 and 1928–1932) and Ricardo Jiménez Oreamuno (president 1910–1914, 1924–1928, and 1932–1936) promoted education, extension of suffrage, and freedom of expression, and, although antagonistic or indifferent to independent labor unions, they permitted new, radical parties to develop. A measure of their tolerance was the creation and growth of the Communist Party from 1929 to 1948. Liberally oriented governments initiated direct election of the president (in 1914), promoted the concept of nonrecognition of new governments coming to power by violence, standardized voting registration, introduced the secret ballot (in 1925), limited terms, and began to regulate campaign activities. In 1945 the National Assembly, responding to popular demand, created the National Tribunal of Elections, making it independent of the executive branch (Blackford 1992:41–42, 45).

The midpoint of the twentieth century, approximately 120 years after separation from the Central American confederation and just before Busey undertook his comparison, is a good place to check the progress of the two countries in their efforts to bring about democracy.

In 1950 Nicaragua was ruled by Anastasio Somoza García and the Liberal Party, now transformed into the very personalist National Liberal Party. Somoza was not lacking in political ability or popular support. Regular elections were held, but Conservatives, because of harassment, co-optation, or indifference, offered little opposition. Conservatives, for the most part, turned to business—cotton was the new export crop of the time—and intellectual pursuits. Twice Somoza stepped down in favor of figureheads, but at the least sign of independence he reclaimed the presidential office. As head of the National Guard as well as president, Somoza kept the primary instrument of coercion under his direct control.

Precisely in 1950 he negotiated the famous Pact of the Generals with the head of the Conservative Party, guaranteeing the Conservatives one-third of the seats in the National Assembly and a share of executive branch positions. Afterward elections were conducted as usual, but they were no longer necessary, as the Somoza family controlled the presidency and determined who held the majority of the legislative seats. The percentage of registered voters who exercised the franchise dropped below 35. The secret ballot, protected by U.S. marines in the elections of 1928 and 1932, disappeared. Municipal elections were still being held in the 1940s, but after 1950 they were suspended in most cities and officers of the National Guard became the most important local authorities. Citizens' input into decisionmaking was minimal at all levels (Fiallos Oyanguren 1969). The Fitzgibbon index of 1950 placed Nicaragua clearly among the least democratic countries of Latin America—in sixteenth position—ahead of only Bolivia, Haiti, the Dominican Republic, and Paraguay. It dropped to eighteenth in 1955. No studies of Nicaragua published since 1950 provide any justification for altering this nondemocratic image of the Nicaraguan government in the 1950s.

The Somoza dynasty survived the assassination of Anastasio Somoza García in 1956, as one son took the presidency and another the National Guard, and continued to dominate the country until 1979. When Anastasio Somoza Debayle took over as president in 1967 the regime grew more repressive and more corrupt. Obviously Nicaragua fell far short of the democratic goals of its founding fathers and its subsequent constitution makers; it had become virtually the private estate of one family.

Costa Rica, which had been second on the Fitzgibbon index in 1945, ranked third in 1950 behind Chile and Uruguay. The timing of the early surveys was unfortunate for Costa Rica because the heretofore peaceful, fledgling democracy was experiencing some transitional strains in the 1940s, strains that erupted in the bloody revolution of 1948. This much-studied event is now generally understood to have been not a social upheaval of the category of the Mexican or Cuban Revolutions but an anticommunist, middle-class movement in favor of political democracy (Bell 1971; Gudmundson 1984; Lehoucq 1991). Or, as Anthony Winson puts it, the events of 1948 marked the transition of Costa Rica's "liberal oligarchic state" to "liberal democratic politics" (1989:1). Led by José Figueres, the rebels fought to preserve the electoral victory of Otilio Ulate. According to the independent electoral tribunal, Ulate had won, but the legislature annulled the election, arrested Ulate, and awarded the presidency to its preferred candidate, Rafael Calderón Guardia. Figueres, once victorious in the field, chose to take advantage of his position as head of a temporary military junta to enact significant institutional changes before handing the government over to Ulate. These reforms included abolition of the army, the grant of full political rights to women, a tax on the wealthy, and nationalization of the banking system.

The Costa Rican Catholic church, which had identified itself with the reformist policies of the 1940–1948 period, found itself on the losing side in the revolution of 1948. Reacting quickly to the changed circumstances, the church lowered its profile and accommodated itself to the Figueres movement. It has not been a divisive factor in subsequent political debate (Williams 1989:119, 172).

The most direct, concrete product of the Costa Rican revolution of 1948 was the Constitution of 1949, which was drawn up by a constituent assembly composed of more opponents of Figueres than supporters. Shocked by the temporary breakdown of order Costa Rican leaders gravitated to the political center and worked together to produce a document that they hoped would prevent future breakdowns. National consensus on this constitution, an agreement among the majority of politically active citizens on basic democratic values and rules of conduct, is perhaps the best evidence of Costa Rica's democratic political maturity.

Theoretically the constitution placed the country among the most democratic countries in the world. Subsequent political practice and refinement of the political system through law and constitutional amendment, though not bringing about a democratic millennium, have enhanced Costa Rica's claim to that position. The constitution strengthened the independent judiciary, fortified the electoral branch of government (the National Electoral Tribunal became the Supreme Electoral Tribunal), weakened the executive, provided for proportional representation, and limited the terms of both presidents and legislators. It further decentralized political power and increased participation in decisionmaking, a major accomplishment in a region where centralization has such deep roots, by giving greater power to municipal government and by encouraging the establishment of autonomous agencies. It is arguable whether the constitutional limitation of the president to one term only is democratic or whether the requirement that deputies in the National Assembly must stand aside for one term before reelection qualifies as a democratic practice, but Costa Ricans argue that it enhances participation. Figueres's preconstitutional reforms concerning the army and women's suffrage were also incorporated in the constitution. As for the church, its low-profile strategy paid off, for the constitution was less restrictive of clerical activity than most Latin American constitutions of the time (Arguedas 1981).

Since Ulate's term ended in 1953 Costa Rican elections have been regular, free of significant irregularities, fair, and competitive. A two-party system has solidified after a few years of uncertainty. Figueres's party, the National Liberation Party (PLN), has won the presidency in seven of the eleven elections since 1953 and has dominated the National Assembly, but the primary opposition party, the Social Christian Unity Party (PUSC) or its predecessor placed its candidate in the presidency in 1958, 1966, 1978, and 1990 (Chalker 1995:103–122).

Since 1962 an average of 80 percent of Costa Rican citizens of voting age have voted (McDonald and Ruhl 1989:178). Compared to other countries this is a very high popular participation. Laws requiring compulsory voting might explain the high percentage, except that there are no penalties for abstention. The responsibility of voting is given heavy emphasis in the school system, and school children participate in polls and vote in mock elections on election day. Many observers have noted the festive atmosphere surrounding election day in Costa Rica; indeed, election day is often called *la fiesta cívica*. Unquestionably, the Costa Rican political system deserves high marks for the regularity and fairness of elections and the high level of citizen participation. The pattern of Costa Rica's political system was determined by the events of 1948 and 1949; subsequent changes have been adopted to improve the system.

Imperfections in Costa Rica's political system have been noted and reforms regularly debated. Problems of violations of human rights, restrictions on press freedoms and campaign finances, corruption among government officials, and militarization are among the controversial issues that relate to democracy (Blackford 1992:54–60). The Costa Rican political system has been buffeted by a lengthy internal economic crisis and by the war between the contras and the Sandinistas, but it has proved to be flexible enough to adapt to change and virtually immune to outside pressures, evidence of the stability of the system.

Studies show significant satisfaction by Costa Rican citizens with the political system. During the domestic economic crisis of the 1980s and the international pressures of the Contra War on Costa Rica some commentators pessimistically predicted that Costa Rica's vaunted democracy would crack or even collapse in the same manner as Chile's and Uruguay's. Charles Ameringer, one of the leading historians of Costa Rica, published his *Democracy in Costa Rica* in the midst of this crisis and dedicated the last few pages of his concluding chapter to a comparison of Uruguay's problems prior to the collapse of democracy with Costa Rica's economic and political problems (1982:126–127). Lowell Gudmundson weighed in with even more alarmist warnings (1985:vol 3, 496–515). But these forebodings proved to be wrong. A few incidents of violence did indeed occur in Costa Rica, but instead of polarizing political thinking, as in Uruguay and Chile, the tension appeared to foster centrist solidarity. In contrast to expected voting behavior in favor of extremist candidates in times of economic crises, Costa Rican voters tended to stay with the major political parties. Even during the presidency of the least popular president of the post–1953 period (Rodrigo Carazo, 1978–1982), polls showed only minimum dissatisfaction with the political system (McDonald and Ruhl 1989; Seligson and Gómez B. 1989; Carvajal Herrera 1978).

Costa Rica's problems in the 1980s seem minuscule compared to those of Nicaragua in the same period. The last years of the Somoza dynasty, in the 1970s, witnessed the end of the Conservative-Liberal dichotomy and the beginning of a new political division centering on such issues as defense, private enterprise, dictatorship, the Catholic church, and communism. The victory of the Frente Sandinista de Liberación Nacional (Sandinista Front of National Liberation, or FSLN) over the dictatorship in 1979 roused great expectations of democracy, soon to be dampened by new rivalries as tempestuous as the old. Sandinista support of the so-called Popular church against the church hierarchy, attempts to identify the FSLN with the national government, and friendly relations with the Soviet bloc contributed to the intensity of conflict. Nicaragua, during the Sandinista revolution, from 1979 to 1990, experienced the most sweeping social change in its history, the most destructive war in its history, unprecedented militarization, repolarization of its politics, and incalculable economic devastation. Ironically, in precisely the same time span Nicaragua made the most substantial progress in its history toward establishing a democratic political system.

One of the highest goals of the Sandinista government was to rule on behalf of the democratic majority rather than, as had been the case in the past, on behalf of the privileged minorities. This is not the place for a review of the accomplishments and failures of the Sandinistas in the area of redistributive justice nor for a review of the fight for survival of the revolution. What is of principal interest in this study is the contradictory Sandinista support of participatory democracy and representative democracy (Coraggio 1985:7–22).

Upon taking power in July 1979 the Sandinistas enjoyed overwhelming popularity because of the euphoria following a victory over a universally despised dictator. As the organization primarily responsible for the defeat of the dictator, the FSLN considered itself the popular vanguard and therefore expected to control and direct the revolutionary government (Brown 1990:46). Mass organizations that had sprung up during the revolution were to be both instruments of control and vehicles of popular participation in government. The Sandinistas gave particular attention to the Committees for the Defense of Sandinismo, which were modeled after similar Cuban committees and whose purpose was to mobilize the citizenry in defense of the revolution and for other specific goals of the FSLN. In effect, Sandinistas saw democracy not in terms of political parties and elections but in terms of participation of citizens in all matters that directly related to them, such as the immediate neighborhood, the school, and the workplace.[7]

For a variety of reasons the mass organizations did not work as planned. There were, of course, instances of success. In 1980 mass organizations participated in a highly successful literacy campaign, in itself promoted as a preliminary step to popular participation. Mass organizations conducted vaccination and other public health campaigns, promoted cultural and sports events, organized fire-fighting and defense brigades, and the like. Public fora and town meetings with Sandinista leaders gave additional opportunities for public expression. But the mass organizations were directed from above and, in general, ultimately failed to become instruments of democratic decisionmaking. As the counterrevolution intensified, as the economy worsened, as opposition to the Sandinista leadership increased, the mass organizations withered. In general, the more independent the organizations were of Sandinista domination, the stronger they were (Stahler-Sholk 1987:86). The FSLN involved a greater percentage of the Nicaraguan population in interest group activities than any previous political grouping, and it remains, even after its defeat in the elections of 1990, the largest political organization in the country, but its success as a promoter of popular participation is mixed.[8]

Sandinistas also publicly committed themselves to elections, but when? What kind? A few Sandinista leaders ridiculed elections as bourgeois sentimentalism and called for their elimination. Ominous signs appeared in Managua's streets in 1979 and 1980 saying, "El pueblo ya votó. Votó por el sandinismo [The people already voted. They voted for Sandinismo]." Others pointed out that immediate elections would have returned an overwhelming Sandinista victory and endangered political pluralism. Sandinistas in favor of delayed elections won out in this internal FSLN dispute, and in August 1980 the FSLN leadership announced that elections would be held in 1985. Later, in 1984, the governing junta established the Supreme Electoral Council by decree and moved the date of elections up to November 4, 1984, when they were indeed carried out.

The elections for president, vice president, and deputies of the National Assembly, despite defects, were the most nearly free, the fairest elections held in Nicaragua up to that time. They were orderly but not necessarily the most orderly nor the most competitive. The residue of popular support for the FSLN and its 1979 victory was the principal factor in the inability of opposition forces to make the election competitive. Other factors, including FSLN coercive tactics, the splintering of the opposition parties, the ongoing counterrevolution, and the indecision of Arturo Cruz, the most attractive personal opponent of the FSLN, helped to account for the 67 percent victory of Daniel Ortega of the FSLN in the race for the presidency. The FSLN won control of the National Assembly by a slightly lesser percentage. Large numbers of international observers confirmed that the campaign had been conducted within reasonable bounds of fairness, that the electoral procedures were sound, and that the votes were counted without evidence of fraud (Booth 1986).

What is often overlooked in the controversy surrounding the elections is that they were Western-style (not Soviet- or Cuban-style) and that they inaugurated significant changes in the political system devised at the moment of Sandinista victory in 1979. Taking advantage of an expanding network of election officials in western Europe and Latin America, Nicaragua's electoral authorities borrowed procedures for the preparation of ballots, registration of voters, organization of the supervision of balloting, and vote counting from many Western countries, including Costa Rica. Elections for regional representatives to the National Assembly (which was to take the place of the FSLN-controlled, corporatist Council of State) took place at the same time, giving a voice to defeated presidential candidates and representatives of opposition parties. Given Nicaragua's electoral history, the elections were a gigantic step in the direction of democracy.

Another significant democratic step taken by Nicaraguan authorities immediately after the inauguration of the new government in 1985 was the initiation of a national dialogue on a new constitution. While the assembly worked on drafting the constitution, the government sponsored a series of open meetings in which constitutional issues were discussed. It is safe to say that no previous Nicaraguan constitution had enjoyed the benefit of such widespread popular participation. The constitution, which was promulgated in 1987, establishes the independence of the Supreme Electoral Council from the executive branch in a manner strikingly similar to the Costa Rican Supreme Electoral Tribunal.[9] This is not surprising in view of the widespread familiarity of Nicaraguans with the Costa Rican electoral process and their admiration of the Costa Rican political system.[10]

That these electoral reforms were more than a temporary political foil or expedient was amply demonstrated by the Nicaraguan elections of February 1990. The 1990 elections not only gave Nicaraguan citizens the opportunity to choose their president and representatives in the National Assembly but also provided them an opportunity freely to elect, for the first time in fifty years, municipal council members. Residents of the Miskito Autonomous Zone, for the first time in a long history of tension between the Atlantic and Pacific regions of Nicaragua, nominated their own candidates and elected their own leaders. At the invitation of the Nicaraguan government thousands of international observers and foreign journalists minutely examined the electoral process from the registration of candidates and parties in August 1989 through the counting of votes. The overwhelming conclusion of these observers was that the elections had been conducted freely and fairly, although with some imperfections due principally to wartime conditions, financial imbalances, abuse of incumbency, and foreign interference (*Electoral Democracy Under International Pressure* 1990). In this case there was competition, opposition candidates campaigned freely, the votes were counted, and the incumbent party, having lost, turned over the government to the victors. Considering Nicaragua's record the elections of 1984 and 1990 marked a more spectacular advance in the direction of democracy than the Costa Rican election of 1889.

In much of the contemporary discussion of the prospects for democracy there is often an optimistic sense of progression toward democratic values. To an extent Costa Rica's experience supports this optimism. It has made steady progress toward the goal of democracy and is more democratic today than it was fifty or a hundred years ago. Nicaragua's experience does not leave the observer with the same sense of optimism. Although Nicaragua today is more democratic than it was twenty years ago, most students would agree that it is too early to tell whether the democratic advances made in the last fifteen years, measured primarily by free elections and greater politicization of citizens, are permanent.

There is also in the contemporary discussion of prospects for democracy often a naive assumption that a democratic system from one country can be implanted in another. Consistent failure of U.S. policy toward Latin America in this regard should make any policymaker wary of attempting to export or transplant a particular concept of democracy. Intervention on behalf of democracy may bring contradictory results. In the same fashion simplistic support of elections and civilian governments over military governments may backfire. If export is possible at all, it should be most likely where the countries share similar cultural backgrounds and political institutions. But we have seen that even in the case of countries so nearly alike as Nicaragua and Costa Rica and where intellectual leaders in Nicaragua in general admired the Costa Rican system and wished to adopt at least portions of it, the delicate Costa Rican democratic plant has not as yet been successfully transplanted in the neighboring soil. Why is there such a difference? It is difficult to resist the conclusion that it is not Costa Rican will nor Costa Rican wisdom, that it is not Nicaraguan lack of will nor Nicaraguan lack of wisdom that produced the different political histories of the two countries. It is, rather, a combination of historical, geographical, social, demographic, and economic circumstances.

Notes

1. Kenneth F. Johnson, personal communication, February 1985. It should be pointed out that the surveys only include countries independent in 1945; former British colonies that are now independent are generally considered Latin American (Jamaica, Barbados, and Belize, for example) and have not been included. For a full explanation of the methodology for the index see Fitzgibbon 1967.

2. It is interesting to note that there is a great deal more scholarly literature on why Costa Rica is democratic than on why Nicaragua is not. John A. Booth has written extensively on Costa Rica's political system; see, for example, his "Costa Rica: The Roots of Democratic Stability" (1989). One of the more recent studies is Dabene 1992. Suzanne Jonas and Nancy Stein (1990), among others, make the case that Nicaragua has become democratic since 1979.

3. Although critics of democracy in Nicaragua and Costa Rica have not been wanting, the overwhelming evidence from the political documentation, and most especially the two countries' constitutions, demonstrates that the citizens of both countries prefer a democratic system to any other.

4. See Burns 1991, especially 16–24. Burns focuses on the nineteenth century, but as late as the 1932 elections the Liberal Party won 90 percent of the votes in the Department of León, and the Conservative Party won 57 percent of the vote in the Department of Granada; see Vargas 1989:162.

5. According to Arend Lijphart, in a consociational democracy "the centrifugal tendencies inherent in a plural society are counteracted by the cooperative attitudes and behavior of the leaders of the different segments of the population" (1977:1).

6. It is true that in the late nineteenth century and in the early twentieth century Costa Rica expended large amounts on military defense. But by 1920 this trend had passed, and Costa Rica reverted to minimum annual military expenditures. Costa Rica's record of military expenditure is graphically displayed from 1882 to 1949 in Muñoz Guillén 1990:27, 99.

7. For example, Minister of Defense Humberto Ortega said on August 23, 1980, soon after the announcement had been made about the holding of elections in 1985: "For the Sandinist Front democracy is not defined in purely political terms, and is not reducible to popular participation in elections. . . . Democracy first appears in the economic order, when social inequalities begin to diminish. . . . Once these goals are attained, democracy immediately spreads to other areas: the field of government is broadened; the people exert influence over its government. . . . At a more advanced state, democracy means workers' participation in the management of factories, co-operatives, cultural centres, and so on" (quoted in Weber 1981:112; Weber cites from the Managua *Barricuda*, August 24, 1980).

8. Even as early as 1980, when Luis Serra wrote a sympathetic account of the mass organizations, the problems noted above were evident. They grew worse afterwards; see Serra 1982:95–113; see also Torres and Coraggio 1987:107–111.

9. The judiciary can overrule the National Electoral Tribunal in Costa Rica under certain circumstances, but the Nicaraguan Supreme Electoral Council cannot be overruled by the judiciary (Blackford 1992:66–71).

10. In a 1988 opinion poll, 41 percent of Nicaraguans polled identified Costa Rica as Central America's most democratic country; only 24 percent selected Nicaragua as the most democratic (Jonas and Stein 1990:33).

Bibliography

Ameringer, Charles. 1982. *Democracy in Costa Rica*. New York: Praeger.

Arguedas, Carlos Manuel. 1981. *Constitución política de la República de Costa Rica: Anotada y concordada*. San José: Editorial Costa Rica.

Bell, John B. 1971. *Crisis in Costa Rica*. Austin: University of Texas Press.

Blackford, Gary S. 1992. Elections and democracy: A comparison of Nicaragua and Costa Rica. M.A. thesis, University of Kansas.

Booth, John A. 1989. Costa Rica: The roots of democratic stability. In *Democracy in Developing Countries* (Larry Diamond, Juan J. Linz, and Seymour Martin Lipset, eds.), 4:387–422. Boulder: Lynne Rienner.

———. 1986. Election amid war and revolution: Toward evaluating the 1984 Nicaraguan national elections. In *Elections and Democratization in Latin America, 1980–1985* (Paul W. Drake and Eduardo Silva, eds.), 37–60. San Diego: Center for Iberian and Latin American Studies.

Booth, John A., and Mitchell A. Seligson. 1994. Paths to democracy and the political culture of Costa Rica, Mexico, and Nicaragua. In *Political Culture and Democracy in Developing Countries* (Larry Diamond, ed.), 99–130. Boulder: Lynne Rienner.

Brown, Doug. 1990. Sandinismo and the problem of democratic hegemony. *Latin American Perspectives* 17:39–61.

Burns, E. Bradford. 1991. *Patriarch and Folk: The Emergence of Nicaragua, 1798–1858*. Cambridge: Harvard University Press.

Busey, James L. 1958. Foundations of political contrast: Costa Rica and Nicaragua. *Western Political Quarterly* 11:627–659.

Carvajal Herrera, Mario. 1978. *Actitudes políticas del costarricense: Análisis de opinión de dirigentes y partidarios*. San José: Editorial Costa Rica.

Chalker, Cynthia. 1995. Elections and democracy in Costa Rica. In *Elections and Democracy in Central America, Revisited* (Mitchell A. Seligson and John A. Booth, eds.), 103–122. Chapel Hill: University of North Carolina Press.

Coraggio, José Luis. 1985. *Nicaragua: Revolution and Democracy.* Boston: Allen and Unwin.

Coronel Urtecho, José. 1962. *Reflexiones sobre la historia de Nicaragua.* 2 vols. Managua: Instituto Histórico Centroamericano.

Dabene, Oliver. 1992. *Costa Rica: Juicio a la Democracia.* San José: FLACSO.

Dodd, Thomas J. 1992. *Managing Democracy in Central America, a Case Study: United States Election Supervision in Nicaragua, 1927–1933.* New Brunswick, N.J.: Transaction Publishers.

Echeverría Morales, Guillermo. 1972. *Breve historia de café: Como llegó a Costa Rica.* San José: Trejos Hermanos.

Electoral Democracy Under International Pressure: The Report of the Latin American Studies Association Commission to Observe the 1990 Nicaraguan Elections. 1990. Pittsburgh: LASA.

Estrada Molina, Ligia María. 1965. *La Costa Rica de don Tomás de Acosta.* San José: Editorial Costa Rica.

Fiallos Oyanguren, Mariano. 1969. The Nicaraguan Political System: The Flow of Demands and the Reactions of the Regime. Ph.D. diss., University of Kansas.

Fischel, Astrid. 1987. *Consenso y represión: Una interpretación socio-político de la educación costarricense.* San José: Editorial Costa Rica.

Fitzgibbon, Russell H. 1967. Measuring democratic change in Latin America. *Journal of Politics* 29:129–166.

Fonseca, Elizabeth. 1984. *Costa Rica colonial: La tierra y el hombre.* 2nd ed. San José: Editorial Universitaria Centroamericana.

Gudmundson, Lowell. 1986. *Costa Rica Before Coffee: Society and Economy on the Eve of the Export Boom.* Baton Rouge: Louisiana State University Press.

[TMBR]. 1985. Costa Rica. In *Latin America and the Caribbean: Contemporary Record* (Jack W. Hopkins, ed.), 3:496–515. New York: Holmes and Meier.

[TMBR]. 1984. Costa Rica and the 1948 revolution: Rethinking the social democratic paradigm. *Latin American Research Review* 19:235–242.

Hall, Carolyn. 1985. *Costa Rica: A Geographical Interpretation in Historical Perspective.* Boulder: Westview Press.

Jonas, Suzanne, and Nancy Stein. 1990. The construction of democracy in Nicaragua. *Latin American Perspectives* 17:10–37.

Lehoucq, Fabrice E. 1991. Class conflict, political crisis, and the breakdown of democratic practices in Costa Rica: Reassessing the origins of the 1948 civil war. *Journal of Latin American Studies* 25:37–59.

Lijphart, Arend. 1977. *Democracy in Plural Societies.* New Haven: Yale University Press.

McDonald, Ronald H., and J. Mark Ruhl. 1989. *Party Politics and Elections in Latin America.* Boulder: Westview Press.

McLeod, Murdo J. 1973. *Spanish Central America: A Socioeconomic History, 1520–1720.* Berkeley: University of California Press.

Mendieta, Salvador. 1934. *La enfermedad de Centro América.* 3 vols. Barcelona: Tip. Maucci.

Muñoz Guillén, Mercedes. 1990. *El estado y la abolición el ejécito, 1914–1949.* San José: Editorial Provenir.

Pinaud, José María. 1979. *La epopeya del civismo costaricense.* 2nd ed. San José: Ministerio de Cultura, Juventud y Deportes.

Sáenz Carbonell, Jorge. 1985. *El despertar constitucional de Costa Rica*. San José: Libro Libre.

Schmitter, Phillippe C., and Terry Lynn Karl. 1991. What democracy is . . . and is not. *Journal of Democracy* 2:75–88.

Seligson, Mitchell A. 1980. *Peasants of Costa Rica and the Development of Agrarian Capitalism*. Madison: University of Wisconsin Press.

Seligson, Mitchell A., and Miguel Gómez B. 1989. Ordinary elections in extraordinary times: The political economy of voting in Costa Rica. In *Elections and Democracy in Central America* (John A. Booth and Mitchell A. Seligson, eds.), 158–184. Chapel Hill: University of North Carolina Press.

Serra, Luis. 1982. The Sandinist mass organizations. In *Nicaragua in Revolution* (Thomas W. Walker, ed.), 95–113. Boulder: Westview Press.

Stahler-Sholk, Richard. 1987. Building democracy in Nicaragua. In *Liberalization and Redemocratization in Latin America* (George A. Lopez and Michael Stohl, eds.), 57–103. New York: Greenwood Press.

Stansifer, Charles L. 1977. José Santos Zelaya: A new look at Nicaragua's "liberal" dictator. *Revista/Review Interamericana* 7:468–485.

Stone, Samuel Z. 1975. *La dinastía de los conquistadores: La crisis del poder en la Costa Rica contemporánea*. 2nd ed. San José: Editorial Universitaria Centroamericana.

Torres, Rosa María, and José Luis Coraggio. 1987. *Transición y crisis en Nicaragua*. San José: Departamento Ecuménico de Investigaciones.

Vargas, Oscar-René. 1989. *Elecciones en Nicaragua: Análisis socio-político*. Managua: Dilesa.

Vega Carballo, José Luis. 1981. *Orden y progreso: La formación del estado nacional en Costa Rica*. San José: Instituto Centroamericano de Administración Pública.

Weber, Henri. 1981. *Nicaragua: The Sandinist Revolution*. Translated by Patrick Camiller. London: Verso Editions.

West, Robert C., and John P. Augelli. 1989. *Middle America: Its Lands and Peoples*. 3rd. ed. Englewood Cliffs, N.J.: Prentice-Hall.

Williams, Philip J. 1989. *The Catholic Church and Politics in Nicaragua and Costa Rica*. Pittsburgh: University of Pittsburgh Press.

Winson, Anthony. 1989. *Coffee and Democracy in Modern Costa Rica*. New York: St. Martin's.

Chapter Ten

Institutional Development, Democratization, and Independence in the Anglophone Caribbean

W. MARVIN WILL

The sociopolitical and labor demonstrations and rebellions that swept Britain's Caribbean colonies during the Great Depression triggered such significant sociopolitical change in those colonies that collectively it could be called a political revolution (Sederberg 1994:46–64; Skocpol 1979:esp. 4). Building on the transplanted values supportive of increased openness following emancipation for the numerically dominant Afro–West Indians the century prior, this largely pre–World War II upheaval contributed directly to a racial shift in the political elite, significant democracy-linked institutional development, and emerging popular pride and national consciousness that contributed to national independence. The region's pre–World War II violence began in British Honduras (now Belize), not in St. Christopher/Kitts as most specialists argue. Also, I contend that the major change-inducing labor disturbances took the form of planned or directed rebellions rather than spontaneous or anomic riots, as these actions almost universally have been labeled. Many who led these worker-linked disturbances were considered charismatic leaders and were often from the middle class.

The Crisis of the 1930s

In the 1930s the privations of the worldwide Great Depression were compounded in the West Indies by economic greed of local colonial-collaborating elites and the relatively closed semi-authoritarian colonial governments. The region's problems were compounded by economic dependence on exported agricultural crops, sugar in most instances—although its profitability was on the wane—petroleum in Trinidad, and timber and related forestry products in the case of Belize. The world price for sugar collapsed from 26s. per cwt. in l923 to 5s. per cwt. in 1934, for example, where it generally remained through 1937. As employer's profits fell, the number of workers and the hours worked were reduced. Workers who remained employed saw their wages pared (Beckles 1990:163; Will 1972). At the same time, taxes were increasing, and this cost was passed along to the working class and consumers. In Trinidad, for instance, the price of food rose 17 percent between 1935 and 1937, while oil field wages remained static. In Belize the 1930s witnessed the collapse of the timber market in addition to severe hurricane damage. Further, for the region, avenues for emigration to the outside world—to Brazil, Panama, Cuba, and the United States—were virtually closed. This combination of factors contributed to a very desperate socioeconomic situation but Whitehall did not seem to detect the early signs of hardship and, especially, the growing unrest. As we shall see, the riots and rebellions that followed eventually captured the attention of the metropolis, helping to trigger an increase in financial and political assistance from Britain, but this help was inordinately late coming, too late for many starving workers.

British Honduras

The initial confrontation involved a series of clashes between forestry and other workers during February and November 1934 in Belize, then known as British Honduras. There "for the first time," writes Peter Ashdown, "the working class masses of the Colony went into open revolt against the Colonial government" (1977a:1). This uprising also marked the beginning of the struggle in the West Indies and was one of the first significant shots across the bow of mighty Britannia's empire that had just reached its zenith (Fieldhouse 1967:242).

On 14 February 1934 "many hundreds of people," calling themselves the Unemployed Brigade, marched to confront the colonial governor with a plea for food and employment. The Governor's response: (1) some inappropriately prepared rice porridge ladled out of much-used laundry tubs at the prison gate, and (2) temporary employment provided for fewer than a hundred individuals in the form of convict-like road gangs and stone-breaking labor for less than a dollar per week (Bradley 1992). This was perceived as an insult, and the brigade leadership walked out in disgust.

Antonio Soberanis Gómez, a local barber of Mexican ancestry but with emotional sympathies for the then largely Afro-Belizean working class, soon mounted the rostrum at the Battlefield, an open space near the middle of Belize Town, the capital, to address a rally that coincided with the release of a report by Sir Alan Pim (1934), an economic traditionalist from the British Treasury. Sir Alan's report proposed public service retrenchment for addressing the crisis that had been spawned in Belize by the desperate conditions produced by the Great Depression coupled with the catastrophic hurricane of 1931, a hurricane that destroyed three-fourths of the housing in the capital and left more than 1,000 fatalities in its wake (U.K. 1934; Pollard 1992).

Soberanis, a "naturally gifted, sincere, . . . charismatic" spokesman of the masses, was outraged. He also delighted his followers by colorfully and forcefully denouncing the government and its leaders (Pollard 1992). Political charisma, in part a divine gift, is also at least two or three parts "being there at the right time" (Rustow 1967) and Soberanis was there when it counted. He attacked government uncaring and corruption, and the collaborating business elites, especially the Belize Estate and Produce Company, Ltd. (BEC) that owned outright one-fifth of the colony.

Most important, a major objective of Soberanis's two-to-three rallies per week was to drive home the urgency of forming labor and political organizations. By mid–1934 he had formed the Labourers and Unemployed Association (LUA), which was both a type of self-help society and as close to a labor union and political party as the severely prohibitive laws of the day permitted. Tony repeatedly attacked those laws and, to the delight of the crowds, hammered the inhumane acts of "King John Crow," Acting Governor John Burton. He also warned Police Superintendent P. E. Matthews to halt his abusive behavior toward the poor or experience "the licking he got in 1919," a direct reference to the beating Matthews experienced from soldiers returning from World War I. Soberanis was arrested for these threats—and a hard-line magistrate was appointed to deal with him (*The Clarion* 1934; *Belize Independent* 1934; Ashdown 1977a:4–9).

Soberanis carried the LUA message from the Mayan- and Spanish-speaking north to the Garifuna—or Caribs—in the south, becoming the first Belizean politician to develop a truly national following. In early September 1934 an estimated 3,000 turned out in a show of force and unity. To elites Soberanis was "that crazy lunatic," but to working-class Belizeans he was "David taking on Goliath" or "Moses before Pharaoh" (Bradley 1992). But government assistance was still not forthcoming.

In a LUA rally on 29 September 1934, Soberanis announced his plan to strike the giant BEC the following Monday, buoyed by having led a successful strike that produced a 300-percent-plus increase in wages for grapefruit loaders of the south. Hopes were high, but the 200 picketing workers who assembled outside the BEC gates at 6:30 A.M. that first day of October were perceived by BEC and the police as so ineffective that the police quickly retired. But the protest was reignited when a fight erupted between a demonstrator and one of the several non-Belizean policeman.

The numbers of workers, now expanded to 500, drove away BEC employees and then moved to storm the warehouse of a coconut exporter, demanding that he increase wages. They then proceeded to a government office, smashing down the gate and manhandling its director as they demanded that he also substantially boost wages. After closing a lumberyard and shutting down a government dredging operation, the rebellious mass marched to the Town Board to confront its deputy, whom they detested. At this point, a battle royal broke out between police armed with heavy batons and some 300 enraged workers armed with sticks. Several shots were fired, but no one was killed although several were injured. At least seventeen were jailed.

This mini-rebellion appeared to end well for workers after the acting governor promising $3,000 in relief aid and ordered the police back to their barracks. Soberanis, who had not been present since the initial picketing and a noontime visit, now bailed out sixteen of the workers. LUA seemed satisfied. But then their leader was jailed and arraigned without bail, and the rebellion nearly exploded to a higher pitch, as more than 2,000 workers poured out to confront the police (Goldson 1992; Matthews 1934:1–7; and Ashdown 1977b:18–24).

The vast majority of LUA's leadership were convicted and sentenced, and Soberanis, although initially freed on bail, was ordered to stand trial and convicted retroactively for violating the Seditions Conspiracy law, a law passed just to nail him. Even though he was released after five months in prison on 5 November 1935, following exoneration by both the lower and higher courts, and was carried home on the shoulders of his overjoyed supporters, thanks to Governor Burton's Machiavellian acts he was soon challenged for the LUA leadership (Bradley 1992; Ashdown 1977b:22–24). Thus, after 1935 a dispirited "lull" fell over the labor movement in the colony.

The Leeward Islands—and Others

Two months after the confrontation in Belize had abated, the second major outbreak erupted in St. Christopher (or St. Kitts), a small island that was essentially one huge sugar plantation from the sea right up to the top of the volcanic peak of Mount Misery. It had less than half Belize's population in the 1930s but with officially the highest mortality rate (36.5 per 1,000 in 1937) and perhaps "the worst social conditions in the West Indies" (Adams 1971a, 1971b; U.K. 1945a). There, in January 1935, a group of frustrated sugar workers went on strike, after which 300 to 400 strikers militantly began to march around the island soliciting workers from each plantation to join their demonstration against low pay and poor working conditions. Violence was initiated when an overseer at Buckley's Estate fired into the assembled workers, wounding three. Then the police opened fire on the protesters, wounding eight and killing three, the first recorded deaths in the prewar West Indian protests. A mini-rebellion then ensued during which plantations were attacked and cane fields set ablaze.

An additional half-dozen workers were injured when the demonstrators were confronted the following day by marines from the warship the HMS *Leander*, which had been requested by the governor (Lewis, 1974:52–57).

By September 1935 protests among the working class had moved to the South American colony of British Guiana (now the independent state of Guyana), where sugar workers burned "canes," raided estates, and "roughed up" management, including at least two white Guianese. There is no doubt that this confrontation was intensified, as it was in several colonies, by the then-occurring invasion of Abyssinia (now Ethiopia) by Italian forces. In Guyana, conditions were not only frequently unhealthy but almost every male worker suffered from malnutrition. Thus there were very strong feelings regarding the lack of government attention to the depressed conditions, and this was compounded by the often openly vocalized disgust with many white overseers of the sugar producers group, who were perceived as racist, and with British behavior in general, not only for its policy in this colony but also for its refusal to deal positively with Italy's invasion of Ethiopia. The official report of the 1935 disorders notes that in one instance a white man was attacked, ordered to wade through a deep ditch and to dance, and then beaten amidst shouts of "bad Abyssinia—you white bitches got no business here—you go back where you come from" (British Guiana 1936:25–35, quote on 35). Such friction continued to fester, although not breaking out in sustained violence until three years later.

The Windward Islands

At the end of October 1935 workers were shot in another labor rebellion, in St. Vincent, this time led by wharf workers and peasant farmers disgruntled by the government's decision to raise custom duties on sea island cotton and its inattention to low prices for arrowroot, both agricultural mainstays. For several days preceding this action, large crowds had been radicalized by inflammatory speeches regarding the indifference shown by Britain and other white Europeans in connection with Italy's invasion of Abyssinia. During the last week in October the workers gathered in Kingstown, the capital city, to address these and the increasingly drastic local labor and consumer concerns. A two-day mini-rebellion followed.

As in Belize, a final triggering element may have been the perceived indifference of the local governor, who, it is alleged, refused to respond positively to local requests relayed by George McIntosh, a labor-sensitive pharmacist who sought to petition the government on behalf of labor (Gonsalves 1992). In the ensuing clashes, as in St. Kitts, at least three workers were killed and a reported twenty-six were injured, including some non-Vincentian police (Lewis 1938:13–14). Again, there was a show of force by the metropolis with the arrival of the HMS *Challenger* and its bayonet-wielding marines (Lewis 1974:58). This proved to be too much for the stick-wielding protesters.

Further demonstrations and strike action took place in the neighboring Windward territory of St. Lucia at the end of 1935, primarily by coal-carrying women, who conveyed this essential fuel to "lighters" that in turn transported it to cargo ships anchored offshore in the relatively shallow harbor. Although locals were accustomed to strikes and strife, what fueled soaring tempers in this instance was what locals perceived to be an inordinate force against peaceful protest, in the form of another British naval vessel summoned by a governor who feared a repeat of the events in St. Kitts and St. Vincent. Marines patrolled the streets of Castries, the capital, day and night, and, most annoying, during the night hours the ship's powerful search lights played up and down city streets, disturbing the sleep of the residents (Lewis 1938:14). Conditions remained tense for months, even after the warship departed, and St. Lucian workers would again go out on strike in 1937.

By mid-1935 violent labor protests were flickering in one colony after another throughout the Caribbean. Within the next two years, running into 1938, the region would literally become inflamed as violence moved into Britain's most populous insular territories: in Trinidad and Tobago and in Barbados in 1937; and in Jamaica from the first hours of 1938. In two of these cases there had been ongoing labor conflicts—Trinidad beginning in 1934 and Jamaica in 1935—and both the size of rebellions and causalities increased dramatically.

Trinidad and Tobago

At midnight 18 June 1937 disturbances in the region flared to their highest peak in the oil fields of Trinidad, a bloody police-labor clash following strike action called by Uriah "Tubs" Butler. Butler had emigrated to Trinidad from Grenada to seek employment in the petroleum industry following his return from service in World War I. He had joined the Trinidad Workingman's Association (TWA) led by A. A. Cipriani, the former captain of Butler's West Indies Regiment. In 1935, while still a member of the captain's organization (by then renamed the Trinidad Labour Party, TLP), Butler helped organize a hunger and protest march of oil workers from the oil fields in southern Trinidad to the capital, Port of Spain. This action brought him into a brief period of cooperation with the more radical Negro Welfare Cultural and Social Association (NWCSA). But if this march brought Butler some legitimacy with NWCSA and at least a spark of recognition from the mostly Asian sugar workers now being sensitized and organized by another TWA/TPL associate, Krishna Deonarine (also known as Adrian Cola Rienzi), it cost Butler dearly with his increasingly anticonfrontation former captain (Barrette and King 1991; Ryan 1974:45–46; Basdeo [1983?]:127–151). Butler soon departed Cipriani's company and joined with Rienzi, who also had just opted out of the TLP, as a cofounder of the Citizens Welfare League (CWL). But within a year Butler had formed his own British Empire Workers and Citizens Home Rule Party (BEWCHRP) (Basdeo [1983?]:134–147).

Butler's messianic demeanor was partly conditioned by his pastoring of the Butlerite Moravian Baptist church, whose congregation consisted chiefly of oil workers. According to Selwyn Ryan:

> Butler [was] a magnificent and fiery orator, [who] had, much more than did Cipriani, the ability to inflame the masses. He not only knew the crowds to whom he spoke

more intimately than did the Captain but had the additional advantage of being able to speak to them in their own idiom. He was of the masses in every sense of the word. He was also a man obsessed with a sense of mission. He believed that God had appointed him to lead the people of the West Indies from the wilderness of colonialism. (1974:45)

Although Governor Sir Murchison Fletcher agreed that Butler and the workers had a valid need for wage increases, he ordered that Butler be monitored by police. It was such a monitoring and the ensuing attempt to arrest the "Chief Servant" that triggered the Trinidadian rebellion.

When police, including Corporal Charlie King, a much detested officer, clumsily attempted to arrest Butler as he addressed some 200 workers in Fyzabad on the afternoon of 19 June 1937, the crowd exploded in anger, freeing their leader. The crowd-turned-mob then ran down the fleeing Corporal King, doused him with kerosene, and incinerated this hated symbol of their oppression. A second policeman was killed as several dozen officers attempted to rescue King's body and capture Butler. Two oil wells were torched as the movement intensified.

Strikes were triggered in almost every part of the island, and workers quickly found themselves facing the first and second battalions of the Trinidad Light Infantry. Although the workers were severely outgunned, one of the battalions used its four machine guns against them, and British warships had been requested to fire on the workers. A number of workers and infantry personnel were casualties in a battle near Penal. Sugar factories were closed as invading strikers drove off factory employees, assaulted management, and smashed furniture.

Eventually, on 22 June, the riot-turned-rebellion that had engulfed San Fernando reached Port of Spain on the other side of the island, spurred on in the capital by NWCSA. There the violence forced closure of many of the commercial establishments (Barrette and King 1991; Basdeo [1983?]). The arrival of two warships, the HMS *Ajax* and the *Exeter*, on 22 and 23 June substantially increased the government firepower and ability to intimidate.

The following day the daily press recorded that multiple deaths had occurred in four separate spots on the island. There were five fatalities at Rio Claro when two bands carrying cutlasses and iron bars were stopped by gunfire. Although agriculture in Trinidad was already secondary to oil, the rebellion spread to the sugar estates just as they were completing the harvest. Several hundred men traversed from estate to estate, disrupting and even shutting down operations. Factories were also closed. By 27 June 1937 the action had encompassed virtually the entire island (*Trinidad Guardian* 1937:1; Singh 1987).

By late July, however, the shared collective rage had run its course, and the British warships were weighing anchor. Government—and then companies—had ordered pay increases during late June and throughout July 1937, improving the atmosphere for negotiated settlements, although many workers remained unhappy with the two-cent-per-hour increase, which they considered paltry and inflation-trailing. Most important, institutional development in the form of new unions was on the way.

Butler, after initially avoiding capture during an island-wide search, was finally arrested in late 1937 when he voluntarily appeared to give testimony before an official panel investigating the rebellion. Despite retaining able counsel, Butler was imprisoned for his alleged role in the insurrection and reincarcerated "for the duration" as a wartime threat—a total of six years (Jacobs 1977; Basdeo [1983?]; Hintzen and Will 1988). The costs of the uprisings in Trinidad were high: fourteen dead and at least fifty-nine injured, with hundreds jailed or imprisoned. The direct cost to workers, businesses, and government was estimated to be $1 million in prewar dollars. This was the largest loss of life and property in any of the labor-related clashes in the British Caribbean to date.

Barbados

Although the fires of rebellion were dying in Trinidad, the embers were hand-carried northeastward to "Little England," as this most easterly Caribbean island of Barbados is known, an island with the reputation of having the region's most conservative culture. By July 1937 one of the most violent "demonstrations of the British Caribbean colonies in the 1930s and 1940s had broken out, triggered by Clement Payne . . . in Bridgetown, . . . when he arrived with the claim that he was 'Minister of Propaganda' from [Trinidad's Youth League]. Payne's fiery speeches stirred the populace of Bridgetown" (Hoyos 1963:63).

Following his arrival in Barbados in March 1937, Payne held seventeen public meetings in which he rallied the workers by railing that the middle class was a "lackey of the employers"; to one conservative middle-class observer, he seemed to recommend the extermination of the middle class. He described the police as "dogs of the capitalists" (Hoyos 1963:63). Of even greater concern to local elites were the efforts by Payne's subordinates to encourage the masses to form trade unions and political parties.

Payne, who was born in Trinidad of Barbadian parents and brought to Barbados at age four, was arrested on the technicality that he had made a false declaration of his place of birth by claiming to be Barbadian. Following Payne's release from custody, secured through the effective argument mounted by Grantley Adams, rallies to protest his legal harassment were held in Golden Square, the heart of the Barbadian capital, Bridgetown. This stimulated a march to Government House to petition Governor Sir Mark Young. "Because he opening we eyes," some were heard to say, "they are trying to lock him up" (Hoyos 1963:63–64; Augier et al. 1960:281). According to the testimony of a conservative publisher, W. A. Beckles, the crowd threatened: "We goin' to do the same thing as Trinidad if anything happens to him" (1937:3). Despite a hard-fought legal victory on appeal, Payne was again arrested and ordered deported on 26 July 1937, after he had already been secretly spirited onto a Trinidad-bound ship (Adams 1971a; Will

1992b). This action incensed Payne's supporters. Although Barbadian workers had lost their leader, other insurrectionists were in the wings to take Payne's place.

Angry workers rampaged through the city on the night of 27 July 1937, destroying the facilities and property of those deemed to be enemies of labor while protecting that of those perceived to be friends of labor. There were repeated attempts to set fire to the headquarters of one insurance company, a perceived enemy of labor, that even went so far as to include physically battling the firemen who were attempting to put out the blaze! Six rebellious workers were killed by police.

The disorders spread to the surrounding countryside during the succeeding two days. In these actions, as in Trinidad, plantations were overrun and operations disrupted. Invectives were hurled at planters especially despised by workers, and plantation provisions were dug up to provide food for the insurrectionists. This multiday action was more a planned, directed, and selectively targeted rebellion than a spontaneous riot, as it has been designated by most local authors. The insurrection was a violent event, resulting in fourteen fatalities, approximately fifty wounded, and more than five hundred arrested by the police (Hoyos 1963:63–64; Beckles 1990; Adams 1971b; Mark 1965: 1–7; U.K. 1945a).

Jamaica

Meanwhile, desperately underpaid workers had begun strike action as early as May 1935 in Jamaica, Britain's most populous West Indian colony. Labor unrest exploded into a dozen or so "general disturbances," primarily between May and June 1938, but continued intermittently throughout the war until 1946. The most intensive and sustained period of violence, however, began with the very first days of 1938 when 1,000 cane cutters at Serge Island in St. Thomas struck to demand higher wages. After the strikers had been dispersed by baton-armed police, the unemployed workers truculently reassembled with machetes and sticks, their numbers now increased to 1,400, to continue their demands (Post 1978).

It was still up to the policy to employ heavy force, and on 5 January 1938 police opened fire as several workers attempted to prevent cane carts from entering or leaving the estate, injuring thirty-four workers and one policeman (Eaton 1975:38). At this point a self-appointed leader emerged, William Alexander Clarke, a tall, charismatic, fifty-four-year-old moneylender using the nom de plume Bustamante, a name he had adopted well before returning to Jamaica three years prior. Since his return to Jamaica he had developed somewhat of a following by writing angry letters to the editor and by providing a loan service in Kingston. Arriving at Serge, he immediately offered to negotiate with management on behalf of labor. This initial effort was as symbolic as it was self-serving, but it was only marginally successful. But the workers realized they now had an activist man of words as their leader, a man who inspired them and then took direct part in their protests and negotiations. Workers who perceived themselves both absolutely and relatively deprived now had a champion for their movement. It was the perfect combination for rebellion (see Gurr 1970).

On 20 April 1937 the "Serge infection" spread to Westmoreland, on the island's opposite (eastern) end, where Tate and Lyle, a British sugar corporation, had widely advertised plans to erect a huge sugar factory. Anticipating more jobs than would be available, and at 40 percent higher wages per week than would be actually offered, thousands of unemployed Jamaicans poured into the area only to experience bitter "grapes of wrath" reality. Anticipating trouble, militia forces had been mobilized at the site and special constables sworn in to aid the police. By 2 May cane fields were being torched and the press reported that the manager was saved from violence only by hiding in a sugar barrel during a skirmish. Police then opened fire into the crowd with rifles, killing four and injuring thirteen, of whom nine required hospitalization. More than a hundred were arrested, and eighty-nine were jailed (*Daily Gleaner* 1938). Although Bustamante again arrived somewhat after the fact, he assumed a prominent leadership position by rallying workers and leading the negotiations.

From mid-May through June strikes and protests literally exploded in both rural and urban areas, north, south, east, and west. As the crisis widened, the Cruiser HMS *Ajax* arrived after being requested by a frightened government. According to W. Arthur Lewis (1938:28–30), it would have been mob rule—or worse—had it not been for the patrolling soldiers, sailors, and police. And in Kingston this was especially the case, as civil order itself was placed in the balance when firemen and other municipal workers not only contemplated striking but sought consultations with Bustamante. Further, the island's external lifeline was also threatened, as shipping was effectively shut down in Kingston by striking wharf workers, Bustamante's most loyal followers. At this point an increasingly physically debilitated Governor Edward Denham declared virtual war by issuing orders for local militias to join with constables, the police, and British regulars—the Sherwood Foresters plus marines from the patrolling cruiser.

Part of the "get tough" approach also saw Bustamante and William Grant, an associate, arrested and incarcerated on 23 May 1938, an act that produced just the opposite effect from that desired by the governor. Being jailed for "his workers" accorded a heroic quality to Bustamante and would substantially boost his leadership stock not only vis-à-vis the government but, ironically, also against his own first cousin, Norman Manley, an athletic record holder and war hero who had returned from study at Oxford and was instrumental in securing Bustamante's early release from prison (on 28 May) and in promoting the development of Bustamante's union during his incarceration. Again, somewhat like the divisions in Belize and Trinidad following the imprisonment of their leaders, a severe rift had developed between these important cousins, who both were labor and political leaders. In the postcrisis period that followed, both Bustamante and Manley would loom large as creators of political parties and unions but would remain fiercely combative national leaders.

British Guiana and the Bahamas

In 1939 and 1942, respectively, two other colonies also experienced significant labor unrest: what is now Guyana and the Bahamas archipelago. Strike action and labor violence developed in Guyana precisely as the Moyne Commission was meeting, while in Nassau, capital of the Bahamas, workers "rebelled" against a U.S. contractor who was accused of discriminatory wage scales during construction of a U.S. base on a site received from the United Kingdom in exchange for submarines. These actions, although not producing either the level of violence nor the institutional results that ensued in the previous three cases, are nevertheless credited with stimulating institutional growth and increased nationalism movements led by men and women of color (Will 1992a; U.K. 1945a).

In summary, the violent uprisings and rebellions throughout the British West Indies during this eight-year period resulted in a minimum of 475 casualties, including at least forty-six dead, plus thousands jailed or imprisoned. Contrasted with one "heated" day of the now concluded civil wars in El Salvador or Guatemala, or even the late July–early August 1990 attempted coup in Trinidad, these are not large numbers, but in the context of the times in this multicolony region, with the relatively conservative cultures in several and low population densities in most, this was indeed a violent and costly display. But these movements also finally captured the attention of Whitehall, the formal, imperial center. At last someone appeared to seriously listen. But why did it take so long?

The Empire Reacts—and Adapts

The Problem of Listening

Communication difficulties between the West Indian colonies and the metropolitan authorities were legend. These difficulties were partially provoked by the inaccessibility of the British Colonial Service (retitled Her Majesty's Overseas Civil Service after 1954), with the inaccessibility of the administration at Whitehall itself being at the forefront. As Adams has noted: "In those days the Secretary of State for the Colonies was a remote and almost inaccessible person who could not be interviewed by anyone from the colonial territories unless he was a high dignitary concerned with matters of the gravest importance" (1971b:10–11).

And this obstacle was not restricted to the service's upper echelons. It was also present in the colonial bureaucracy. Thus even at the colonial bureaucratic level, one found unresponsiveness and unrepresentativeness, especially in the smaller territories (Jeffries 1956; Poole 1951:59–60). This situation not only made West Indians ruinously critical but also fostered "innate resistance to government and all its ramifications" (Poole 1951:59–60). And alienated subjects who are "ruinously critical" likewise protest and rebel.

The violence in the West Indies broke through the metropolis's resistance and produced a major attempt to contain the damage, an attempt that was driven largely by Britain's need for West Indian produce and manpower and, especially, Trinidadian oil in the coming world war and by the desire to avoid conspicuous propaganda losses to the Axes Powers that might accrue from ongoing open rebellions by black and brown subjects. This response was implemented in the form of parliamentary reports followed by a fact-gathering, policy-advising, investigatory Royal Commission.

The Metropolis Investigates: The Moyne Commission

Lord Walter Moyne chaired the ten-member West Indies Royal Commission created by royal warrant in London on 5 August 1938. Its mandate was to investigate and to offer recommendations on social and economic conditions in "all" the West Indian territories. In the succeeding fifteen months, the commission did just that: probing, interviewing, analyzing. The first stop on its 9,900 mile journey was Jamaica on 1 November 1938; its last stop in spring 1939 was in what is now Guyana. Hearings were held in twenty-six locations in the West Indies, with the commissioners receiving formal testimony from individuals and groups, including newly formed trade unions and political parties. The commission accepted almost 800 memoranda of evidence and 300 individual grievance statements.

Attempts were made to coordinate the reports that were to be presented by the various colonial "working-class" groups. In addition, the West Indies Labour Congress prepared and presented a four-point economic plan. From this evidence the commissioners produced a long and comprehensive report that covered topics as diverse as agriculture, administration, public health, communications, labor problems, social needs, political integration, political and constitutional issues, and local government. In fact the findings of the commission were deemed so censorious of British policy toward the oldest part of its remaining empire that the full report was officially withheld until after World War II to avert any potential for unfavorable wartime propaganda.

Recommendations: A Push for Mass Institutions and Policy Directives

Testimony relating to social problems monopolized much of the commission's time. It documented the hunger, disease, and grinding poverty in the region, particularly in Belize and in the larger cities: Bridgetown (Barbados), Kingston (Jamaica), and Port of Spain (Trinidad). There, even those children fortunate enough to obtain public education followed a depressing pattern of leaving an overcrowded house to go to an overcrowded and poorly equipped school, only to be thrust at age fourteen or fifteen into an overcrowded labor market (U.K. 1945a:4–7, 34–35, 134–137, 215, 261–312). Such frustration piled upon frustration is yet another contributory factor in the buildup to political violence and insurrection.

If the social conditions in the West Indies were as desperate as the commission found, equally serious problems related to political conditions were also prevalent (U.K. 1945a:190–196, 215–254). The Moyne investigators pinpointed lack of political representation as a most significant concern. Suffrage was inordinately restrictive in all of the colonies, and the Moyne Report reiterated that the Crown system, with its considerable faults, continued to dominate most territorial governance. The version of Crown government in pre-1946 Trinidad, for instance, gave virtually no representation to the popular cultures, which were largely unfamiliar with the subtleties of English constitutional forms despite the long-term colonial tutelage. Authority continued to rest almost solely in the hands of the governor in much the way it had since the end of the nineteenth century, when the island's first governor restricted the elective assembly for Trinidad's and Guyana's racially and ethnically heterogeneous populations (U.K. 1945a:190–255; Williams 1964:69–72). And those without Crown governance, Barbados and the Bahamas, were dominated by white elites and had very limited suffrage. Thus there were major indices of lethargic or inflexible colonial institutions, all of which negatively affected Whitehall's ability to hear the sounds of alarm, whether emanating from the 1932 conference in Rosseau, Dominica, or from W. M. Macmillan's *Warning from the West Indies* (1936), authored in the midst of the 1930s crisis, even though the latter was widely circulated and read in Whitehall.

Among its recommendations, the Moyne Commission urged that political parties and labor unions be established, and beseeched the institution of additional political changes such as improved civil service, increased governmental centralization in the less compact territories, expanded interisland integration, and, most important, local governmental authorities who could bolster attitudinal support and promote the development of mass institutions. The report heavily emphasized increased financial responsibility by Britain.

That the findings of the portions of the Moyne Report that were released in 1940 were taken seriously is evidenced by Britain's establishment of a £1 million per annum twenty-year West Indian Welfare Fund financed by the economically hard-pressed British parliament (U.K. 1940, 1945b). By 1951 in excess of 22 million of Britain's hard-to-obtain pounds had been sent to these colonies, supplemented by still other monies for special projects and disasters. A majority of these funds were issued as outright grants. In addition, the recent insurrections brought policy adaptations by the colonial governments. Notable was the expanded number of social programs passed into law by the "more responsible" administrations. By the 1940s and 1950s, locally led movements toward political independence had also been instituted, a development directly attributable to the new mass unions and political parties but perhaps even more so to the new mass consciousness (see Ryan 1974).

The Moyne Report had concluded, in a most sophisticated argument, that West Indian poverty was poverty heightened by declining capability, and resultant attitudes of relative deprivation (see Gurr 1970). The commission found that "[the] cumulative effect of education, the press, wireless, the spectacle of the standards of living of white people, and the reports of West Indians who have lived and worked abroad, particularly in the United States of America, has been to create a demand for better conditions of work and life. This demand has found expression from time to time in disorders and bloodshed" (U.K. 1945a:422–425, quote on 422).

A strong effort must be made to increase popular support for island governments, the report continued. One of the most effective means proposed was encouragement of greater participation and, concomitantly, mass political institutions to channel the participation: "A substantial body of public opinion in the West Indies is convinced that far-reaching measures of social reconstruction depend, both for their initiation and their effective administration, upon greater participation of the people in the business of government" (U.K. 1945a:438–451, 198–210, 373, quote on 303). The crisis was awakening the West Indian masses— and now also a lethargic British Colonial office.

Mass Movements, Mass Leaders, and the Emergence of Union and Party Institutions

Of the two relatively modern institutions, trade unions and political parties, the development of unions was of utmost importance in the Caribbean due to the need to elevate the abysmally low wages of workers and, in the process, broaden opportunities for suffrage in these income-restricted systems (Will 1972:124–168; 1992a:13, 53–55, 546, 556; 1992b:9–18, 66–84). Political parties, too, are multifunctional institutions with at least two primary functions: (1) They serve as systems to link voters and thus to help legitimate fledgling governments, and (2) of perhaps even greater importance, they further the nomination and election processes. And party-driven elections are the principal nonviolent means for changing governments and protecting against coups (Huntington 1968).

Once the prewar labor strife in the West Indies had finally gained long-delayed metropolitan attention, key funding was forthcoming, as noted, even during the money-restricted war years (U.K. 1940; 1945b). More important, however, there were key policy shifts that placed pressure on still-recalcitrant local elites—the time-honored collaborators of empire—as well as some hands-on participation from London in building both union and party institutions (with all contributing to the general darkening of the complexion of these colonial governments as a result of expanded franchise and suffrage) and the presentation of new role models. This is not to say there were no alternate role model pioneers. Certainly, there were those men of color who were active in liberal groups of the nineteenth century, and in the 1920s many of the colonies experienced party-like and proto–union movements promoted by Creoles linked to the Jamaican activist Marcus Garvey (Will 1972). But the crisis of the 1930s and early 1940s contributed to both institutional development and role model development in most of the West Indian colonies and directly to party building and the institutionalization of semiministerial government in two West Indian colonies, Jamaica, the most populous of the Anglophone colonies in the West Indies, and Barbados, the third most populous. In this concluding section I shall sketch such a development in these two colonies. I shall also discuss the substantial development in Trinidad and Tobago, the West Indies islands that together have the second largest population, as well as make fragmentary mention of union and party development in other colonies.

Jamaica

Jamaica was the first West Indies territory to directly benefit politically from the prewar labor upheavals. This island, in fact, received substantial hands-on assistance from Britain, both positive and negative, in the formation of political parties. The negative input came in the form of Britain's decision to imprison Bustamante, initially for his role in the labor unrest of 1938, followed by much longer imprisonments for his perceived threat to the war effort. As noted, this action had the effect of promoting his reputation for martyrdom and building his leadership charisma, which, according to Max Weber (1964), Seymour Martin Lipset (1979), and Dankwart Rustow (1967), is an important albeit uncertain aspect of the political authority system.

The positive impact of British policy was twofold, coming in the form of (1) a hard push for expanded suffrage from the new Labour government in the United Kingdom through the colonial governor in Jamaica, and (2) strong personal inducements for the formation of labor unions and parties from individual Labour parliamentarians at the inaugural meeting of the People's National Party (PNP), 18 September 1938 (Cripps 1938). The PNP, whose founder and first leader was Norman Manley, is today the well-institutionalized governing party in Jamaica. The "loyal" opposition party, the Jamaica Labour Party (JLP), was also founded in the aftermath of the labor uprising in 1943 as an offshoot of the largest union on the island, the Bustamante Industrial Trade Union (BITU), which was founded in early 1938 largely as a result of Bustamante's paternal efforts following his short stint as a member of the PNP (Eaton 1975). The BITU too is very much alive today.

Bustamante's work with the early labor movement had made him by far the most popular leader among the masses in Jamaica. Projecting the role of a messiah, Bustamante promised the workers not only higher wages but also hope and self-respect. He protected his elite support by giving homage to the empire, Christianity, and anticommunism. His appearance furthered his image: He was tall and robust with bushy hair that gave him the appearance of a orchestral conductor, and occasionally his well-fitting clothing was adorned with a brace of revolvers. His JLP was—and long remained—a poorly differentiated segment of the BITU. But Bustamante was also a fighter whose charisma often pushed him to the edges of power, and even legality, as was the case with his contemporary labor leader in Trinidad (Butler). When Jamaica's leading daily, the *Gleaner*, was mildly critical of

Bustamante's policies, for example, he made the following response to the editor: "Now, just understand one thing. I believe in ruthless industrial warfare. . . . You are always hitting at the port workers. Well, I shall instruct the port workers not to land any newsprint coming to the country for the *Gleaner* newspaper" (quoted in Blanchard 1947:94–96, quote on 96).

As noted, Norman Manley, a Rhodes Scholar and leading barrister as well as a leading intellectual on the island, also courted the labor vote by forming a PNP-connected labor union, assembled in the Trade Union Congress (TUC), since he also was fully aware that until there was an increase in wages it would be difficult to win voters whose right to suffrage was tied to property. He thus devoted considerable effort to the battle for lowered restrictions on suffrage, for only by this means could potential voters be brought into his PNP in sufficient numbers to win elections and provide the basis for a legitimated mass party. Manley worked hard for the ministerial status of government in Jamaica. Largely because of his efforts, semi–home rule cabinet government was pledged in the 1943 constitution (which went into effect the year following). But due to his middle-class predilections, and probably more because of the success of his cousin Bustamante, Manley's PNP constituency moved more and more away from the workers toward the growing but still comparatively small Jamaican middle class. This not only hurt his PNP but, because of the crucial loss to the JLP at a sensitive time during the formation of the 1958–1962 West Indies Federation (WIF), it indirectly doomed early collective independence for the region.

However, with the expansion of suffrage from less than 6 percent to more than 80 percent, effective party government became increasingly possible in Jamaica since for the first time there was the possibility that black and brown Jamaicans would form a majority in the government. This occurred in the general election of 1944 when, in a considerable reversal of form, only one white Jamaican was elected to a parliamentary seat as the JLP defeated Manley and the PNP, capturing twenty-two of thirty-two seats. In 1944, as is so often the case, votes were cast less on reasoned appeals than on gut reactions to clientelist-based perceptions. The 1944 victory produced a new constitution with a modified home rule government. This was a major step toward singular independence, which was realized, as noted, in 1962 immediately following the demise of the region's most important effort at collective independence, the four-year-old WIF.

Not only have the two Jamaican parties established as a direct outgrowth of the violent 1930s continued to compete to this day, but they also have alternated in power each two terms without fail, the most consistent turnover in the region. One remaining legacy is more negative, however. The positive postrebellion political changes did not end political violence in Jamaican politics, as evidenced in the very violent election in 1980 and since. The noted color- and class-linked divisions, the massive poverty, and the island's penchant for violence are all factors, but one of the most important ingredients has been the role of both major parties in recruiting gangs, allegedly to defend against each other.

Barbados

Barbados, the most easterly and the most densely populated of the West Indian colonies, also began union and party activity in the 1930s and began to experiment with modified home rule governance during the subsequent decade. During the 1930s, electoral eligibility in Barbados was less than 4 percent. Whites were predominant in the legislature until 1944. Nonetheless, labor unions and political parties had begun "to mobilize and direct the upsurge of political enthusiasm and energy released as a result of the disturbances of 1937 and the announcement of the appointment of the Royal Commission" (Barbados Progressive League, 1944:1). The new movement, called the Barbados Progressive League (BPL), was founded in October 1938. It combined union, party, and social functions in one umbrella organization with the slogan "Three units, one aim: Raising the living standards for the working classes." Grantley Adams was chosen president (Will 1972).

The league soon divided into two groups, with the league faction supporting Adams's more gradualist approach. A second labor faction, the Congress Party (CP) led by W. A. Crawford, pushed for more radical representation of labor. In somewhat of a reversal from Jamaica, in Barbados the most charismatic of the two leaders, Grantley Adams, promoted the slower course. Crawford withdrew from the league to form the CP, just as Bustamante broke from the PNP to form the JLP—and each proceeded to form a rival union. Nonetheless, the Barbados Labour Party (BLP) and the Barbados Workers' Union (BWU), which were the two major wings of the BPL, have each survived and prospered. The BPL's principal opposition, the Democratic Labour Party (DLP), is also linked to this period, breaking from the BLP but picking up the mantel—and many members—from Crawford's CP.

The twin route to mass party and union status in Barbados, as in Jamaica, led to an increase in the wages of workers and a reduction in suffrage requirements. Adams had the ear of the governor on the suffrage issue, and a new constitution with expanded suffrage was presented in December 1943, slated for implementation in 1944. This action, which passed the Barbadian House of Assembly by just one vote, expanded voter eligibility in Barbados from 7,600 voters to 16,000. Although this was a much smaller electoral expansion than in Jamaica, it still enabled Barbadians to elect their first nonwhite government as the so-called labor parties of Adams (BPL) and Crawford (CP) garnered eight seats each (of twenty-four).

By 1940 the BWU had separated from the BPL/BLP and was registered as the largest federated union on the island. It continues to function in this dominant capacity today. As suffrage expanded, the league's political arm also differentiated itself from the league under the name Barbados Labour Party, and in 1946 this party won its first legislative plurality. The following year a modified version of home rule government was introduced in Barbados. Complete home rule status would come to Barbados in 1954 with Grantley Adams as premier, a position he held until he assumed the premiership of the WIF in 1958.

The BLP suffered a major schism in 1955 when its more progressive wing withdrew to form the DLP under the leadership of Errol Barrow, who took the island to singular independence in 1966 following the failure of collective independence via federation (Will 1989:321–342).

Trinidad and Tobago—and Others

Jamaica and Barbados were not alone in gaining substantially from the prewar uprisings. In Belize, our first case, two union-like organizations were founded in 1939, well before there was permissive legislation in this elite-dominated colony, although neither of these proto-unions survived beyond the mid-1940s. During the 1930s unions and parties were also formed on two additional islands that had experienced significant labor disturbances, St. Vincent and St. Lucia, as well as in Antigua and Barbuda and in Montserrat, also in response to the uprisings. On these islands, as well as in St. Kitts–Nevis and Grenada in the 1940s and 1950s, respectively, labor and party groups initially formed as a single entity that later subdivided, albeit without the early differentiation that occurred in Barbados.

In Trinidad and Tobago, as noted, there were already functioning political parties and unions before the 1937 uprising. In addition, before the smoke from the rebellion had settled, it was announced that an oil field workers union was being formed. On 29 July 1937 the *Trinidad Guardian* noted that 150 delegates "from practically all oil fields in the colony" had formed the Oil Workers Trade Union (OWTU) to better focus their grievances: "Oil workers through this new organization will have a united front with an Executive Committee of 21 [persons] under the Presidency of Adrian Cola Rienzi, [who will] represent them on all matters of dispute between their employers and themselves" (1937:1).

Cola Rienzi, an experienced unionist (since 1924), who at age eighteen had already been elected president of the San Fernando branch of TWA and later served as mayor, had been catapulted into leadership of the fledgling trade union movement partially as a result of "Tubs" Butler's incarceration. This multitalented leader would be severely tested as a designated but not universally supported replacement for Butler.

Before the end of the year six unions had formed in Trinidad, thirteen by the end of the decade. Several, including the OWTU, continue to survive. At the party level, however, neither the Butler nor the Cipriani party remains, and it was not until 15 January 1956 that Eric Williams formed the People's National Movement (PNM), the country's most institutionalized mass party (Oxaal 1968). And by the end of the 1950s party development had occurred or was occurring throughout the Commonwealth Caribbean.

Summary and Conclusions

The violent demonstrations and confrontations during the Great Depression in the Anglophone Caribbean induced massive destruction and inflicted hundreds of casualties. This underscored political failures by both metropolitan and local elite-influenced governments, and the quickening winds of World War II no doubt speeded and changed the metropolitan response. These crises also played a significant role in positive regional change by establishing an environment in almost every regional colony for mass politicization, thus providing a raison d'être for institutional representation of worker grievances and for organizing and channeling the political enthusiasm and energy generated through the formation of trade unions and political parties.

This change was long enduring: The basic foundations of the labor unions and political party systems that exist today in Jamaica, Barbados, and several other Caribbean states were established in the late 1930s and early 1940s as a direct outgrowth of the crisis and metropolitan adaptations. Charismatic leadership also played an important, albeit very uneven, role in the development of unions and political parties throughout the region. Lastly, the seeds of independence movements were sewn during this period.

Collective independence was the initial vision, but following the breakup of the ill-fated 1958–1962 WIF—with the insular-looking Bustamante of Jamaica providing much of the negative "leadership"—Jamaica and then Trinidad and Tobago gained independence in 1962. Guyana and Barbados also opted for separate independence four years later after the Little Eight federation had also failed. All but the smallest of the remaining colonies gained independence between 1972 (the Bahamas) and 1983 (St. Kitts). A countermove to resurrect the federation ideal took place almost with the first move toward singular independence, however, but this remains an ideal (Will 1991).

To conclude, the 1930s represented both the apex of the formal British Empire and the beginning of its end, both in the Caribbean and globally. More important for the subject of this chapter, the mass protests in the Caribbean gave rise to class consciousness among the black and brown workers, encouraging them to democratization after labor movements had increased suffrage, and the added presence of popular classes then elected to governments added their voices and votes for further changes in suffrage and constitutional rules. Independence followed for twelve of the thirteen newest states in the Americas. In a word, the change produced was revolutionary.

Notes

This chapter is essentially an abstract of a forthcoming book.

Bibliography

Adams, Sir Grantley. 1971a. Personal interview by author, St. Michael Home, Barbados, 6 September.

Adams, Sir Grantley. 1971b. Blunders, struggles, and regrets. Part 2 [Barbados]. *Sunday Advocate-News* (24 January):Part 3; continued as Part 4, 7 February.

Ashdown, Peter. 1978. Antonio Soberanis and the disturbances in Belize, 1934–1937. *Caribbean Quarterly* 24:61–74.

———. 1977a. Antonio Soberanis and the 1934–35 disturbances in Belize. Part 1. *Belizean Studies* 5:1–11.

———. 1977b. Antonio Soberanis and the 1934–35 disturbances in Belize. Part 2. *Belizean Studies* 5:16–27.

Augier, F., et al. 1960. *The Making of the West Indies*. London: Longmans, Green.

The Bahamas, party and community leaders, including Pindling, Ingrahm, and Sanders. 1982, 1992. Interviews by W. Marvin Will, Nassau, May, August.

Barbados Progressive League (BPL). 1944. *Past, Present, and Future: Policy and Programme*. Bridgetown, Barbados: BPL.

Basdeo, Sahadeo. [1983?]. *Labour Organization and Labour Reform in Trinidad, 1919–1939*. St. Augustine, Trinidad: Institute of Social and Economic Research, University of the West Indies.

Barrette, Jim, and Christina King. 1991. Personal interviews (jointly) by author in their John-John home, Port of Spain, Trinidad, 14 November.

Beckles, Hilary M. 1990. *A History of Barbados*. Cambridge: Cambridge University Press.

Beckles, W. A. 1937. *The Barbados Disturbances: Review, Reproduction of the Evidence, and the report of the Committee*. Bridgetown, Barbados: Advocate Company.

Belize Independent. 1934. 10–30 May and intermittent issues through November.

Blanchard, Paul. 1947. *Democracy and Empire in the Caribbean*. New York: Macmillan.

Bradley, Leo. 1992. Personal interview by author, Belize City, Belize, December.

British Guiana. 1936. *Report of the Commission to Enquire and Report of the Labour Disputes in Demerara during the Months of September and October, 1935*. Georgetown: Argosy.

The Clarion (Belize). 1934. 5 May–19 July and intermittent issues through November.

Craig, Susan. 1988. *Smiles and Blood*. London: New Beacon Books.

Cripps, Sir Stafford. 1938. Call to Jamaica. Speech given at Ward Theatre, Kingston, Jamaica, 18 September. Printed as a twenty-page pamphlet by People's National Party.

Daily Gleaner (Jamaica). 1938. 3 May.

Davies, James C. 1962. Toward a theory of revolution. *American Sociological Review* 27:5–19.

de Boissiére, R. 1952. *Crown Jewel*. London: Picador, by Pan Books.

Eaton, George E. 1975. *Alexander Bustamante and Modern Jamaica*. Kingston, Jamaica: Kingston Publishers.

Fieldhouse, D. K. 1967. *The Colonial Empires*. New York: Delcourte Press.

Fox, Annette Baker. 1949. *Freedom and Welfare in the Caribbean: A Colonial Dilemma*. New York: Harcourt, Brace.

Goldson, Philip. 1992. Personal interview with author, Belize City, Belize, December.

Gonsalves, Ralph E. 1992. Personal interview with author, Kingstown, St. Vincent, May.

Grant, C. H. 1976. *The Making of Modern Belize*. Cambridge: Cambridge University Press.

Gurr, Ted Robert. 1970. *Why Men Rebel*. Princeton: Princeton University Press.

Hart, Richard. 1989. *Rise and Organize: The Birth of the Workers and National Movements in Jamaica (1936–1939)*. London: Karia Press.

Hintzen, Percy C., and W. Marvin Will. 1988. "Butler." In *Biographical Dictionary of Latin American and Caribbean Political Leaders* (Robert J. Alexander, ed.), 83–84. New York: Greenwood Press.

Hoyos, F. A. 1963. *The Rise of West Indian Democracy: The Life and Times of Sir Grantley Adams*. Bridgetown, Barbados: Advocate Press.

Huntington, Samuel P. 1991. *The Third Wave: Democratization in the Late Twentieth Century*. Norman: University of Oklahoma Press.

_____. 1968. *Political Order in Changing Societies*. New Haven: Yale University Press.

Jacobs, W. Richard. 1977. The politics of protest in Trinidad: The strikes and disturbances of 1937. *Caribbean Studies* 1:5–50.

Jeffries, Sir Charles. 1956. *The Colonial Office*. London: Allen and Unwin.

Johnson, Howard. 1975. Oil, imperial policy, and the Trinidad disturbances, 1937. *The Journal of Imperial and Commonwealth History* 4:29–54.

Lewis, Patrick Albert. 1974. A historical analysis of the union-party system in the Commonwealth Caribbean, 1935–1968. Ph.D. diss., University of Cincinnati.

Lewis, W. Arthur. 1938. *Labour in the West Indies: The Birth of a Workers' Movement*. Research series no. 44. [London?]: Fabian Society.

Lipset, Seymour Martin. 1979. *The First New Nation: The United States in Historical and Comparative Perspective*. New York: Norton.

Macmillan, W. M. 1936. *Warning from the West Indies: A Tract for Africa and the Empire*. London: Faber and Faber.

Mark, Francis. 1965. *The History of the Barbados Workers' Union*. Bridgetown, Barbados: Advocate Press.

Matthews, P. E. 1934. *Report of the Superintendent of Police on the Disturbances of October 1st 1934*. Report to the governor, 27 November, Belize City, Belize. CO 123/346/35524.

Munroe, Trevor. 1972. *The Politics of Constitutional Decolonization: Jamaica, 1944–62*. Kingston, Jamaica: Institute of Social and Economic Research, University of the West Indies.

Oxaal, Ivar. 1968. *Black Intellectuals Come to Power: The Rise of Creole Nationalism in Trinidad and Tobago*. Cambridge, Mass.: Schenkman.

Pollard, Sir Nicholas. 1992. Personal interview by author (including three pages of his typed notes), Belize City, Belize, December.

Poole, Bernard L. 1951. *The Caribbean Commission: Background for Cooperation of the West Indies*. Columbia: University of South Carolina Press.

Post, Ken. 1978. *Arise Ye Starvelings: The Jamaican Labour Rebellion and Its Aftermath*. The Hague, London: Martinus Nijhoff.

Rueschemeyer, Detrich, Evelyne Huber Stephens, and John D. Stephens. 1992. *Capitalist Development and Democracy*. Chicago: University of Chicago Press.

Rustow, Dankwart A. 1967. *A World of Nations: Problems of Political Modernization*. Washington, D.C.: The Brookings Institution.

Ryan, Selwyn D. 1974. *Race and Nationalism in Trinidad and Tobago*. Port of Spain, Trinidad: University of the West Indies Press.

Sederberg, Peter. 1994. *Fires Within: Political Violence and Revolutionary Change*. New York: HarperCollins.

Shoman, Assad. n.d. The making and breaking of the UGWU. Unpublished paper, Belize City, Belize.

Simey, T[homas] S. 1946. *Welfare and Planning in the West Indies*. Oxford: Clarendon Press.

Singh, Kelvin. 1987. The Trinidad labour riots of 1937. In *The Trinidad Riots of 1937: Perspectives 50 Years Later* (Roy Thomas, ed.), 57–67. St. Augustine, Trinidad: Extra-Mural Studies Unit, University of the West Indies.

Skocpol, Theda. 1979. *States and Social Revolutions: A Comparative Analysis of France, Russia, and China*. New York: Cambridge University Press.

Thomas, Roy, ed. 1987. *The Trinidad Labour Riots of 1937: Perspectives 50 Years Later*. St. Augustine, Trinidad: Extra-Mural Studies Unit, University of the West Indies.

Trinidad Guardian. 1937. 18 June–27 July.

United Kingdom (U.K.). 1945a. *West India Royal Commission Report, 1938–39*. Cmd. 6607. London: HMSO. Often referred to as "Moyne Report."

_____. 1945b. *West India Commission 1938–39: Statement of Action Taken on the Recommendations*. Cmd. 6646. London: HMSO.

_____. 1940. *Recommendations*. Cmd. 6174. London: HMSO.

_____. 1934. *Report on the Financial and Economic Position of British Honduras*. Honduras. Report by Sir Alan Pim. Cmd. 4586. London: HMSO.

Weber, Max. 1964. *The Theory of Social and Economic Organization*. New York: Free Press.

Will, W. Marvin. 1997. NGOs and IGOs as promoters of liberal democracy in the Caribbean: Cases from Nicaragua and Guyana. In *Democracy and Human Rights in the Caribbean* (Ivelaw Griffith and Betty Sedoc, eds.), 51–73. Boulder: Westview Press.

_____. 1992a. The Bahamas. St. Lucia. St. Vincent and the Grenadines, et al. In *Political Parties of the Americas, 1980s to 1990s* (Charles Ameringer, ed.), 53–75, 546, 556. Westport, Conn.: Greenwood Press.

_____. 1992b. Insurrection and the development of political institutions . . . in Barbados. *Journal of the Barbados Museum and Historical Society* 40:9–18, 66–84.

_____. 1991. A nation divided: The quest for Caribbean integration. *Latin American Research Review* 26:3–37.

_____. 1989. Democracy, elections, and public policy in the Eastern Caribbean: The case of Barbados. *The Journal of Commonwealth and Comparative Politics* 27:321–346

_____. 1972. Political development in the mini-state Caribbean. Ph.D. diss., University of Missouri-Columbia.

Williams, Eric. 1964. *History of the People of Trinidad and Tobago*. Rev. ed. New York: Praeger.

Wolf, Eric R. 1969. *Peasant Wars of the Twentieth Century*. New York: Harper and Row.

Chapter Eleven

Passion and Democracy in Cuba

DAMIÁN J. FERNÁNDEZ

Will Cuba adopt a democratic system in the future? Yes, I expect it will. I arrive at this conclusion based on a number of factors, not on wishful thinking, Pollyannaishness, or teleology. On the contrary, my argument as to the type of democracy Cuba is likely to establish is anything but utopic.

The question of whether Cuba will be democratic begs other questions: When? How? And, most important, what type of democracy? It is the last question I wish to address in this chapter. The "when" and "how" questions are intriguing but require playing the scenario game, something of a bore after so many others have tried their hand at it. The "what" question is more substantial, although when and how the Cuban government takes a turn toward democracy will influence the succeeding regime. The focus, therefore, is on post-transition politics.

For the purpose of my argument, I use a simple and orthodox definition of liberal democracy. A democracy is a system of government that, *at a minimum,* meets the following criteria: (1) holds competitive multiparty elections among an enfranchised citizenry; (2) guarantees the civil liberties (that is, freedom of speech and freedom of association, among others) of all members of society, including minorities; and (3) is based on and observes the rule of law. Moreover, as will be explained later, democracy requires a public space in which individuals and groups exercise their rights and organize in associations.

As a general theoretical point of departure I echo Di Palma's claim about the indeterminacy of politics: "In political matters, particularly in matters of regime change, causal relations are only probable and outcomes uncertain. We can make broad probabilistic predictions about categories, but we cannot make firm predictions about individual cases. In any single case, unless relevant circumstances cumulate in the extreme, the end result is not inescapable" (1990:4). He adds:

"Whatever the historical trends, whatever the hard facts, the importance of human action in a difficult transition should not be underestimated" (1990:9). Therefore, in my discussion I will resort to probabilistic terms such as "likely" in recognition of the fact that my topic by definition is speculative. At the moment that I write this chapter (1997) the Cuban political system continues to be an authoritarian/totalitarian one.

To reach conclusions as to the qualitative aspects of Cuban politics in the posttransition era, I will examine aspects of political culture as they relate to the formation and practices of civil society in democracy. Political culture covers those aspects of behavior, attitudes, *and feelings* that influence how individuals relate to politics. From this angle one can interpret some key dimensions of politics in particular settings. The approach is partial and selective, although it relies on generalizations. It only provides a taste of the political system, but that piece is one of the ingredients that gives the politics of a country, or an area, its distinct flavor.

This approach does not dismiss other types of factors as unimportant. Structural factors, for instance, are basic factors to be considered in any analysis. Attitudes and values alone are not the principal causes of democracy. On the contrary, a transition to democracy (and its consolidation) depends on a multiplicity of factors, including elite decisions, institutional arrangements, pacts between competing social actors, a constitution and organizations typical of liberal democracies, a favorable moment in world history, supportive international structures, and a measure of good luck. Political and economic factors also impinge on the likelihood of democratic transitions and survival. But political and economic factors determine per se neither transition to democracy nor democratic stability. The impact of the economy on democracy is not automatic, unidirectional, or necessarily predictable. Democracy is the product of multiple causes working together.

Democracy requires a public sphere, preferably marked by positive civic attitudes (that is,, tolerance, moderation, collaboration for the common good), on the one hand, and by associations that incorporate multiple identities and interests, on the other. It is this public sphere that I refer to as civil society, with its qualitative (political cultural attributes) and quantitative (host of associations) dimensions.

My interest is the osmosis of the cultural attributes, values, behavior, and *affective expression* into civil society and their impact on democratic governance. Usually civil society is seen as either shaping democracy (that is, through voluntary associations, social movements, or the civic culture it embodies) or shaped by democratic regimes (that is, through norms). In practice both relationships are at work. Though some scholars argue that political culture (or the civic culture as one of its modalities) contributes to democracy, others contend that democracy, specifically participatory democracy, fosters democratic values in the population (that is, active citizenship). In short, there is no consensus as to whether the political culture of society is a cause or a consequence of democracy (or any other form of government). From my perspective, political culture is both cause and effect, an input and an output (if we wish to use a functionalist lexicon) of the political system.

Political culture can change over time; it is not immutably fixed, but it is not easily malleable because individuals are not clay. Political culture is embodied in living people and it is reproduced; it is not out in an imaginary world. Although political culture does not explain all, it helps explain some dimensions of the democratic experience. At its worst the political culture approach is patronizing, deterministic, and blanketing. At its best it brings in the cultural specificity of a place, avoids the universalism of other theories, and recognizes that individuals have cultural predispositions and frames of reference that influence their actions. The political cultural approach that I advocate, one that includes emotions, helps embody the process of political change by bringing people (thinking and feeling entities, the ultimate actors in politics) back into the analysis.

Despite the modern emphasis on avoiding the emotions and harping on rational self-interest, politics is inherently emotional in societies facing transitions and other foundational questions. Not only are emotional appeals a useful tool in political campaigns, but people's actions are largely based on feelings, not exclusively on cost-benefit analyses (Mansbridge 1990).

Ronald Inglehart, a prominent student of the role of political culture in fostering democracy, concluded that "a long-term commitment to democratic institutions among the public is . . . required in order to sustain democracy when conditions are dire" (quoted in Mattiace and Camp 1996:7). Among the values relevant to democracy are tolerance of opposition, moderation, and a high level of trust in the system and in other citizens. These values are what I refer to as the qualitative dimensions of civil society because they are the essence of civility and presume an emotional infrastructure that can help sustain democracy. In contexts where the system confronts unresolved foundational issues and consensus is elusive—on such matters as how the political community is defined, who has authority, what the rules of the game are—political questions become an affair of the heart, lending themselves less to compromise and pragmatism. As a result civility tends to be endangered, particularly in places where institutional democratic norms are weak and personalism is high. This is likely to occur in Cuba after Fidel Castro (as it has before and during the socialist years).

Jean Cohen and Andrew Arato's broad definition of civil society is useful for my argument and for the scope of my work because it does not divorce the personal/private from the public. They define civil society as

> a sphere of social interaction between economy and state, composed above all of the intimate sphere (especially voluntary associations), social movements, and forms of public communications. Modern civil society is created through forms of self-constitution and self-mobilization. It is institutionalized and generalized through laws, and especially subjective rights, that stabilize social differentiation. . . . in the long term both independent action and institutionalization are necessary for the reproduction of civil society. (1992:xvi)

Civil society is part of the social world but is not all encompassing of social life. It is distinguishable from political society (political parties) and economic society (firms). Whereas political and economic society emerge from civil society, civil society emerges from society at large.

This chapter argues that though democracy will be established in Cuba sometime in the future, Cuban democracy will not conform to normative models of liberal democracy. Democracy à la *cubana* will be characterized by features of incivility in civil society. Incivility, an aspect of Cuban political culture, is born from two main sources: the politics of passion and the politics of affection. In turn, the politics of passion and the politics of affection emanate from six sources: (1) the historical legacy of competing normative paradigms in Cuban political culture, (2) the origins of organized groups forming civil society after the demise of the socialist state, (3) *"lo informal,"* or the culture of informality, (4) the codes of passion, (5) the retreat to the personal (or the shifting involvement cycle), and (6) the charged political economy of transition.

This chapter will first present a theoretical reconsideration of the role of emotions in democracy in order to set the foundation for the argument that passionate politics and the politics of affection are likely to be detrimental to democracy and civility. Next it will sketch the reasons why democracy will be established in Cuba in the future. And, third, it will analyze the six dimensions of emotional politics already mentioned to conclude that there is a strong tendency for incivility in the island's future.

The democracy that is most likely to emerge on the island will be far from perfect, will share striking continuities with the past, and will dash the hopes of many who dream of democracy with a capital D. This disappointing view of democracy is part of a long tradition in the literature on democratic governance dating to the nineteenth century, even by some authors who are proponents of democratic practices. The cynicism about democracy also has a long genealogy in Cuban intellectual history. As far back as the nineteenth century cultural pessimists on the island have remarked on the frustration that has followed modern projects of independence, nationalism, republicanism, and democracy. These writers point to culture, with its affectivity, as the principal reason for the tarnished results of even the most promising of political projects. I would add that the normative models that have been aspired to—creations of modernity, by and large—have contributed to their own frustration because they have been intrinsically flawed, primarily by their utopianism and their neglect of the importance of affect. More important, they have been in logical competition with contending paradigms that are part and parcel of Cuban political culture.

A Theoretical Reconsideration:
Passion and Democratic Politics

To speak about democracy, more often than not, has been an exercise in normativity: in considering the ideal system of elections, representation, legal equality, separation of powers, and citizen participation. A far less optimistic perspective grounds democracy in concrete experience and in the less than savory history of democratic practice. This perspective questions the rational bases of politics and incorporates emotions as important influences in all human epistemology and ontology.

The politics of passion is key to understanding the social world and particularly to explaining civility (and incivility) in democracy. A discussion that neglects the role of the personal, of the nonrational, of affection and disaffection, and of the informal misses the heart of politics. Politics is not exclusively or primarily motivated by rational calculation, contrary to the claims of the dominant paradigm in political science. Primordial feelings of group membership (whether in the family or in the nation) are powerful forces of high emotional charge, which can (and do) steer politics in specific directions, frame issues in particular terms, and tend to undermine the institutions and the civility of a civil society (Holmes 1995; Mansbridge 1990; Frank 1988).

Emotional expressions are value judgments that people make about their surroundings (Solomon 1976). As such they are valuable indications of how people feel about politics and what they expect from the political system. Collective emotions of disaffection generated with the political system are the result of expectations that are not matched by reality. The gap between the real and the ideal makes individuals and groups react in affective ways. In the case of Cuba the gap between the ideal and the real revolves around three cultural paradigms that coexist in tension: the modern, the corporatist, and the informal. These three set the goals the society aspires to but are also the bases of their own unraveling as they contradict each other.

Modernity proposes lofty projects (liberal democracy and capitalism), but the other paradigms undermine the realization of those aspirations. Corporatism, a legacy of Spanish colonialism, favors a centralized authority and harmonious social relations orchestrated from above. The informal is an instrumental framework in which everything goes as long as it benefits oneself and usually those one loves. *"Lo informal"* bypasses the legal institutions of the society in favor of the personal and expedient (and usually the legal). It is in the informal that one finds the politics of affection. The logic of each paradigm is in conflict with the logic of the others. As a consequence the high goals of modernity—which induce great passion, as they are vital foundational issues—have proven unreachable in Cuba (and elsewhere) not only because the paradigm itself is utopic but also because the conduct implied by the norms of modern democracy run against those prescribed by the other paradigms, which are very much part of Cuban political culture. As political actors pursue lofty goals (such as democracy) for the community at large, along the way they resort to the instrumental procedures of the informal (and the politics of affection—who one knows, who one loves) and the authoritarianism of corporatism, undermining the intellectual foundation of the modern project.

Whereas democracy is expected to establish legal equality among the citizenry, that is, universalisms, the informal operates based on kinship and friendship, that is, affection and personal exceptionalism. Corporatism favors order rather than democratic competition and adjudicates special treatment of distinct social groups rather than allowing political laissez-faire. Corporatism also advocates a strong and good-hearted state that provides the good life for the people. The politics of affection, both of the informal and corporatist paradigms but especially in the informal sphere of daily life, challenges the modern tenets of a bureaucratic legal rational order on which democracy should rest. The connections among *amigos, socios* (buddies), and *familia* usually operate against the precepts of modernity. These primordial affective ties contribute to undermining modern aspirations, specifically by creating trust in small circles rather than in broader organizations and by pursuing personal benefits through instruments that do not benefit society at large. Therefore the politics of affection contributes to an uncivil society on a broad scale and to the undoing of projects such as democracy. The politics of passion does so as well.

Dissatisfaction with the unmet expectations of modernity in turn fuels the fire of those who search for a better tomorrow (usually middle-class elites educated in modern normative frameworks). That search is an emotional one—for meaning and identity—and a moral one. As foundational issues of the national political community remain unsettled (partly because there is no consensus on how to resolve them), they continue to be volatile. The immediacy of politics, the personalism of the political system and the political culture, and the challenges confronted in the international arena inject politics with high dosages of affectivity. The political discourse becomes hyperinflated as political dilemmas are conceived of as a struggle between good and evil. Politics becomes passionate, a search for the moral order that should be, almost a national religion. The political crusade can readily trample values that in theory it holds dear as its leaders resort to an instrumental logic in which the ends justify the means (typical of the informal sphere). In the process they corrode their own normative desires.

However, democracy and a democratic civil society need what Harry Eckstein (1992) called "balanced disparities." Among the balanced disparities required for democratic stability is the opposition between, on the one hand, affective attachment to the political system and, on the other, affective neutrality. Gabriel Almond and Sidney Verba argue that "politics must not be so instrumental and pragmatic that participants lose all emotional involvement in it." On the other hand, "the level of affective orientation to politics ought not to become too intensive" (1963:488). As anemic as the statement is, it deals with a necessary and delicate balance. The participant's emotional intensity as well as the type of polemical issues confronted (particularly morally charged ones and foundational ones related to the constitution of the political community) raise the stakes of politics. These sorts of issues increase the potential for instability, polarization, and witchhunts against adversaries (who are seen as "traitorous," "evil," "inhuman"), contributing to the conception of politics as zero-sum, winner-takes-all games. In such cases, civil society tends to lose its civility, especially if institutions that could prevent incivility are weak.

The Uncivil Society

Before turning to the sources of incivility in the democratic future of Cuban society, the notion of uncivil society must be defined. The uncivil society is characterized by high degrees of personalism (despite the existence of institutions) in social relations and high affectivity over political issues. Both of these traits result in
a variety of negative effects on democracy. Personalism values individual relations
over universalism, legal equality, and institutional standard operating procedures.
High affectivity, in turn, contributes to a political climate of high emotional
charge, where the stakes are increased and where moderation and negotiated solutions based on compromise are hard to achieve. Civil discourse and the effective
performance of the political system suffer as a consequence.

Uncivil society is prone to mass politics and is conducive to the emergence of
charismatic leaders who appeal to the emotions as they promise to deliver the nation from crisis. Although highly personalized, uncivil societies show a distrust of
those outside the affective networks. Lack of trust is manifested toward institutions and norms. The beliefs of individual exceptionalism and the informal politics of affection run counter to the universalism implied in democratic norms.
Uncivil societies share the amoral familism that Banfield identified in southern
Italy (Banfield 1958).

Why Democracy Is Likely to Return to Cuba

Democratic aspirations have a long history on the island, as long as the trajectory
of their frustration. The notion is not as alien to Cuban soil as many believe. The
ideological founders of the Cuban nation, José Martí among them, aspired to
democracy and nationalism, two pillars of the modern cosmography. Their definition of the term has been contested, problematic, and pliable, cloaking with legitimacy many an undemocratic project. José Martí's idealism, on the one hand, and
his emphasis on unity above all, on the other, were an ill-suited basis for the pragmatic compromises between divergent interests on which democratic government must stand.

After its independence in 1902, Cuba experienced periods of elected governments in a competitive party system until the 1952 coup of General Fulgencio
Batista. During the years of independence before Batista's takeover, Cuban
democracy, far from perfect, did not live up to the expectations of many, including the United States. Frustration with the state of affairs was rampant. The Constitution of 1940 was a response to the derailed national democratic project of the
past. The constitution enshrined the desire for democracy of the great majority of
Cubans, but it fell prey to overly ambitious promises (and failure to deliver on
those promises), corruption, and finally to General Batista's intervention.

The restoration of the constitution was the principal initial goal of those fighting against the military dictatorship of General Batista. Fidel Castro, then the

young leader of the July 26 Movement, pledged to return to an improved democracy and to forge a moral nation after the dictator's ouster. His would be an emotional (read moral) revolution. Although once in power the revolutionary leaders did not reinstate the 1940 Constitution, pursuing a Marxist-Leninist course instead, they never eliminated the notion of democracy and morality from their lexicon. Socialism would bring the democracy and the higher moral order the Cuban people sought. Or so it seemed.

In the 1990s, confronted with an unparalleled economic and political crisis, the regime has had to wrestle once again with issues associated with democratic governance (that is, pluralism, participation, and human rights) as a way to muster popular support and to respond to dissidents and critics. Under the banner of human rights, groups of activists on the island have urged the government to take steps toward liberal democracy by observing civil liberties and holding multiparty elections. Within the state and the Communist Party of Cuba (PCC), reformers have advocated greater political and economic liberalization. Outside Cuba governments and international organizations have echoed the call for a transition to democracy, some offering carrots while holding (weak and ineffective) sticks in an attempt to sway the Cuban leaders. The historical moment seems to favor those, inside and outside Cuba, who advocate democracy; the end of the twentieth century appears propitious for democratic transitions, particularly in Latin America and in socialist regimes.

Authoritarian and totalitarian regimes throughout the world have failed to provide important material and nonmaterial benefits to their populations (not that democracies always fare better). Moreover, international norms on human rights undermined the bases of nondemocratic governance. Civil society and social movements worldwide challenged authoritarianism. A new generation of leaders, including those in the former Soviet Union, unfurled the banners of transparency and accountability, key components of good democratic practice.

Cuba has not been immune to developments outside its borders. The breakup of the socialist camp had not only economic repercussions but dramatic political ones as well. The Cuban government has had to begrudgingly adopt economic measures that gingerly, and not so gingerly at times, move toward a mixed economy. The economic shock and the consequent decline in the state's ability to deliver goods led to a loss of social control of *la calle* (the street) as ordinary Cubans resorted to a host of informal mechanisms, usually illegal, to make ends meet. At the same time dissident groups proliferated and the youth became increasingly discontented with the regime's performance (Fernández 1993).

On the other side of the Florida strait, the United States touted democracy as the goal of its policy toward the island and passed laws proclaiming such. (Whether the means chosen are adequate is doubtful.) Though opposing economic isolation, Canada, Europe, and Latin America have tried unsuccessfully to promote democracy through softer tactics (that is, through dialogue with the government and through engagement rather than disengagement). Regardless of differences in means, the goal of the international community vis-à-vis Cuba is the same: democracy. Several factors, however, indicate that the normative presumptions of advocates of democracy both inside and outside the nation stand on shaky ground.

Looking Back Before Looking Forward: The Uncivil Past of Civil Society

Democracy and civil society in Cuba have had a checkered past, which is not unusual when compared to the rest of the world. Though a liberal discourse is woven throughout the history of the nation, its threads run alongside an antiliberal discourse characterized by a teleological reasoning in which the ends justify the means (Rojas 1993:20). Throughout the island's history observers have remarked on the lack of civic spirit among the Cuban people. Father Felix Varela, one of the founding fathers of this school of thought, probably inaugurated this mode of thought when he complained that islanders seemed to care exclusively about money (1996). Other observers have remarked on the opportunism, lack of social discipline, and lack of civic responsibility of Cubans (Varona 1914:13).

In the Republican years (1902–1958), Cuba's public sphere met one of the criteria—multiplicity of associations—of civil society. Seldom did one find the quantitative and qualitative dimensions of civil society concurrently. Civil society (as well as political and economic society) was identified with corruption, gangsterism, opportunism, and personalism. The 1940 constitutional convention—in spite of infighting and personal attacks hurled among some of its leaders—was an exception to the general run of civil society when it successfully gathered representatives of all the important political and social currents on the island and managed to craft a consensus. With the advent of the Revolution of 1959 a process unfolded of homogenizing the organizations of civil society and subjugating them to newly created revolutionary umbrella organizations. Individuals and groups who resisted were silenced through repression, exile, or imprisonment. The majority embraced the new regime for emotional, moral, and economic reasons.

The emotional bases of the support for the regime rested on the charismatic leadership of Fidel Castro and on nationalism. Nationalism, more than a set of beliefs, is a sentimental posture vis-à-vis the world. It provides a sense of self that is felt, not necessarily reasoned. Charisma and nationalism were the pillars of a political religion inaugurated by the Revolution. Politics became a passionate moral struggle against the evil of corruption, U.S. imperialism, inequality, and dependency on sugar monoculture.

A return to the Constitution of 1940 appealed to many Cubans, particularly in the middle and upper sectors of society, but such a desire was no match for the passion generated by a man (who appeared to be a superman) promising the rebirth of the Cuban nation. The promise, and the delivery, of social benefits for the less fortunate constituted another source of support.

Civil society, which had contributed to the struggle against Batista, was relatively quickly subsumed by mass politics in the institution of the new state. In the process much of what was supposed to be civil in civil society was lost. Not only was civil society in Cuba during the 1959–1961 period unable to steer the course of the Revolution toward the liberal democracy of the 1940s but, in practice, it helped the revolutionary leadership consolidate unity and conformity by silencing nonconformists. The example of the closing of Catholic churches in these years reveals the inability of civic organizations and norms to protect the rights of citizens in the face of mass support for the *lider* and his/their cause. In the 1990s the *acto de repudio* (state orchestrated public acts of shunning nonconformists) became emblematic of the uncivil dimension of Cuban society.

The Origins of Civil Society in a Post-Socialist Cuba

The roots of civil society are found in the private sphere and in informal politics within and without the institutions of the state. The politics of affection and disaffection, usually perceived as belonging exclusively to the private lives of individuals, is an initial arena where public life is articulated and mediated. Affective bonds of kinship, friendship, and clientelism glue groups together in domestic society (and in political society as well). These groups represent a proto–civil society. From the arena of affection, groups organize into associations in the public sphere. Some human rights groups in Cuba, for example, have their genesis in small groups of friends, as trust is a necessary component of such organizations. (In Argentina, Las Madres de la Plaza de Mayo epitomizes the role affection can play in mobilization). As groups expand their membership in the public arena, a redefinition of the basis of membership usually ensues, away from affection.

In Cuba civil society will emerge, slowly and with great difficulty, from two principal sources: from the state (its bureaucracy, affiliated organizations, and policies—such as the promotion of Sociedades Anónimas) and from the informal practices of individuals in their everyday lives (the black market, cultural reaffirmation of subgroups and networks of *socios*). There is a domestic society in Cuba, largely informal and outside state boundaries (although informality is also prevalent within state bureaucracies). But there is hardly a civil society (despite the presence of several independent organizations on the island). Both sources of civil society formation, the state and informal politics, present serious problems for civility in public life. Given the qualities of state structures and policies, on the one hand, and of informal behavior, on the other, instead of a civil society what might reemerge in Cuba is an uncivil society.

The institutional history of the Cuban state casts a dark shadow on the prospects for a civil society. During the past three decades state agencies or the top leaders have tended to close spaces when attempts are made to open them.

The trajectory of the intellectuals is illustrative. Artists and scholars have tried to carve a sphere of autonomy within the system, but time after time the attempt has been frustrated as periods of relative openness are followed by closure. Diverse opinions (ranging from the correct interpretation of Marxism to the benefits of the free farmers' market) have been repeatedly silenced, at least temporarily. The institutionalization of incivility took a turn for the worse in the *actos de repudio* coordinated by the government during the Mariel exodus and once again since the late 1980s against dissidents.

The Cultural Basis of Civil (and Uncivil) Society in Cuba: Choteo, Informality, and Passion

Scholars have argued that the Latin American Iberian heritage is an unsuitable ground for liberal democracy to take hold. Corporatism, one of the main theories advanced to explain the politics of the region, emphasizes the penchant for authoritarian political structures and identifies the Catholic and Aristotelian-Thomist traditions as the principal source of Latin political culture. Glenn Caudill Dealy (1996) takes the argument a step further, arguing that a two-track moral code is responsible for the lack of public civic consciousness, on the one hand, and the love and fraternity of private life in the region, on the other. The result is that whereas private personal relations are guided by an ethos of empathy and piety, public matters are conducted on the basis of expediency and opportunism. The public realm is devoid of familiarity and as a consequence is marked by lack of trust and the possibility of hostility.

Recognizing the binary logic of the public and the private renders understandable the fact that Latin Americans try to deal with public challenges through familiarity. That is, Latin Americans' dealings in the public sphere tend to be marked not only by trepidation but also by patterns of behavior typically associated with their private life: making the public familiar, personalizing the impersonal. The process involves establishing networks of buddies, patrons, or clients within and without the institutions of the state. These personal relations help deal with the bureaucracy of institutional life, usually by circumventing their norms.

The specific cultural modality of this phenomenon in the Cuban case is, first, the type of humor known as *choteo* and, second, the tendency towards informality. The *choteo*'s comic peculiarity is that it targets authority, undermining order and debunking formality in all settings. The *choteo* is the expression of a society that relishes unbridled individual exceptionalism and pervasive familiarity in social relations, at the expense of authority and order. (Remember: Familiarity breeds contempt.) By "privatizing" social relations (making them more accessible, at least momentarily), the *choteo* infuses social life with informality and indiscipline. In short, the Cuban *choteo* both manifests and breeds contempt for norms, the pillars of civil society (Manach 1969).

The Culture of Informality

Informality at the grass roots has a paradoxical impact on the emergence of civil society. On the one hand, ties of friendship, networks of *socios,* and bonds between patrons and clients foster important elements necessary for civil society, namely, trust, collaboration outside the state, and the recognition of separate identities, passions, and interests not recognized by the government. On the other hand, informal mechanisms provide advantages to the system (for example, increased flexibility, reduction of bottlenecks, satisfaction of some needs) that might help it survive. Above all, informal politics socializes individuals in a culture of illegality and underscores elements of a political culture that undermine what would be an ideal democratic set of attitudes. Informality is likely to contribute to an uncivil civil society.

Informal politics is based on personalism. Although they often carry with them affection and reciprocity, they are also often set on patron-client (or corporatist) bases. Informal politics breeds mistrust of political organizations, and despite the networks formed, it also generates anomie behavior, mistrust, and unregulated competition (that is, it's a jungle out there). Moreover, individuals try to deal with the imposition of the formal public life by "escaping" to the private and informal, which is more familiar, more malleable. This withdrawal from the public does not bode well for a democratic civil society, in which individual participation and institutions are vital. By privatizing public life, the informal contributes to a political culture akin to clientelism and to attitudes of exceptionalism ("I am above the law; I obey but I do not comply").

The Codes of Passion

The other side of *choteo* and informality is the fact that Cuban politics has also revolved around a moral and passionate quest for political utopia. Nelson Valdes (1992) has uncovered four important codes in the political culture of Cubans: (1) the generational theme (the notion that the youth, the embodiment of courage and idealism, can regenerate the island's political system), (2) the moralism-idealism syndrome (the idea that politics is driven by questions of honor, duty, and dignity), (3) the theme of betrayal (the conviction that loyalty and truth are absolute, that any deviation is a violation of group integrity), and (4) the politicization of Thanatos (the belief that the willingness to die for political ideals is the highest manifestation of altruism).

These codes can be summarized by the notion of the politics of passion and the passion of politics, which encapsulate one of the two most important dimensions of the political culture of the island. They reveal a political culture characterized by a high affectivity and personalism, on the one hand, and a moral imperative, on the other. This combination makes politics passionate, rendering democratic pragmatism less tenable and placing democratic stability in jeopardy. Moreover, though the moral imperative demands passion for the pursuit of a better political community, the logic of political utopia is quite different from the logic of personalism. The first is motivated by the pursuit of normative goals (disregarding practical means), and the second is instrumental, using whatever means necessary to satisfy the ends. The combination of these two logics, normative and instrumental, results in a situation in which individuals tend to justify any means to achieve the morally higher end.

The Shifting Involvement Syndrome

In Cuba the politicization of the masses since 1959 has given way to depoliticization as Cubans have become increasingly disillusioned with collective participation. Depoliticization has been coupled with a retreat to the personal, away from the public. As individuals grow disenchanted with the political life they will seek other spheres in which to invest time and energy and through which they can construct their own sense of self and meaning. The process leads to apolitical and antipolitical attitudes manifested in a retreat from politics, which contradicts the traditional image of the participatory citizen in democracy.

What Albert Hirschman (1982) called the cycle of shifting involvement is likely to occur in Cuba (and elsewhere in the former socialist countries and in liberal democracies as well). As their expectations regarding participation in collective politics are dashed, people will be disenchanted with the public and concentrate on the private, devoting themselves to individual and family pursuits. In the long run, the pendulum will shift toward collective involvement once again. In the post-transition period, disengaged citizens will be more prevalent than the engaged. These individuals will seek to exercise his or her freedom from politics.

As positive as this development may be for Cubans tired of the demands of mass mobilization and politics in general, it is an auspicious beginning for democracy. A retreat to the personal gives greater room to elites, who might become less representative and accountable. It also does not empower citizens in the public domain, although their choice to not participate is understandable and, after all, a choice.

The Political Economy of Transition

Complicating the picture is the possibility that market reforms in the context of economic crisis might result in a merciless capitalism. As the socialist safety net is in tatters, and the laws of supply and demand overtake the laws of socialist equity, civility in social relations is likely to suffer. Criminality, mafia-type activities, class and race conflict, and corruption, all with a long history before and during socialism, are likely to spread.

If the corporatist paradigm still holds sway in Cubans' relations to the political, as I think it does, one can expect that Cubans will continue to perceive the state as a source of distribution of material and nonmaterial benefits in the post-transition period. They are eventually likely to want a big state with a big heart. It is unlikely that such a state will have the big pockets necessary to distribute material benefits to the society.

Conclusion

Democracy and civil society are not only descriptive concepts but normative projects as well. As a modern individual with his fair share of disenchantment, I question the utopian subtext that a reconstruction of democracy and civil society is expected to produce on the island. Political cultural factors (not to mention structural ones) will tend to conspire against liberal democratic norms. A transition from one regime to another per se is unlikely to usher in a transformation in the way Cubans relate to politics. Although change is possible, desirable, and likely at some level, its magnitude and direction does not warrant the conclusion that it will contribute to civic attitudes and behavior conducive to democracy to the extent that people inside and outside the country desire and expect.

This does not mean that civil society in practice and in theory will not play a significant role in Cuban politics and in the transition to democracy. On the contrary, it will be the handmaiden, if not the midwife, of democratic transition, but down the line it is likely to challenge the ideal mental map of many who expect democracy in the post-transition period. Incivility will likely raise its head once again in the new context.

The corporatist, clientelistic, informal, instrumental, passionate, moralistic, and idealistic characteristics of Cuban political culture are likely to be reproduced once more, regenerating many of the modes of being, feeling, and understanding that do not mesh with the modern theory of democratic practice. As they have in the past these factors will contribute to incivility and to an uncivil civil society, fragmented, competitive, myopic. Transition will arouse great passion. Democracy might become the next crusade. Those responsible for the past might be made to pay for their "mistakes," and thus a new dynamic of conflict, zero-sum politics, and incivility might be unleashed.

Moreover, after the transition popular expectations of material and nonmaterial benefits will be heightened at a time when the state will be facing severe economic and political constraints. Cubans will resort to the politics of affection—who one knows, who one loves—as a mechanism to make ends meet and to secure some of the things they want but that the system in its institutional legal mode is unlikely to provide. In so doing, they will bypass and undermine the legal and ideal moral order. Many will be disappointed by the inability (or unwillingness) of the new state to deliver goods. Many will long for and demand a stronger and bigger state with a generous heart (an echo of the corporatist legacy). In short, consensus in civil society (not to mention political society) will be hard to craft, as will be civility in such a scenario. The stage will be set for another round of disappointment as the script of democracy-as-utopia starts to unravel, and politicians will find plenty of reasons to render politics passionate once again.

Bibliography

Almond, Gabriel, and Sidney Verba. 1963. *The Civic Culture: Political Attitudes and Democracy in Five Nations*. Princeton: Princeton University Press.

Banfield, Edward C. 1958. *The Moral Basis of a Backward Society*. New York: Free Press.

Cohen, Jean, and Andrew Arato. 1992. *Civil Society and Political Theory*. Cambridge: MIT Press.

Dealy, Glenn Caudill. 1996. Two cultures and political behavior in Latin America. In *Democracy in Latin America: Patterns and Cycles* (Roderic Ai Camp, ed.), 49–66. Wilmington, Del.: Scholarly Resources.

Di Palma, Giuseppe. 1990. *To Craft Democracies: An Essay on Democratic Transitions*. Berkeley: University of California Press.

Eckstein, Harry. 1992. *Regarding Politics: Essays on Political Theory, Stability, and Change*. Berkeley: University of California Press.

Fernández, Damián J. 1993. Youth in Cuba: Resistance and accommodation. In *Conflict and Change in Cuba* (Enrique Baloyra and James Morris, eds.), 189–214. Albuquerque: University of New Mexico Press.

Frank, Robert. 1988. *Passions Within Reason: The Strategic Role of the Emotions*. New York: Norton.

Hirschman, Albert O. 1982. *Shifting Involvements: Private Interests and Public Action*. Princeton: Princeton University Press.

Holmes, Stephen. 1995. *Passions and Constraint*. Chicago: University of Chicago Press.

Manach, Jorge. 1969. *Indagación del Choteo*. Miami, Fla.: Mnemosyne Publishing.

Mansbridge, Jane J. 1990. *Beyond Self-Interest*. Chicago: University of Chicago Press.

Mattiace, Shannain, and Roderic Ai Camp. 1996. Democracy and development: An overview. In *Democracy in Latin America: Patterns and Cycles* (Roderic Ai Camp, ed.), 3–19. Wilmington, Del.: Scholarly Resources.

Rojas, Rafael. 1993. Viaje a la semilla: Instituciones de la antimodernidad cubana. *Apuntes Postmodernos* 4:3–20.

Solomon, Robert C. 1976. *The Passions*. Garden City, N.Y.: Anchor Press.

Valdes, Nelson. 1992. Cuban political culture: Between betrayal and death. In *Cuba in Transition: Crisis and Transformation* (Sandor Halebsky and John M. Kirk, eds.), 207–228. Boulder: Westview Press.

Varela, Felix. (1996). *Cartas a Elpidio*. Miami, Fla.: Editorial Cubana.

Varona, Enrique José. 1914. Nuestra indisciplina. *Cuba Contemporanea* 4:12–16.

Chapter Twelve

Haitian Democracy: Oxymoron or Emerging Reality?

RICHARD L. MILLETT

In 1957 a Haitian newspaper, commenting on the violence and intimidation that had characterized the election of Dr. François Duvalier (Papa Doc) as president, declared that democracy in Haiti was "dead, almost without having lived" (Trouillot 1986:160). More than twenty-seven years later, President Jean-Bertrand Aristide, on his return to Haiti in the wake of a U.S.-led intervention, told his supporters: "Today is the day that the sun of democracy rises to never set" (Klarreich 1994:1). This declaration that democracy had finally been resurrected in Haiti, following the prolonged nightmare of Duvalier family rule and military oppression, represents the most optimistic view of the current status and future prospects for the poorest nation in the western hemisphere. Haiti has clearly made important strides toward establishing a more democratic political system. The rampant abuses of the past have been dramatically curbed, basic freedoms are generally observed, and the curse of militarism has, at least for the moment, been removed.

But the sustainability of this transition remains open to question. What progress has been made seems heavily dependent on the presence of a multinational armed force combined with constant pressures from international aid donors. Public frustrations are rising as hoped-for development fails to materialize, crime spreads, and political divisions grow. For a nation as poor as Haiti, with its lack of any democratic heritage, to develop sustainable democratic institutions would be an almost unprecedented development. Yet the situation of Haiti is not without some elements of hope. If democracy in Haiti is not nearly so certain as

Aristide's declaration would make it, neither is it so totally hopeless as it appeared in 1957.

Any assessment of Haiti's prospects for developing an effective and sustainable democratic system will be risky at best. To begin with, the task requires a clear definition of what it is we are talking about, what we mean by democracy in the context of Haitian realities.

Democracy is clearly more than simply having contested elections in which the votes are cast and counted relatively fairly and freely. Several additional criteria need to be emphasized. First, it must mean that the power of the state and its agents is limited, limited by law, by countervailing power, and by some measure of accountability. Next there must be broad freedom to criticize government policies, to organize opposition movements and groups, to compete effectively for public support, and to be protected from reprisals for engaging in such activities. Basic human freedoms must be guaranteed, and when a state violates such rights there must be a real possibility of redressing such violations. This necessitates an effective, credible, and independent justice system under which political "losers" as well as "winners" have rights. Finally, as James Madison argued in the tenth of the *Federalist Papers*, there must be protection for minority rights within the context of majority rule.

Haiti's history in these areas is dismal at best. Force has been the traditional arbiter of power, and the justice system has been little more than an instrument of protection for the privileged and of oppression for government opponents. Until this decade elections were rarely either open or honest. Death, imprisonment, or exile were the traditional options open to those who made unsuccessful efforts to challenge ruling regimes.

Other nations had done little to help the situation. The French colonial legacy provided a heritage of slavery, class and caste divisions, and warfare (James 1989). The United States treated Haiti as a pariah state until the Civil War and then began to compete with European powers for economic advantages and access to naval bases. Haitian elites tried to manipulate this rivalry to their own advantage, in the process further compromising national sovereignty and undermining whatever democratic prospects may have existed (Plummer 1988). The United States occupied Haiti from 1915 until 1934 and installed some of the trappings of democracy, but the heavy-handed mixture of paternalism and racism that characterized the intervention ensured that the results would be superficial at best (Schmidt 1971).

Internally, a series of factors worked against the development of democracy in Haiti. First and perhaps foremost was the nation's abysmal poverty. Long the poorest nation in the western hemisphere, conditions for Haitians deteriorated even further during the long (1957–1971) dictatorial regime of François (Papa Doc) Duvalier and again during the political turmoil that dominated from 1981 until 1994. From 1981 through 1990 Haiti's gross domestic product per capita fell by 20 percent, and from 1991 through 1995, despite a small increase in 1995, it fell by an additional 33 percent (UN Economic Commission for Latin America and the Caribbean 1995:48).

The nation's economic plight is compounded by two factors. First, Haiti is an ecological disaster, with arguably the worst pattern of soil erosion in the hemisphere. Second, the nascent tourism industry, so vital to much of the Caribbean, has been devastated by a combination of security concerns and the identification of Haiti with the problem of AIDS. About the only thing Haiti's economy has had going for it in the past decade has been remittances from those who managed to migrate.

Also hampering democratic development is the deep class/caste division between the minority French-speaking mulattoes, known as the "elite," and the overwhelmingly African descent, Creole-speaking majority. The gap reflects economic status, education, ingrained prejudices, and decades of frequently race-based political conflicts (Leyburn 1966:88–112). It has also contributed to what Mats Lundahl has characterized as "the predatory nature" of the Haitian state where "ruling politicians have acted on the assumption that the nation exists for the sake of the polity and not vice versa" (1989:2; also Trouillot 1994:46–51). Indeed, the state reinforced the gap, going so far as to issue separate classes of birth certificates, giving higher status to those born in urban areas than to the majority of poor peasants (Maguire 1995:12).

The final factor that blocked democratic development in Haiti was the military, the Forces Armées d'Haiti (FADH), a hybrid combination of police and military forces that not only dominated internal security but also acted as a virtual occupying force, suppressing dissent, engaging in massive corruption and criminal activities, and, in an effective alliance with intransigent elite sectors, ensuring that no meaningful reforms would take place. The military had declined in power notably during the reign of Papa Doc, who created as a counterweight the infamous "volunteers in national service," popularly known as the Tonton Macoutes. Originally fierce rivals, the military and the Macoutes eventually formed a working partnership in which both controlled and abused the bulk of the population (Maguire 1994).

The September 1994 U.S. intervention effectively removed the last of these obstacles and also curbed the power of the traditional elite. But it did little to restart the economy, nor could it deal with the lack of infrastructure, low educational levels, rampant malnutrition, and ecological disaster that undermine Haiti's development efforts. Perhaps most fundamentally, it could not provide Haiti with any of the traditions and civic values that are needed to undergird and consolidate democratic progress.

The lack of such traditions was clearly evident in the events leading up to the intervention. When Jean-Claude Duvalier fled into exile on February 7, 1986, there were hopes that Haiti might, at last, be able to create at least the semblance of a democratic government. A five-member National Government Council (CNG) was installed, headed by General Henri Namphy but including the founder of Haiti's Human Rights League. It ordered the dissolution of the Tonton Macoutes, freed all political prisoners, and allowed exiles to return (Abbott 1988:296–335). But corruption, political divisions, and continued violence soon undermined the popularity of the CNG. Within a year General Namphy was publicly declaring that "Haiti is not ready for democracy" (Abbott 1988:341).

Nevertheless, a new constitution was drafted and approved, and presidential elections were scheduled for late 1987 with thirty-five candidates competing. As election day approached political violence increased, largely instigated by former supporters of the Duvaliers but tolerated when not actively abetted by the military. This reached a crescendo on election day, November 27, and gave the regime an excuse to cancel the elections, rescheduling them under much more restrictive conditions for the following January. These "elections," boycotted by most major candidates and denounced by much of the international community, saw the military's choice, Leslie Manigat, win a poll boycotted by nearly 90 percent of Haiti's eligible voters. Manigat lasted only four months before, caught in the middle of rival military factions, he was overthrown and General Namphy returned to power (Plummer 1992:222–226). On September 18, 1988, he, too, was toppled by the military following growing popular protests against his rule.

The military regimes that followed Manigat found themselves internationally isolated, dealing with a steadily deteriorating economy, and confronting rising popular protests. The latter reflected both the growing power of a wide variety of grassroots nongovernmental organizations (NGOs), active in rural as well as urban areas, and the emerging leadership of an outspoken, antigovernment Roman Catholic priest, Father Jean-Bertrand Aristide. In March 1990 spreading disturbances forced the military to allow the appointment of an interim civilian government charged with holding new elections later that year. To the surprise of many observers, this regime managed to hold relatively peaceful and open elections in December. These produced an overwhelming victory (67 percent of the vote) for Aristide, who had left the priesthood to run for president.

Aristide's victory produced both hope and concern. Hope was generated because the elections had genuinely expressed popular will, bringing to power the nation's leading critic of the military and the elite establishment. For once Haiti had an administration that appeared genuinely dedicated to enhancing the welfare of the impoverished masses rather than to simply maintaining order while lining its own pockets. Concerns related to Aristide's alleged endorsement of political violence, to his outspoken praise for Fidel Castro and his tendency to blame the United States for much of Haiti's ills (Aristide 1990:11, 47, 59, 97, 104), to his total lack of administrative experience, and to the chaotic political party structure that had given a congressional majority to Aristide's opponents. In addition the military was still intact, suspicious, and determined to protect its privileges.

Inaugurated on February 7, 1991, Aristide was in power for less than eight months before being overthrown on September 30 by a military coup. The coup reflected a host of grievances, including allegations of the president's refusal to abide by constitutional requirements in his dealings with the Congress (much of which supported the coup); his complicity in or at least inability to prevent human rights abuses, including the murder in prison of a prominent opponent and Duvalier supporter, Roger Lafontant; his efforts to disband the oppressive local government structure dominated by corrupt *chefs de seccion*, all appointed by previous antidemocratic regimes and closely linked to the military; and his threats to begin taxing the rich elite (Taft-Morales 1993:4–8).

Aristide's ouster precipitated nearly three years of internal conflict and international pressures for his return. Haiti was subjected to steadily increasing international sanctions, further destroying the economy. The military and its Macoute allies, in turn, resorted to brutal force against those perceived as Aristide supporters, and repeated efforts to negotiate a political solution broke down. All of this further polarized Haitian society, and severely damaged the network of NGOs that had been developing. Finally, in September 1994, with U.S. armed intervention imminent, an agreement was reached providing for the peaceful insertion of an international (largely U.S.) military force under a UN mandate, the retirement of the military leadership, the end of international economic sanctions, and, implicitly but not explicitly, the return of President Aristide (Fauriol 1995:204–210).

At first it appeared that U.S. forces would coexist with the Haitian military, undertaking a program of extensive retraining and formally separating the military and the police but preserving the bulk of the armed forces. Incidents of brutality against the civilian population by the FADH, however, led to rapidly mounting political pressures to disarm the bulk of its forces. By October 15, when President Aristide returned, the FADH had lost its power and authority and the nation was essentially occupied by the international force (Caught in the middle 1994:36–40). When the military collapsed, so did the authority of the rural section chiefs, creating something of a vacuum of authority in rural areas but also opening up the possibility of progress toward democracy at the local level (Belsie 1994:6).

Aristide's politics had apparently modified during his years in exile. In any case, his power was effectively constrained by the presence of the international force and the nation's near total dependence on promised international assistance. Aristide had agreed that his term as president would end, as scheduled, on February 7, 1996, and that he would not be a candidate for immediate reelection. A feared a wave of popular vengeance against those associated with the previous regime largely failed to materialize, a new police force was created and the FADH disbanded, and a series of elections were held with varying degrees of success. On February 7, 1996, he turned over the presidency to an elected successor, Rene Preval.

In the period from President Aristide's return till the start of 1997 a host of developments have shaped and reshaped the Haitian political landscape. Many of these seem promising for the future of that nation's democratic development; others remain the basis for serious concern. In order to understand the extent to which Haiti has been able to overcome its profoundly antidemocratic political heritage and to evaluate its prospects for maintaining and consolidating a democratic political system, it is necessary to examine both positive and negative trends and to focus on the critical uncertainties of the next few years.

There is no shortage of positive developments, especially when they are judged against the heritage of the past. Perhaps most dramatic, the military has been, for all practical purposes, eliminated, the Tonton Macoutes have disappeared, and the apparatus of state repression, dominant for decades, no longer exists. A new civilian police force has been created with extensive international funding and training (Neild 1995). Though it was deemed necessary for some time to incorporate members of the FADH into an interim police force, they had been largely removed by the end of 1996. For the first time in recent memory, those accused by the state have the right to a public trial with at least the possibility of an effective defense, and torture as an instrument of state policy has ended.

In another break with tradition, political opponents, many of whom had actively collaborated with the military dictatorship, remain free, and in some cases continue to engage in politics. While much of the old military leadership found it prudent to leave the country in the weeks following the intervention, forced political exile has not been an instrument of official policy. The fact that there has been no major outbreak of revenge attacks and no systematic effort to use the resources of the state to deprive supporters of the previous regime of their liberty or property is a clear step forward. President Aristide, himself, took the lead in promoting this climate, repeatedly urging national reconciliation and discouraging attempts at exacting vengeance (Schulz 1996:5).

Combined with this has been a general climate of press and media freedom. Criticism of the government has been constant. In addition basic freedoms of religion and assembly have been respected. Labor strikes are increasingly frequent, even including labor actions by government employees. Haitians have never had greater freedom to form political organizations, recruit members, and pursue goals than they have had for the past two years. Grassroots organizations and other NGOs have begun to revive, although they continue to suffer the effects of the repression of the early 1990s. The rural poor are showing signs of a growing interest and involvement in politics (Maguire 1995:20–27). Church and other international charitable organizations have also increased programs, many of which are aimed at promoting popular organizations and leadership.

In June 1995 Haiti held elections for Congress and for local officials. These elections were controversial and far from perfect, but in laying the foundation for elected local government they represented yet another fundamental break with the past. No longer are local officials simply allies of a predatory central government or allies of a repressive military apparatus. They now come from the local population, have at least some degree of responsibility to that population, and have elements of real authority. The electoral process left much to be desired, but the change in the nature of local authority is at least potentially salutary.

Finally, Haiti has marshaled more international support in the past two years than at any previous time in its history. This has been facilitated by the fact that international organizations and other donor groups are now able to operate in Haiti without fear of repression or the necessity of paying endless bribes to public officials. From October 1994 through December 1995, government and multilateral organizations disbursed aid to Haiti totaling $534 million. This came from a wide variety of donors, including the Inter-American Development Bank, the World Bank, and the European Economic Community (EEC), as well as from the governments of the United States, France, Canada, Japan, and many other nations. This total does not include major amounts contributed by private NGOs, notably church-related groups. Haiti has also received massive technical assistance, on everything from holding elections to rural health. The assistance in training new police forces has already been mentioned, but other aspects of the Ministry of Justice have also benefited significantly (Haiti: Radio reports 1996). The continued presence of the UN force in Haiti has also been of great importance in maintaining a level of public order and security. The mandate for this force has been extended twice, most recently on December 5, 1996, for a period through May 1997.

Unfortunately, some negative aspects are also quite apparent. Common crime has risen alarmingly over the past two years. Gangs attack cars, assault merchants, and pillage the pitiful possessions of the poor, while the police all too often seem unable to respond (Haiti: Gangsters attack vehicles 1996). This has kept public confidence in the new police at a low level and has contributed to the rise of vigilante-type violence, especially in the poorest slums of the capital. The activity of criminal gangs inhibits business, discourages tourism, and leads many to long for a return to a more authoritarian style of government.

Though Haiti's army has been disbanded, this does not mean that there is no danger of a return to government by force. Ex-members of the FADH have been accused of involvement in numerous plots against the current government. There is even evidence of plotting within the president's own guard, which in September 1996 led to increased U.S. involvement in presidential security (Haiti: Under protection 1996:A8).

The situation is made worse by the general weakness of the entire administration of justice system. This is especially true when cases of human rights violations are involved. As late as March 1996 the Haitian National Police had demonstrated neither the will nor the capability to conduct a serious investigation of cases, regardless of whether they occurred under the military or the restored civilian governments (U.S. General Accounting Office 1996:14–15). Even when alleged perpetrators are apprehended, the courts are frequently unable to conduct fair or effective trials. Aristide's justice minister reportedly declared that only a third of the judges were capable, with perhaps another third trainable (Haiti: Not quite normal 1996:38). An international consultant noted that "most judges and prosecutors are poorly trained and lack motivation" then added: "Most Haitians view lawyers, judges—virtually anyone connected with the justice system—with well deserved scorn and contempt. People will avoid contact with the system unless it is the last resort" (National Coalition for Haitian Refugees 1995:3). As a result justice functions sporadically, if at all. In September 1996 Human Rights Watch reported that in the major coastal town of Gonaives no criminal court sessions had been held since 1991 (Human Rights Watch Americas Report 1996:24).

Not only has the Haitian government made little progress in investigating crimes committed under the military dictatorship, but it has also been increasingly criticized for not investigating attacks on opposition politicians in the postintervention period (Human Rights Watch Americas Report 1996:16–27; International Republican Institute 1995:Section 6). Though political freedom is clearly greater then before, the persistence of such reports is disturbing and, if not addressed, the situation could easily become a major obstacle to democratic consolidation.

If the government has its shortcomings, so too does the political opposition. Haiti has no tradition of a responsible opposition that plays within the rules of the system, and the current crop of opposition politicians has done little to change this image. The immediate reaction of many to problems in recent elections was to boycott the entire process and to focus their efforts on gaining support from external actors. Anthony Maingot, a leading analyst of Haitian political behavior, has attributed much of that nation's political problems to a political culture that emphasizes individualism, discourages lasting political alliances, and undermines efforts to cooperate for national goals (1994a:2; 1994b:204–205, 223–224; 1996:151–155). Others blame the corrupting heritage of the Duvalier era, the persistence of foreign intervention in Haitian politics, or the traditional alienation of the masses from the political process. Whatever the root causes, it is clear that the foundations of Haitian political culture derive from anything but democratic sources and that it will be extraordinarily difficult for the current generation of political leadership to fully overcome this heritage.

Though Haiti has held elections—first, in June 1995, for legislative and municipal officials and then, on December 17, 1995, for president—these elections have been marred by numerous problems, including widespread charges of political favoritism by the government-controlled Provisional Election Commission (International Republican Institute 1995:Sections 1, 10). Though conditions were somewhat better in December than in June the presidential elections also saw a significant drop in voter participation, something that does not bode well for the future of the democratic process.

As previously noted, Haiti has very limited resources, either economic or human, available for its effort to construct democratic structures. The economy has remained profoundly depressed over the past two years. The decline of the previous decade has been halted but not effectively reversed. All too much of what resources are available remain concentrated in the diaspora, those Haitians who fled the country in preceding decades, often settling in the United States and Canada or securing employment with a variety of international organizations. Neither they nor their economic resources have returned to Haiti in anything like the hoped-for amounts, and there is little reason to expect this pattern to change in the near future.

Foreign governments have contributed significantly to efforts to help rebuild Haiti's economy and support its democratic transition, but the amounts of assistance made available have been far less than those originally pledged and these in turn were, not surprisingly, well below Haitian expectations. In over two years, less than half of the $1.2 billion pledged for reconstruction has been delivered. Much of this is attributable to United States policies that have held up multilateral as well as bilateral assistance. This reflects a general tightening of the U.S. budget combined with extremely low levels of public support for foreign aid. It also reflects Republican suspicions of the economic and political orientation of the Aristide and Preval governments, suspicions that became much more significant following the January 1995 Republican congressional victories. Finally, it derives from the Clinton administration's efforts to pressure Haiti in adopting economic reforms, especially those relating to privatization (Schulz 1996:19–25; Farah 1996:16).

There is growing reason to doubt the durability and depth of international commitments to Haiti. The December 1996 struggle to extend the UN forces mandate for another six months underscores this reality. It is worth noting that when it was finally approved, this extension was specified to be a "final period" (Mader 1996). With rising concerns in other parts of the world, declining aid budgets in the United States, Canada, and elsewhere, and a tendency to assume that short-range stability is the most that can realistically be expected in Haiti, aid levels are likely to continue to decline in coming years. There is some hope that private investment will make up for this shortfall, but to date little evidence to support such assumptions.

Finally, hope, like most other things, is a scarce and fragile resource in Haiti. The failure to restart the economy is generating growing skepticism and frustration. Many of those with the energy and contacts are beginning again to seek opportunities to migrate. Declining levels of electoral participation are another sign of rising apathy and even despair, attitudes that are the exact opposite of those conducive to democratic consolidation.

It is still too early to make definitive judgments about the long-range prospects for democracy in Haiti. As Robert Pastor has noted: "The current situation in Haiti has an artificial quality due to the presence of U.N. forces" (1995:10). Furthermore, as Anthony Bryan of the North-South Center has written: "The road map to a democratic tradition in Haiti is by no means precise" (1995:65). The current president, Rene Preval, has demonstrated a pragmatic and serious approach to constructing democracy in Haiti and in the process has proved far more independent of former-president Aristide than many had expected (Robbins 1996:8; Farah 1996:16). But he has also encountered mounting obstacles both at home and abroad. What can be said is that, for now at least, democracy is still alive in Haiti.

Keeping it alive will depend on several factors. There will have to be some economic improvement; even if limited and halting, as is probable, it must be enough to nourish the hope of a better future for Haiti's next generation. At the same time the outside world needs to set realistic expectations and not adopt an all-or-nothing approach to the question of democracy in Haiti. Aid donors and external analysts of Haitian events have an obligation to be critical but not overly discriminating; they must avoid the temptation to see any individual failure as part of an inevitable deluge that will drown the nation's democratic prospects. Problems, failures, and frustrations are inevitable, but they do not mean that the process itself is doomed to failure. Haiti must be judged in its own context, within the limitations imposed by its past heritage and present condition, not against some theoretical model for democratic transitions (Merrill 1996:31–52).

Haiti will need prolonged significant international support. Though Anthony Bryan's declaration that "Haiti's future now depends almost completely on outsiders" may be overstated, it underscores the extent to which, without effective external support, Haiti's prospects are bleak indeed (1995:69). This does not necessarily mean prolonged high levels of financial contributions, but it does mean preferential access to credit, technical assistance, and public support for Haiti's democratic leaders. In one sense, at least, international support seems relatively assured. The world community will clearly not support or even tolerate a return to predatory, authoritarian politics of the past. Any attempt to do so would ensure economic disaster, a lesson that even the most recalcitrant of Haiti's elite has probably absorbed during this decade.

Patience, understanding, and international support are all vital, but the ultimate responsibility for democracy rests with the Haitians themselves, most notably with those who aspire to political leadership. It is they who must demonstrate an ability to break with the traditional political culture and, at least on some occasions, to subordinate short-range personal to long-range national interests. They must accept that in today's world only power limited by the rule of law can truly be effective. Their task is monumental, and based on past precedents the odds would seem to be against them. But the situation is by no means without hope. And hope, not optimism, is perhaps as much as can be reasonably expected when trying to discern the future of democracy in Haiti.

Bibliography

Abbott, Elizabeth. 1988. *Haiti: The Duvaliers and Their Legacy.* New York: McGraw Hill.

Aristide, Jean-Bertrand. 1990. *In the Parish of the Poor: Writings from Haiti.* Maryknoll, N.Y.: Orbis Books.

Belsie, Laurent. 1994. Their backing gone, Haiti's rural chiefs flee. *Christian Science Monitor* (October 13):6.

Bryan, Anthony T. 1995. Haiti: Kick starting the economy. *Current History* 94:65–70.

Caught in the middle. 1994. *Newsweek* (October 10):36–40.

Farah, Douglas. 1996. When a "twin" goes it alone. *Washington Post National Weekly Edition* (August 19–25):16.

Fauriol, George A., ed. 1995. *Haitian Frustrations: Dilemmas for U.S. Policy.* Washington, D.C.: Center for Strategic and International Studies.

Haiti: Gangsters attack vehicles, pedestrians along roads. 1996. Port-au-Prince Radio Metropole. Translation published by Foreign Broadcast Information Service (FBIS), December 16, 1996.

Haiti: Not quite normal. 1996. *The Economist* (July 27):38.

Haiti: Radio reports on international aid received by Haiti. 1996. Port-au-Prince FM Radio in Creole, November 29. Translation produced by Foreign Broadcast Information Service (FBIS), Daily Report, December 4, 1996.

Haiti: Under protection. 1996. *The Economist* (September 21):47.

Human Rights Watch Americas Report. 1996. *Haiti: Thirst for Justice.* New York: Human Rights Watch. September.

International Republican Institute. 1995. *Haiti: Election Observation Report, December 17, 1995.* Washington: International Republican Institute, Sections 1, 6, 10.

James, C. L. R. 1989. *The Black Jacobins: Toussaint L'Overture and the San Domingo Revolution.* 2nd ed. New York: Vintage.

Klarreich, Kathie. 1994. Back in Haiti, Aristide calls for new democratic order. *Christian Science Monitor* (October 17):1.

Leyburn, James G. 1966. *The Haitian People.* 2nd ed. New Haven: Yale University Press.

Lundahl, Mats. 1989. History as an obstacle to change: The case of Haiti. *Journal of International Studies and World Affairs* 31:1–21.

Mader, Jan. 1996. Associated Press, December 5.

Maguire, Robert E. 1995. Bootstrap politics: Elections and Haiti's new public officials. Paper prepared for the Briefing Paper Series of the Johns Hopkins–Georgetown Haiti Project, November.

———. 1994. Haiti: State terror in mufti. *Caribbean Affairs* 7:78–95.

Maingot, Anthony. 1996. Haiti: Four old and two new hypotheses. In *Constructing Democratic Governance: Latin America and the Caribbean in the 1990s* (Jorge I. Dominguez and Abraham F. Lowenthal, eds.), part 4, 135–158. Baltimore: Johns Hopkins University Press.

———. 1994a. *Grasping the Nettle: A National Liberation Option for Haiti.* Miami, Fla.: North-South Center, North-South Agenda Papers #6, March.

———. 1994b. *The United States and the Caribbean.* Boulder: Westview Press.

Merrill, John. (1996). Vodou and political reform in Haiti: Some lessons for the international community. *The Fletcher Forum of World Affairs* 20:31–52.

National Coalition for Haitian Refugees. 1995. *No Greater Priority: Judicial Reform in Haiti.* New York: National Coalition for Haitian Refugees.

Neild, Rachel. 1995. *Policing Haiti: Preliminary Assessment of the New Civilian Security Force.* Washington, D.C.: Washington Office on Latin America.

Pastor, Robert. 1995. The status of Haiti's democratic transition. Prepared statement of Dr. Robert Pastor, director, Latin American Program, the Carter Center, for the Subcommittee on Western Hemisphere Affairs, Committee on International Relations, U.S. House of Representatives. October 12.

Plummer, Brenda Gayle. 1992. *Haiti and the United States.* Athens: Georgia University Press.

_____. 1988. *Haiti and the Great Powers, 1902–1915.* Baton Rouge: Louisiana State University Press.

Robbins, Carla Anne. 1996. Haiti tastes freedom, but efforts to rebuild run into roadblocks. *Wall Street Journal* (October 30):A8.

Schmidt, Hans. 1971. *The United States Occupation of Haiti, 1915–1934.* New Brunswick, N.J.: Rutgers University Press.

Schulz, Donald E. 1996. *Wither Haiti?* Carlisle, Pa.: U.S. Army War College, Strategic Studies Institute.

Taft-Morales, Maureen. 1993. *Haiti: Background to the Overthrow of President Aristide.* Washington, D.C.: Congressional Research Service, Library of Congress. (October 22). CRS 4–8.

Trouillot, Michel-Rolph. 1994. Haiti's nightmare and the lessons of history. *NACLA Report on the Americas* 27:4,46–51.

_____. 1986. *Les Racines Historiques de L'etat Duvalierien.* Port-au-Prince: Editions Deschamps.

UN Economic Commission for Latin America and the Caribbean. 1996. *Preliminary Overview of the Latin American and Caribbean Economy, 1995.* Santiago, Chile: United Nations Economic Commission for Latin America and the Caribbean.

U.S. General Accounting Office. 1996. *Haiti: U.S. Assistance for the Electoral Process.* GAO/NSIAD–96–147. July).

Chapter Thirteen

The Dilemmas of Democracy in the Dominican Republic: A Paradigm for All of Latin America?

HOWARD J. WIARDA

The Dominican Republic has rather consistently over the years ranked in the lower third of the Latin American countries on the Fitzgibbon-Johnson-Kelly five-year surveys of democracy. It is usually grouped with the smaller, less institutionalized countries of South America (Bolivia, Ecuador, Paraguay, Peru) and Central America (El Salvador, Guatemala, Honduras, Nicaragua) where democracy is "problematic" or where there have been repeated alternations between wobbly democratic regimes and often similarly unstable authoritarian ones.

My own assessment is that there is greater freedom and stronger democracy in the Dominican Republic than the periodic surveys have indicated. I attribute the disjuncture between the survey results and my own views to the facts that the democracy surveys call for a level of detailed and specific knowledge on the part of the Latin American experts polled that few of them have about each individual country and that in the absence of very specific or current knowledge about a particular country, some respondents rely on the country's past history and general reputation in framing their evaluations.

Be that as it may, it *is* clear that the Dominican Republic, and *almost all the other Latin American countries*, lie at some intermediate points on the authoritarian-democracy spectrum. That is, most of these are countries that are partly democratic but not fully so. They rank lower than the United States or western or central Europe on virtually every index of democratization but considerably above most of the African countries and those of the Islamic world. The question we pose here is: Why? Why after some 175 years of independent life and considerable economic, social, and political development are the countries of Latin America still only partially and incompletely democratic? Why do we still have guided democracy, controlled democracy, "tutelary democracy" (Oropeza 1983), "delegated democracy" (O'Donnell 1994:55–69), or "Rousseauism democracy" (Wiarda 1995)—democracy with adjectives instead of the real, purer thing?

This chapter, mainly in the realm of speculation and as a set of suggestions for further study, seeks to provide some at least partial answers to those questions. It uses the Dominican Republic and its history, fears, and developmental experiences as a paradigm for the rest of Latin America. For even with all its many differences from other countries, the Dominican Republic is probably more typical, even representative, of the rest of Latin America than we, or the other countries, might suspect. I wish here to use the Dominican experience as a metaphor, with appropriate reservations and allowances for national differences, for what ails democracy in *all* of Latin America.

Political Culture and the Colonial Past

The Dominican Republic was the first country in the Americas to feel the imprint of Spanish colonialism. All the experiments in colonial administration later used throughout the Americas were first tried out on Hispaniola. The colony had a two-class system reinforced by racial criteria, a church that served as an arm of the state in subduing the indigenous population, a top-down and authoritarian political system reaching from king to captain-general to local *hacendado*, an exploitative, semifeudal, milk-cow economic system based on plantation agriculture and slavery, and similarly rigid top-down, educational and legal systems. *All* the main features of a destructive, exploitative Spanish colonial system were present. Yet ironically it is this system of an ordered, hierarchical, stable, authoritarian, comparatively prosperous society that Dominicans would later look back to, from an even lower existence, as their ideal, the high point of their history. Elsewhere (1993) I have termed this the "Hapsburgian model."

For after 1550, with the greater attractiveness of the lands, precious metals, and indigenous populations to be enslaved of other colonial territories, Hispaniola was all but abandoned by the Spanish Crown. Its population declined, its economy reverted to a more primitive existence, its colonial institutions fell into neglect, and it suffered as the ignored, tail end of the vast Spanish colonial empire. The result for the later Dominican Republic was the worst of all possible worlds: Because of the rapacious Spanish colonial system, it had absolutely no training in democratic self-government; because of its abandonment by the Crown, it lacked even the institutions of colonial government that might have eased and provided a stable transition to independence; and its ideal remained the ordered, stable, authoritarian, hierarchical, relatively prosperous colony of 1492–1550—hardly a democratic model.

The Independence Period

After independence things went from bad to worse in the Dominican Republic. On the one side were important factions that wished to restore the Spanish system, the Hapsburgian model, to reunite with Spain, or to find another outside and powerful "protector" like France or the United States. On the other side were republicans, who had such an idealized view of independence that their visions had no basis in Dominican realities and whose governments usually collapsed into confusion and anarchy after only a few months in power. Meanwhile, only a few weeks after the declaration of independence in 1821, armies made up of former slaves from next-door Haiti invaded the country, destroying farms, burning and looting, and eliminating the few viable institutions still left over from colonial times. The Haitian occupation lasted from 1822 until 1844; thereafter and throughout the rest of the nineteenth century, Haiti's assaults on the Spanish-speaking part of the island were virtually continuous, preventing renewed economic development, discouraging immigration and investments, keeping the country from stabilizing politically or developing functioning institutions of its own, and renewing the now often-desperate calls for a foreign protector.

While the rest of Latin America did not in its early decades of independence have to contend with anything comparable to the repeated Haitian invasions, it did have comparable problems. These included the legacy of a colonial system that provided no training in self-government or democracy, rigid and authoritarian institutions and practices left over from colonial days, a vast and frequently anarchic interior where the hand of the central government reached at best unevenly, large indigenous populations only weakly (if at all) integrated into national life, and a weak institutional and associational life (now called "civil society") that was incapable of holding society together, which frequently resulted in the newly independent countries disintegrating still further (Sarmiento 1990).

Faced with such overwhelming difficulties, what were these poorly and woefully underinstitutionalized Latin American countries to do? They wrote liberal and republican laws and constitutions even while clinging to authoritarian institutions and emergency laws as the best hope against chaos. They supported separation of powers and at the same time realistically recognized the need for a powerful executive and strongman rule. They sought to reduce the power of some of the corporate interests (such as the church) left over from colonial days but then created larger armies to help fill the institutional void. Much like today, the liberal laws, constitutions, and facade democratic institutions provided respectable legitimacy and were for the outside world to admire and applaud; but the realities of governing underinstitutionalized, often chaotic, strife-torn countries call for a pragmatic recognition of harsher realities and the use of measures that were not consistently democratic.

In the Dominican Republic another phenomenon was at work in the nineteenth century—and one not entirely unknown in the rest of Latin America. The Dominicans discovered that their democratic interludes were not only brief but also inefficient, chaotic, and productive mainly of disorder. In contrast their strong and authoritarian regimes—those of Pedro Santana, Buenaventura Báez, and eventually Ulises Heureaux (1882–1899)—not only were more stable but also brought foreign investment, infrastructure growth (highways, railroads, port facilities, and so on), and economic development. Faced with a choice between a weak, wobbly, chaotic, and short-lived democratic government and a strong regime, often authoritarian, that brought stability and prosperity (and also warded off Haiti's advances), most Dominicans preferred the latter—as long as it stayed within acceptable bounds of behavior and did not become, in Aristotelian or Thomistic terms, an unacceptable tyranny.

In the regimes of Porfirio Díaz in Mexico, Juan Vicente Gómez in Venezuela, and many others during these same time periods, one can find both comparable, strong-arm but development-oriented regimes *and* the justification for them (Vallenilla Lanz 1920). In the U.S. Marine occupation of the Dominican Republic of 1916–1924, incidentally, one can find similar features: a regime that was unacceptable in some quarters on nationalistic grounds but that was very much like the order-and-progress dictators of the nineteenth century.

The regime of Rafael L. Trujillo, 1930–1961, was a continuation, perhaps a culmination, of this tradition. Trujillo ruled as an authoritarian, and often a bloody one. He was in the long tradition of Dominican and Latin American "Caesars": strongmen or caudillos who used authoritarian techniques to hold their underinstitutionalized countries together. But Trujillo did not rule by blood and authoritarianism alone; he was also a developer like Heureaux, Díaz, Gómez, Vargas, Caría Andino, Somoza the elder, Ubico, and others who brought much-needed economic growth, infrastructure development (water supplies, highways, public buildings, electrification, port facilities, and so on) and modernization (however perverted by corruption and bloody reprisals) to his country. Eventually Trujillo's excesses went beyond the bounds of often-permissive Dominican (and Latin American) strong-arm rule; his regime became one of full-fledged tyranny, thus justifying resistance to it. When that fateful transition occurred, the opposition to Trujillo mounted, and he was repudiated and eventually assassinated (Wiarda 1970).

The Transitions to Democracy and the Three Incarnations of Joaquín Balaguer

Almost everyone who has written about the Dominican Republic in the last thirty-five years (myself included) has concentrated on the country's transition to democracy, the emergence of new social and political groups and movements, the holding of regular elections, and the change process. All these aspects are in fact true and have occurred. But the real story in the Dominican Republic for over three decades may well be not so much the changes that have taken place but the continuities, the persistence of more traditional ways of doing things, or the complex blends, fusions, and overlaps of traditional and modern, of authoritarianism and democracy.

No one personifies these blends, or the Dominicans' continuing ambivalence about democracy, better than longtime president Joaquín Balaguer. In the early years of the post-Trujillo transition it appeared that Juan Bosch, the democratic caudillo, would be the dominant force. But in the long run it turned out that Balaguer was the most important political figure. Indeed, the period 1960–1996, comparable in length to the political rules of Fidel Castro or Alfredo Stroessner, is now routinely referred to as the "Era of Balaguer."

But I wish here to make an ever stronger and perhaps more controversial case. Recognizing that all analogies are imperfect as well as the problems of generalizing from a single case, I want to suggest that Balaguer's long political career, from the 1930s to the 1990s, personifies and at some level is a metaphor for *all* of Latin America's ambivalence toward, conflict over, and (even now) limited and partial commitment to political democracy. For it is clear, despite the heartening transitions to democracy in Latin America over the last two decades, that most of these are still incomplete transitions, partial democracies, (sometimes) facade democracies, "democracies" for the outside world and domestic voters to applaud, unimplemented or only partially implemented democracies, limited democracies. Whether one is speaking of Argentina, Bolivia, Brazil, Colombia, Central America, Mexico, Paraguay, Peru, Venezuela, or even Chile, one has to be struck these days by how fragile, incomplete, and precarious democracy is in all these countries.

Balaguer's career is instructive not only because he exemplifies the general Latin American ambivalence about democracy but because his long career spans just about every political movement that Latin America has experienced in the last sixty-five years. He is almost the personification of the "living museum" concept that Charles Anderson (1967) used to characterize Latin America. Let us review Balaguer's career in its three incarnations: from authoritarianism and state corporatism to more open forms of corporatism coupled with facade democracy to a more pluralist and freer but still limited democracy.

First, as a general comment, it needs to be said that Balaguer is a master at manipulative, Machiavellian politics. One need not admire all his policies (I do not) to recognize that he is one of the shrewdest politicians of all time, in any country. Balaguer has been inaugurated president of the Dominican Republic on seven occasions (thus surpassing the previous "leaders," Arnulfo Arias of Panama and José M. Velasco Ibarra of Ecuador), he is a master politician who has not only dominated Dominican national life for over thirty years but forces all other politicians to react to *his* moves and agenda, and he runs circles around all other political groups and movements in the Dominican Republic as well as the U.S. embassy.

Balaguer is a godfather, a patronage politician to end all patronage politicians, a combination of Mayor Richard Daley (the elder) of Chicago and the Mexican Institutional Revolutionary Party (PRI) (Atkins 1981).

This is not intended as a biography of Balaguer, but we need to know enough of his background to understand his later political career. He was born in Navarete, a suburb of Santiago in the conservative Cibao, along one of the historic Haitian invasion routes where considerations of race and class were always important and interrelated. His family tradition was strongly Catholic and devout, and the young Balaguer was an excellent student, excelling in the traditional Latin American secondary and university specializations of literature, philosophy, oratory, and law. There is a pattern in this early history: conservative, Catholic, anti-Haitian, and focused on law, philosophy, oratory, and the Roman conception of a hierarchical, centralized, and functionally representative state.

Balaguer joined the Dominican foreign service in the early 1930s; his early postings were to Madrid, Paris, and Colombia. All of these were hotbeds of Catholic, authoritarian, corporatist politics of the 1930s and 1940s, of the Falange in Spain, the *Action Française* in France, and of conservative Laureano Gómez in Colombia. Balaguer was caught up in these movements while at the same time admiring the oratory of their chief spokesmen.

Returning to the Dominican Republic, he occupied a number of low-level government positions where his intellectual acumen and administrative capacities attracted the attention of dictator Trujillo. Balaguer became an admirer of Trujillo's undoubted leadership qualities and was part of a group of Dominican intellectuals and policy advisers who admired Spain, Franco, and his philosophies of *Hispanismo*, including its stress on authority, hierarchy, discipline, traditional Catholicism, and the corporatist organization of society. Indeed, it was Balaguer and his colleagues who first gave the shrewd but not well-educated Trujillo a political ideology (which he had lacked before) stressing these same themes, who wrote the pamphlets and speeches on state corporation that appeared under the dictator's name, who drafted the corporatist labor law of 1952 and other major pieces of legislation, and who helped convert the Trujillo regime from a rough-and-ready caudillismo to a more sophisticated and modern dictatorship.

This was Balaguer's first political incarnation, as a 1930s and 1940s–style authoritarian and corporatist. In these respects, he was not very different from a whole host of Latin American leaders and movements of that same time period: Perón, Vargas, Ibáñez, and so on. Balaguer went on in the 1950s to become a cabinet minister, vice president, and eventually president of the country in 1960 when the incumbent (Trujillo's brother) resigned.

Balaguer tried to bridge the transition from the Trujillo to the post-Trujillo regime after the dictator was assassinated in May 1961. But the anti-Trujillo sentiment then sweeping the country was too strong, and in January 1962 he was forced to leave office, pushed by both domestic and U.S. pressures. He settled in exile in the United States, from which he watched the election of Bosch in 1962, the overthrow of democracy in 1963, and the buildup to revolution, civil war, and U.S. military intervention in 1965. Ironically, after having helped oust him from power in 1962, it was the United States that brought Balaguer back to the Dominican Republic in 1965 and helped him win the presidential elections of 1966, defeating Bosch and the Democratic Revolutionary Party (PRD).

Thereupon began Balaguer's second incarnation. Recognizing that the old Trujillo-style authoritarianism verging on totalitarianism would no longer do and that to compete with Bosch and the PRD in the new democratic climate he would need a similarly mass-based political party, Balaguer created a political machine called the Reformist Party (PR). The PR was used as an instrument to rally Balaguer's supporters and to help him reacquire power, but it was generally devoid of program or ideology. Rather, it was a personalistic apparatus that, after Balaguer's election and then reelection (without opposition in 1970 and again in 1974) was used mainly as a vast national patronage agency doling out toys to children, charity to the indigent, peso notes to voters, sewing machines to widows, land titles (often worthless) to peasants, and vast public works projects to "the deserving." Bowing to realities and the new times, Balaguer was careful all during this "*docenio*" to rule constitutionally, legally, with regular "elections" (which were really ratifications of Balaguer's continuation in office), and through a "party" system.

Recall that this period, from the mid–1960s through the late–1970s, was the high point of military authoritarianism or, as it was often called, bureaucratic-authoritarianism, and corporatism throughout Latin America (Malloy 1977; O'-Donnell 1973; Wiarda 1981, 1973:206–235). At least fourteen, depending on how it is measured perhaps seventeen, of the twenty Latin American countries were under authoritarian rule. The Dominican Republic was not immune to these currents—except that Balaguer was more skillful at hiding his authoritarianism than were other military regimes and more clever at manipulating it. He allowed repressive military and police factions to beat up trade union, peasant, and PRD leaders, even while ascribing the excesses to "uncontrollable forces" and never allowing the repression to be connected to him personally. He allowed cronies to engage in massive corruption, meanwhile avoiding being tainted himself and holding past involvement in corruption as a club against them. He regularly violated freedom of the press, of speech, of assembly, of association as well as habeas corpus, but he nevertheless stayed within a constitutional facade that he called "true democracy."

Meanwhile, through patronage and vast public works programs, he built up a huge following that owed their jobs, livelihoods, and well-being directly to him (the late 1960s and early 1970s—before the 1973 oil crisis—saw yearly economic growth rates of 6, 7, and 8 percent in the Dominican Republic: the "Balaguer miracle," it was called). This was an improvement over Trujillo's megalomania and bloody rule, but it was a long ways from democracy. Nevertheless, in this second incarnation Balaguer could call his rule "constitutional," and at some levels it was (Kryzanek 1977:83–103).

In 1978, in a period of falling sugar prices, Balaguer's popularity waned, and he faced a serious opposition candidate from the PRD. When early returns showed him trailing, Balaguer's henchmen responded by shutting down the vote count. Only massive internal protests as well as protests from the international community forced the regime to resume the electoral tabulation, which resulted in Balaguer losing. From 1978 until 1986 the PRD was back in power.

At this stage Balaguer's third incarnation as a political leader and his presiding over a transition to a new form of "democracy" began. Ever a realist and maneuverer, Balaguer recognized he needed to go a step further toward democracy than in his previous incarnations. Indeed, to this point each of his incarnations had involved a creative but usually halting and often reluctant step, reflecting new realities, toward democracy and pluralism. Acknowledging that he needed more in the democratic 1980s than just an old-fashioned, PRI-like political machine, Balaguer now moved to create a merger between his PR and the small but respectable Revolutionary Social Christian Party (PRSC). The PRSC had a Christian Democratic ideology; it had a progressive but moderate program; it had ancillary groups for organized labor, peasants, women, youth, and businessmen; and it had ties to the money, expertise, and organization of the Christian Democratic "internationale."

Hence in one fell swoop the skillful Balaguer had put together a new organization, now called the *Partido Reformista Social Cristiano* (PRSC), which consisted of his old political machine—still skillful at patronage and electoral manipulation—and the moderation and respectability of the Revolutionary Social Christian Party. With this new coalition, Balaguer returned to office in 1986 and served as president for another ten years, making a total of twenty-four in the presidency, winning the elections of 1986, 1990, and 1994—although the latter two were often considered fraudulent victories.

In 1996, at the age of eighty-nine, blind, enfeebled, unable to walk without assistance but still with a razor-sharp political mind, Balaguer left office—but not power. Indeed, one can say that for him the current situation represents still another, or fourth, incarnation. For even though he was constitutionally prohibited from seeking still another term, by throwing his support in a runoff election to the eventual winner, Leonel Fernández, Balaguer maximized his power. Fernández's party has only minuscule support in the Congress; he cannot get any of his legislation passed without the approval of Balaguer's legislative bloc. Even out of office, Balaguer thus retains a hammerlock on the political process through his ability to exercise veto power over all legislation.

Summing Up: Broader Implications

The 1990 and 1994 Dominican elections were marred by such fraud that Dominicans were ashamed, and the raft of international observers that descended on the country to oversee the process denounced them. Hence in 1996 the elections were squeaky clean, pronounced by one and all to fair, honest, transparent, and democratic. For some, a clean *process* is enough; but for Dominicans the more important questions are still unanswered. Let us review the issues here and briefly summarize the broader Latin American implications.

First, though the electoral process was clean, the Dominican Republic (and most of Latin America) still has a vast problem of ungovernability. The country still lacks institutions, infrastructure, a web of associational life, and a civil society capable of knitting the society together, enabling it to modernize, filling the organizational void, and avoiding chaos. The elections were *"para que los Americanos puedan ver* [for North Americans to see, that is, window dressing]," but the harder problems of governing and policy implementation, of making up for what Dominicans call their *"falta de civilización* [lacking civilization]," must still be faced.

Second, though a generational shift has not yet occurred from the aging, infirm Balaguer to a new set of leaders, many thoughtful Dominicans are not sure that the new leaders coming up are capable of filling Balaguer's gigantic shoes. Can they control the military and police the way Balaguer did, can they manage a vast patronage system as he did, can they make the wheels of government turn as he did, can they hold the ever-present and often intrusive U.S. embassy at bay the way he did, can they maneuver and manipulate to get things done in this woefully underinstitutionalized nation as he did? Dominicans recognize that it was time for a political change, but they are very apprehensive about the future.

The third issue has to do with the nature of elections themselves, particularly those of 1996. Fair elections are based on Lockean, individualistic, Jeffersonian, one-person-one-vote principles. But the Dominican Republic has historically been based on principles that are organic, integralist, corporatist, Rousseauian. It opts for this in part for historical and cultural reasons ("it has always been this way") but also for very practical reasons. For an organic, integralist, corporatist society under strong leadership like Balaguer's helps fill the organizational and associational void that has long plagued Latin America. It enables the hemisphere to give the appearance of democracy while also enabling it to govern itself through some often decidedly undemocratic means (emergency laws, decrees, "rules of exception"). But now, to satisfy both domestic and international pressures, the Dominican Republic—and Latin America—has opted for an inorganic, individualistic, non-Rousseauian form of democracy. Whether it can hold a fragmented society together and effectively govern under these new rules, however, remains highly uncertain.

Dominican uncertainties in these regards, repeated in recent surveys in virtually all other countries of Latin America, are reflected in a recent survey of public opinion attitudes, which is the best, most empirical study of political culture ever done in the country (Duarte et. al 1996; *Cultura Democrática en Venezuela* 1996). On the one hand, it is clear that Dominicans overwhelmingly (over 80 percent) think of liberal, democratic, representative government as the best form of government. But they are not certain that democracy works well in their context. For equally overwhelmingly (over 80 percent), they also prefer strong, paternalistic government—precisely what Balaguer provided for all these many decades. But these are the two forks in the road, are they not, not only for the Dominican Republic but for all of Latin America? Can one have both democracy and strong government at the same time? Are they compatible? Are they reconcilable? If one opts too strongly for either one over the other, is not one's country likely to get in political trouble?

Balaguer, a master politician, was able skillfully to reconcile these two opposing tensions for over three decades. He balanced one against the other; he sometimes went too far or lagged behind and got into political difficulties, but he survived by juggling these two opposed tendencies in the body politic, meanwhile constantly adjusting to new conditions. He went from being an authoritarian corporatist in the 1930s sense to an advocate of freer but still controlled constitutional government in the 1960s to a kind of patrimonialist democrat in the 1980s and 1990s. Few other Latin American leaders have lasted as long or personified as many epochal changes as Balaguer did. But isn't this constant tension between democracy and strong government precisely the history of Latin America over the last two centuries and continuing even today? And isn't this ambivalence about democracy even now precisely what we see in presidents Menem of Argentina ("delegated democracy"), Fujimori of Peru ("authoritarian democracy"), and Caldera of Venezuela (corporatist democracy), in the Mexican PRI (one-party democracy), *and in virtually every other government in Latin America?*

We need, therefore, in addition to this book's measurements of democracy, a set of conceptual tools—with important policy implications as well—for various intermediate stages between authoritarianism and democracy. We need measures for gauging the various halfway houses on the route to democracy, the crazy-quilt patterns of democracy, corporatism, and patrimonialism. A new conceptual framework of this kind would not only enable us to understand better the wide spectrum of regimes strung out, so to speak, between authoritarianism and democracy but also would allow policymakers a more nuanced set of responses when, as happens more often than not, a regime falls short of U.S.-style democracy (Wiarda 1996).

Bibliography

Anderson, Charles W. 1967. *Politics and Economic Change in Latin America: The Governing of Restless Nations.* Princeton: Van Nostrand, 1967.

Atkins, G. Pope. 1981. *Arms and Politics in the Dominican Republic.* Boulder: Westview Press.

Cultura Democrática en Venezuela. 1996. Caracas: Fundación Pensamiento y Acción.

Duarte, Isis, Ramonina Brea, Ramón Tejada, and Clara Báez. 1996. *Cultura Política y Democracía en República Dominicano.* Santo Domingo: Pontificia Universidad Católica Madre y Maestra.

Kryzanek, Michael J. 1977. Diversion, subversion, and repression: The strategies of anti-regime politics in Balaguer's Dominican Republic. *Caribbean Studies* 17:83–103.

Malloy, James, ed. 1977. *Authoritarianism and Corporatism in Latin America.* Pittsburgh: University of Pittsburgh Press.

O'Donnell, Guillermo. 1994. Delegative democracy. *Journal of Democracy* 5:55–69.

O'Donnell, Guillermo. 1973. *Modernization and Bureaucratic Authoritarianism.* Berkeley: Institute of International Studies, University of California.

Oropeza, José. 1983. *Tutelary Pluralism: A Critical Approach to Venezuelan Democracy.* Cambridge: Center for International Affairs, Harvard University.

Sarmiento, Domingo. 1990. *Facundo: Civilización y Barbarie.* Madrid: Catedra (Edición de Roberto Yahni).

Vallenilla Lanz, Laureano. 1920. *Caesarisme Démocrátique en America Latine.* Paris: Revue de L'Amerique Latine.

Wiarda, Howard J. 1996. The political systems of Latin America: Developmental models and a topology of regimes. In *Latin America: Perspectives on a Region* (Jack W. Hopkins, ed.), 243–256. New York: Holmes and Meier.

_____. 1995. U.S. policy and democracy in the Caribbean and Latin America. Washington, D.C.: Policy Papers on the Americas, Center for Strategic and International Studies.

_____. 1993. *Politics in Iberia: The Political Systems of Spain and Portugal.* New York: The Little Brown Series in Comparative Politics, Harper and Row.

_____. 1981. *Corporatism and Development in Latin America.* Boulder: Westview Press.

_____. 1973. Toward a framework for the study of political change in the Iberic-Latin world: The corporatist model. *World Politics* 25:206–235.

_____. 1970. *Dictatorship and Development: The Methods of Control in Trujillo's Dominican Republic.* Gainesville: University of Florida Press.

Part Three

Assessing Democracy in South America

The impact of political culture upon democracy is raised by David J. Myers in Chapter 14, "The Emergence of a Dominant Political Culture: Venezuelan Professionals and Post-1958 Democracy." In 1957, the final year of General Marcos Pérez Jiménez's dictatorship, a fragmented culture was observed, one supportive of three distinct orientations: modernizing oligarchy, developmental socialism, and reconciliational democracy. By 1973, after three successive and successful democratic administrations, political culture among professionals had "crystallized" predominately to reconciliational democracy. Hence the suggestion that successful performance influenced affective orientations, or competent constitutional governments brought a supportive cultural direction.

Robert E. Biles, in Chapter 15, "Democracy for the Few: Ecuador's Crisis-Prone Democracy," reports that democracy in Ecuador is "fragile," with "outward appearances of democracy but little of its substance." Basically, the elite continue to rule because of ineffective governance, political and cultural disunity, limited state resources, divided political parties, deadlock between Congress and the president, and authoritarian political cultures. Biles provides three possible explanations for Ecuador's "exclusionary" political system: (1) the very slow transition from authoritarian to democratic political values; (2) the continuation of elite dominance of the system; and (3) the poor performance of democratic institutions in reform and in the economy reinforcing a poor image of democracy. In contrast, the military possesses a much better image in these latter respects.

The limitations of leadership and the Shining Path guerrillas are primarily responsible for the recent weakness of democracy in Peru, argues David Scott Palmer in Chapter 16, "Democracy in Peru?" The tenure of President Alan García (1985–1990) failed to institute constructive responses to economic decline and to terrorism. His successor, Alberto Fujimori, has ruled more authoritatively than democratically, further discrediting the image of constitutionalism. Hence, "democracy remains fragile" in Peru, according to Palmer, and he does not see in Fujimori's "direct democracy" model a successful "formula for future democratic consolidation."

In two of our strongest cases of democracy, in Chile and in Uruguay, Ronald H. McDonald in Chapter 17, "Democratic Crises and Assumptions in Chile and Uruguay," seriously questions "the resiliency of democratic systems." For both countries, he finds stalemate leading to eventual decline into military rule when constitutional governments become confronted with economic decline, social mobilization, and political fragmentation and frustration. Ironically, democracy had performed so well in Chile and Uruguay that it became doomed to failure.

In Chapter 18, "The Military and Democracy in Argentina," Jack Child traces the relationship between the Argentine military and the functioning of democracy since 1945, noting that until recently the military in one role or another has dominated national politics. Factors affecting the military's political activism are examined in a later section. Child feels "cautious optimism" in a shift away from intense military involvement, as long as the current "period of reasonably competent and legitimate civilian regimes lasts."

Bolivia and Paraguay contrast starkly with Chile and Uruguay in democracy ratings. Neither country, according to Philip Kelly and Thomas Whigham in Chapter 19, "Democracy in Bolivia and Paraguay: A Comparison," possesses a good record in having stable constitutional government. Nonetheless, these writers conclude that "Progress is amply shown in the tenures of recent civilian presidents, in better adherence to constitutions, in the reigning in of the armed forces, in increased civic participation, in regional and international pressures favoring progressive government, and in like examples, attainments that could eventually encourage stronger institutions of democracy and contribute to possible improvement in their Fitzgibbon index standings."

In the final chapter, "Democracy and Development in Brazil: Cardoso's Catch-22," Jan Knippers Black focuses on the "challenge of maintaining [both economic] growth and democracy in the midst of [Brazil's] great poverty and inequality." Since 1945, no economic strategy attempted has reduced the gap between rich and poor, and reform within the current neoliberal policies could frighten away the international sources that buttress the present economic and political stability. Black finds Brazil's main hope in its two outstanding political leaders, President Fernando Henrique Cardoso and his rival, Luis Inácio "Lula" da Silva.

Chapter Fourteen

The Emergence of a Dominant Political Culture: Venezuelan Professionals and Post-1958 Democracy

DAVID J. MYERS

Political culture has been described as "one of the two still viable general approaches to political theory and explanation proposed since the early 1950s to replace the long-dominant formal legalism of the field" (Eckstein 1988). The touchstone of culturalist theory, the postulate of oriented action, views actors as responding to situations through mediating orientations rather than directly (Putman 1971:651–653; Eckstein 1988; Almond 1990; Mayer 1989:183–84). Orientations can be differentiated from attitudes. The latter are more specific; the former appear as cultural dispositions. Orientations, the "mind stuff" of politics, vary cross-nationally; but in addition, within the same country different groups may possess distinctive orientations (Gaenslen 1986; Lane 1992). Interaction between these particular orientations shapes the polity's processing of experiences into action. Culturalists, in their theory of oriented action, have identified three kinds of critical mediating orientations: cognitive, affective, and evaluative.[1]

Following publication in 1963 of Gabriel Almond's and Sidney Verba's revolutionary *The Civic Culture*, enthusiasm over the possibility of advances beyond traditional national culture studies gave rise to a current of research employing the culturalist perspective. In their assessment of this perspective two decades later Almond and Verba (1980:1–36) acknowledged that political culture research was controversial from the beginning and remained so. Most important, Ronald Rogowski (1974), Carole Pateman (1980), and Robert Lane (1992) had highlighted shortcomings in the culturalist approach when they pointed out that there were obvious cross-national differences in political behavior that could not be accounted for by culture and that furthermore the culturalist methodology was unable to handle political change in other than an ad hoc manner.

Partisans of political culture responded to both criticisms. First, they conceded that this approach was never intended to explain all differences in political behavior, declaring it to be sufficient that political culture accounted for some important differences. Culturalists also pointed out that political culture should be viewed as one of several useful lenses, along with theories of choice and institutional behavior. In addition culturalists began crafting an explicit general cultural theory of change consistent with their assumptions (Eckstein 1988; Inglehart 1988; Wildavsky 1987; Thompson, Ellis, and Wildavsky 1990:261–273). More recently, defenders have argued that to expand the predictive power of the culturalist approach, research should build on the second or "unnoticed" tradition in political culture research, that pioneered by Lucien Pye and Sidney Verba (1965) in *Political Culture and Political Development* (see Lane 1992:363–366).

The Pye and Verba tradition, in contrast to the one advanced in the *Civic Culture*, is disaggregative, focusing on the mediating orientations of critical elites and masses in order to study the inner structure of political culture (Laitin 1978; Lichter 1979; Lockhart 1984). Our research looks to this second perspective in its focus on Venezuelan professionals. We want to know if the mediating orientations of this critical elite underpinned the post-1958 democratic regime in 1974, at the beginning of President Carlos Andrés Pérez's first term. This moment is widely viewed as marking the consolidation of Venezuelan democracy, a perception echoed by contributors to the Fitzgibbon-Johnson Index when they ranked Venezuela as Latin America's second most democratic country in 1975. During the dictatorship of General Marcos Pérez Jiménez, in contrast, Fitzgibbon-Johnson contributors ranked Venezuela thirteenth.[2] Concern with understanding the evolving mediating orientations that accompanied this shift leads us to examine two central postulates, shared by both the Almond and Verba and the Pye and Verba traditions, about how political culture evolves and crystallizes.

The first postulate encompasses two assumptions concerning the responsiveness of political culture to abrupt social discontinuities: (1) that for a considerable period of time, political culture becomes entropic, that is, incoherent in individuals and fragmented in aggregates; and (2) that eventually political culture will diverge from revolutionary attempts at transformation toward the mediating orientations that prevailed in the old society or regime (Eckstein 1988:796–801). Second is a postulate that carries the assumption that preferences spring from the dynamics of living. It asserts that for political regimes that have attained power without a great legitimizing revolution (Venezuela's post-1958 democracy), the crystallization of positive affect for regime processes will depend on positive evaluations of regime output (Almond and Verba 1963:18–35; Davis and Speer 1991:325; Pye and Verba 1965:543; Wildavsky 1987; Putnam, Leonardi, and Nanetti 1988).

The perspective of this research is longitudinal, profiling mediating orientations between 1957 and 1973. Its first data point, a time of accelerated political decay, is the eve of General Marcos Pérez Jiménez's fraudulent November 1957 plebiscite. The general intended that this vote, a yes/no referendum on whether he should continue as president for five more years, would resolve the succession crisis occasioned as the 1953–1958 constitutional period drew to a close. However, falsification of plebiscite results (officially, 95 percent voted yes) so discredited his regime that within nine weeks of the balloting a popular uprising forced Pérez Jiménez into exile. This produced a situation that culturalists view as breeding an entropic political culture.

The second data point falls during the 1972–1973 presidential election campaign. Here electioneering culminated in voting that transformed Venezuela's political regime and party system. A succession of tenuously installed democratic governments seeking to reconcile interests that historically viewed each other's political demands as illegitimate finally congealed into a reconciliation regime dominated by two broadly aggregative political parties, the Acción Democrática (Democratic Action—AD) and the Social Christian Party (Comité de Organización Política Electoral Independiente—COPEI).[3] In other words, the experience of three democratic presidents (Rómulo Betancourt, 1959–1964; Raúl Leoni, 1964–1969; and Rafael Caldera, 1969–1973) proved sufficiently positive to consolidate the norms of reconciliation democracy.[4] From the perspective of culturalist theory, Venezuela's situation in 1972–1973 is propitious for probing relationships between the mediating orientations of affect and evaluation that characterize and facilitate the consolidation of a political regime. In addition, comparison of this situation's mediating orientations with those surrounding the fraudulent 1957 plebiscite should expedite identifying patterns and paths of crystallization for regime-supportive mediating orientations.

To summarize, this research examines the political culture of Venezuelan professionals, beginning just prior to the overthrow of General Pérez Jiménez and continuing through the consolidation of a new democratic political regime. Its primary purpose is to refine and deepen culturalist postulates about how a political culture congeals following revolution and how the structural components of that reconstituted culture relate to each other and to regime legitimacy. Finally, it appraises the capability of cultural postulates to explain observed changes in professionals' mediating orientations, briefly contrasting them with insights provided by the perspectives of institutionalism and strategic choice.

Professionals and the Data on
Their Mediating Orientations

Venezuelan professionals, like their counterparts throughout Latin American, are high status and privileged.[5] Critical to professionals' political and economic influence are their *colegios*, the state-chartered organizations empowered to confer membership in the profession. *Colegios* also assist members in obtaining bureaucratic employment and provide them with a broad array of social benefits. Thus, in societies where a majority live on the margins, professionals possess advanced education, hold high-status jobs, and enjoy great influence. They command the knowledge and expertise on which social, economic, and political modernization depends. Their importance in Latin America has increased as policy elites have sought to emulate the industrialized North Atlantic. Professionals, however, are a diverse lot, and this has discouraged social scientists from studying them. Passing references to their political proclivities suggest diversity; service to democratic regimes has been matched by support for authoritarianism (Martz and Myers 1994).

The work that follows draws on data from diverse sources. These include scholarly and participant histories, focus groups, elite interviews, and a public opinion survey sponsored by the National Science Foundation. These data do not emerge from research designed to shed light on the political culture of Venezuelan professionals. Yet each source contains information that facilitates the piecing together of relevant mediating political orientations. The 1957 data, not surprisingly, are least satisfying. They consist of secondary accounts and retrospective evaluations by professionals active at that time. Of special importance are findings from a project directed by Professor Ildemaro Martínez of Venezuela's Instituto de Estudios Superiores de Administración (IESA). In 1972–1973 Martínez probed the attitudes and behavior of professionals toward post-1958 democracy.[6] Critical data for 1972–1973 come from a National Science Foundation survey exploring Venezuelan political attitudes (Baloyra and Martz 1979).

To summarize, this study assembles data that describe the mediating political orientations of professionals in 1957 and 1973. It relies on diverse sources crafted originally for a variety of purposes. The information describing professional political culture at our two data points, therefore, is not identical. Nevertheless, it is sufficiently comparable to allow for longitudinal comparisons of affective and evaluative orientations.

Professional Political Culture at a Time of Tumult

Culturalists, as suggested above, would be surprised if a dominant political culture underpinned the political regime embedded in the tumult surrounding General Pérez Jiménez's 1957 plebiscite. Between 1935 and 1957 Venezuelans experienced five distinct political regimes.[7] General Pérez Jiménez came to power in 1952 promising a progressive and populist political order. His government, however, rested on political quicksand: the forcible overthrow of a popularly elected president, political killings, and electoral fraud. Many, but by no means all, viewed the Pérez Jiménez government as illegitimate at its inception in 1953 (Betancourt 1967:657–777; Lott 1957; Pacanins 1965; Rodríguez Campos 1991:191–261).

Venezuelan professionals in 1957, as well as in 1973, emerge as knowledgeable about the institutions, decision processes, and policies of government (Albornoz

1976:129–132; Martz and Myers 1994; Pacanins 1965:11–112; Vallenilla Lanz 1967:400–443). Culturalists would describe their level of cognitive political orientation as high. This is not surprising given professionals' advanced education and concentration in Caracas, Venezuela's primate city. Their soliciting of favors and contracts, planning and construction of public works, and the publicizing of government accomplishments (not to mention practices needed to obtain payment for work completed) brought professionals into daily contact with the powerful. In other words, the affective and evaluative orientations of professionals toward the political regime derived from an intimate knowledge of policy process and output.

Our data describing attitudes and behavior comprising Venezuelan political culture in 1957 profile only selected mediating political orientations. To repeat, the data are also retrospective. The first major social science project of the postrevolutionary period focusing on political attitudes, the 1963 CENDES—MIT collaboration,[8] found that six years after Pérez Jiménez's fraudulent plebiscite, Venezuelans lacked a "clearly crystallized ideological stance" (Bonilla and Silva Michelena 1967:371). In addition, middle-sector attitudes did not differ significantly from those of the general population (Bonilla 1970:315–321). These findings support Harry Eckstein's contention that no dominant political culture underpins postrevolutionary situations (1988:796–797).

A decade later, when Martínez interviewed seventy-eight professionals, he focused on whether professionals remained nostalgic for the Pérez Jiménez era and only weakly supported post-1958 reconciliation democracy. Project findings with direct relevance to this research concerned professionals' view of which kind of political system provided the best opportunities for them. Table 14.1 compares the retrospective perceptions of professionals about their orientations at the time of the 1957 plebiscite with those held when they were interviewed (during the 1973 election campaign). Political orientations toward three kinds of political systems are compared: one like Pérez Jiménez said he would make during the 1952 election campaign (cf. Lott 1957); the actual post-1958 Venezuelan democratic regime; and the political system Fidel Castro had established in Cuba.[9]

Table 14.1 compares professionals' evaluations of output from political systems widely viewed as major competitors for the allegiance of Venezuelans during the 1950s and 1960s (Betancourt 1967:941–960; Karl 1986; Pacanins 1965:3–10). Respondents, when recalling their 1957 orientations, differ in their evaluations of which political system would provide the best opportunities for them. One in five remembers themselves as enamored with the oligarchic modernization originally promised by Pérez Jiménez, and one in three recalls favoring some kind of system like Venezuela the one was then experiencing (reconciliation democracy). The distribution of preferences among professionals had changed by 1972. Six in ten then considered they would be best off under a government like the one they were experiencing. Finally, as of 1972, fewer respondents viewed either a developmental socialist or modernizing oligarchic regime as best for professionals.

TABLE 14.1   Political System Providing Best Opportunities for Professionals

	Retrospective (during late 1957)	Contemporary (during 1972–1973)
Like Pérez Jiménez promised in 1952	21%	6%
Like AD and COPEI created in 1972–1973	32%	61%
Like Fidel Castro has created in Cuba	16%	9%
Don't know/didn't answer	31%	24%
N = 78		

Sources: Compiled from Ildemaro J. Martínez, Profesionales y la nueva democrácia. (Caracas: IESA: Mimeo, 1974).

Table 14.1, even taking into account that retrospective reconstructions may introduce distortion, reveals the existence of a fragmented political culture among professionals in 1957. Several political cultures, each with a significant following, competed to shape mediating orientations. To state it differently, just prior to the fraudulent plebiscite on whether Pérez Jiménez should continue in office, seven in ten professionals made one of three political regimes (modernizing oligarchy, reconciliation democracy, and developmental socialism) the object of their positive affective political orientation. None was preferred by more than 32 percent of the respondents.

Each of the above regimes sought political stability by forming coalitions of individuals embedded in at least two of the "active ways of life" described by culturalists: hierarchy, egalitarianism, and individualism (Thompson, Ellis, and Wildavsky 1990:86–93; Wildavsky 1987:5–7). In these terms, Pérez Jiménez's modernizing oligarchy rested on a coalition uniting hierarchy and individualism.[10] Cuba's developmental socialism joins egalitarianism with hierarchy, and Venezuela's post-1958 reconciliation democracy initially attempted an unstable alliance involving all three ways of life. By the regime-consolidating election of 1973, however, egalitarians found themselves marginalized.

From this point forward, I will label professionals most favorably disposed toward the early Pérez Jiménez regime "authoritarian progressives." I will also refer to sympathizers with a regime like Cuban socialism as "Leninists" and to advocates of post-1958 Venezuelan democracy as "limited pluralists." Keeping this in mind, I shift from definitional concerns to a more detailed comparison of the mediating political orientations toward regime institutions and regime processes of each of the three professional currents.

In interviews, authoritarian progressives described themselves as direct descendants of Venezuela's historic professional community. By and large they belonged to extended families of the historic elite, and they were concentrated in Caracas. Authoritarian progressives initially overlooked Pérez Jiménez's fraudulent election to the presidency as the price to be paid so that egalitarians, especially the 1945–1948 leadership of AD, could be suppressed. They grudgingly tolerated the general's arbitrary executive, emasculated Congress, and secretive policing of dissidents. In the words of a prominent authoritarian progressive professional:

> When the AD ran Venezuela the first time (between 1945 and 1948) we almost became communist. The government wanted a say in everything, and if you wouldn't actively support the party you had no voice. Although [Rómulo] Gallegos was president, [Rómulo] Betancourt called the shots; he wanted to control what everyone did; even how I would raise my children. This was an attack on the family and the church. If we hadn't accepted PJ [Pérez Jiménez] we would have ended up like Cuba long before anyone ever heard of Fidel Castro.[11]

After a few years in power, however, Pérez Jiménez's incompetence dismayed progressive authoritarian professionals, and they grew increasingly frightened of his security police. None of the progressive authoritarian professionals interviewed by Martínez or by me admitted to supporting Pérez Jiménez in the 1957 plebiscite.

Leninist professionals, unlike progressive authoritarians, came largely from the Interior's[12] middle class, but they too had been trained at the Central University in Caracas. Initially some Leninist professionals were AD activists. Others joined and withdrew from the Venezuelan Communist Party (PCV) and the Democratic Republican Union (URD). Retrospection by Pompeyo Márquez, a militantly leftist lawyer and politician, summarizes the perceptions that Leninist professionals retained of their orientations toward competing political regimes in 1957:

> Most lawyers, doctors and engineers supported Pérez Jiménez in 1953, but by 1957 they had turned against him. Bourgeois professionals suddenly found themselves subjected to secret police terror, just like everyone else. The small band of heroic professionals in our party [PCV] knew from the beginning that Pérez Jiménez was a tyrant. His government represented international capitalism. We believed then and we believe now that bourgeois democracy is a screen for imperialism. We have always wanted a strong government that is truly democratic; it is the only path to social justice.[13]

Professionals claiming to have favored reconciliation democracy in 1957, with few exceptions, described themselves in 1972 as card-carrying members of AD and COPEI or as independents associated with these political parties. They remember themselves in that earlier time as disenchanted with military rule. More than half claim to have engaged in some kind of antiregime activity. The remembrances of a prominent agrarian engineer, subsequently the Caldera government official responsible for agrarian reform, profile this current's political orientations:

> We [professionals oriented toward COPEI] never supported Pérez Jiménez. Perhaps we sat back in 1953 and 1954 because of the way AD behaved when it was in power the first time. Adeco [or AD] governments used ideology to decide technical matters. This alienated many professionals, even some with sympathy for them. By the time of the plebiscite, however, we all knew that Pérez Jiménez was a petty gangster. For example, during October 1956 I exhibited my prize turkeys in Caracas. In December some gov-

ernment officials came to my farm and confiscated 150 of my birds for the Colonel's Christmas party. Incidents like this persuaded professionals that the dictatorship had to go. They also convinced those of us who wanted a United States style government that we would have to become involved in building the new democracy.[14]

To summarize, the affective orientations described above suggest that Eckstein's characterization of political culture structure in revolutionary situations is misleading. Professionals in 1957 held well-defined sets of affective orientations toward three distinct political regimes. Their political culture was not entropic, or, as Eckstein suggests, "formless." "Fragmented" seems a truer description. Also, the culturalist focus on conditions under which a preexisting political culture "reemerges" appears to be misplaced when the polity has just experienced far-reaching modernization, as had Venezuela between 1945 and 1948 (Cárdenas 1987:chaps. 2–8; Alexander 1982:195–293). Whatever mediating political orientations existed toward the authoritaran Andean political regime that dominated Venezuela prior to the 1945–1948 provisional government, our interviews uncovered no evidence of affinity toward its leaders, institutions, or processes. Neither was their any affect toward the political regime that Pérez Jiménez delivered, in contrast to the one that he promised in 1952.

Professional Political Culture and the Regime Consolidated

Politics had changed dramatically by the end of 1973. Reconciliation regime democrats, still laboring to integrate questionably loyal leftists and rightists into their system, had just conducted Venezuela's third successful presidential election since 1958. The incumbent COPEI president was ending a term during which the AD had conducted a constructively loyal opposition. Though some important political parties seemed indifferent or hostile to reconciliation democracy, Venezuelans had just elected AD's Carlos Andrés Pérez as president. Support for Pérez and his COPEI rival approached 90 percent of the total presidential vote. These results, as suggested earlier, have been interpreted widely as marking the consolidation of Venezuela's post-1958 democracy (Levine 1978:93–101; Martz 1980:7–16).

In the context of consolidation I now probe professionals' affective and evaluative orientations toward the three political regimes that were the objects of their support in 1957. We want to know if 1957's fragmented political culture had changed, as well as whether professionals' political orientations differed from those of other Venezuelans. I also will explore possible explanations for the condition of professionals' mediating orientations in 1973: the legacy of earlier political culture, the impact of role playing in post-1958 political institutions, and professionals' strategic choices.

TABLE 14.2   Affective Orientations Toward Reconciliation Democracy (1973)

	Identifying with Political Parties—The Central Regime Institution			Best Characterization of Post-1958 Governmental Decision Makers as Political Actors		
	Professionals 5%	Others 95%			Professionals 5%	Others 95%
AD	18	23	Honorable		11	13
COPEI	27	27	Shameless, some		53	44
MAS	14	6	Shameless, all		36	43
MEP	1	4				
CCN	1	3				
Other	—	1				
None	38	35				
N = 1395			N = 1427			
Pearson's r –.02			Pearson's r –.02			
Somer's D^a –.06			Somer's D^b –.05			

Note: Differences between professionals and others not significant at .1 level

[a]Somer's D (asymmetric with party affinity dependent)

[b]Somer's D (asymmetric with quality of decision maker dependent)

The Baloyra and Martz VENEVOTE survey conducted during Venezuela's 1972–1973 presidential election campaign provides my principal data for disaggregating the political culture of regime consolidation. Data interpretation begins with the widely shared view that political parties were the most important national institutions integrating Venezuela's post-1958 reconciliation democracy (Coppedge 1988; Karl 1986; Myers 1980). I also follow the lead of others (Davis 1989:chap. 8; Davis and Speer 1991:329–330) in assuming that attitudes toward the two political parties that elected presidents under the 1961 constitution, AD and COPEI, serve as surrogates for orientations toward the regime itself. Table 14.2 profiles the affective orientations of professionals and others toward political parties and toward the process characteristic that sums up the behavior of post-1958 government decisionmakers.

Table 14.2 reports that after fifteen years of reconciliation governments, 45 percent of all professionals named one of the two regime-sustaining political parties as the object of their positive affective orientation. Just under 15 percent of professionals claimed positive affective orientation toward the Movement Toward Socialism (MAS), a political party closely identified with developmental socialism (Ellner 1988). Only 1 percent of professionals identified with the National Civic Crusade (CCN), a grouping that sought to elect General Pérez Jiménez as president. This minuscule proportion of professionals identifying with the CCN confirms the near-total rejection of Pérez Jiménez's government that emerged from our 1972–1973 interviews with professionals. The People's Electoral Movement (MEP), a leftist faction, garnered just 1 percent of the total, equal to the CCN. Rejection, however, did not necessarily imply disapproval of modernizing oligarchy. Four professionals in ten classified themselves as "independents," and one-third of self-styled independents asserted that Venezuela would be better off under a strong leader than with the existing system of political parties.

Though the Baloyra-Martz survey contained no questions designed to measure affect toward regime processes, we asked participants in our 1973 focus groups if any of several VENEVOTE questions provided a valid measure of affect toward the political process. Most selected the question that characterized the orienting quality of post-1958 government decisionmakers. The responses to this question, presented in Table 14.2, are mixed. Roughly one-third of all professionals characterized all government officials as "shameless," and only 11 percent viewed them as "honorable." Slightly more than half of all professionals chose a middle course, characterizing "some" government officials as "shameless." When participants in our focus groups were shown the Martz-Baloyra questions, they volunteered that a response that described only "some" government officials as "shameless" should be viewed as a mildly positive orientation toward how the regime was operating.

I turn to evaluative orientations. Culturalists conceptualize them as judgments and opinions about political objects that typically involve the combination of value standards and criteria with information and feeling. To a large extent they are assessments of performance, of quality of life provided by the system, of the fairness of its processes, and of the impact of its policies. Table 14.3 compares professionals' evaluative orientations toward post-1958 reconciliation democracy with those of others. Evaluative orientations are more strongly positive than affective orientations.

An overwhelming proportion of professionals, like other Venezuelans in 1973, viewed AD or COPEI as the institutions best able to govern during the next constitutional period (1974–1979). Professionals' evaluations of post-1958 regime processes, like their affective orientations, proved mixed: One-third responded that Venezuelan governments "frequently or always" behaved correctly when exercising power, and one-quarter viewed them as "almost never" having behaved correctly. The remaining 45 percent saw reconciliation governments as occasionally having behaved correctly. A willingness to circumvent reconciliation processes surfaced when almost two-thirds of professionals replied that they could envision circumstances in which a military coup would be justified. On the other hand, three-quarters of VENEVOTE professionals viewed elections as politically efficacious mechanisms for influencing government policy, 96 percent perceived a strong connection between democracy and elections, and 80 percent supported the right of opponents to criticize those in power. There were no significant differences between the opinion of professionals and of other Venezuelans along any of these dimensions evaluating the processes of reconciliation democracy.

Professionals' evaluative orientations toward the output of post-1958 governments were more positive than those of other Venezuelans and of their own affec-

TABLE 14.3 Evaluative Orientations Toward Reconciliation Democracy (1973)

	Institutions		Process		Output	
	Political Party That Will Govern Best in Next Five Years		*Have the Post-1958 Governments Behaved Correctly in What They Have Done?*		*Have the Post-1958 Governments Been Beneficial to the Country?*	
	Professionals 5%	*Others* 95%	*Professionals* 5%	*Others* 95%	*Professionals* 5%	*Others* 95%
AD	32	35				
COPEI	44	41				
MAS	17	11				
MEP	5	7				
CCN	2	6				
Total	100%	100%				
Frequently/always			32	27		
Occasionally			45	43		
Almost never			23	30		
Yes					59	45
Depends					16	19
No					25	36
	N = 1049		N = 1434		N = 1477	

[a] Somer's D (asymmetric with govern-best dependent)

Pearson's r -.01
Somer's D[a] -.01

[b] Somer's D (asymmetric with behavior dependent)

Pearson's r -.04
Somer's D[b] -.05

[c] Somer's D (asymmetric with governments-beneficial to country dependent)

Pearson's r -.06*
Somer's D[c] -.15

*Significant at .07 level

tive orientations toward process. The internal structure of mediating political orientations resembles what Almond and Verba (1963:364) found in West Germany. It led them to speculate that, should West German democracy's output continue to be perceived positively, a greater proportion of citizens would have positive feelings toward its processes. Measurements of West German affective orientations in 1978, following twenty more years of prosperity and positive performance by regime institutions, confirmed this prediction (Conradt 1980:230).

To summarize, between 1957 and 1972–1973 a dominant political culture supportive of reconciliation democracy crystallized among Venezuelan professionals. A small but important minority of professionals favored development socialism, and an even smaller number looked fondly on the modernizing oligarchy they remembered Pérez Jiménez as having promised. Within the newly ascendant political culture, affective and evaluative orientations toward reconciliation democracy's central sustaining institutions, AD and COPEI, were positive. Orientations toward processes were mixed, and toward outputs they were strongly positive. In other words, regime-supportive political culture among professionals in 1972–1973 rested on positive orientations toward AD and COPEI as institutions and toward their accomplishments in government.

Comparing Explanations

Three important social science paradigms currently compete to explain changes in political culture. The first, favored by culturalists, looks to the earlier structure of political culture itself. A second views political culture transformation as adaptation to political institutions that remain in place for extended periods. A third perceives modifications as strategic choices by those who have purposefully altered their mediating orientations. These alternatives, though not mutually exclusive, have distinct emphases.

Culturalists from both traditions begin their search for explanation with the structure of earlier mediating orientations. They assume that orientations change slowly; thus even in revolutionary situations there is a clinging to preexisting political culture. Decay may lead some individuals to adopt new sets of mediating orientations and others to become indifferent, but historical mediating orientations also persist. Eckstein (1988:796–798) has argued that when revolutionary impulses exhaust themselves society's innate conservatism predisposes postrevolutionary political culture toward its prerevolutionary form. Though no studies exist of pre-1957 Venezuelan political culture, accounts of the twentieth-century's first six decades agree on the absence of any societal consensus favoring reconciliation democracy (Alexander 1982; Clements et al. 1959; Lott 1957; Silva Michelena 1971; Vallenilla Lanz 1967). Thus Eckstein's theory does not adequately portray the course of professionals' political culture between 1957 and 1973.

My findings do reveal an ascendant political culture in 1972–1973. A comparison of its structure with what existed in 1957 shows that this ascendant political culture was coalescing, not beginning to unravel. The focus on political culture's internal structure also yielded supportive evidence for the postulate of Pye and Verba (1965; also cf. Thompson, Ellis, and Wildavsky 1990:69–99) that political culture in all polities results from the clash of differing sets of mediating orientations. However, culturalism appears powerless to explain how clash transforms.

Institutionalist perspectives stress recurring patterns of action and the roles of individuals in pattern maintenance (March and Olsen 1984, 1989; Searing 1991). Between 1935 and 1959 Venezuela experienced extreme turbulence and little pattern maintenance. Strong political actors viewed each of the transitory constitutions proclaimed during this period as illegitimate. The casting of a broad net by those who shaped post-1958 regime institutions and norms suggests that elites, many of whom were professionals, sought an escape from this destructive spiral. COPEI spokesman, Allan R. Brewer-Carias, reflecting on the 1961 constitution, noted that its drafters intended to create broadly acceptable arrangements. The system was "built upon the experience of absolute power suffered in the past and the subsequent claim for democracy, which gave rise to specific political institutions. Hence it is the result of a compromise to establish a formal—but not rigid—regime to govern the economic and social system, and it is here that the compromise between the various political forces is evident" (Goldwin and Kaufman 1988:386).

My data suggest that fifteen years of institutional continuity assisted the set of mediating orientations that led reconciliation democracy to become ascendant. Facilitating patterns of action had weathered violent assaults. Reconciliation democracy's champions (AD and COPEI) had beaten back all electoral challengers and critical actors, and early reservations had been co-opted. Constitutional norms prevailed; business groups participated in the National Planning Council; the subsidized church lent support to education policy; the military deferred to civilians in matters of governing; and even U.S. presidents spoke glowingly of Venezuela's democratic experiment. In other words, striking shifts in the behavior of those directing powerful institutions preceded congruent changes in the political culture. Only a minority of professionals, however, made policy for societally pivotal institutions. Many were self-employed or scattered among small firms. At best, role socialization within powerful regime-supporting or co-opted institutions is a partial and unsatisfactory explanation for changes in the political culture of Venezuelan professionals between 1957 and 1973.

The strategic choice perspective draws upon Guillermo O'Donnell's "game" of regime consolidation between "consolidators," those who prefer "breakdown," and "neutrals" (Collier and Norden 1992). Here it focuses attention on the choices made by professionals identifying with AD and COPEI, the two regime-supporting political parties. Those identifying with COPEI disdained Pérez Jiménez's ill-fated 1957 referendum and solidly backed movement toward reconciliation arrangements.[15] Thus for COPEI-oriented professionals to view the post-1958 regime positively required only that they not change their 1957 orientations. All

COPEI-oriented professionals interviewed in 1972–1973 expressed strong support for the reconciliation experiment.

AD professionals admitted in the Martínez-IESA interviews to the presence of
numerous developmental socialists within their ranks in 1957. However, cooperation with establishment interests to overthrow Pérez Jiménez softened this faction's opposition to experimentation with reconciliation norms. Also, after AD's
1959 return to power the official party position made support for the new regime
a higher priority than redistribution (Gil Yepes 1978; Levine 1978; Martz 1966).
Most of the AD professionals interviewed described the benefits of governing as
more than counterbalancing their unhappiness over their party's failure to resurrect earlier developmentally socialist policies.

Among professionals claiming to have favored a regime "like the one Pérez
Jiménez promised," those interviewed in 1972–1973 reported reduced hostility
toward the post-1958 democracy. They cited President Betancourt's willingness to
rule in coalition and AD's relinquishing of the presidency to COPEI's Rafael
Caldera in 1969 as important in overcoming their misgivings. In addition, they
singled out Fidel Castro's success in Cuba as evidence that a military seizure of
power might pave the way for developmental socialism. Nevertheless, throughout
the 1960s most authoritarian progressive professionals remained neutral specta-
tors in the "game" of regime consolidation.

Four in ten professionals responding to VENEVOTE (Table 14.2) claimed no
affinity with any political party, but in elections three months later the presidential candidates of AD and COPEI received 84 percent of the total vote. Although
conclusive data are lacking, the professionals interviewed in 1973 suggested an explanation in keeping with the strategic choice framework. With two exceptions,
professionals claiming to be "independent" volunteered that they intended to vote
for a presidential candidate of the two pro-system political parties. Interviewees
portrayed this choice as deriving from their concern that an antisystem presidency would be destabilizing, possibly a repeat of Chile's disastrous experience
with the Allende government. Thus skeptical "neutral" professionals intended to
behave like supportive "consolidators." In contrast to the preference affirmation
underpinning choices by "consolidator" professionals, these "neutrals" or "independents" sought to minimize risk.

Leninist professionals, as of 1972–1973 roughly one in seven, identified overwhelmingly with the MAS. Born as a breakaway from the Venezuelan Communist
Party after the Soviet Union crushed Czechoslovakia's Prague Spring, MAS entered the electoral arena as an opponent of the post-1958 regime. MAS leaders
spoke openly of their prominent role in the 1960s insurgency. Throughout the
1972–1973 election campaign, party propaganda disparaged reconciliation, or
"bourgeois," democracy. Focus group professionals of all political persuasions
agreed that AD and COPEI were allowing this questionably loyal opposition because they preferred a contest for votes over one decided by bullets. Reconciliation democracy benefited from this choice. By abandoning the armed struggle

MAS inadvertently legitimated the structures and processes it opposed. This process continued after 1973, when professionals allied with MAS accepted bureaucratic positions offered by the newly inaugurated AD government (Ellner 1988:111–115). Thus, despite the tortured logic with which MAS defended this participation, the behavior of its professionals approximated that of identifiers with AD and COPEI.

Conclusions

This research examined the political culture literature and followed its admonition to test culturalist ideas in representative ethnographic studies. The concern was with the mediating political orientations of Venezuelan professionals, a privileged elite most often studied in their role as bureaucrats. This analysis, in contrast, focused on professionals as a political group in their own right.

The first major finding is that, contrary to the culturalist assumption, the political culture of professionals during the turmoil surrounding the decay of General Marcos Pérez Jiménez's government was not entropic in individuals; however, it could be viewed as fragmented in the aggregate. Specifically, three sets of mediating orientations were detected: one favorable to modernizing oligarchy, a second supportive of developmental socialism, and a final one sympathetic to reconciliation democracy. Professionals portrayed themselves as partisans of one of these sets. A contest between sets replaced the dominant way of life that underpinned the primitive terrorism permeating the Gómez dictatorship (1908–1935). By 1973 the set favorable to reconciliation democracy predominated. There seemed to be no evidence that mediating orientations diverged back toward support for any "dominant game rules" that characterized the Andean dictatorships of 1908–1945. The diversity we detected also supports theorizing by Michael Thompson, Richard Ellis, and Aaron Wildavsky (1990:chaps. 4, 5) that sets of mediating orientations favorable to competing ways of life are present in all polities.

The second finding derives from the internal structure of professional political culture at the time of regime consolidation. In this context can be detected strong positive affect for the central regime institutions (AD and COPEI), highly positive evaluative orientations toward their governing capabilities, and a positive evaluation of reconciliation democracy's overall output. This confirms the second postulate. Also compatible with this postulate are findings that affective and evaluative orientations toward regime processes were mixed, and that a low percentage of respondents identified with political parties advocating developmental socialism (MAS) and modernizing oligarchy. However, the process of political culture crystallization appears to be less straightforward in light of the finding that affective orientations toward the two regime-sustaining political parties approached 50 percent for professionals and for others. This suggests that Venezuela's 1973 regime-supportive political culture rested as much on orientations toward AD and COPEI as on evaluations of regime output.

Finally, probes using strategic choice, institutionalism, and political culture expanded understanding of why political culture's internal structure changed between 1957 and 1973. Initially, strategic choice helped by focusing attention on the behavior of regime-supportive professionals, especially their efforts to deter ambivalent independents from joining antiregime conspiracies. This provided breathing space during which orientations favoring reconciliation democracy could become the norm, thus isolating partisans of modernizing oligarchy and developmental socialism.

Little in the literature of cultural theory contributed to an understanding of why the fragmented internal structure of professional political culture in 1957 became predominately regime supportive by 1973. Institutionalism proved more helpful. During constitution drafting in 1959 and 1960, dominating political elites rejected the alternatives of modernizing oligarchy and developmental socialism. Their 1961 constitution incorporated reconciliation patterns of action, and it remained the law of the land. In order to function in the new political order professionals took clues from the social relations inherent in reconciliation democratic patterns of action. Thus role validation began to shape the mediating orientations of professionals into orientations supportive of the post-1958 regime's institutions, processes, and possibly outputs.

In the final analysis, this research demonstrates the utility of the "second" political culture tradition's emphasis on comparing the mediating orientations of a polity's critical elites and masses. It also confirms the wisdom of describing political culture's internal structure and of analyzing how its components evolve as regimes change and incremental modifications occur. These findings increase culturalists' ability to construct their theory of political change.

Notes

1. Cognitive mediating orientations center on knowledge and benefits about the political system: its roles and the incumbents of these roles, its processes, and its outputs. Affective mediating orientations are feelings with respect to the political system's institutions, roles, personnel, process, and performance. Evaluative mediating orientations embody judgments about whether the political system's process and output reflects those values (Parsons and Shils 1951:58–60; Almond and Verba 1963:14; Bill and Hargrave 1981:86–88; Eckstein 1988:801–803).

2. The index ranks twenty countries.

3. For conceptual clarity, "reconciliation democracy" in this research will follow the definition devised by Helio Jaguaribe (1973:166–169) when he crossed the macro variables of political superordination and developmental orientation. The regime designation Jaguaribe assigns to this variation is "national capitalism." Other variables falling in this classification include Chile under Eduardo Frei and the Institutional Revolutionary Party's Mexico. Venezuela's COPEI began as an amalgam of independents opposed to AD. Its origin is recounted by Donald Herman (1980). We also follow the Jaguaribe classificatory scheme when we label as a "modernizing oligarchy" the dictatorship of General Marcos

Pérez Jiménez (1952–1958). Jaguaribe classifies this arrangement as an "ordination regime," "capitalistic," "reactionary," and "modernizing." For Fidel Castro's Cuba we accept the label "developmental socialism." Jaguaribe views developmental socialism as the archetypal "mobilization regime."

4. Analysts have labeled regime consolidation the second transition. In contrast, the first transition begins with the initial stirring of crisis under authoritarian rule. It ends with the establishment of a government elected in an open competitive contest (Mainwaring, O'-Donnell, and Valenzuela 1992:2–3).

5. The literature on Latin American professionals is reviewed in Martz and Myers 1994, a companion piece to this research that focuses on relationships between Venezuelan professionals and the political parties. Peter Cleaves's (1987) work on Mexican professionals is the only book-length study of Latin American professionals in English. The comprehensive description by Orlando Albornoz (1976) of Venezuela's professional community emphasizes the centrality of state-recognized professional *colegios* in separating out professionals as interest articulators from other educated and wealthy Venezuelans; for example, entrepreneurs and merchants. Though Albornoz views medical doctors, engineers, lawyers, accountants, architects, and journalists as professionals, he portrays university professors in the sciences and humanities as being less than full professionals, at least from the perspective of being political demand makers (101–103). This is because few academic specialties have their own state-chartered *colegio*, and most university professors interact with the political elite through the Education Bureau of the political parties rather than through the Secretariat of Professionals and Technicians. Finally, university professors comprise a minuscule strata when compared with mainline professionals (113–114).

6. Martínez examined the political attitudes of professionals, a group that at that time was commonly viewed as only weakly committed to the post-1958 democratic system. With the assistance of several graduate students, Professor Martínez and I organized six focus groups and interviewed seventy-eight professionals. We selected interviewees from the following *colegios*: lawyers, 25 percent; medical doctors, 20 percent; journalists, 20 percent; engineers, 20 percent; and accountants, 15 percent. Table 14.1 is compiled from a question asked of every interviewee. Survey data profiling professional attitudes in 1973 were derived by recoding results from the Baloyra-Martz VENEVOTE survey. Those interested in the exact wording of the questions used in Tables 14.1, 14.2, and 14.3 are encouraged to write me at the Department of Political Science, Penn State University, University Park, PA 16802.

7. The primitive Gómez regime ended in 1935. Unsuccessful oligarchic modernization marked the decade that followed. A revolutionary military junta ruled between November 1945 and February 1948 before giving way to a short-lived modernizing democracy headed by a popularly elected president, Rómulo Gallegos. A military coup toppled Gallegos, but within two years its perpetrator, Colonel Delgado Chalbaud, was assassinated under mysterious circumstances. Fraudulent elections in November 1952 opened the presidency to General Marcos Pérez Jiménez; in turn, a popular uprising on January 23, 1958, overthrew the general. G. Bigler (1981:62–63) assembles a comprehensive chronology of twentieth-century regime changes.

8. Three volumes flowed from this effort (Bonilla and Silva Michelena 1967; Bonilla 1970; Silva Michelena 1971). Inexplicably, the authors failed to include professionals in their listing of elite political actors, and they appeared to be unaware of the evolving political culture literature. Analysis of this project's data became mired in controversy, includ-

ing charges that findings would be used by the U.S. government to prevent revolutionary change in Venezuela. Its hypotheses cannot be reassessed in light of subsequent methodological advances, for most of the original data disappeared under mysterious circumstances.

9. I consulted with Professor Martínez, and we exchanged data during 1972 and 1973. I asked questions of relevance to Martínez's project in my elite interviewing for other purposes. The three political systems of Table 14.1 are specific examples of the political system types discussed in note 3. Martínez's designation of a political system "like the one Pérez Jiménez said he would make in 1952" assumes that though the dictator himself had been discredited by 1957, the modernizing authoritarian system he promised in 1952 remained popular with the professionals.

10. Jaguaribe's formulations of modernizing oligarchy, developmental socialism, and reconciliation democracy imply these way-of-life alliances. Evidence that Pérez Jiménez's regime sought to legitimate itself by allying hierarchicals with individualists permeates Rodríguez Campos (1991:210–251) and Vallenilla Lanz (1967:378–430). Leninism as an alliance of egalitarianism and hierarchy is analyzed directly by culturalists (Thompson, Ellis, and Wildavsky 1990:157–158). For post-1958 Venezuela, Martz (1966:174–183), Myers (1973:55–60), and Hellinger (1991:107–119) describe how egalitarians were marginalized as coordination increased between individualists and hierarchialists.

11. Quoted from an interview with one of the authors by Oscar Gil Santana, a prominent engineer who built some of General Pérez Jiménez's most important projects, September 16, 1972. At the time of this interview, Gil portrayed himself as an "independent," adding he had no intention of joining a political party.

12. Venezuelans refer to all locations outside of Caracas as the Interior.

13. Interview by the author, October 23, 1972.

14. Interview by the author with Juan Guevara Benso, November 6, 1972. Also see Alexander 1982:392–397,490–491.

15. All COPEI-oriented professionals interviewed in 1972–1973 expressed contempt for the 1957 referendum. In an interview with the author (November 22, 1972), José Curiel, a leading COPEI engineer, stated that after May 1957 his party's professionals were working to create a consensus in their respective *colegios* against continuation of the Pérez Jiménez government.

Bibliography

Albornoz, Orlando. 1976. Las profesionales en Venezuela. In *La Sociedad Venezolana* (Orlando Albornoz, ed.), 97–134. Caracas: Editorial Arte.

Alexander, Robert J. 1982. *Rómulo Betancourt and the Transformation of Venezuela*. New Brunswick, N.J.: Transaction Books.

Almond, Gabriel. 1990. The study of political culture. In *A Discipline Divided: Schools and Sects in Political Science* (Gabriel Almond, ed.), 138–154. Newbury Park, Calif.: Sage Publications.

_____. 1980. The intellectual history of the civic culture concept. In *The Civic Culture Revisited* (Gabriel Almond and Sidney Verba, eds.), 1–36. Boston: Little, Brown.

Almond, Gabriel, and Sidney Verba. 1963. *The Civic Culture*. Princeton: Princeton University Press.

Almond, Gabriel, and Sidney Verba, eds. 1980. *The Civic Culture Revisited.* Boston: Little, Brown.

Baloyra, Enrique A., and John D. Martz. 1979. *Political Attitudes in Venezuela: Societal Cleavages and Political Opinion.* Austin: University of Texas Press.

Bermeo, Nancy. 1992. Democracy and the lessons of dictatorship. *Comparative Politics* 24:273–292.

Betancourt, Rómulo. 1967. *Venezuela: Política y Petróleo.* Caracas: Editorial Senderos.

Bigler, G. 1981. *La Política y el Capitalismo de Estado en Venezuela.* Madrid: Tecnos.

Bill, James A., and Robert L. Hargrave. 1981. *Comparative Politics.* Washington, D.C.: University Presses of America.

Bonilla, Frank. 1970. *The Failure of Elites.* Cambridge: MIT Press.

Bonilla, Frank, and José Agustin Silva Michelena. 1967. *A Strategy for Research on the Polity.* Cambridge: MIT Press.

Cárdenas, R. 1987. *COPEI en el Trienio Populista 1945–1948.* Madrid: Ronda de Toledo.

Cleaves, Peter S. 1987. *Professions and the State.* Tucson: University of Arizona Press.

Clements, J., et al. 1959. *Report on Venezuela.* New York: n.p.

Collier, David, and Deborah L. Norden. 1992. Strategic choice models of political change in Latin America. *Comparative Politics* 24:229–241.

Conradt, David P. 1980. Changing German political culture. In *The Civic Culture Revisited* (Gabriel Almond and Sidney Verba, eds.), 212–272. Boston: Little, Brown.

Coppedge, Michael. 1988. Strong parties and lame ducks: A study of the quality and stability of Venezuelan democracy. Diss., Yale University Department of Political Science.

Davis, Charles L. 1989. *Political Control and Working Class Mobilization.* Lexington: University of Kentucky Press.

Davis, Charles L., and John G. Speer. 1991. The psychological bases of regime support among urban workers in Venezuela and Mexico. *Comparative Political Studies* 24:319–343.

Eckstein, Harry. 1988. A culturalist theory of political change. *American Political Science Review* 82:789–804.

Ellner, Steve. 1988. *Venezuela's Movimiento al Socialismo: From Guerrilla Defeat into Innovative Politics.* Durham, N.C.: Duke University Press.

Frente Nacional Democrática (FND). 1966. *El F.N.D. y el Gobierno de Colaboración.* Caracas: n.p.

Gaenslen, Fritz. 1986. Culture and decision making in China, Japan, Russia, and the United States. *World Politics* 39:78–103.

Gil Yepes, José Antonio. 1978. *El Reto de los Elites.* Madrid: Editorial Tecnos.

Goldwin, Robert A., and Art Kaufman. 1988. *Constitution Making: The Experience of Eight Nations.* Washington, D.C.: American Enterprise Institute for Public Policy Research.

Hellinger, Daniel. 1991. *Venezuela: Tarnished Democracy.* Boulder: Westview Press.

Herman, Donald L. 1980. *Christian Democracy in Venezuela.* Chapel Hill: University of North Carolina Press.

Inglehart, Ronald. 1988. The renaissance of political culture. *American Political Science Review* 82:1203–1230.

Jaguaribe, Helio. 1973. *Political Development: A General Theory and a Latin American Case Study.* New York: Harper and Row.

Karl, Terry Lynn. 1986. Petroleum and political pacts: The transition to democracy in Venezuela. *Latin American Research Review* 22:63–94.

Laitin, David D. 1978. Religion, political culture, and the Weberian tradition. *World Politics* 30:563–592.

Laitin, David D., and Aaron B. Wildavsky. 1988. Political culture and political preferences. *American Political Science Review* 82:589–604.

Lane, Robert E. 1992. Political culture: Residual category or general theory. *Comparative Political Studies* 25:362–387.

Levine, David H. 1978. Venezuela since 1958: The consolidation of democratic politics. In *The Breakdown of Democratic Regimes: Latin America* (Juan D. Linz and Alfred Stepan, eds.), 82–109. Baltimore: Johns Hopkins University Press.

Lichter, S. Robert. 1979. Young rebels: A psychopolitical study of West German male radical students. *Comparative Politics* 12:27–48.

Lockhart, Charles. 1984. Explaining social policy differences among advanced industrial societies. *Comparative Politics* 16:335–350.

Lott, Leo B. 1957. The 1952 Venezuelan elections: A lesson for 1957. *Western Political Quarterly* 10:541–558.

Mainwaring, Scott, Guillermo O'Donnell, and J. Samuel Valenzuela. 1992. *Issues in Democratic Consolidation: The New South American Democracies in Comparative Perspective.* Notre Dame, Ind.: Notre Dame University Press.

March, James G., and Johan P. Olsen. 1989. *Rediscovering Institutions: The Organizational Basis of Politics.* New York: Free Press.

————. 1984. The new institutionalism: Organizational factors in political life. *American Political Science Review* 78:734–749.

Martz, John D. 1980. The evolution of democratic politics in Venezuela. In *Venezuela at the Polls: The National Elections of 1978* (Howard Rae Penniman, ed.), 1–29. Washington, D.C.: American Enterprise Institute for Public Policy.

————. 1966. *Acción Democrática.* Princeton: Princeton University Press.

Martz, John D., and Enrique A. Baloyra. 1976. *Electoral Mobilization and Public Opinion: The Venezuelan Campaign of 1973.* Chapel Hill: University of North Carolina Press.

Martz, John D., and David J. Myers. 1994. Technological elites and political parties: The Venezuelan professional community. *Latin American Research Review* 29:7–27.

Mayer, Lawrence C. 1989. Micro-level analysis: Culture, violence, and personality. In *Redefining Comparative Politics: Promise Versus Performance* (Lawrence C. Mayer, ed.), 178–233. Newbury Park, Calif.: Sage Publications.

Movimiento de Liberación Anticomunista de Venezuela. 1959. *Proof of the Communist Domination of Venezuela.* Caracas: privately published.

Myers, David J. 1980. The elections and the evolution of Venezuela's party system. In *Venezuela at the Polls* (Howard Rae Penniman, ed.), 218–252. Washington, D.C.: American Enterprise Institute for Public Policy.

————. 1973. *Democratic Campaigning in Venezuela.* Caracas: Fundación La Salle.

Pacanins, G. 1965. *Siete Años en la Governación del Distrito Federal.* Caracas: Lit. y Tip. Vargas.

Parsons, Talcott, and Edward Shils. 1951. *Toward a General Theory of Action.* Cambridge: Harvard University Press.

Pateman, Carole. 1980. The civic culture: A philosophic critique. In *The Civic Culture Revisited* (Gabriel Almond and Sidney Verba, eds.), 57–102. Boston: Little, Brown.

Putnam, Robert D. 1971. Studying elite political culture: The case of ideology. *American Political Science Review* 65:682–693.

Putnam, Robert D., Robert Leonardi, and Raffaella Nanetti. 1988. Institutional performance and political culture: Some puzzles about the power of the past. *Governance: An International Journal of Policy and Administration* 1:221–242.

Pye, Lucien, and Sidney Verba. 1965. *Political Culture and Political Development*. Princeton: Princeton University Press.

Rodríguez Campos, Manuel. 1991. *Pérez Jiménez y la Dinámica del Poder (1948–1958)*. Caracas: Editorial El Dorado.

Rogowski, Ronald. 1974. *Rational Legitimacy*. Princeton: Princeton University Press.

Searing, Donald. 1991. Roles, rules, and rationality in the new institutionalism. *American Political Science Review* 85:1239–1260.

Silva Michelena, José Agustin. 1971. *The Illusion of Democracy in Dependent States*. Cambridge: MIT Press.

Silvert, Kalman H., and Leonard Reissman. 1976. *Education, Class, and Nation: The Experiences of Chile and Venezuela*. Amsterdam: Elsevier.

Thompson, Michael, Richard J. Ellis, and Aaron Wildavsky. 1990. *Cultural Theory*. Boulder: Westview Press.

Vallenilla Lanz, Luis. 1967. *Escrito de Memoria*. Caracas: Garrido.

Wildavsky, Aaron. 1987. Choosing preferences by constructing institutions: A culturalist theory of preference formation. *American Political Science Review* 81:2–21.

Chapter Fifteen

Democracy for the Few: Ecuador's Crisis-Prone Democracy

ROBERT E. BILES

Since its transition from military rule in 1978–1979 Ecuador has enjoyed its longest period of continuous democratic rule. Throughout the period, Latin Americanists from North America have ranked it ninth among the twenty nations on the Fitzgibbon-Johnson-Kelly Image-Index of Latin American democracy. The one exception was in 1985, early in the period, when it dropped to eleventh under the government of León Febres Cordero, who often showed only minimal respect for democratic processes.

This chapter is an attempt to assess the quality of Ecuadorean democracy. It finds that Ecuador has the outward appearances of democracy but little of its substance. Ecuador has most of the forms and some of the practices of democracy; however, democracy is not supported by either an elite or mass consensus, its practice is erratic, its success is limited, and its life is fragile. The hope is that Ecuador can produce a more substantive and less fragile democracy through longevity and perhaps enhanced performance.

Prior to 1979 Ecuadorean politics appeared chaotic. Since independence the nation has had eighteen constitutions. From 1900 to 1979, there were forty-eight chiefs of state, serving an average of 1.7 years each. Fifteen were extraconstitutional de facto leaders for all or part of their time in power (Ecuador Tribunal Supremo Electoral [TSE] 1989:147–151). Coups were carried out by individual military leaders, the military as an institution, presidents, and on one occasion the Congress. There have been only two periods of sustained democracy: 1948–1961 and 1979 to the present. Nevertheless, there was actually considerable continuity.

The government responded mainly to a narrow stratum of elites. For the mass of the population, most of the major issues had little relevance: They consisted of regional conflicts between the Guayaquil merchant class and the *sierra* landowners, questions about the status of the church, and personal squabbles among the elite (Schodt 1987:68). Moreover, the state was relatively weak. It had difficulty extending its power very far into society. Thus for much of the population governmental changes made little difference.

Economic development and the socioeconomic changes that it commonly brings came later to Ecuador than to most of Latin America. Thus a significant middle class, an industrial working class, and the institutions and values that represent popular interests were late in developing. Though there were stirrings in the 1920s and 1930s, significant class development, modern parties, and popular organizations have occurred largely in the decades following 1950, and such groups are still small, weak, and disunited (Hurtado 1990:259–268). Popular groups came into a political environment in which formal, constitutional rights had increased over time, and some groups, notably women, were formally given the vote earlier than in other parts of Latin America. However, the political system had long been essentially exclusionary. The large illiterate population, for example, was not permitted to vote until 1984. Thus until the 1980s the participant population—those who voted or were represented by effective organizations—remained small compared to that of most other Latin American nations.

Not surprisingly, when the reform-minded military junta led by General Rodríguez Lara came to power in 1972, economic reforms were easily beaten down by the elites. In 1976 more-conservative generals replaced Rodríguez Lara with a triumvirate of the three service commanders and abandoned socioeconomic reform. However, the new junta sought not just a transition to civilian rule but political reforms that would improve the capability of democratic institutions, particularly the political parties and the presidency. Though the democratic transition has produced an unbroken series of government turnovers based on elections, it does not appear to have increased the civic-mindedness of the elite, the representation and responsive capabilities of the system, or the respect for the rules of the democratic game among the key participants. Today most of the population is formally included in the political process, but both the culture and the institutions produce low effective participation and low responsiveness.

What Is Democracy?

There is no universal agreement as to the exact meaning of democracy. However, there are some common themes. Traditionally scholars have defined democracy in procedural and institutional terms (for example, Schumpeter 1950; Huntington 1991). For them, democracy implies the consent of the governed through free, fair, and periodic elections in which there is universal suffrage, competition, and freedom to organize and oppose. A second traditional concern is that government power be limited in the sense that individual and minority rights are protected from oppression by the majority.

Robert Dahl (1971) and Francis Hagopian (1990) add a third requirement, that mechanisms be present to articulate the interests of subordinate groups. Fourth, Valerie Bunce (cited in Mattiace and Camp 1996:6) adds that "Democratic elections . . . are nice, but democratic governance is crucial." Democratic government is simultaneously representative, accountable, and sufficiently powerful to rule effectively. It also requires "a Weberian bureaucracy—that is, a bureaucracy that is rational, rule-bound, merit-based, and subject to control by elected officials" (Mattiace and Camp 1996:6). Fifth, in Latin America the one group that is generally most critical to the survival of democracy is the military. Ideally, one might wish for a military establishment that valued civilian rule and had a strong ethos of nonintervention. However, in the short run, perhaps the best that can be expected is a military that in fact abstains from armed intervention and does not use its power to direct the civilian authorities. Thus the definition of democracy used here requires (1) free, competitive elections, (2) civil liberties, (3) effective representation of subordinate groups, (4) responsive government in its several dimensions, and (5) a military that allows the first four to happen.

How Well Does Ecuadorean Democracy
Meet These Five Standards?

Elections

The forms of contemporary Ecuadorean democracy match the definition of democracy, as does some of the substance. Beginning with the 1978–1979 democratic transition, there have been five consecutive presidential elections, three off-year congressional elections, and regular provincial and local elections. With the partial exception of the transition elections, competition has been free and vigorous. Presidents of quite different ideology have alternated in office with no military intervention. In sequence, presidents have been populist/Christian democrat, conservative, democratic socialist, conservative, and populist. Moreover, on two occasions voters rejected presidential initiatives in plebiscites. Thus, Ecuadorean democracy passes the test of holding regular elections, allowing competition, and respecting the results.

In February 1997 the nation underwent an event that can be interpreted as indicating either the resilience or the weakness of Ecuadorean democracy. In the six months following his August 1996 swearing in, President Abdalá Bucaram saw his popularity plummet because of the severe austerity measures he implemented in violation of his populist promises, because of his erratic behavior, and because of the obvious corruption surrounding his administration. He had become unpopular with the masses who elected him and an embarrassment to the elite. Nevertheless, he ignored calls for his resignation, and opponents appeared to be unlikely to obtain the two-thirds congressional majority required to impeach him. Instead, in the midst of popular demonstrations, the Congress removed him from office on grounds of mental incapacity, which required only a simple majority. The final vote was 44–34 for removal. Because the constitution was deliberately left unclear as to succession, Ecuador lived through several days in which three persons claimed to be president: Bucaram, Vice President Rosalía Arteaga, and the president of the Congress, Fabián Alarcón, who was chosen by Congress to be the new president. The military stayed neutral but played a key role in persuading the civilians to work out an arrangement in which Bucaram would step down and Arteaga would become president but would immediately resign to allow the Congress to select Alarcón as interim president until elections in 1998. After the fact, voters approved the decisions in a May 1997 plebiscite. Three-fourths supported the removal of Bucaram and two-thirds the selection of Alarcón as interim president. The process was messy, but legal forms were more or less observed, if stretched, and negotiation was used instead of force.

Civil Liberties

In spite of some major problems, this is the current Ecuadorean democracy's other strong area. There is a relatively free and vigorous press, both print and electronic, that is critical of the government and that covers a range of views. Even during the military governments of the 1970s, the press remained free and served as a major outlet for criticism of the government. Although military leaders recognized that the storm of criticism in the press shortened their rule, they refrained from repressing it. There appears to have been only one major case of press censorship during the period of military rule. With the exception of the Febres Cordero government, there has been substantial freedom of speech and organization during the current democratic period. Working-class, peasant, and student organizations have not been totally free of government persecution, but they have enjoyed a considerable degree of freedom to organize and present their views.

Prior to 1979 repression and violation of human rights were common features of many regimes. For example, when the populist José María Velasco Ibarra was returned to the presidency by a leftist coup in 1944, he systematically destroyed most of the small influence acquired by the Left during the 1930s and early 1940s. Leftists were purged from the government, students and workers beaten, and the opposition press suppressed (Schodt 1987:77). When he assumed dictatorial powers during his fifth and last presidency in 1970, he closed the universities and exiled Assad Bucaram, who seemed the probable winner of the 1972 elections.

The military has acted in a repressive fashion on various occasions. However, its two most recent governments were commonly seen as *dictablandas,* or mild dictatorships, for their relatively low level of repression. Nevertheless, the military did quit approving new labor unions and repressed strikers and students during the 1970s. There was a massacre of rural workers in 1977, and the leader of the Radical Alfarista Front (FRA), Abdón Calderón, was assassinated by military hard-liners seeking to derail the democratic transition. The 1963–1966 military regime was sufficiently repressive that there was fear of retribution when civilian rule resumed. However, repression was particularly light under General Rodríguez Lara's regime (1972–1976), and although rights violations increased under the 1976–1979 junta, amnesty for human rights violations was not an issue in 1978–1979. In this area, Ecuadorean military regimes stand in sharp contrast to those of the southern cone of Latin America and of Brazil.

Reports of human rights violations today occur primarily in areas related to the security forces, both police and military (for example, Panchana 1996; Cornejo Menacho 1994:192–194). The situation is made worse by problems with the judicial system. The judiciary is commonly manipulated by the executive and receives poor evaluations from the public and many lawyers for the quality of justice (Villavicencio 1994:106). The system of justice has been severely criticized by Amnesty International for the failure to prosecute members of the security forces who commit human rights violations (Amnesty International 1995).

Thus, by Latin American standards, Ecuador has a good record of permitting open debate and a better than average record for permitting organized opposition. On the other hand, the record for protection of the individual from abuse by police and security forces is much weaker. In the 1985 Fitzgibbon-Johnson-Kelly Image-Index of Latin American democracy, Ecuador had its highest ranking in the area of freedom of speech, press, assembly, and public communications—fifth among the twenty nations. In the 1995 Image-Index, these freedoms and "free elections" were Ecuador's two highest-ranked areas among the fifteen categories used to assess democracy.

Representation of Subordinate Groups

This is one of the weakest areas of Ecuadorean democracy. Ecuador still has a political system that the elites dominate because they are well organized and have substantial and effective access to decisionmakers. Popular groups, on the other hand, are relatively few, disunited, and lacking in effective access. Geographic, social, and organizational fragmentation have kept the popular sectors weak and given the better-organized, more-cohesive elites the advantage (Mills 1991:209). Though the overwhelming proportion of Ecuador's population falls into the "popular" category, it is nevertheless severely divided. The urban working class has at least three divisions: in order of increasing size, the industrial working class, the artisans, and the informal sector. Because of Ecuador's late industrialization, the nation still has a relatively small industrial working class, the most readily organizable portion of the working class. It is represented by three competing national confederations. However, since the 1970s they have coordinated their action through the Unitary Workers' Front (FUT), carrying out their first successful twenty-four-hour general strike in 1985. Nevertheless, the substantial diversity within the ranks of organized labor—running the gamut from rural laborers to industrial workers to government bureaucrats—makes it difficult for labor to place effective specific demands on government. Labor is further weakened by the attachment of much of its leadership to the leftist parties, which have had little electoral success in Ecuador (Mills 1984:127–190). Thus "labour's ties to institutional politics are weak and its influence inside policy-making bodies in the state is marginal" (Conaghan and Espinal 1990:568). FUT appears to function "largely as a defensive and reactive pressure group that views workers' interests in relation to their status as consumers" (567). Whereas labor has limited ability to influence the state, government influence over labor increased after the 1970s oil boom. The influence is greater in rural areas (Nurse 1989). Moreover, unions represent only a small portion of the working class.

Artisans are much more numerous than industrial workers, but the conditions under which they work make them much more difficult to organize. In addition, under the law, they are in a much weaker position with respect to their employers (Middleton 1982). The largest urban working-class group is the informal sector, the large mass of unemployed, underemployed, and self-employed poor. Parts of the informal sector are represented through neighborhood associations and small organizations such as associations of street vendors. However, the number who are organized is small, their coordination minimal, their resources few, and their access to policymakers negligible. Thus the urban working class is only partly organized, and that sector suffers significant division. Several unions have also sought to organize peasants and rural wage laborers, but the numbers recruited are small.

The most neglected and oppressed segment of Ecuador has long been its indigenous population, which makes up a fourth of the nation. Divided into numerous ethnic groups and isolated in rural areas, the indigenous population had long been difficult to organize. However, the Confederation of Ecuadorean Indigenous Nationalities (CONIAE) has operated effectively in the 1990s and was able to extract some concessions during both the Rodrigo Borja and Sixto Durán Ballén governments. Because it initially had minimal access, CONIAE used militant tactics, occupying the Congress in 1991 and blockading national highways in 1994. However, it has grown in political sophistication and access. During the 1996 elections it created a political organization and ran candidates for office in conjunction with other groups. CONIAE leader Luis Macas was elected to the Congress. Its position is still weak in terms of affecting policy but appears to be improving.

Not only are worker and peasant organizations weak, the party system also provides them little effective representation. Ecuador has a strong tradition of populism, to which the working class responds. However, it has provided few concrete responses to working-class needs. There have been two major populist movements, one associated with five-time president Velasco Ibarra and one associated with the Bucaram family. Velasco Ibarra was a powerful and demagogic orator who was able to capture the frustration and needs of the poor and working classes, but in office he did little to benefit those who elected him. He was unskilled as an executive, he had no program of reform that would improve the long-term lot of the poor, and he served the interest of the elite of the moment, the traditional economic elite who dominated the old Conservative and Liberal Parties (Cueva 1982:74–75). Assad Bucaram and his nephew, Abdalá Bucaram, continued the tradition of fiery oratory aimed at the marginal population but added effective clientelistic party organization. They were long successful in Guayaquil and the coast, but by 1966 Abdalá had added sufficient support in the *sierra* to win the presidency.

Abdalá Bucaram began his presidency much as had Velasco Ibarra. During the campaign, he described himself as the "leader of the poor" and the "scourge of the oligarchy," but once he had won he said that the country needed good businessmen and foreign investment (Cisternas 1996). His actual policies were closer to those of his neoliberal predecessor, and in some cases even harsher.

Paul Drake has argued that populism in other Latin American nations provided their working-class constituencies "concrete benefits well in excess of those delivered by most other political systems" (1982:235). However, this has not been the case of Ecuadorean populism, which is more comparable to early than to later Latin American populism.[1] Popular groups in Ecuador have received rhetoric and a few public works but little substantive response from the populists.

During the 1970s, two programmatically oriented parties, Democratic Left (Izquierda Democrática—ID) and Popular Democracy (Democracia Popular—DP), attempted to develop programmatic national, mass-based organizations. Both, coming from the center left, are ideologically disposed to represent popular interests. However, with the fragility of attachments to parties by both followers and leaders and the competition from clientelist populist parties, the two parties have had trouble maintaining an electoral base. With the DP barred from the 1978 transition election, its leader, Osvaldo Hurtado, was elected vice president with the populist Jaime Roldós and became president on his death in 1981. The ID won the presidency in 1988 and in alliance with the DP had a congressional majority. However, the majority steadily declined, and in 1992 both parties suffered a major defeat. In 1996 the DP had its largest congressional bloc ever, twelve members, while the ID had only five out of the total of eighty-two deputies. Popular interests have also been represented by the radical left and other center left parties. However, the Left, which was never strong, declined markedly in 1996, and other nonpopulist parties appealing to the working class have been small and sporadic. It would seem that Ecuador does not yet adequately meet the democratic standard of adequate representation of subordinate groups.

Responsive Government

The fourth democratic standard is a government that is representative, accountable, and sufficiently powerful to rule effectively. It should also have a rational, responsive bureaucracy. Ecuador has problems on all these counts.

Representative?   The electorate was long kept small by exclusion of much of the working class, but these legal barriers have been largely eliminated. Thus, with near universal adult suffrage for selection of the president, Congress, and local government, one could argue that government is representative. However, its functioning is not. The fourth of the population that is indigenous has always been treated as the objects of rule, not as participants in the process. This is only recently beginning to change. The pervasive elitism of the society also makes representation difficult. Most of the parties are organized to carry messages from the top down. They commonly lack a popular base of participant members who can articulate working-class interests to be represented by their party. The substitution of elite opinion for actual representation is found even on the Left, which generally has actively sought to represent popular interests. For example, in an interview, a local union leader told me of her frustration that the leftist party with which the union was affiliated regularly subordinated the union members' concerns to the broader issues that the party leaders felt were oppressing the workers (Biles 1993–1994).

Accountable?   Neither is the government very accountable. Populist leaders have long been accustomed to voicing popular discontent in order to win elections but then governing in the interests of the elite. Yet they maintain their popularity. One reason may be a disconnection between the vote and expectations of policy implementation. Amparo Menéndez Carrión's extensive field research in Guayaquil, for example, found lower-class voters responded to populist leaders for rational reasons such as expectations of material benefits rather than because of charisma or populist ideology (1986). The interest group system gives elite interests substantial access to elected officials and the bureaucracy. This is reinforced by habits of corporatism. Earlier, Ecuador utilized functional representation of groups such as agriculture, commerce, industry, and labor in the Congress. This has been abolished, but it is still the custom of many city councils that the chairs of certain committees should be from the appropriate profession (Biles 1993–1994). Close informal ties still exist between associations and the government agency making decisions in their area. All of this means that government is accountable more to elites and corporate groups than to the public at large.

Effective Rule?   In several senses Ecuadorean government is too weak to rule effectively. Some authors, such as John Martz (1996, 1987, 1972) see a political and cultural disunity based in substantial measure on the regional differences and conflicts between the coast and the *sierra* that reduce the sense of national identity and the effective reach of the national government. The authority of the state is relatively weak, and the system is effectively decentralized. In many ways the mayor of Guayaquil, the largest city and the commercial center of the nation, is the second most important elected official in the country. The *tenientes políticos* (political lieutenants) are still powerful figures in many rural areas. Though they are appointed by the executive, they commonly enjoy great discretion, unchecked by the government in Quito (Martz 1996:333).

The state is also limited by the lack of revenue. Tax evasion is pervasive in Ecuador, and the state is resource starved. The discovery of large petroleum reserves in 1967 gave a temporary boost to the financial capability of the Ecuadorean state in two ways. First, it provided a great deal of money directly to the state, which then did not have to tax Ecuador's private sector. It also reduced the leverage of Guayaquil's commercial and export sector on the economy and thereby on the government. The 1970s was a boom period for Ecuador. Direct linkages between oil production and the domestic economy were relatively small, but government expenditures grew substantially. Unfortunately, government expenditures grew faster than revenues, and like other oil producers Ecuador borrowed heavily from international lenders, planning to pay back the debts from continued high oil revenues. Though oil revenues grew until 1983, the increased rate of government expenditure was dependent upon continued international borrowing, which was cut off in 1982 as a consequence of Mexico's threatened default (Schodt 1987:99–112; Rouquié 1987:327–330). Industry and commerce had grown during the 1970s but were not able to take up the slack. The democratic governments of the 1980s were thus faced with the politics of austerity.

Two political patterns significantly weaken the ability to govern effectively in Ecuador: the weakness of the party system and the disarticulation between the president and the Congress. Political parties in Ecuador find it difficult to carry out their functions of representing public interests and keeping public officials in line with public sentiment because the parties have a small base, are held in low esteem by both leaders and followers, and have been significantly replaced by interest groups in the representation of interests.

For almost a century, the party system consisted largely of the two traditional parties of the oligarchy, the Conservatives and the Liberals. The parties served the elite, and most of the population was little involved in or served by them. The traditional parties were supplemented in the 1930s to 1950s by populism, the loose *velasquista* movement, and the more organized Concentration of Popular Forces (CFP). Although the small Socialist and Communist Parties were formed in 1926 and 1931, most of the modern parties (those that are programmatic and mass based) arose as a consequence of the economic development of the 1950s to 1970s. Modern parties generally draw their cadre and much of their following from people in the more technologically advanced parts of the society. Even though these sectors grew in this period, they were still a very small constituency. For example, at the end of 1993, 79 percent of the population was in poverty, including the 51 percent who were chronically poor (*El Comercio*, September 19, 1993:A1). The nonpoor represented only 2.3 million persons, a small constituency for the modern parties.

The parties' base was further limited by repression from the military governments of the 1960s and 1970s. Though the parties' organizational activities continued, they were hampered, and the new parties lost valuable experience in negotiation, governmental leadership, and democratic opposition. During the 1972–1979 military government the parties were replaced by interest groups as the primary source of interest representation, a significant change. The military jailed party leaders, exiled them to the Amazon area, or refused to deal with them. However, the military was willing to deal with interest groups. The business community was well organized to lobby the military through their Chambers of Agriculture, Commerce, and Industry, but particularly through the newly created umbrella organization, the National Federation of Chambers of Production. Organized labor also played a significant, though lesser, role in representation.

Once the military regime ended the parties were unable to regain primacy in interest representation or to command the respect that would enable them to effectively govern. The modern parties emerged in an era when parties were held in low esteem. The elites long used the Liberal and Conservative Parties to present their wishes to government, but they readily abandoned the parties when their interest associations offered better channels. Effectively left out of the traditional party system, the masses had little incentive to value the parties. Neither were the parties associated with major reform, a sustained struggle for popular participation, or opposition to a tyrant that could give them a heroic image. On the contrary, Velasco Ibarra's ability to get the country temporarily through elite impasses and his vocal disdain for parties retarded their development and institutionalization. Just as Velasco's followers were opportunistic, supporting or abandoning him when it seemed to give them advantage (Cueva 1982:80), so too both the followers and the leaders of the parties in the modern period have more a pragmatic than an affective attachment to their parties. The parties have experienced dramatic shifts in their electoral fortunes as well as major shifts in the loyalty of party members in congress. The effect of these party weaknesses is to weaken the ability of government to rule effectively.

During the last years of their rule, the military made a serious effort to reform the parties and to produce a system in which the parties would be healthier and stronger and in which presidents could govern effectively within a democratic framework of party competition. To limit the proliferation of parties they were required to have official recognition, and parties not receiving at least 5 percent of the vote in two successive elections would lose their certification. To reduce the role of personalism and to strengthen the parties, candidates had to be put forward by parties; independent candidacies were not permitted. And to strengthen the president in dealing with Congress, he or she had to be elected by a majority. It was hoped that the need to form electoral coalitions for the second round would produce majority congressional coalitions for the president.

None of these goals have been achieved. Proliferation of parties continues: Since the mid-1980s the number of parties has fluctuated around seventeen; after the 1994 midterm elections there were thirteen parties and two independents in Congress; and in the four presidential elections between 1984 and 1996 there were from nine to twelve president–vice president slates. Even before the prohibition against independents was effectively ended, it had little effect on the low level of attachment to the parties. In fact, it forced ambitious politicians into temporary marriages of convenience with parties to which they felt no attachment. Following election by a party, members of Congress have regularly abandoned their party of election for other parties or independence, a process referred to as a *cambio de camisetas* (change of undershirts). Party leaders have continued the process in an unsuccessful attempt to create party discipline. In August 1993, for example, Abdalá Bucaram expelled seven deputies from the Ecuadorean Roldosisto Party (PRE) for voting against the bloc in electing the president of the Congress. The lack of party attachment is illustrated by Sixto Durán Ballén. Twice the presidential candidate of the Social Christian Party (PSC), he abandoned the party in 1992 when it became clear that Jaime Nebot would be the party's candidate. He formed the Republican Unity Party (PUR) and soundly defeated Nebot.

Finally, the military government of the 1970s correctly saw that the president was weak in dealing with Congress, but their solution, the requirement of majority election for the president, did not provide a cure. The two top presidential candidates in the first round of elections do have to form coalitions for the second round; however, these coalitions quickly die in the heat of congressional politics.

The resultant disarticulation between the president and the Congress makes policymaking difficult and increases the temptation to rule in a nondemocratic fashion. Ecuador's Congress has been relatively strong and assertive during the democratic period, which is generally a positive development. However, none of the five presidents through 1996 have been able to maintain a congressional majority that would allow them to pass a coherent program. Rather, Congress has been so divided and has displayed so much conflict within its own ranks and toward the president that the president's ability to carry out any significant program of change has been destroyed.

A brief history of the relations between Congress and the presidency reveals the role of the proliferation of parties, the weakness of party attachment and discipline, and the strength of personalism and crude pragmatism. In 1978 Jaime Roldós became the nominee of the populist CFP when CFP leader Assad Bucaram was banned from running for president. Roldós won, the party obtained a solid congressional majority, and Bucaram became the president of Congress. But rather than allowing the president to govern with the assistance of a pro-government majority, the victory was followed by a bitter fight between the two leaders not over issues but over their personal status as leaders and over control of the party and its patronage. The conflict produced fragmentation of the party and a legislative-executive stalemate. It led to the Congress passing unsound legislation and rejecting reforms proposed by Roldós. When Vice President Osvaldo Hurtado assumed the presidency, his reform proposals were also stymied by a hostile Congress, in spite of a series of transitory legislative coalitions. Hurtado was also unable to gain the support of the center left, which agreed with his ideas but wanted to avoid identification with an unpopular government during the 1984 presidential elections.

Conservative León Febres Cordero of the PSC was elected president in 1984 but faced a Congress controlled by the center left Bloque Progresista, which initially opposed his programs. However, patronage and individual advancement won over ideology, and eleven deputies defected to the government coalition. Febres Cordero enjoyed a brief pro-government majority but lost it in the midterm elections. His relations with Congress are routinely described in terms such as "tumultuous," "embittered," and "pitched battles." Febres Cordero dealt in part with the legislative impasse by ignoring congressional actions and ruling in a more authoritarian manner than any of the other presidents of the democratic period. For example, it was his refusal to recognize the congressional amnesty for General Frank Vargas that led to the president's kidnapping by air force paratroopers in 1987 (discussed later).

Rodrigo Borja of the ID was elected president in 1988 with a congressional majority based on a coalition with DP. However, the coalition broke down before the midterm elections, and little of his ambitious social program was actually implemented. The opposition was more personalist than ideological. The leftist Popular Democratic Movement (MPD) and Broad Front of the Left (FADI), for example, voted with the conservative opposition as Congress voted to impeach several cabinet members (Cockcroft 1996:448). Supporters of Abdalá Bucaram focused on securing an amnesty for Bucaram, who had fled to Panama following charges of misuse of public funds. Febres Cordero, for his part, sought revenge for alleged persecution by the Borja government and the Supreme Court (Isaacs 1993:129).

Sixto Durán Ballén entered the presidency in 1992 with a clear conservative majority, although his own party was third after his vice president's PSC and Bucaram's PRE. Feuding between the PSC and his own PUR caused a breakdown of the coalition within a few months. Durán Ballén did accomplish his goal of stabilizing the economy, but his ambitious neoliberal program for major structural reforms of government and the economy was largely derailed by the ambitions of the PSC and populist leaders, by ideological opposition from the center left, and by Durán Ballén's own ineffective leadership.

In 1996 Abdalá Bucaram entered the presidency with a Congress divided among three minority blocs and almost a dozen miniblocs. His own PRE had the second-largest delegation, nineteen, after the PSC's twenty-six in the eighty-two member Congress. Both parties sought a majority through alliance with parties from the center left. Within six months of taking office, Bucaram's plummeting popularity, his erratic behavior, widespread corruption by his appointees, and the opposition of the congressional majority led to his removal from office.

The history of presidential-legislative stalemate shows a variety of structural and value impediments to the broad acceptance of the idea of a loyal opposition in which the nongovernment parties see it as their duty to oppose the government but do not carry opposition to the point of deadlock. As a consequence, compromise and concern for the national good too seldom temper opposition in Ecuador.

The combination of the limited financial resources of the state and the lack of cooperation between Congress and the president has contributed to the relatively small variation in the actual impact of the different governments, populist, democratic socialist, and neoliberal. The Borja government, for example, had a strong commitment to social programs but was hamstrung by opposition and the need for austerity. Durán Ballén sought major reforms in the other direction—neoliberalism—but he too was stymied by opposition. Even so, there were indications that his plans for the economy were bearing fruit when the border war with Peru broke out in 1995. The war produced a temporary truce with the opposition but wreaked havoc with the economy.

A final requisite of effective democratic government is a Weberian bureaucracy. Because studies of Ecuador's bureaucracy are so sparse (Dent 1990:156), the present evaluation is highly subjective. Several criticisms that are made of bureaucracy in other parts of Latin America appear to apply in Ecuador as well. There have been attempts to reduce the number of government agencies outside of the control of elected officials, but a large number still appear to be independent and thus subject to little public control. Patronage and clientelism are strong forces in Ecuador's politics, which reduces competency levels and responsiveness to the public interest. Pay is low, which encourages corruption and a minimal commitment of time. Finally, Ecuador's bureaucracy appears to have retained more of the colonial mentality. The bureaucracy tends to see its purpose as controlling and directing the public rather than serving it. It tends to be highly legalistic, applying the rules without thought to goals or consequences. And it tends to be rigid and resistant to change. Such a bureaucracy serves authoritarianism better than democracy. On the whole, it appears that Ecuador fails the test of effective democratic government.

The Military

The final test of democracy is the role of the military. Respect for democratic processes by the military is critical to the survival of democracy in any Latin American country, and this is clearly so in Ecuador. Overt military involvement in civilian politics in Ecuador appears to have declined since the military juntas of the 1970s. In the transitional elections of 1978–1979 the long-time populist leader Assad Bucaram, who would probably have been elected president, was barred from participating by the military junta. The junta also barred two parties: the center left Christian democratic DP and the leftist MPD. In 1981, when President Roldós was killed in a plane crash, the military hesitated a few hours before accepting the ascension of Vice President Osvaldo Hurtado. Hurtado had run with Roldós but was a leader of the proscribed Christian Democrats. Under the government of the conservative León Febres Cordero, there was constant conflict between the military and the civil authorities because of Febres Cordero's scorn for the military's institutional autonomy and his promotion of favored officers. The conflict became particularly heated in 1986 when the chief of the joint command,

General Frank Vargas, was arrested after bringing charges of corruption against the Febres Cordero government. Unsuccessful bargaining and heated exchanges led to the brief seizure of the president by pro-Vargas paratroopers. Subsequent presidents have respected the military's autonomy and dealt carefully with them. Military respect for democratic processes was again tested in 1988 when Abdalá Bucaram reached the presidential runoff. Bucaram, nephew of Assad and also a fiery populist, was highly critical of the military (Martz, 1996:334), and a *golpe de estado* (coup d'état) was rumored if he were elected. However, he was not proscribed in 1988, and when he was elected president in 1996 there was apparently no serious thought of intervention by the military, even though he greatly worried conservative elites. Rumors of coups have marked all of the civilian governments, but none have borne fruit.

At least two military figures have achieved national prominence, but they do not represent a military intervention in civilian affairs. General Frank Vargas left the military following the conflict with Febres Cordero and made three races for the presidency as leader of a nationalist, popularly oriented center left party, Ecuadorean Revolutionary Popular Action (APRE). After backing Bucaram in the 1996 runoff, he became a minister of government. The 1995 border war with Peru brought national popularity to the troop's commander, General Paco Moncayo. Moncayo has used his prominence to denounce the corruption and inefficiency of civilian leaders but claims to support democracy and has made no move toward military intervention.

In sum, overt military intervention has declined during the period of civilian rule, and though some military leaders may comment on civilian matters, the military does not appear to attempt to dictate policy or behavior outside of national security matters, broadly defined. The military does remain autonomous and resistant to subordination to civilian leaders, who tend to tread carefully when dealing with the military. The military's independence is also enhanced by its control over various industries that bring it revenue directly. Many retired officers have entered the private sector, which increases concerns of military ties to the business elite. Military *golpes* remain a possibility that must be considered by civilian regimes. The possibility of a military *golpe* is enhanced by the low level of popular legitimacy of civilian politicians (Bustamente 1988). In her excellent study of the Ecuadorean military, based heavily on interviews with military and civilian officials, Anita Isaacs (1993:143) concludes that military coups remain a real possibility. Another careful student of the Ecuadorean military, J. Samuel Fitch (1986; 1977) sees the coup as an integral part of Ecuador's political system. This is true because of both military and civilian attitudes. Finally, as we saw earlier, there are also questions raised about the military's respect for human rights.

Political Culture

Although not part of the definition of democracy, the values and beliefs about democracy among the public and elites may reinforce or weaken a democratic

TABLE 15.1   Public Evaluation of Democracy and Dictatorship: A Close Race
(1988–1989)

	Guayaquil	Quito
Do you prefer democracy or dictatorship?		
Democracy	44%	66%
No difference	5%	7%
Dictatorship	51%	27%
Is democracy or dictatorship better at solving problems?		
Democracy	54%	65%
No difference	8%	10%
Dictatorship	38%	24%
Is democracy or dictatorship more corrupt?		
Democracy	49%	30%
No difference	26%	31%
Dictatorship	25%	40%

Source: Instituto de Estudios Sociales y de la Opinión Pública, *Informe Confidencial,*
quoted in Anita Isaacs, *Military Rule and Transitions in Ecuador, 1972–1992* (Pittsburgh:
University of Pittsburgh Press), 134. Adapted by author.

system (Inglehart 1988:2; Mattiace and Camp 1996:6–10). These values and beliefs may also be taken as a reflection of the success or failure of democracy (Seligson 1996). Latin America's colonial period implanted a political culture featuring
authoritarianism, elitism, personalism, and corporatism, among other values.
The independence period has added beliefs in democracy and republicanism and
more recently socialism, Marxism, and social democracy. Some see democratic
values currently gaining ascendancy (Wiarda and Kline 1996:13). However, others
find nondemocratic values still dominant (Dealy 1996; Harrison 1985).

   There is strong evidence that neither democracy nor authoritarianism is clearly
dominant among the masses or elites of Ecuador. As Table 15.1 shows, when the
people of Guayaquil and Quito were asked to evaluate democracy and dictatorship, two-thirds of Quito residents preferred democracy and thought it was better
at solving problems. However, half of Guayaquil residents preferred dictatorship
and thought democracy was more corrupt.

   On the whole, Ecuador's citizens show less support for democracy than do
other Latin Americans. When fourteen Latin American nations were surveyed in
1993, an average of almost half the public reported being satisfied with democracy in their country. However, Ecuadorans had the lowest level of satisfaction
among the nations polled—29 percent (Table 15.2).[2] Similarly, when Latin Americans were asked if they had confidence in their major institutions, most expressed confidence in the church, the educational system, and the communications media. However, only a minority had confidence in the major institutions of
government and politics, such as parties, Congress, and the justice system.
Ecuadorans followed this pattern but rated the political and governmental insti-

TABLE 15.2   Democracy and the Economy: Public Satisfaction (1993)

	Percent Satisfied with	
	Democracy	Economic Situation
High for Latin America[a]	67	43
Mean for Latin America	47	[b]
Ecuador	29	17
Low for Latin America	29	17

Source: Barómetro Iberoamericano; Ecuadorian agency, Cedatos. Reported in *El Comercio* (October 31, 1993): B6.

[a]Fourteen states: Bolivia, Brazil, Colombia, Costa Rica, Chile, Dominican Republic, Ecuador, El Salvador, Guatemala, Mexico, Peru, Puerto Rico, Uruguay, and Venezuela.

[b]Not available in source.

tutions markedly lower than the average for the fourteen nations. Parties were seen in a particularly bad light (Table 15.3).

Ecuador's leaders also show mixed support for democracy. In the author's national surveys of political leaders in Ecuador, whose results are reported in Table 15.4, respondents were asked to indicate their agreement or disagreement with questions and statements that measure democratic attitudes. One, asked only of women political leaders, showed substantial support for freedom of speech, which is in keeping with the practice in Ecuador: "If someone wishes to speak against our system of government, should it be permitted?" A second statement was presented to female and male political leaders as well as to women in the professions and business. It touched on deference to authority figures and respect for the rule of law: "A few strong and decisive leaders would accomplish more for our country than all the laws and political discussions." Just over half of the political leaders of both sexes chose the less democratic response, which again appears to be in keeping with the mixture of democracy and authoritarianism in actual practice. On the other hand, more than three out of four business and professional leaders chose the less democratic answer, indicating less understanding and support for democratic practice.

Among the women political leaders, it was possible to form a scale with the two questions. A third of the leaders gave a democratic response to both questions, and only one in eleven gave undemocratic responses to both questions. The majority gave one democratic and one undemocratic response. It would appear that Ecuador's political leaders have a mixture of democratic and undemocratic values and that perhaps there is even less democratic orientation among private sector elites.

In summary, democracy in Ecuador since the democratic transition of 1979 meets two of the criteria for democracy: regular, competitive elections and, to a significant degree, respect for civil liberties, especially those having to do with freedom of debate. However, it largely fails on two others: effective representation

TABLE 15.3   Public Confidence in Politics and Government

	Latin America	Ecuador
Percent Expressing Confidence in the Institution 1993[a]		
Catholic church	60	73
Armed forces	[b]	65
Educational system	52	59
Communications media	58	58
Electoral system	46	28
Police	28	25
Justice	28	16
National Congress	28	11
Political parties	17	8

Evaluation of the Performance of the President 1993[a]
(1 = very bad; 10 = excellent)

High for Latin America	7.7
Mean for Latin America	5.8
Ecuador	4.3
Low for Latin America	3.9

Do Political Parties Care About Your Problems? (1993)[c]

	Guayaquil	Quito
Yes	11%	18%
No	89%	82%

[a]*Source:* Barómetro Iberoamericano; Ecuadorian agency, Cedatos. Reported in *El Comercio* (October 31, 1993): B6, table 15.2, which lists states surveyed.

[b]Not available in source.

[c]*Source:* Instituto des Estudios Sociales y de la Opinión Pública, *Informe Confidencial,* quoted in Anita Isaacs, Military Rule and Transition in Ecuador, 1972–1992 (Pittsburgh: University of Pittsburgh Press), 133.

of subordinate groups and responsive government. Its performance on the fifth criterion is less clear. The military has largely stayed out of civilian affairs when the civilians respected military independence and prerogatives; the only president to have serious problems was Febres Cordero, who openly interfered in what the military considered its own affairs. On the other hand, the possibility of a military coup remains real and is an option that some prefer. Such a possibility affects the behavior of leaders and appears to reduce the likelihood of developing widespread consensus on democratic rules of the game. Ecuador also has a political culture in which democratic and authoritarian values conflict. Thus Ecuador has the outward appearance of democracy and some of the substance, but it has yet to achieve a democratic reality across all the democratic criteria.

TABLE 15.4   Respect for Democratic Rules of the Game Among Ecuadorean Leaders

A. *"If someone wishes to speak against our system of government, should it be permitted?"*

	Women Political Leaders
Democratic response (agree)	87%
Undemocratic response (disagree)	13%

B. *"A few strong and decisive leaders would accomplish more for our country than all the laws and political discussions."*

	Men and Women Political Leaders	Women Business and Professional Leaders
Democratic response (disagree)	43%	22%
Undemocratic response (agree)	57%	78%
X^2 Significant at .005		

C. *Scale of Democratic Attitudes Among Women Political Leaders (number of democratic responses to A and B).*

No democratic response	9%
One democratic reponse	57%
Two democratic responses	34%

Source: Author's national surveys of female and male political leaders (Ns = 120 and 70, respectively) and of women business and professional leaders (N = 70), 1993–1994.

The Future of Ecuadorean Democracy

A quick review of three explanations for Ecuador's mixed state of democracy may help to put the preceding analysis in context. One explanation emphasizes Ecuador's lack of experience with democracy. Since the Liberal seizure of power under Eloy Alfaro in 1895, Ecuador has gone through a gradual process of increasing rights and participation. However, the authoritarian political culture matched much of the actual practice until the 1980s. Prior to the current period, there was only one other period of peaceful transfer of elected presidents, 1948–1961, and that was still a period of democracy largely by and for the elite. Thus it should take some time for democratic values and practices to take hold throughout the range of citizens and leaders.

Variations of a second explanation have been accepted by several North American scholars (Schodt 1987; Isaacs 1993; Conaghan and Espinal 1990). It develops in part from James Malloy's (1977) argument that delayed dependent capitalism and populism are important structural factors in the emergence of authoritarian regimes. In Ecuador the argument combines the impact of economic development with elite and political trends. It is well established that the development of democracy is assisted by economic development (Burkhart and Lewis-Beck 1994; Lipset, Seong, and Torres 1993). In particular, economic growth, industrialization, and urbanization produce a variety of social forces that promote more participation, increased political competition, challenges to authoritarian values, and democratic vehicles such as parties, unions, and peasant organizations. In Ecuador economic development came decades later than the average for Latin America, not until after 1950. This meant that the elites could continue to control the political process without much challenge until the 1950s. As popular organizations were emerging during the 1950s to 1970s, the continuing presence of the populist Velasco Ibarra and the major role of the military (which ruled twice in the period) depoliticized the system and delayed the development of popular democratic mechanisms. Both Velasco Ibarra and the military were deeply suspicious of politics, both voicing their distrust and acting to repress it. Thus the current democratic period began with democratic institutions and practices still in their infancy, the elite still exercising a dominant role in policy, and authoritarian values still strong.

The third explanation looks at the current period and asks whether the poor performance of democracy in improving the economy and reforming the polity to make it more representative contributes to the lack of support for democracy. Writers such as Adam Przeworski (1991) and Juan Linz (Diamond, Linz, and Lipset 1990) argue that economic growth enhances the legitimacy of democracy. The belief is that the practical attachment to democracy produced by economic growth will eventually lead to affective attachments that will carry the regime through periods of poor performance. This is supported by survey data from Ecuador that show a positive correlation between perceptions of "how things are going" in the country and satisfaction with democracy (U.S. Information Agency 1993:12). Giuseppe Di Palma (1990) and Samuel Huntington (1991), on the other hand, see experience with democratic processes as more important than economic performance. In either case, Ecuador's democracy may have problems. The civilian governments inherited a host of economic problems, including slow growth and heavy inflation, from the military regime. The military regimes, on the other hand, were times of growth and relative prosperity. The bill for the prosperity did not arrive until the civilians were in power. Thus the civilian governments' inability to resolve the economic crises causes many to view military rule with nostalgia. Moreover, both the 1963–1966 and 1972–1979 military regimes were seen as *dictablandas*, not marked by heavy repression. Thus military rule retains a positive image for many. Anita Isaacs argues that "because military rule remains a viable alternative, the performance of civilian regimes will be more closely scrutinised and tied to regime stability" (1993:137).

What, then, are the prospects for democracy in Ecuador? It would be easy to assume from what we have seen here that Ecuador's masses and elites will readily respond to a crisis by turning to authoritarianism. Support for democracy does seem fragile. However, Ecuador has successfully muddled through seventeen years of democracy. For its part, Ecuador's military appears to be cognizant of the costs of intervention in terms of dissension within its ranks and diversion from its national security role (Isaacs 1993:106, 140). It is possible that Ecuador may continue to muddle through as what Catherine Conaghan and Rosario Espinal call a "crisis-prone democracy" (1990:574).

Notes

The author thanks the U.S. Department of Education Fulbright-Hays Faculty Research Abroad Program, the Council for International Exchange of Scholars Fulbright Scholar Program, and the Faculty Development Leave Program of Sam Houston State University for support for field research in Ecuador during 1993–1994.

1. Rafael Quintero (1980) has argued that the populism of Velasco Ibarra was different from populism in the rest of Latin America and that therefore populism is not an adequate model for studying change in Ecuador. Iván Fernández Espinosa (1992:187) sees Ecuador's populism as different from classical populism in Latin America because of the less-developed socioeconomic environment in which it developed. Agustín Cueva (1982), on the other hand, sees Velasco's caudillismo and populism as a product of the conditions of the time and as important to understanding the period.

2. Surveys of the urban population conducted for USIA (1993:7) in 1991 and 1992, while showing higher levels of satisfaction with democracy, support the findings of a relatively low level of satisfaction and its fluctuation. In 1991, thirty-three percent of Ecuadorians were very or somewhat satisfied with the way democracy was functioning in Ecuador; in 1992, the percentage was fifty-four.

Bibliography

Amnesty International. 1995. Ecuador: Judicial authorities fail to clarify human right crimes. *Amnesty_International@io.org* July 12.

Biles, Robert E. 1993–1994. Interviews by author. Data from national surveys of female and male political leaders (Ns = 120 and 70, respectively) and of women business and professional leaders (N = 70).

Burkhart, Ross E., and Michael S. Lewis-Beck. 1994. Comparative democracy: The economic development thesis. *American Political Science Review* 88:903–910.

Bustamente, Fernando. 1988. Fuerzas armadas en Ecuador: ¿Puede institucionalizarse la subordinación al poder civil? In *Democracia y fuerzas armadas* (Fernando Bustamente, ed.), 129–160. Quito: Corporación de Estudios para el Desarrollo.

Cisternas, Carlos. 1996. Ecuador president reached poor. Associated Press News Service. July 10.

Cockcroft, James. 1996. *Latin America: History, Politics, and U.S. Policy.* 2nd ed. Chicago: Nelson-Hall.

El Comercio. 1993. Iberoamérica: cómo y hacia dónde (October 31):B1–B10.

_____. 1993. Aumenta la pobreza (September 19):A1.

Conaghan, Catherine M. 1987. Party politics and democratization in Ecuador. In *Authoritarians and Democrats: Regime Transition in Latin America* (James M. Malloy and Mitchell A. Seligson, eds.), 145–163. Pittsburgh: University of Pittsburgh Press.

_____. 1988. *Restructuring Domination: Industrialists and the State in Ecuador.* Pittsburgh: University of Pittsburgh Press.

Conaghan, Catherine M., and Rosario Espinal. 1990. Unlikely transitions to uncertain regimes? Democracy without compromise in the Dominican Republic and Ecuador. *Journal of Latin American Studies* 22:553–574.

Cornejo Menacho, Diego. 1994. Agenda pública y clima de opinión en la democracia: El papel de los medios de comunicación. In IDIS and ILDIS. In *Democracia y desarrollo,* 191–208. Cuenca: IDIS and ILDIS.

Cueva, Agustín. 1982. *The Process of Political Domination in Ecuador.* Translated by Danielle Salti. New Brunswick, N.J.: Transaction Books.

Dahl, Robert A. 1971. *Polyarchy: Participation and Opposition.* New Haven: Yale University Press.

Dealy, Glen Caudill. 1996. Two cultures and political behavior in Latin America. In *Democracy in Latin America: Patterns and Cycles* (Roderic Ai Camp, ed.), 49–66. Wilmington, Del.: Scholarly Resources.

Dent, David W. 1990. Ecuador. In *Handbook of Political Science Research on Latin America: Trends from the 1960s to the 1990s* (David W. Dent, ed.), 149–161. New York: Greenwood.

Diamond, Larry, Juan J. Linz, and Seymour Martin Lipset. 1990. Introduction: Comparing experiences with democracy. In *Politics in Developing Countries: Comparing Experiences with Democracy* (Larry Diamond, Juan J. Linz, and Seymour Martin Lipset, eds.), 1–38. Boulder: Lynne Rienner.

Di Palma, Giuseppe. 1990. *To Craft Democracies: An Essay on Democratic Transitions.* Berkeley: University of California Press.

Drake, Paul W. 1982. Conclusion: Requiem for populism. In *Latin American Populism in Comparative Perspective* (Michael L. Conniff, ed.), 217–245. Albuquerque: University of New Mexico Press.

Ecuador Tribunal Supremo Electoral (TSE). 1989. *Elecciones y democracia en el Ecuador, Tomo 1, El proceso electoral ecuatoriano.* Quito: Corporación Editora Nacional.

Fernández Espinosa, Iván. 1992. Los contenidos sociológicos del populismo. In *Populismo* (Blasco Peñaherrera Padilla and others, eds.), 179–195. Quito: ILDIS, El Duende, and Abya-Yala.

Fitch, John Samuel. 1977. *The Military Coup d'Etat as a Political Process: Ecuador, 1948–1966.* Baltimore: Johns Hopkins University Press.

———. 1986. The military coup d'état: the Ecuadorian case. In *Armies and Politics in Latin America,* rev. ed. (Abraham F. Lowenthal and John Samuel Fitch, eds.), 151–164. New York: Holmes and Meier.

Fitzgibbon-Johnson-Kelly Image-Index of Latin American Democracy. 1985, 1990, 1995. Mimeo. Phil Kelly, Emporia State University, Emporia, Kansas.

Hagopian, Francis. 1990. Democracy by undemocratic means: Elites, political pacts, and regime transition in Brazil. *Comparative Political Studies* 23:147–170.

Harrison, Lawrence E. 1985. *Underdevelopment Is a State of Mind: The Latin American Case.* Lanham, Md.: Madison Books.

Huntington, Samuel P. 1991. *The Third Wave: Democratization in the Late Twentieth Century.* Norman: University of Oklahoma Press.

Hurtado, Osvaldo. 1990. *El poder político en el Ecuador.* Quito: Letraviva-Editoria Planeta del Ecuador.

Inglehart, Ronald. 1988. The renaissance of political culture. *American Political Science Review* 82:1203–1230.

Isaacs, Anita. 1993. *Military Rule and Transition in Ecuador, 1972–1992.* Pittsburgh: University of Pittsburgh Press.
Lipset, Seymour Martin, Kyoung-R Seong, and John C. Torres. 1993. A comparative analysis of the social requisites of democracy. *International Social Science Journal* 136:155–175.
Malloy, James M., ed. 1977. *Authoritarianism and Corporatism in Latin America.* Pittsburgh: University of Pittsburgh Press.
Martz, John D. 1972. *Ecuador: Conflicting Political Culture and the Quest for Progress.* Boston: Allyn and Bacon.
_____. 1987. *Politics and Petroleum in Ecuador.* New Brunswick, N.J.: Transaction Books.
_____. 1996. Ecuador: The fragility of dependent democracy. In *Latin American Politics and Development,* 4th ed. (Howard J. Wiarda and Harvey K. Kline, eds.), 326–340. Boulder: Westview.
Mattiace, Shannan, and Roderic Ai Camp. 1996. Democracy and development: An overview. In *Democracy in Latin America: Patterns and Cycles* (Roderic Ai Camp, ed.), 3–19. Wilmington, Del.: Scholarly Resources.
Menéndez Carrión, Amparo. 1986. *La conquista del voto en el Ecuador: De Velasco a Roldós.* Quito: Corporación Editora Nacional and FLACSO.
Middleton, Alan. 1982. Division and cohesion in the working class: Artisans and wage labourers in Ecuador. *Journal of Latin American Studies* 14:171–194.
Mills, Nick D. 1984. *Crisis, conflicto y consenso. Ecuador: 1979–1984.* Quito: Corporación Editora Nacional.
_____. 1991. Sector privado y estado nacional en el Ecuador democrático, 1979–84. In *La Cuestión regional y el poder* (Rafael Quintero, ed.), 207–245. Quito: Corporación Editora Nacional.
Nurse, Charles. 1989. Ecuador. In *The State, Industrial Relations and the Labour Movement in Latin America* (Jean Carrière, Nigel Haworth, and Jacqueline Roddick, eds.), 1:99–127. New York: St. Martin's.
Panchana, Rolando. 1996. El SIC 10. *Vistazo.* August 29. *Http://www3.vistazo.com.ec/ago29_96/html/pais3.html.*
Przeworski, Adam. 1991. *Democracy and the Market: Political and Economic Reforms in Eastern Europe and Latin America.* Cambridge: Cambridge University Press.
Quintero, Rafael. 1980. *El mito del populismo en el Ecuador: Análisis de los fundamentos del estado ecuatoriano moderno, 1895–1934.* Quito: FLACSO.
Rouquié, Alain. 1987. *The Military and the State in Latin America.* Translated by Paul E. Sigmund. Berkeley: University of California Press.
Schodt, David W. 1983. Republic of Ecuador. In *World Encyclopedia of Political Systems and Parties* (George E. Delury, ed.), 275–285. New York: Facts on File.
_____. 1987. *Ecuador: An Andean Enigma.* Boulder: Westview.
Schumpeter, Joseph. 1950. *Capitalism, Socialism, and Democracy.* 3rd ed. New York: Harper and Row.
Seligson, Mitchell A. 1996. Political culture and democratization in Latin America. In *Democracy in Latin America: Patterns and Cycles* (Roderic Ai Camp, ed.), 67–89. Wilmington, Del.: Scholarly Resources.
U.S. Information Agency (USIA), Office of Research. 1993. Andean publics prefer democracy. Opinion Research Memorandum. Washington: USIA, April.

Villavicencio, Gaitán. 1994. Democracia formal, ciudadanía y violencia cotidiana en el Ecuador: Entre la amenaza y el miedo. In IDIS and ILDIS, *Democracia y desarrollo*, 103–120. Cuenca: IDIS and ILDIS.

Wiarda, Howard J., and Harvey F. Kline. 1996. The Latin American tradition and process of development. In *Latin American Politics and Development*, 4th ed. (Howard J. Wiarda and Harvey F. Kline, eds.), 3–68. Boulder: Westview.

Chapter Sixteen

Democracy in Peru?

DAVID SCOTT PALMER

Peru is one of those Latin American countries that has only infrequently done very well on *anybody's* "index of democracy." Over its history as an independent country, in fact—since 1821—Peru has been able to maintain long periods of formal democratic governments (that is, elected and civilian) only twice: 1895–1914 and 1980–1992. If we do a rough calculation of the proportion of all the years since independence that the government of Peru has been in the hands of elected civilian authorities, we find that it is about 60 of 175, or 34 percent, among the lowest of the Latin American countries (Palmer 1980:table 3.5, p. 37).

There was no civilian head of state for more than a few months until 1872. When civilian presidents did take over in the 1870s, by most accounts they did not acquit themselves well. In fact, historians assign these governments with much of the responsibility for Peru's absolutely catastrophic failure in the War of the Pacific (1879–1883) against Chile, which brought economic ruin as well as the loss of the nitrate-rich southern Department of Tarapacá (Werlich 1978:106–137). This disaster further postponed any democratic opening, until the mid-1890s as it turned out, far later than its neighbors and most other countries in the region.[1]

A further political distinction setting Peru apart in the area is the emergence of a military versus civilian party competition over the course of the nineteenth century rather than the conservative versus liberal competition that appeared and dominated politics almost everywhere else. However, the country did finally settle down politically with a limited liberal electoral democracy under the Civilistas, starting in 1895. At last there occurred successive four-year presidential elections and completed terms—six in all. There was just one brief interruption (a 1914 *golpe* [coup]) until the 1919 *autogolpe* (a self-administered nonconstitutional takeover by the sitting head of state) by elected president Augusto Leguía. He ushered in at this juncture an authoritarian, if civilian, *oncenio* (eleven-year rule) that lasted until a military *golpe* in 1930. Over the course of the next fifty-five years, only one elected civilian government completed its term of office (Manuel Prado, 1939–1945). Even that election was not completely open and aboveboard, for Peru's only mass-based party at the time, the American Popular Revolutionary Alliance (Alianza Popular Revolucionaria Americana—APRA), was not allowed to participate in the 1939 elections (Werlich 1978:218–222).

Only in 1980 was democratic rule reestablished (understood as electoral and civilian and not necessarily in terms of its policy orientation toward satisfying citizen needs), now fully open and participatory. But twelve years later, in April 1992, President Alberto Fujimori repeated the Leguía maneuver with an *autogolpe* of his own. Although democratic forms were restored within some twenty months under international pressure led by the United States and the Organization of American States (OAS), to this day a cloud hangs over the reestablished democratic processes and procedures in Peru (LASA 1995; McClintock et al. 1995; Tuesta Soldeville 1996). The perception lingers that President Fujimori, as one of only two elected heads of state in Latin America who secured consecutive second terms in office after constitutional changes permitting immediate reelection of an incumbent (Carlos Menem of Argentina is the other, though Fernando Henrique Cardoso of Brazil appears likely to follow suit), has in fact mounted a personalized and populist apparatus permitting an approach to governance that is at root not very democratic at all. As of 1997, furthermore, indications suggest that President Fujimori is working diligently to set himself up for a third election in the year 2000 in spite of considerable public opposition.

The Fitzgibbon-Johnson Index and Its Limitations

Through the case of Peru—and various others in the region as well—we can appreciate the challenges presented in attempting to "measure" levels of democracy in Latin America by means of the Fitzgibbon-Johnson Index. First of all, the fifteen-point index asks for assessments of a variety of intranational phenomena. As the criteria make clear, several relate to societal variables (educational level, internal unity), others to economic criteria (standard of living and external economic domination), and some to politics and its context (freedom of speech, free elections, and absence of foreign domination).

Second, the assessments of the degree of democracy present at a given point in time are determined every five years by Latin American specialists who are usually political scientists but who are unlikely to be completely knowledgeable on the specifics of the multiple Fitzgibbon criteria for each of the twenty countries that comprise the region. This means that subjective and impressionistic judgments inevitably creep into the index through the individual assessments.

A third limitation is that the twenty Latin American countries have always been rank ordered from 1 to 20 under the terms of the Fitzgibbon-Johnson Index assessment procedures. As long as a wide variety of regional political types and policy modes obtained in the region, this could be done. With the virtual universalization of democracy by the 1990s, however, and the concomitant convergence of the policy approach, rank-order differentiation becomes much more difficult and problematic. In other words, a 15 in 1970 is most unlikely to mean the same thing as a 15 in 1995.

A fourth problem in measurement occurs through the necessarily arbitrary five-year assessment of levels of democratic practice at junctures that inevitably favor some countries and penalize others simply because of the year in which the evaluation takes place. As an example, Peru's only "high" ranking over the entire fifty-year period—1945–1995—covered in the index (fifth out of twenty in 1980) occurred because that happened to be the year in which a *docenio* (twelve-year period) of military regimes gave way to the country's first elected civilian government based on open elections that included the entire adult population, and the year that followed two years of democratic opening, including constitutional convention elections.

Were the evaluative index to be based only on electoral criteria rather than on assessments of government performance and economic development as well, Peru quite probably would have found itself with considerably higher relative ratings in 1945, 1960, 1985, 1991, and 1995. In each of these years the country was functioning within the context of an elected civilian government. To provide one comparative illustration if the same electoral criteria were the only ones used: Cuba would have been placed at or close to the bottom of the list from 1960 through 1995. Presumably that country's relatively high ranking since the victory of the Fidel Castro's Revolution in 1959 (as high as sixth in 1980) has to do with the government's relative success in responding to a variety of citizen needs. By including performance criteria, a functioning democracy confronting economic crisis for whatever reason is penalized in the Fitzgibbon evaluative framework. Peru is affected adversely when these performance considerations are taken into account because government programs suffered almost continuously after 1975 due to a combination of government policy reform overreaching, mismanagement, and very high levels of foreign indebtedness (Thorp and Bertram 1978:318–320).

Explaining Peru's Politics in the Context of the Fitzgibbon Index

Whatever the limitations of the Fitzgibbon index, Peru is a fascinating case of the multiple challenges to implementing democratic practices. The long and the short of it is that the country never established a fully functioning democracy under the rules in effect in different historical periods—including the 1945–1995 years covered by the index. Why this is the case has been the subject of many assessments.

The Big Picture

One of the most persuasive assessments focuses on the nation's history as a center of Indian civilization, the location of major mineral deposits valued by the Crown of Castile and Aragon, and its resulting placement as the administrative center of Latin America during most of the 289 years under Spanish control. This argument presents Peru, as a central area of the Spanish Empire, in a long-term hierarchical relationship in which the authoritarian values of Iberia and its leading administrators permeated deeply into the society, the economy, and the polity. Such a long-standing dynamic, the argument continues, made it more difficult for the Crown's subjects to develop any meaningful political relationship based on bargaining, exchange among equals, and civil society (Haring 1963:chap. 3; Morse 1964:123–177).

However, the application of colonial administrative control was not uniform throughout Spanish America. Peru, as a core region under Spanish control, was more affected by these authoritarian values and procedures of Spanish governance than were other, more peripheral areas of the empire that were less subject to close day-to-day administrative oversight and control. One result, then, was a delayed and reluctant independence in Peru. Another was the retention, after the establishment of the Republic of Peru, of a more hierarchical and authoritarian perspective on citizen-state relations than in those areas of Spanish America where centralized control had been exercised less pervasively, where settlement had been less oriented toward responding to the needs of the metropole, and where a smaller proportion of the population was Indian.[2]

Another explanation offered for Peru's lack of success with democratic procedures and practices is based on the degree to which the country depended on outside investment, exports, and foreign loans and on its own private sector over the years. Because the government did not have control over its own economic destiny, the argument goes, it could not count on a stable economic base to build a responsible civilian democracy (Cotler 1978:Perú Problema 17). As one extreme example, it has been noted that as late as the early 1960s the Peruvian government, one of the smallest of public bureaucracies in Latin America, continued to rely on private contractors to collect public taxes (Hunt 1971:375–428). In examining the historical record, however, it turns out that the country's only extended period of elected civilian rule, from the mid-1890s until the late 1910s, happened to coincide with many of its years of greatest economic dependency (Palmer 1980:44–51). This suggests that dependency by itself may not have the systematic destabilizing effects on politics attributed to it; rather, it may interact with other factors.

Peru's relatively low levels of social mobilization and rates of change until the 1960s should have increased the possibilities that the government would have the political space necessary to effect incremental changes that would aid in establishing and consolidating democratic practices (Chaplin 1968). That this did not occur says more about the political and economic elites' willingness to maneuver to keep the country's only mass-based party (APRA) out of power for over fifty years than to the supposed salutary effects of specific macro phenomena (Graham 1992:23–71). In fact, it appears that this consideration—political leadership and its limitations—seems to provide the analyst with the best overall explanation, perhaps in combination with the weight of the authoritarian Hispanic colonial tradition, as to why Peru has had such difficulty in making democracy take root and function with reasonable effectiveness over the years and down to the present.[3]

"The Fitzgibbon Years," 1945–1995

Our focus is on the fifty-year period encompassed by the Fitzgibbon-Johnson Image-Index of Democracy, 1945–1995. Over these years Peru has experimented with a variety of political arrangements, some quite democratic, others frankly authoritarian, but none very long-lasting. A tumultuous reformist democracy under José Luis Bustamante y Rivero from 1945 to 1948 gave way before it could effectively implement its popular mandate for change to a personalistic conservative dictatorship under General Manuel Odría (known as the *ochenio*, or eight-year period) to mid-1956.

Conservative democratic restoration (that is, national politics that continued, as under General Odría, to eschew social programs and to favor elites, but with elections) with the election of Manuel Prado to a second term in 1956 might have taken hold under the *convivencia* (living together, or cohabitation) that included a tamed APRA behind the scenes. However, the 1962 elections, which continued to be open only to the literate adult minority, produced a virtual three-way tie among the leading contenders—conservative Manuel Odría and his National Odriist Union (Unión Nacional Odriista—UNO), Víctor Raúl Haya de la Torre and his recently centrist APRA, and Fernando Belaúnde Terry and Popular Action (Acción Popular—AP), the new claimant to the reformist democratic left (Werlich 1978:256–274). As a result, the military, having undergone significant internal change of its own, cut the electoral knot with its first institutionalist and reformist *golpe de estado* (coup d'état) in July 1962. Nevertheless, it was itself cut short by strong international pressure—particularly from the Kennedy administration in the United States—to hold new elections as soon as practicable and by its own internal divisions (Masterson 1991:173–201).

The result in 1963 was a clear mandate for AP and Belaúnde and a modestly reformist administration with sometime AP support.[4] The outside observer had reason to expect this democratic iteration to survive and to have consolidated electoral governance, given its concern for agrarian reform, a modest expansion of the state, the reestablishment of municipal elections, and continuing economic growth. However, a Castro-sponsored *foquista* guerrilla outbreak in 1965 (though short-lived), growing inflation (up to 37 percent annually by 1968, though modest indeed by the triple- and even quadruple-digit increases of the 1980s), and an ill-fated attempt to nationalize a U.S. oil company (Esso's International Petroleum

Company, IPC) over U.S. objections provoked another institutionalized reformist military *golpe* in 1968 (Masterson 1991:203–235).

This time, however, the military's action was much better organized and had far fewer internal divisions, and the reformist impulse was a core component. So one of the multiple ironies of Peruvian political history, compared to that of most of Latin America, was that it was the military rather than civilian governments that ushered in significant social and economic change. Over the *docenio* of military rule between 1968 and 1980 Peru underwent significant agrarian reform, the nationalization of many key industries and mining and fishing enterprises, and experimentation with a top-down "popular participation" initiative designed to replace traditional political party activities with workplace and community-based cooperative ones.[5] Government employment and participation in the national economy moved from being one of the smallest in the region to one of the largest in just a few years (Fitzgerald 1976). Traditional political parties were considered irrelevant anachronisms as military-directed bureaucracies took on the tasks of determining popular needs as they emerged from the new local participation entities, such as cooperatives and communities, and responded to them (Dietz and Palmer 1978:172–188; Woy 1978:189–208).

Reformist military rule may have been a great model, but it suffered from two ultimately fatal flaws. On the one hand, there was the inevitable tension between the military's tendency to seek to maintain strong, hierarchical, central control and the local organization members' desire to determine their own destiny. On the other, the military leaders lacked the resources to fully implement their reforms, could generate little enthusiasm among domestic or foreign private investors to provide the economic wherewithal, and turned to international lenders on such a massive scale that Peru became the first of the Latin American countries to experience a severe foreign debt crisis (in 1977 and 1978, almost five years before the August 1982 Mexican foreign debt emergency signaled the onset of what was to become a general problem for the entire region). As a result, the military saw no option but to help usher in a new era of civilian democracy, beginning with constitutional convention elections in 1978 and a full transition to electoral democracy two years later under the new 1979 constitution (Masterson 1991:265–269).

The democratic *docenio* began auspiciously with a fully involved citizenry, significant representation by the Marxist left, a reasonably strong set of parties, an experienced civilian president (Belaúnde was elected again), and a Congress with a majority in both houses from the president's party, AP. In addition, the military had been thoroughly disabused of its long-standing view that it could step into power during moments of crisis to do a better job than the civilians at managing the government. Their own chastening experience served to raise significantly their "threshold of intervention." Democracy in Peru appeared to be poised for reasonably clear sailing on into the future. Who could have anticipated, then, the debacle that ensued? Certainly few of us social scientists and specialists on Peru! What happened? And why?

The world economic downturn beginning in 1981–1982 that provoked what came to be called "the lost decade" for Latin America was certainly one important contributing factor. However, most of the reestablished Latin American democracies of the late 1970s and early 1980s survived this challenge—Peru was one of only two that did not (Haiti is the other Latin American country over the course of the region's "Third Wave of Democracy"—1978 to the present—to experience a nonconstitutional takeover after democratic forms had been put in place) (Huntington 1991; Palmer 1996a). The underlying reasons for the failure of democratic procedures to take hold in Peru continue to be the subject of ongoing debate, but at least three factors stand out.

One was failure of leadership at the top. Both Fernando Belaúnde (1980–1985) and his successor, Alan García (1985–1990), were unable to take advantage of strong popular support and congressional majorities to consolidate democratic practices through realistic policies that might have set more modest but more attainable goals at a time calling for economic restraint. Though democratic forms and procedures continued at both the national and the municipal levels during their administrations, their actions served over time to discredit both parties and the democratic process itself. For some time it seemed possible that democratic practice could generate solutions rather than aggravate the problems. For as one party and its administration faltered over the democratic *docenio*, a different party received the popular mandate to right the wrongs of its predecessor in each successive national election.[6]

As most of us observed at the time, this was nothing more than democracy at work in a multiparty system. When one party fails to meet popular needs and expectations, the public can turn to another—and in the case of Peru, it did. At the municipal level as well, a similar rotation occurred, with AP, United Left (Izquiera Unida—IU, a grouping of left, mostly Marxist parties), APRA, and the Democratic Front (Frente Democrático—FREDEMO, a grouping of right, essentially conservative parties) gaining pluralities nationwide in succession over the 1980, 1983, 1986, and 1989 municipal elections.[7] Unfortunately, over time the political, economic, and social situation in Peru continued to deteriorate whichever party was in power, and this decline eventually led to the election for president in 1990 of a candidate whose signal virtue in the minds of the electorate was that he had never been a politician. University president Alberto Fujimori's main rival was a similarly endowed individual, the leading novelist Mario Vargas Llosa.

Several factors and individuals share the blame for contributing to the erosion of public acceptance of the legitimacy of the formal democratic process and party politics. However, no individual bears more of the burden of political failure than President García. During his five-year administration, inflation increased by a cumulative 2 million percent, absolute poverty more than doubled, Peru's international credit ratings dropped to zero, political violence reached unprecedented levels, and over half a million citizens migrated abroad legally (Crabtree 1992:121–216; Graham 1992:99–126). His public approval ratings peaked after a year in office at over 80 percent, but at the end of his term they were in single dig-its, and many saw the country on the verge of collapse (Palmer 1990:5–8).

Yet President García had many advantages that one would have expected to lead to a much more positive outcome. He was young, dashing, and charismatic and a superb orator. In the early 1980s he had brought his party back to its re-formist roots by eschewing the tactical conservatism that his mentor and party founder, Víctor Raúl Haya de la Torre, had taken with him to the grave in 1979. He infused Peru's most institutionalized political party with new life and pro-pelled APRA into the presidency and a majority in Congress in 1985 for the first time in its sixty-one-year history. This political breakthrough carried over into the first two years of his government as well, with economic growth, agricultural expansion, decentralization, and reduced political violence all part of the scene (Crabtree 1992:25–120).

In 1987, however, his plan and program came unstuck. Problems began with his attempted nationalization of the banks and continued with rampant inflation and indiscriminate printing of the currency, a resurgence of guerrilla activity, and major problems with drug trafficking. It was rumored, furthermore, that Presi-dent García suffered from a serious mental disorder that contributed to his erratic exercise of leadership. By the time he left office in July 1990 his approval ratings in the polls had bottomed out at single-digit levels, the treasury was bare, and the Shining Path guerrillas were advancing rapidly. Even the other, much smaller guerrilla group operating in Peru, the Tupac Amaru Revolutionary Movement (Movimiento Revolucionario Tupac Amaru—MRTA), succeeded in humiliating Peruvian authorities as President García's term was ending by engineering the es-cape of more than forty top leaders from the country's newest maximum security prison, Canto Grande—and recording it all on videotape!

The effect of successive failures of elected governments was to discredit the de-mocratic process itself as it had been constituted in 1979, including the political parties that formed it. Much of the population, cast adrift by the errors of the elected leaders and their parties, was forced to cope on its own through a variety of ad hoc local organizations, from neighborhood soup kitchens to self-defense groups (Burt 1997; Starn 1993). Political crises, in effect, produced informal poli-tics much as the ongoing economic problems had generated a rapid expansion of the informal economy (Stokes 1995; Soto 1986).

The failures of political leadership do not by themselves explain Peru's acute crisis as of 1990, however. The other significant domestic contributor was the Shining Path guerrilla organization. Over the decade of elected government be-ginning in 1980, political violence, largely inspired by Shining Path, had ac-counted for some 23,000 casualties and over $10 billion in damages to the coun-try's economic infrastructure (Comisión Especial sobre Violencia y Pacificación del Senado 1991). Such guerrilla activity would appear on its face to be incompat-ible with the practice of an open and inclusive democracy and flies in the face of theories of revolution (Goldstone 1980; McClintock 1994).

In practice, however, the Maoist guerrilla organization—which gestated over almost two decades in one of Peru's poorest and most isolated *sierra* departments, Ayacucho—gradually created through its own operations the conditions of generalized violence and central government repression that it asserted had always existed in the country. To its discredit, the government often responded inappropriately and ineffectively to the guerrilla challenge, thereby aiding and abetting Shining Path's objective of creating a Maoist-style "New Democracy" through revolutionary violence in Peru. The destructive dynamic was sufficiently advanced by the early 1990s, in fact, that Shining Path spokespeople began to predict an "imminent" victory after long holding that their struggle could take decades to bear fruit (Palmer 1994).

Such predictions proved to be premature. However, the costs incurred in gaining the upper hand over Shining Path were high. Democratic procedures and practices were among the casualties. Ironically, however, their progressive abandonment had substantial popular support. In 1990 the public turned away from traditional parties to elect the "apolitical" neophyte Alberto Fujimori. Once in office, the new president launched a dramatic economic shock program that was quite at odds with his electoral promises but that soon gained substantial support because it produced results. Within a year, hyperinflation had been tamed even though extreme poverty increased dramatically. Slowly, Peru's international credit standing was restored and prospects for renewed economic growth began to glimmer on the horizon.

However, unlike his elected predecessors, President Fujimori did not enjoy a majority in Congress, and the judiciary was dominated by former-president García's appointees. Shining Path continued to advance on its destructive course, and states of emergency were in effect in about half of Peru's 180-odd provinces, which put the military in charge of wide swaths of the country and contributed to a wide variety of human rights abuses. Most observers believed that under President Fujimori Peru's beleaguered democracy was slowly regaining some operational capacity by 1991 and early 1992 and could have moved forward through executive-legislative crisis management negotiations to something resembling a normal state of affairs, but that was not to be. On April 5, 1992, President Fujimori surprised almost everyone by suspending the constitution, dismissing Congress, and declaring a reorganization of the judiciary. His *autogolpe* abandoned democracy in favor of rule by presidential decree. Almost universally opposed abroad, his initiative met with overwhelming support at home (McClintock 1993).

Nevertheless, this was a most dangerous course to pursue and could easily have proven disastrous. Foreign economic and military assistance was slashed; international creditors suspended significant planned new resource infusions, thereby setting back Peru's international economic reinsertion plan and any possibility of renewed economic growth; and political parties lost their access to the policy process and with it their raison d'être with the citizenry. Shining Path, smelling new opportunity, increased the pace of its violent actions, repeatedly embarrassing the government and further disquieting the population. The guerrilla leadership began preparations for massive attacks, which were scheduled to get underway in October 1992. Under these multiple strains, President Fujimori's popularity began to erode.

What saved him and his country from Shining Path, many agree, was the culmination of a shift in military and police strategy for combating terrorism, including new methods of intelligence gathering and new approaches to working with local communities, that had begun amidst the chaos of the final year of the García government. The new strategy enabled the Fujimori government to strike a devastating blow against the guerrillas in September 1992 by capturing Shining Path's key figure, founder, ideologue, and strategist, Abimael Guzmán Reynoso, as well as key files on the organization's membership. Within days, Peru went from depression to euphoria, with President Fujimori the immediate beneficiary. Continuing counterguerrilla actions succeeded in reducing Shining Path to a shadow of its former self—as one indicator, by 1996 levels of political violence had decreased to less than one-fifth of their 1992 pace (Palmer 1996b).

Riding a new crest of popular support, President Fujimori was able to set the parameters of a revised democratic process under a new constitution, his reelection in 1995 with over 60 percent of the valid vote, and a congressional majority (McClintock 1995:13–20). He has also been able to advance dramatically the economic liberalization program that had stalled with the *autogolpe* through privatization of scores of public enterprises, major infusions of private capital, and the normalization of international credit. Reduced inflation, economic growth, multiple local infrastructure rebuilding projects, and slowly declining levels of absolute poverty can be counted among the government's economic accomplishments in the mid–1990s.

However, democracy remains fragile, largely because it is based on a variety of mechanisms and procedures that enhance recentralization of political power even as they reduce pluralistic institutional approaches to problem solving. President Fujimori has made it very clear that he favors what he calls "direct democracy," that is, a system that works without parties or intermediaries and permits a personal relationship between the president and the population to solve the country's problems. Although Peru clearly has benefited for now from President Fujimori's approach, many analysts do not see in this model of citizen-state relationships a formula for future democratic consolidation. Although Peru may well be an extreme case of a modern Latin American "partial democracy," this pattern of incomplete transition to stable, institutionalized, elected civilian rule continues to be the norm rather than the exception in the region.

Conclusion

To conclude, a brief recapitulation of the Fitzgibbon-Johnson Image-Index as applied to the Peruvian case circa 1997 highlights the multiple limitations that continue to apply to political democracy in Peru.

1. Educational level sufficiently high: Literacy has increased in Peru, as has the number of university graduates. There is a widespread view, however, that the national public educational system is desperately in need of reform and has been less and less able over time to meet national needs.

2. Standard of living reasonably adequate: The modest improvement since 1994 has been significant but far from sufficient to improve most Peruvians' lives. In fact, absolute levels today are still significantly below those of the mid-1970s.

3. Internal unity and cohesion: Peru remains a bifurcated country by most accounts, with a growing, largely Spanish-speaking urban sector amidst a significant rural minority, largely Indian-language speaking.

4. Mature political system: By many accounts Peru's political system has deteriorated over time and has become more personalistic and less institutionalized and routinized.

5. Absence of foreign domination: On the face of matters the combination of economic liberalization with substantial new foreign investment and a counter-drug policy dictated by the United States constitutes increased levels of foreign economic influence and control, according to many. For others, Peru has been emerging successfully from the worst set of crises in this century and as a result is more often able to call its own shots on issues central to internal growth and development.

6. Freedom of speech: Though a robust print media has developed under democracy, individual journalists have been harassed, driven into exile, and even killed. Television is often subject to arbitrary interference by the government.

7. Free and popular elections: Most observers believe that elections have been genuine expressions of popular will, though it is also true that the Fujimori government has changed many of the ground rules in ways that tend to favor its continued control. The most recent machinations to do whatever it takes to get another term in office illustrate the limitations of fixed electoral laws and procedures. Elections are free, but the rules are less than impartial and the adjustments have been made sufficiently in advance so that voter intimidation or dishonest voting procedures have not been necessary up to now.

8. Freedom of party organization: Multiple parties abound and are encouraged in Peru, which gives the voting public options. (There were thirteen parties with presidential candidates and twenty-two parties supporting candidates for Congress in the 1995 elections.) However, that also helps to undermine traditional parties and enhances the incumbent's advantage. As for the effective party opposition in a legislative arena that permits scrutiny of and challenge to the executive branch, Peru, as most Latin American countries, is an executive-dominant, not a balance-of-powers political system. Thus it does not respond well to legislative or judicial scrutiny.

9. Independently functioning judiciary: In Peru the judiciary has been consciously and specifically placed in a subordinate position to the executive, in part because it might oppose the president's initiatives and in part because this subor-

dinate and less-prestigious position is where the judiciary has always been. Since Latin America is a civil rather than a common law region, the judiciary is more subordinate to executive authority. This reality places the judiciary in a clearly deficient position with regard to international norms but may also be a reflection in part of a U.S. ethnocentric view.

10. Accountability for the administration of public funds: Though some corruption exists, Peru has not been plagued during the Fujimori administration by the scandals of its predecessors or in comparison to a number of other Latin American governments, and this honesty has been one of the factors generating popular support.

11. Social legislation: Peru, like many Latin American countries, lives under a constitution that embodies advanced levels of social consciousness as statements of principle rather than enforceable statutes. The commitment is there in principle, in other words, but in Peru, as elsewhere in the region, fiscal constraints plus free-market principles have tended to limit and reduce the social welfare net.

12. Civilian supremacy over the military: Peru is a country with a strong tradition of military intervention in politics—in fact the nineteenth- and early-twentieth-century political cleavage was between civilian and military parties rather than between conservative and liberal parties. Though there is wide variation among countries and time periods, analysts tend to characterize Peru as continuing to be subject to significant military influence.

13. Limitations on religious activity in politics: Peru is a Catholic country but has a long-standing tradition of separation of church and state. Even so, the church plays a role in politics at the national level and influences political outcomes. But with a Vatican policy of the 1980s and 1990s that emphasizes the distinction between the spiritual and the political, de facto separation is significant.

14. Professionalization of government administration: Peru has passed through one of the most severe political crises in its history, and the administrative apparatus has been decimated as a result. The Fujimori government has worked to restore some degree of professionalism to the public bureaucracy, but severe problems remain in most areas.

15. Local self government: Since 1993, after a period of delegating fiscal capacities and administrative responsibilities to local government during the first years of the Fujimori administration, there has occurred a progressive recentralization of fiscal control by central government even though municipal elections continue.

This brief review of the Fitzgibbon indicators of democracy reflects the limited degree to which Peru meets the standards established. It also reflects, however, the difficulty of making objective evaluations, as many of the indicators are both multifaceted and difficult or impossible to subject to straightforward and comparable measurement. True, Peru falls far short, but the measurements themselves are fraught with limitations.

Notes

1. Elected civilian rule and elected successions had been established in Chile by the 1840s, in Ecuador in the 1860s, and in Bolivia in the 1880s. Only Venezuela, the Dominican Republic, and Haiti lagged behind Peru in getting democratic reforms underway (Banks 1971:segment 1, field D).

2. See Wiarda 1973 on the political implications for Spanish America of the weight of the Iberian tradition and Palmer 1977:379–384 and passim on the differences among Latin American countries within this tradition.

3. This conclusion forms part of a larger study I am preparing, *Latin American Macropolitics*, under contract with St. Martin's Press and due to be completed in 1998. Earlier elaborations appear in the "Authoritarianism in Spanish America" chapter and in *Authoritarian Tradition*.

4. The support was conditioned by various bilateral issues of the day; St. John. 1992:193–198.

5. Lowenthal 1975 and Lowenthal and McClintock 1983 are perhaps the most comprehensive treatments of this period.

6. Such a turnover is an absolutely essential requisite of democracy according to Larry Diamond, Juan J. Linz, and Seymour Martin Lipset (1989:8–43).

7. Tuesta Soldevilla 1995 contains the election results from the 1930s to the mid-1990s, presidential congressional, and municipal, both at the national and provincial levels. It is the best available reference work.

Bibliography

Banks, Robert A. 1971. *Cross Polity Time Series Data.* Cambridge: MIT Press.

Burt, Jo Marie. 1997. Vigilantes, guerrillas, and electric fences: Responses to crime in urban Peru. Paper presented to the 1997 Latin American Studies Association meeting, Guadalajara, Mexico, April 17–19.

Chaplin, David. 1968. Peru's postponed revolution. *World Politics* 19:393–420.

Comisión Especial sobre Violencia y Pacificación del Senado (Comisión Bernales). 1991. *Reporte anual.* Lima: Senado del Perú.

Cotler, Julio. 1978. *Clases, estado, y nación en el Perú.* Lima: Instituto de Estudios Peruanos.

Crabtree, John. 1992. *Peru under García.* Pittsburgh: University of Pittsburgh Press.

Diamond, Larry, Juan J. Linz, and Seymour Martin Lipset, eds. 1989. *Democracy in Developing Countries: Latin America.* Vol. 4. Baltimore: Johns Hopkins University Press.

Dietz, Henry A., and David Scott Palmer. 1978. Citizen participation under innovative military corporatism in Peru. In *Political Participation in Latin America.* Volume 1: *Citizen and State* (John A. Booth and Mitchell A. Seligson, eds.), 172–188. New York: Holmes and Meier.

Fitzgerald, E. V. K. 1976. *The State and Economic Development in Peru since 1968.* Cambridge: Cambridge University Press.

Goldstone, Jack A. 1980. Theories of revolution: The third generation. *World Politics* 32:425–453.

Graham, Carol. 1992. *Peru's APRA: Parties, Politics, and the Elusive Quest for Democracy.* Boulder: Lynne Rienner.

Haring, C. H. 1963. *The Spanish Empire in America.* New York: Harcourt, Brace, and World.

Hunt, Shane. 1971. Distribution, growth, and government economic behavior in Peru. In *Government and Economic Development* (Gustav Ranis, ed.), 375–428. New Haven: Yale University Press.

Huntington, Samuel P. 1991. *The Third Wave: Democratization in the Late 20th Century.* Norman: University of Oklahoma Press.

Latin American Studies Association (LASA). 1995. *The 1995 Electoral Process in Peru.* Pittsburgh: LASA and the North-South Center.

Lowenthal, Abraham F., ed. 1975. *The Peruvian Experiment: Continuity and Change Under Military Rule.* Princeton: Princeton University Press.

Lowenthal, Abraham F., and Cynthia McClintock. 1983. *The Peruvian Experiment Reconsidered.* Princeton: Princeton University Press.

Masterson, Daniel M. 1991. *Militarism and Politics in Latin America: Peru from Sánchez Cerro to Sendero Luminoso.* Westport, Conn.: Greenwood Press.

McClintock, Cynthia. 1994. Theories of revolution and the case of Peru. In *Shining Path of Peru,* 2nd ed. (David Scott Palmer, ed.), 243–258. New York: St. Martin's.

[TMBR]. 1993. Peru's Fujimori: A caudillo derails democracy. *Current History* 92:112–119.

McClintock, Cynthia, Catherine M. Conaghan, Bruce H. Kay, and David Scott Palmer. 1995. Articles on the 1995 Peruvian election. *LASA Forum* 26:9–20.

Morse, Richard. 1964. The heritage of Latin America. In *The Founding of New Societies* (Louis Hartz et al., eds.), 123–177. New York: Harcourt, Brace, and World.

Palmer, David Scott. 1996a. Peru: Collectively defending democracy in the hemisphere. In *Beyond Intervention* (Tom Farer, ed.), 257–276. Baltimore: Johns Hopkins University Press.

_____. 1996b. "Fujipopulism" and Peru's progress. *Current History* 95:70–75.

_____. 1994. *Shining Path of Peru.* 2nd ed. New York: St. Martin's.

_____. 1990. Peru's persistent problems. *Current History* 89:5–8, 31–34.

_____. 1980. *Peru: The Authoritarian Tradition.* New York: Praeger.

_____. 1977. The authoritarian tradition in Spanish America. In *Authoritarianism and Corporatism in Latin America* (James M. Malloy, ed.), 377–412. Pittsburgh: University of Pittsburgh Press.

St. John, Ronald Bruce. 1992. *The Foreign Policy of Peru.* Boulder: Lynne Rienner Publishers.

Soto, Hernando de. 1986. *El otro sendero: La revolución informal.* Lima: Editorial el Barranco.

Starn, Orin. 1993. Hablan los ronderos: La búsqueda por la paz en los Andes. *Documento de trabajo 45, IEP talleres.* Lima: IEP.

Stokes, Susan C. 1995. *Cultures in Conflict: Social Movements and the State in Peru.* Berkeley: University of California Press.

Thorp, Rosemary, and Geoffrey Bertram. 1978. *Peru, 1890–1977.* New York: Columbia University Press.

Tuesta Soldevilla, Fernando. 1996. *Los enigmas del poder: Fujimori 1990–1996.* Lima: Fundación Friedrich Ebert.

_____. 1995. *Perú político en cifras.* Lima: Fundación Friedrich Ebert.

Werlich, David P. 1978. *Peru: A Short History.* Carbondale: University of Southern Illinois Press.

Wiarda, Howard J. 1973. Toward a framework for the study of political change in the Iberic-Latin tradition. *World Politics* 25:206–235.

Woy, Sandra. 1978. Infrastructure of participation in Peru: SINAMOS. In *Political Participation in Latin America.* Volume 1: *Citizen and State* (John A. Booth and Mitchell A. Seligson, eds.), 189–208. New York: Holmes and Meier.

Chapter Seventeen

Democratic Crises and Assumptions in Chile and Uruguay

RONALD H. MCDONALD

The panel surveys of democracy in Latin America that were initiated by Russell H. Fitzgibbon in 1945 reflected his personal belief and commitment to democratic societies and values, as well as the preeminent concerns and aspirations of his generation. The defeat of fascist dictatorships in the agonizing struggles of World War II encouraged a preoccupation with democracy as a means of preventing a repetition of that catastrophe. The survival and increasing world influence of a totalitarian, communist regime merged with the obsessive preoccupation of global struggle and the need to encourage democratic institutions and to strengthen prosperity following the war. The Fitzgibbon survey was a measure of the status of those values and realities in Latin America and by implication an agenda for their realization. Out of the survey data came a provocative evaluation of "democracy" in the region, which over subsequent years generated awareness, debate, and discussion.

For several decades two countries, Chile and Uruguay, consistently ranked in the surveys among the most democratic, although during the period after the war economic and political trends were emerging in each that led inexorably to the collapse of their democratic institutions and the imposition of military rule. The surveys generally failed to sense these trends and continued to rank both countries among the most democratic even as each came closer to military rule.[1]

In the first five surveys (1945–1965) the highest ranking country was consistently Uruguay, although it tied for first with Costa Rica in 1965. Chile ranked third behind Uruguay and Costa Rica in each survey except for 1950, when it ranked second; Costa Rica at that time was having its own problems with democracy, however minor and transient. By 1965 Chile and Uruguay were in the early stages of profound political upheaval, and by 1973 both were under the control of particularly brutal, repressive military regimes. Their democracies had failed. By 1975 the survey reflected the changes, ranking Chile tenth and Uruguay sixth, just above Cuba. The 1980 survey, incorporating the new realities of the previous seven years, ranked Uruguay thirteenth and Chile fourteenth among the twenty countries. Their rank decline indisputably would have been more precipitous were it not inflated by relatively high educational levels, standards of living, and internal unity scores, whose levels were not immediately affected by the political changes or the military regimes. In the 1985 survey Chile still ranked fourteenth, but Uruguay had risen to third within the context of proliferating military regimes and violence throughout the region.

My purpose here is not to review in detail the process of democratic collapse in Chile and Uruguay—those have been described elsewhere—but, rather, to place the experiences within the framework of the questions raised by the survey data and more generally to raise the question of how these historically democratic nations could have changed so rapidly and profoundly during the 1950s and 1960s. Why did their democracies fail, why had they continued to receive high scores in the surveys, and what did their experiences reveal about the viability of democratic values, processes, and institutions as conceptualized in the assumptions of the survey? The changing nature of their institutional status clearly was related to changing political behavior in the countries, but the question is: How did institutions and behavior influence each other, and what was causing the changes?[2]

Background to Democratic Collapse in Chile and Uruguay

There were intriguing similarities and differences between the contexts and the experiences of Chile and Uruguay. By comparison generally with other Latin American nations, they sustained an almost unbroken history of democratic government and politics in the twentieth century until 1973. True, there were instances of irregularities and even dictatorship in each: a military dictatorship in Chile (1927–1931) under Carlos Ibáñez and a civilian one in Uruguay under Gabriel Terra that lasted less than a year (1933). Neither appeared to have had a profound or lasting impact on their democratic traditions, but those traditions were very much in an uncertain state of evolution before and after the brief dictatorships.

In both countries there was a deeply rooted suspicion of strong executive government institutions, and in each there had been efforts through different ways and at different times to diminish or at least control and balance administrative power. Both countries had small populations in the early 1950s, Chile with about 5.8 million people and Uruguay with 2.3 million inhabitants. Chile's population increased rapidly afterward, reaching about 14.3 million in 1996; Uruguay's population rose only slowly, reaching about 3.2 million the same year. Both countries were abnormally urban; today Chile is about 82 percent and Uruguay 84 percent urban. About one-third of the Chilean population today live in the capital city, Santiago, and about 70 percent live in Central Chile in or near the capital city. About one-half the Uruguayan population this century has lived in its capital city, Montevideo. Urbanization and population increased rapidly in Chile following World War II, but Uruguay was always dominated demographically by its capital city and maintained low population growth. Demographic factors, including population growth, urbanization, and age distribution, often affect politics and exacerbate political stresses. That occurred in Chile and Uruguay, although in different ways. Both countries established viable public education systems in the late nineteenth century, achieving high levels of literacy that were unusual at the time in Latin America. Education levels and particularly institutions of higher education had important political consequences subsequently in both Chile and Uruguay.

The countries were different economically, but there were some similarities that led to economic dysfunction following World War II. Both were dependent on exports for economic growth, and for different reasons their exports became less viable over time. Both tried to industrialize but were too small to do so rationally, which created chronic economic problems with monopolies, inflation, and foreign investment and provoked relatively high government spending for ambitious public programs. Their military organizations, by Latin American and world standards, were under civilian control and had no tradition of military intervention. Their officer corps was largely middle class and shared a commitment to professionalism and to political stability but also increasingly to "anti-Marxism."

Chile and Uruguay reached unusually high levels of social mobilization early in the century and a relatively high level of democratic institutionalization. The latter emerged even as new political issues were arising, a periodically awkward and frustrating experience. Eventually institutional renewal and renovation failed to keep pace with growing levels of political participation or with gradually rising frustration and alienation in the population. The widening gap between participation and institutionalization weakened the ability of institutions to function and led to the institutional crises of the late 1960s and early 1970s. The politics and government of the two countries were significantly different but produced similar results during the same critical decades. Both countries failed to meet escalating political challenges, which in Chile produced polarization and ultimately confrontation and in Uruguay fragmentation and paralysis.

Military organizations became increasingly fearful of political chaos, paralysis, terrorism, and civil war. Their leaders became convinced that the civil institutions "were not working" and that civilian leaders were incompetent, corrupt, and untrustworthy. They came to believe that survival of the nation ultimately depended on their initiatives and actions and that economic and political conditions had to be stabilized and institutions renovated and cleansed of pernicious influences, specifically civilian politicians and political parties. Military intervention was becoming inevitable.

Confrontational Democracy in Chile

Significant trends after World War II began to affect Chilean politics and contributed to the decay of its democratic institutions. An analysis of all of these is
beyond the scope of this chapter, but a few of the more important ones can be
mentioned.[3]

Demographic changes were among the most fundamental. Chile experienced a
rate of population growth in the postwar decades that averaged about 2.5 percent,
high even by Latin American standards. The political effects of this were important. It lowered the median age in the country significantly to the point at which
about half the population was under eighteen years of age. This in turn accelerated demands for jobs by the comparatively well-educated burgeoning youth
population, demands the economy could not satisfy. Chile had long achieved a
high level of literacy and educational attainment through its innovative public
school system, but in the early twentieth century educational opportunities expanded even further, as did higher education. Two great universities flourished in
the capital city, the National University run by the state and the Catholic University affiliated with the Church. These institutions, like their counterparts elsewhere in Latin America, produced a new generation of university-trained leaders.
Those coming from the National University had been exposed to radical, mostly
Marxist dogma, and those from the Catholic University to liberal Catholic dog-
mas. The political fate of the country was to a considerable extent in their hands
by the 1960s. By that time there also had been created a reservoir of relatively
well-educated, informed, and discontented adolescents and young adults who
were ready for significant political and economic changes and leaders who would
implement it.

The country was also becoming more urban through urban migration and natural population growth. In 1940 Chile was about 50 percent urban, by the mid-
1960s it was 67 percent urban, and today it is about 84 percent urban. Central
Chile, dominated by the capital city, Santiago, grew to about 70 percent of the national population, and Santiago from a city of about 1.3 million in 1950 to 4.0
million by the late 1960s. Urban dwellers were increasingly discontented and frustrated despite a reasonably high standard of living compared to the poorer areas
of the country and Latin America more generally. Demands for jobs, housing, and
higher living standards placed increased strains on the political and economic
systems.

To solve some of these urban economic and political problems, Chile tried to
increase its industrialization after World War II but at high costs. Capital for industrial growth could be generated only by international means, specifically from
export revenues or direct foreign investment. Chile was dependent on a single export, copper, which was in turn notoriously unstable in its international price and
made long-term economic planning difficult. Moreover, the production of copper
remained in the hands of foreign corporations that were primarily interested in

repatriating their profits, not in reinvesting them either in a copper industry that had become inefficient and expensive by world standards or in other areas of the Chilean economy. Less-expensive sources of copper were available worldwide, and for the foreign corporations the return on reinvesting in Chile was too low economically and the risk too high politically. Foreign control of its primary export was a dilemma for Chileans. On the one hand most Chileans wanted it under national control, whether public or private. Yet to impose that on the foreign owners would threaten Chile's access to world markets, which were largely controlled by the same foreign companies. The industry was in dire need of modernization if it was to remain competitive in world markets.

Chilean industrialization became a patchwork of import-substitution industries, protectionist trade policies, monopolies, and low-efficiency industries that produced low-quality consumer goods at high cost that could neither compete in export markets nor, for that matter, satisfy frustrated Chilean consumers. Efforts to expand public services to ease the frustrations created chronic government deficits financed by expanding the money supply, and with that higher levels of inflation that constantly threatened the middle classes. Chile became a country of anxious and angry consumers whose relatively high level of social mobilization and economic aspirations and expectations could not be met. The hostility was focused on the government, politics, and more generally the democratic system.

Chileans had once rebelled at strong administrative power in a short but significant revolt against President José Manuel Balmaceda in 1890. The revolt abruptly changed Chilean government from a strong presidential to a parliamentary system, in which the Congress and the emerging and diversifying political parties prevailed. The result was often chaotic. Cabinets came and went much as they did in the Third and Fourth French Republics. Parties proliferated and fractionalized around individual leaders who, if they were not allowed parity in party leadership, left the party and formed a new one. The institutional paralysis was addressed by a new constitution in 1925, the first in ninety-two years. The strong presidency was reestablished, congressional controls over ministries were eliminated, and a clear separation between church and state was established. Parties, however, continued to proliferate, fractionalize, and diversify as new sectors of the society gained entrance to the political system, forcing presidents to try to govern through party coalitions that usually failed to achieve enough cohesion for effective and consistent policy. In 1927 the minister of war, Colonel Carlos Ibáñez del Campo, exasperated by the continuing devolution of power, seized control of the presidency and ruled the country until 1932. Alienation and cynicism about politicians and their governments, especially within the context of economic frustrations and stagnation, transformed national elections into campaigns for "reform" and "renovation" of the government, which were slow to come.[4]

By the early 1950s the parties had proliferated to the point that several dozen were represented in Congress, but new leaders also emerged during that decade. They tried to mobilize the masses of urban and rural poor people into the parties and the political system, a significant development in Chilean politics. Slowly the number of parties winning congressional representation began to decline and to arrange themselves on a clear ideological continuum from left to right. At first these parties were dominated by centrist groups, most importantly by the Radical Party, which was a middle-class organization that had been around since the beginning of the twentieth century. A leftist, largely Marxist coalition was formed for the 1958 elections led by Salvador Allende, a physician and graduate of the National University who had been elected to the Senate in the mid-1940s. At the same time a small center leftist group inspired intellectually by reformist Catholic theology gained political support under the leadership of Eduardo Frei, a graduate of the Catholic University, who like Allende had been elected Senator in the mid-1940s. The group, eventually known as the Christian Democratic Party, was modeled after its Italian and German counterparts and grew rapidly in popularity. In 1963 Eduardo Frei was elected president by a majority of voters, and two years later the Christian Democrats elected a majority of the lower house. It was rare for any presidential candidate to receive a majority of the vote, and this was the first time in the century that any political party had gained a majority in the lower chamber of Congress. Chilean politics during the late 1950s and the 1960s consolidated and became increasingly ideological and to that extent more confrontational.

By the mid-1960s yet another change was occurring in Chilean politics: The center parties began to lose influence and support and national politics polarized, with a stronger political right and left and a weaker center. The centrist Radical Party, which had long played a mediating role in Chilean politics, fragmented over policy, ideology, and personalities. The Christian Democrats were unable to make fundamental changes or to improve conditions in Chile during the five years (1965–1970) they held the presidency since they lacked a majority in the Senate and had too little time to achieve major reforms. Christian Democrats, like the Radicals, increasingly fragmented over policy, ideology, and personal ambitions, and their national influence waned. During the same period the rightist parties coalesced and strengthened their position. Polarization encouraged extremist solutions to the habitual economic and political dilemmas in Chile and brought with it confrontation, increasing political conflict, and instability.

The presidential election of 1970 (presidential, legislative, and municipal elections were staggered and held in different years) was won by Allende and his leftist coalition, Popular Unity, but by only 1 percent of the vote; the rightist candidate (former President Jorge Alessandri) won second place in a three-way race that included the Christian Democratic candidate, Radomiro Tomic. Under the constitution, the Senate had to select the new president from among the two leading candidates when no one received a majority. Although controlled by the opposition, the Senate chose Allende, sustaining a long practice of selecting whichever candidate received the plurality. Three years later in the congressional elections of March 1973, Popular Unity picked up a few seats in both houses but still lacked a majority in either. The stalemate between the Congress and the president was a bad omen for the military, suggesting to them the possibility that the Marxist regime might try to circumvent the legislature, and even the next elections, and impose its reforms by force.

The military intervention of September 11, 1973, occurred about six months after the legislative elections, initiating an agonizing and brutal regime in Chile that lasted until a new civilian president was elected in December 1989. The military officers were divided over the intervention. Some enthusiastically supported it, including the head of the army, General Augusto Pinochet; a few opposed it; many were ambivalent. By the time it occurred there was sufficient agreement about its inevitability to create a consensus among most of the officers. The country was run briefly by a military junta, but General Pinochet ultimately assumed the presidency and ran the country for the duration of the dictatorship. His power was more corporate than personal. Once the coup had been executed professional careers and the viability of the armed forces were at stake. Officers had little choice but to accept the new reality.

Pinochet was never able to build popular support for the dictatorship, but through draconian measures he was able to reform the economy following the advice of free-market advisers from the United States. The economy did rebound, something of an economic miracle in Latin America. But the price for most Chileans was very high, as rampant inflation was replaced by massive unemployment, diminishing public services, and declining living standards. The price for Chile as a country was the collapse of its democratic institutions and heritage and enduring one of the most onerous military regimes ever in Latin America.[5]

The failure of Chilean democracy raised many questions beyond its implications for Chile. The country's democracy had been universally recognized and admired, including by respondents to the Fitzgibbon survey, who recognized its historically high levels of education, living standards, internal unity, and political maturity, as well as its freedom of press, elections, and party organizations, social legislation, civilian supremacy, and ecclesiastical freedoms—all important indicators in the survey. The collapse of democracy occurred not as a result of a revolution or terrorism but from actions by a military inexperienced in intervention. The obvious question was why Chile's democracy failed. Conspiracy theories were common in the aftermath of the event in the absence of other explanations. Greedy military leaders, the wealthy upper class, multinational corporations, and the United States among others were nominated as conspirators and sometimes coconspirators. Many of the conspiracy theories are still believed, and there may be some truth in some of them, but the collapse of Chilean democracy is not so easily nor simply explained.

There are other explanations, most of which raise troubling questions. Chilean democracy failed partly because it had worked so well. What triggered the military intervention was the selection of Allende as president in 1970. The election reflected the political realities in Chile: The country truly was divided ideologically in thirds—the right, the center, and the left. The polarization was not caused by the democratic system; rather, it was reflected through it. The failure of successive regimes to address the major economic, social, and political problems of the country and the eventual political paralysis were the result of the political divisions in the country that had created a stalemate that had existed for generations and worsened over time. The paralysis of the political system was an accurate translation into institutional structures of the divisions of the society, and it led increasingly toward confrontation and polarization and, in the eyes of some military officers, increasingly toward coercion, violence, and perhaps eventually to civil war.

The potential for greater political participation in Chile was also rising due to the high level of social mobilization in the country. Higher political participation at all levels of the society overwhelmed the capacity of institutions to absorb it, let alone reconcile or ameliorate its diverse objectives. The balance between presidential and legislative power remained a significant political issue as Chilean democracy evolved. Before 1890 the country had a strong president and a weak or at least subservient legislature, but until then political parties based on the assumption of "mass politics" had not yet emerged, nor had the conditions that would support it. The rebellion against the strong presidency in 1890 produced a parliamentary system dominated by the legislature, which in turn supported the evolution of "mass parties" and their eventual proliferation. The 1925 constitution tried to strike a balance between the "excessive sensitivity" to public opinion of the parliamentary system and the "excessive rigidity" of the previous strong presidential system, and that new balance was exactly what occurred. The "balance," however, became stalemated as the electorate evolved, increasingly polarized, politically active, and ideological. The failure of democracy in Chile was not due to its ineffectiveness nor solely to the despicable motives of those who ultimately destroyed it. The system was overwhelmed by the issues and the levels of political tension and participation imposed on it. Too much preoccupation with political issues and too high a level of political participation can overwhelm the institutions that designed to absorb them and become politically destabilizing. In Chile they did.

The Incremental Decay of Uruguayan Democracy

Russell H. Fitzgibbon had a special knowledge and affection for Uruguay, and in 1953 he published the first book-length study in English of the nation's politics, *Uruguay: Portrait of a Democracy.*[6] His analysis identified many of the characteristics and trends in the country and was the first to describe some of the country's unique political institutions. Many of his themes, not all of them fully explored, provided ample hypotheses for subsequent studies and analyses.

Like the Chileans, and at about the same time, the Uruguayans tried to sift through the question of balancing the presidency and the legislature. The solutions pursued were different, as were the results. The country came under the political and intellectual influence of a remarkable leader, José Batlle y Ordóñez, who served twice as president (1903–1907, 1911–1915) and was responsible for designing one of the most unusual party and electoral systems in the world. Batlle wanted to avoid the tendency he saw for Latin American nations to become dictatorships at the end of the nineteenth century, and he tried to remedy the causes of that pattern through a unique institutional framework. Batlle's analysis of the problem was elaborate and clearly thought out. He believed that dictatorships arose out of the unchecked ambitions and greed of leaders, who too often viewed government as an avenue to expand their personal power and wealth, an assumption that was based on his perception of "human nature" if not human psychology.

The unusual electoral system he proposed was adopted and provided a balance within the structures of the parties and the electoral system between personal ambitions of leaders (*personalism*) and the corporate organization, actions, and responsibility of parties.[7] His plan established a system of institutionalized factions (*sub-lemas*) within the structures of the political parties (*lemas*). He also believed that the only sure way to prevent dictators was to eliminate the presidency, and he advocated replacing it with an administrative structure known as the "National Council," with two-thirds of its members from the party receiving the most votes and the other third from the party coming in second. This plan was partially implemented in 1919, creating a bifurcated system with both a president and a National Council that endured until 1934, when the National Council was eliminated. The presidential elections presumed multiple candidates from the parties, the winner being the candidate with the most votes from the party with the most votes. It was a unique system that combined a primary and a general election in one event. Through yet another constitutional referendum the National Council was reestablished in 1952, this time without the presidency. It lasted only through two elections, 1958 and 1962, and was repealed in a joint referendum and national election in 1966 that reestablished a presidential system.

All Batlle's proposals were based on a rather common and naive nineteenth-century assumption of the inevitability of "progress," usually meaning economic growth, industrialization, and the mass politics of democracy. It also was optimistically assumed that economic growth under reasonable conditions would be automatic as long as a "healthy" social and political environment was provided in which it could occur, which meant rising living standards and expectations for all sectors of the society. Batlle wanted to foster such an environment by initiating public programs of education, social security, retirement pensions, health care, and a variety of other benefits that were visionary even by world standards and were far more comprehensive than what had been tried at the time in Europe or the United States. Even before Batlle, Uruguay, like Chile, had initiated an effective system of publicly financed education from elementary through university levels that expanded literacy and educational attainment. Not coincidentally, Batlle's political base, the Colorado Party, was concentrated in the capital city of Montevideo, and soliciting the interests of its residents expanded the strength of his party's support there. Montevideo was growing rapidly from European immigration in the late nineteenth century and already constituted about half the national population. The urban dwellers wanted industrialization and economic growth and were responsive to his ideas for what would later be called a welfare state.[8]

As in Chile, democracy collapsed in Uruguay in 1973 with a military dictatorship. The fundamental cause of the collapse was rooted in Batlle's assumptions about democracy, the threats to it, and the inevitability of "progress," specifically economic growth and rising living standards. The failure of Uruguayan democracy had occurred very slowly over several generations, largely the result of an extended period of economic stagnation and decay that began following World War II and continued through the next several decades. Unlike in Chile, where the end of democracy occurred with the dramatic and horrific events of September 1973, the political decay of democracy in Uruguay began in the mid-1960s as military leaders brought one national institution after another slowly under their control. The last elected president, who had cooperated with the military leaders in their increasingly authoritarian plans, was finally removed from power in June 1976 and replaced by a military officer. Democracy in Uruguay realistically had been lost to military meddling in national politics and government by 1973, and the final 1976 coup de grâce merely ratified the obvious.[9]

The incremental decay of Uruguayan democracy had several origins, including an extended period of economic stagnation and decay beginning after World War II and a political paralysis induced largely by the reintroduction in 1952 of the Collegial Executive, a plural or multiple executive of nine elected presidents, which was unable to exert strong leadership during a period of mounting economic crises. The traditional democracy was also eroded by the emergence of a revolutionary (or, as some viewed it, a "terrorist") Marxist movement in the mid-1960s known as the Tupamaros. Any one of these causes would have challenged the viability of Uruguayan democracy, but under their simultaneous and collective pressure there was little other outcome possible than the failure of democracy.

The economic prosperity of Uruguay in the first half of the twentieth century depended on its exports, primarily sheep (lamb, mutton, wool), cattle (meat, leather), and some grains, mostly exported to Europe. These export revenues subsidized an ineffectual industrialization, which was an essential part of Batlle's plan for self-sufficiency of the small nation. Industrialization created urban jobs, but it also produced all the negative characteristics of import-substitution industrialization. Organized labor grew and played an important role in the industrialization efforts, as did government protection, subsidization, and regulation. Export revenues also helped pay for the extensive social welfare programs the country had adopted. As long as the exports held firm, the fragile economic balance which underlay the political assumptions about democracy could be maintained.

After World War II export revenues slowly declined. As Europe recovered, new alternative sources for what had been imported from Uruguay, especially beef and lamb, emerged within Europe and beyond. Demand for wool textiles declined as synthetic fibers such as nylon, rayon, dacron, and others became more popular. Uruguayan manufactured goods could not be exported because they were not competitive in world markets, but the nation's dependence on imported capital goods, energy, and many consumer goods made it difficult to reduce imports. Government revenues stagnated or declined as budgetary and trade deficits increased, causing higher inflation and requiring reductions in government programs and spending, either directly or through inflationary monetary policies.

Uruguay's demography was also a contributing factor. Unlike Chile, Uruguay had no population explosion after World War II; in fact it has had for years the lowest rate of population growth in Latin America. The result was an aging population, similar to the situation now developing in the United States, and social and welfare programs that were bankrupting the country. Many Uruguayans, including females, could retire at full salary at age fifty-five. There were extensive social security, education, and health care programs, and government price controls over many consumer necessities kept prices and consequently production unrealistically low. Uruguay was living beyond its means. There was no dramatic economic crisis such as a depression of the 1930s, merely a gradual economic decay beginning in the late 1940s and continuing on through the critical period of the 1950s and 1960s.

Many Uruguayans received at least some higher education, mostly through the National University at Montevideo. University students became increasingly pessimistic about their own economic futures as well as the country's. The university, like many in Latin America, had a strong Marxist tradition that provided simple explanations and solutions for essentially complex economic problems. It produced a generation of alienated, cynical, and hostile university students, a few of whom formed the nucleus for the Tupamaro movement in the 1960s.

Batlle's Colorado Party had dominated Uruguayan politics, winning the presidency and a majority of the Congress in every election until 1958. The abolition of the presidency and substitution of the National Council in 1952 could not have come at a worse time. The council was not designed to provide imaginative or aggressive leadership, which was exactly what was needed in Uruguay by the 1950s to reverse the economic decline. The decay was so gradual that most Uruguayans failed to perceive or understand its long-term implications until it was too late. The victory of the opposition (the National Party, more commonly known as the Blancos) in the 1958 election, its first national victory in ninety-three years, was an early expression of discontent and national anxiety. But the Blancos, unaccustomed and inexperienced in running the country, could not, especially within the context of the National Council system, address the problems, let alone solve them. The Blancos also won the 1962 elections, but barely, and they failed to achieve a majority in either legislative chamber. Political paralysis set in, nothing could be done by the government, and widespread dissatisfaction with the political system escalated rapidly. When in 1966 the presidential system was reestablished through constitutional referendum, the Colorados returned to power but with only a thin majority in Congress. Unfortunately they remained committed to the premises and programs of the past and either could not or would not deal with the increasingly obvious economic problems and political stalemate. The new Colorado president, Oscar Gestido, was not a career politician but a career military officer, a retired general, which was symbolic and perhaps symptomatic of the national malaise. Gestido died unexpectedly of a heart attack in December 1967, shortly after taking office, and his vice president, Jorge Pacheco Areco, assumed the presidency. Pacheco was a hard-nosed, partisan, career politician, and it was under his regime that the military, impatient with and exasperated by the civilian paralysis and inaction, began to impose its priorities on the civilian leaders and to short-circuit the Uruguayan democratic political system.

By the mid–1960s yet another threat to Uruguayan democracy emerged, the Tupamaros, who were the most sophisticated, imaginative, and successful such movement at the time in Latin America and who seriously accelerated the process of political decay. Military officers in collaboration with some civilian leaders responded forcefully and energetically to the Tupamaros, slowly extending their increasingly oppressive influence and control over the population and placing limits on Uruguayan democratic institutions. They imposed censorship on the press, forbidding mention of the Tupamaros, they declared a state of emergency, and they subsequently proclaimed "temporary security measures" that constituted a virtual state of siege that suspended most individual rights. Eventually the military declared that a state of internal war existed in Uruguay and took over from the civilian police the responsibility for dealing with the Tupamaros. They also pressured, coerced, and even threatened members of the legislature to pass stronger measures supporting their efforts and limiting political liberties and constitutional processes.

Uruguayan politics became increasingly violent and acrimonious. The newly formed Broad Front, a coalition of leftist parties, along with prominent Blanco leaders and even some Colorado leaders, regularly attacked the president for his oppressive policies and cooperation with the military. At one point the lower house of Congress tried to impeach the resident, but the effort ultimately failed. A conservative Colorado, Juan María Bordaberry, was elected president in 1972 in a widely disputed election. The next year, 1973, the military seized control of television stations, threatened party leaders, forced Bordaberry to close the Congress, and arrested thousands of political dissidents. By 1973 the military effectively controlled the country after a gradual process of absorbing power that had taken at least seven or eight years. In 1976 the military "fired" President Bordaberry, ending and confirming the slow, painful process of bringing Uruguayan democracy under their total control. Despite censorship and authoritarian measures, the public was very much aware of what was occurring. In so well educated and so small a country political secrecy if not coercion was all but impossible.

Military intervention was as unprecedented and shocking in Uruguay as it was in Chile. Though the military did not assume formal power until 1976, it had totally controlled the country since 1973. The "coup," like the country's economic decay, was a gradual and incremental process that extended over years. There was no single, dramatic event as there was in the Chilean coup. As in Chile not all military officers supported the intervention, but eventually those who did were unable or unwilling to come up with any alternative. The political system had degenerated and was paralyzed by inaction, increasingly polarized, and, in the eyes of the military officers, on the brink of civil war.[10]

As was the case in Chile, the Uruguayan democratic system had not failed. It worked as it was designed to work, to maintain a "stable" if inflexible division of political power among traditional political elites and interests, discouraging radical (or "innovative") changes. The "stability" inevitably prevented the system from responding to changing conditions or initiating critical political and economic reforms. The cause of the Uruguayan democratic collapse was embedded in the principal assumptions of Batlle: that progress—economic growth and modernization—was certain and inevitable as long as the political system precluded a strong, authoritarian leader from being president and as long as the public received economic and social benefits from the system. Economic growth and the modernity it can stimulate, contrary to Batlle's assumptions, turned out to be neither certain nor inevitable. At the beginning of the twentieth century that possibility had probably never occurred to Batlle, and only very slowly did it occur to the Uruguayan people, their political leaders, and their governments.

The Fragility of Institutional Democracies

By the 1980s significant global political and economic changes were beginning to occur, and the two military regimes were well aware that military rule in their historically democratic countries could not endure forever. The Brazilian military, which was no more experienced in direct governance than they were, was stumbling toward restoration of civilian rule. The Argentine military officers were experienced with intervention and governance, but in disarray and disrepute following their disastrous Falklands War with England. They left power in 1982 facing an uncertain future of trials, imprisonment, and general retribution. Their fate was not lost on their Chilean and Uruguayan counterparts, who also feared retribution and particularly the loss of their pensions.

A referendum in Chile in 1980 set the country on a course to restore civilian rule. The military hoped to maintain a strong role in the future, but negotiations with civilian leaders and a 1988 plebiscite that would have extended military rule failed. Civilian government was eventually restored in 1990. Uruguayan military leaders held a referendum on a new constitution in 1980 under strict controls and censorship that would have maintained their influence after "normalization," but their proposal was defeated. That led to intense negotiations with civilian political leaders and an election in 1985 that finally restored civilian control. The negotiations between military and political leaders in the two countries were critical to restoring civilian control, but the compromises fell short of serious retribution against the military officers.

There are aspects of the experiences of Chile and Uruguay that raise serious questions generally about the resiliency of democratic systems. These two cases clearly illustrate the notion that even long-established, functioning democracies under sufficient stress can fail. Their failures were not the result of conspiracies or of the withering of democratic values; rather, they were the result of the inability of their political systems to function, to resolve conflicts within their institutional frameworks, and, most important, to withstand and absorb rising levels of political participation.

Even the strongest democratic institutions and traditions are limited by the level and kind of participation they can tolerate over any period of time. In the cases of Chile and Uruguay they were stretched to their limits and beyond in the 1960s, the symptoms in both cases being similar: stalemate, political and governmental paralysis, radicalization, polarization, alienation, confrontation, and eventual military intervention. In both, military intervention was more a symptom than a cause of their malaise. Career military officers as a result of their personalities and socialization commonly value order above everything else. They cannot accept, tolerate, nor cope with the chaos and politics that are inevitable symptoms of stress created by democratic institutional decay.[11]

Democratic systems both presume and require some minimum degree of consensus within a society or the ability to reach it through political means. The balance between authoritative and authoritarian decisionmaking is a precarious one that both Chile and Uruguay struggled with as they tried to avoid the authoritarianism so common in Latin America. The institutional devices for protecting democracy and discouraging authoritarianism worked in the two countries as long as the assumptions of continued growth, modernization, and rising living standards remained viable and sustained a national consensus. In the post–World War II period the assumptions proved unrealistic in both countries, as consensus declined and the democratic institutions that were based on it were unable to respond to the new challenges. That democracies can fail is not a new idea; there had been obvious European precedents earlier in the century and many examples more recently, but most of them were relatively recent attempts at democratization. Chilean and Uruguayan democracies were well rooted in their history and culture. Their experiences underscore the need to reevaluate historic assumptions, renovate institutional frameworks as political behavior changes and intensifies, and find ways to generate and recruit effective, national political leadership.

Notes

1. These questions are discussed more fully in Fitzgibbon 1967:129–133.
2. See the general discussion in Huntington 1968:191–236.

3. Comprehensive analysis of this period can be found in Valenzuela and Valenzuela 1976, 1986.

4. A concise summary of Chilean political history for the pre–World War II era is in Gil 1966:34–139.

5. These changes are well documented in Sigmund 1977.

6. The Fitzgibbon book on Uruguay (1954) was preceded by a study by George Pendle (1952) that included discussion of both politics and government, but it was on balance a more general and less analytic exercise.

7. The unusual electoral system has been reviewed in greater detail in Taylor 1955 and McDonald 1989:91–110.

8. Batlle's ideas have been widely explored, notably in the early biography by Enrique Rodríguez Fabregat (1942).

9. The final collapse of democracy in 1973 is discussed in greater detail in Weinstein 1975 and McDonald 1975.

10. Reconstruction in Uruguay is extensively discussed in Kaufman 1978; Handelman 1981, 1986; Gillespie 1986; Weinstein 1988 among others so identified in the bibliography.

11. The general problems and patterns of democratization in the late twentieth century are explored with compelling results in Huntington 1991.

Bibliography

Campiglia, Nestor. 1969. *Los Grupos de Presión y el Proceso Político*. Montevideo: Arca.

Caviedes, Cesar N. 1990. *Elections in Chile*. Boulder: Lynne Rienner.

Constable, Pamela, and Arturo Valenzuela. 1991. *A Nation of Enemies: Chile Under Pinochet*. New York: Norton.

Fitzgibbon, Russell H. 1967. Measuring democratic change in Latin America. *Journal of Politics* 29:129–166.

_____. 1954. *Uruguay: Portrait of a Democracy*. New Brunswick, N.J.: Rutgers University Press.

Gil, Federico G. 1966. *The Political System of Chile*. Boston: Houghton Mifflin.

Gillespie, Charles G. 1986. Activists and floating voters: The unheeded lessons of Uruguay's 1982 primaries. In *Elections and Democratization in Latin America, 1980–1985* (Paul W. Drake and Eduardo Silva, eds.), 215–244. San Diego: Center for Iberian and Latin American Studies, Center for U.S.-Mexican Studies Institute of the Americas.

Gonzalez, Luis E. 1991. *Political Structures and Democracy in Uruguay*. Notre Dame, Ind.: University of Notre Dame Press.

Handelman, Howard. 1986. Prelude to elections: The military's legitimacy crisis and the constitutional plebiscite in Uruguay. In *Elections and Democratization in Latin America, 1980–1985* (Paul W. Drake and Eduardo Silva, eds.), 201–214. San Diego: Center for Iberian and Latin American Studies, Center for U.S.-Mexican Studies Institute of the Americas.

_____. 1981. Uruguay. In *Military Government and the Movement Toward Democracy in South America* (Howard Handelman and Thomas G. Sanders, eds.), 215–284. Bloomington: Indiana University Press.

Huntington, Samuel P. 1991. *The Third Wave: Democratization in the Late Twentieth Century*. Norman: Oklahoma University Press.

_____. 1968. *Political Order in Changing Societies.* New Haven, Conn.: Yale University Press.

Kaufman, Eli. 1978. *Uruguay in Transition.* New Brunswick, N.J.: Transaction Books.

McDonald, Ronald H. 1996. Uruguay: Redefining normalcy. In *Latin American Politics and Development,* 4th ed. (Howard W. Wiarda and Harvey F. Kline, eds.), 270–284. Boulder: Westview Press.

_____. 1989. Chile. Uruguay. In *Political Parties and Elections in Latin America* (Ronald H. McDonald and J. Mark Ruhl, eds.), 91–109, 185–207. Boulder: Westview Press.

_____. 1987. Redemocratization in Uruguay. In *Liberalization and Redemocratization in Latin America* (George A. Lopez and Michael Stoh, eds.), 173–198. Westport, Conn.: Greenwood Press.

_____. 1975. The rise of military politics in Uruguay. *Inter-American Economic Affairs* 28:25–43.

_____. 1971. Legislative politics in Uruguay: A preliminary analysis. In *Latin American Legislatures: Their Role and Influence* (Weston H. Agor, ed.), 113–135. New York: Praeger.

Oppenheim, Lois Hecht. 1993. *Politics in Chile: Democracy, Authoritarianism, and the Search for Development.* Boulder: Westview Press.

Pendle, George. 1952. *Uruguay: South America's First Welfare State.* London: Royal Institute of International Affairs.

Portes, Alejandro. 1976. Occupation and lower-class political orientations in Chile. In *Chile: Politics and Society* (Arturo Valenzuela and J. Samuel Valenzuela, eds.), 201–237. New Brunswick, N.J.: Transaction Books.

Prothro, James W., and Patricio E. Chaparro. 1974. Public opinion and the movement of the Chilean government to the left, 1952–1972. *Journal of Politics* 36:2–43.

Rial, Juan. 1986. The Uruguayan elections of 1984: A triumph of the center. In *Elections and Democratization in Latin America, 1980–1985* (Paul W. Drake and Eduardo Silva, eds.), 245–272. San Diego: Center for Iberian and Latin American Studies, Center for U.S.-Mexican Studies, Institute of the Americas.

Rodríguez Fabregat, Enrique. 1942. *Batlle y Ordóñez: El Reformador.* Buenos Aires: Editorial Claridad.

Sigmund, Paul E. 1996. Chile. In *Latin American Politics and Development,* 4th ed. (Howard J. Wiarda and Harvey F. Kline, eds.), 144–172. Boulder: Westview Press.

_____. 1977. *The Overthrow of Allende and the Politics of Chile, 1964–1976.* Pittsburgh: University of Pittsburgh Press.

Taylor, Philip B. 1963. Interests and institutional disfunction in Uruguay. *American Political Science Review* 58:62–74.

_____. 1955. The Electoral System in Uruguay. *Journal of Politics* 17:19–42.

_____. 1951. The executive power in Uruguay. Diss., University of California, Berkeley.

Tulchin, Joseph S., and Augusto Varas. 1991. *From Democracy to Democracy: Rebuilding Political Consensus in Chile.* Boulder: Lynne Rienner.

Valenzuela, Arturo, and J. Samuel Valenzuela. 1976. *Chile: Politics and Society.* New Brunswick, N.J.: Transaction Books.

Valenzuela, J. Samuel, and Arturo Valenzuela. 1986. *Military Rule in Chile: Dictatorship and Oppositions.* Baltimore: Johns Hopkins University Press.

Weinstein, Martin. 1988. *Uruguay: Democracy at the Crossroads.* Boulder: Westview Press.

_____. 1975. *Uruguay: The Politics of Failure.* Westport, Conn.: Greenwood Press.

Chapter Eighteen

The Military and Democracy in Argentina

JACK CHILD

Ever since the early 1930s the Argentine military has been a major factor in the viability, and sometimes absence, of functioning democracy in Argentina. In the postwar years there have been four extended periods of direct military rule, along with two other periods in which the military either exercised a veto or shared power with an elected president. The last such period of direct rule (the so-called Proceso de Reorganización Nacional from 1976 to 1983) was so disastrous in economic, political, military, and human rights terms that it resulted in a dramatic loss of prestige for the military and opened up space for elected civilian presidents in a way that may have permanently altered their political roles. As Peter Snow (1993) points out, of the twenty-seven chief executives from 1928 to date, seventeen were professional military men, and only ten were civilians; furthermore, since 1928 only one civilian (Menem) has served a complete term in office.

This chapter will examine the relationship between the military and democracy in Argentina since the early World War II years and will attempt to analyze some of the factors involved in that relationship.

Figure 18.1[1] provides a chronological summary of the political roles played by the Argentine military since 1943, along with the Fitzgibbon-Johnson Index figures for the country from 1945 to 1995. The names of presidents are also provided (some short-term transitional figures are omitted for the sake of simplicity). As can be seen, the Fitzgibbon Index figures vary from a low of 11 (during the 1976–1983 "Proceso") to a high of 3; the most extended period of high ratings (3, 5, and 4) has been the period of elected civilian rule under Presidents Raúl Alfonsín and Carlos Saúl Menem that began at the end of the Proceso in 1983. Beyond the numbers and graphic presentation lies the reality that since 1930 democracy in Argentina has been strongly influenced by the political role of the military. Civilian politicians have consistently had to ask themselves how the mil-

Fitzgibbon Index		Military Role	President
	1943		
	1944	**Direct rule**	Gens. Ramírez, Farrell
5	1945		
	1946		
	1947		
	1948		
	1949		
8	1950	**Partner**	Juan D. Perón
	1951		
	1952		
	1953		
	1954		
8	1955		
	1956	**Direct rule**	Gen. Aramburu
	1957		
	1958		
	1959		
4	1960	**Veto power**	Arturo Frondizi José Guido
	1961		
	1962		
	1963		
	1964	**Pressure group**	Arturo Illia
6	1965		
	1966		
	1967		
	1968		
	1969		
7	1970	**Direct rule**	Gens. Onganía, Levingston, Lanusse
	1971		
	1972		
	1973		
	1974	**Pressure group**	Juan D. Perón
5	1975		Isabelita Perón
	1976		
	1977		
	1978		
	1979		Gens. Videla,
11	1980	**Direct rule**	Viola, Galtieri
	1981		
	1982		
	1983		
	1984		
3	1985		
	1986		Raúl Alfonsín
	1987		
	1988	**Pressure group**	
	1989		
5	1990		
	1991		
	1992		Carlos Saúl Menem
	1993		
	1994		
4	1995		
	1996		

Figure 18.1 Argentina: Military Role, Presidents, Fitzgibbon Index

itary would react to their initiatives, and frequently the military launched its own vision of what the country's government and policies should be. Civilian politicians have also frequently sought out the military as a political ally to bring down an adversary or to support them in power.

Some caveats are in order. As is true in many of the Latin American nations, there is no such thing as a single unified and homogeneous "military." For a variety of reasons, it is the Argentine army that has played the primary (and sometimes almost exclusive) political role. A further caveat is that the political role of the military is usually defined by its officer corps, and in particular by a relatively small group of senior generals and flag officers. Enlisted men, noncommissioned officers, and junior commissioned officers generally have little say in the political direction the military takes, although there have been important exceptions.

Political Roles of the Argentine Military

Origins, Nineteenth-Century Developments, and Professionalization

Most of the hemisphere's military establishments proudly claim to have been "born with the nation" in the process of fighting for independence from the European colonial mother country. The Argentine military claims an even earlier origin, based on the hastily organized popular militias that repelled the British invasions of 1806 and 1807, events that have entered Argentine military lore as the first in a series of victories over the English.

But perhaps more relevant was the formal creation and growth of the Argentine army under the leadership of the liberator General José de San Martín, know as "el Santo de la Espada."

Besides the play on his name, the honorific is emblematic of the close ties between the Catholic church and the Argentine military, in which most units have a patron saint and in which the army is formally dedicated and devoted to the Virgin Mary. As the founding father of his nation and its military, San Martín provided an example of democratic republican virtue; unlike Simón Bolívar, he refused a postindependence political role and instead went into European exile after his victories. San Martín also was reputed to have called the military "a tiger which must be kept caged until the day of battle" (Whitaker 1962:36).

It is difficult to specify the political roles of the military for the first fifty years after independence for the simple reason that a regular professional military did not exist in a period characterized by anarchy and local warlords (caudillos) who fought each other with rag-tag improvised forces. The process of national consolidation after the fall of the caudillo Juan Manuel de Rosas (1829–1852) permitted the professionalization of the Argentine military and the emergence of its fundamental political role as a pressure group devoted to protecting and preserving itself as a national institution. This professionalization included the creation of basic military academies for the army and navy and the requirement that all combat and line officers begin their careers as cadets in these academies. Late in the century Prussian and German military officers were brought in to establish a War College and a general staff, to set up the draft, and to oversee the acquisition of German military equipment, tactics, and doctrine. Up until the outbreak of World War I significant numbers of key Argentine army officers were also sent to Germany for training and service. In contrast, the principal foreign influence on the Argentine navy in this period was British.

One enduring legacy in the Argentine army from this period of Prussian professionalization was the transfer of geopolitical ideas then in vogue in Germany, and in particular the concept that the nation-state was an "organic" living thing that needed protection from other organic states that competed with it for survival and scarce resources.

The late-nineteenth-century process of professionalization brought with it a series of real roles and missions, especially for the army, which gave it a sense of self-confidence and a feeling that it was a vital part of the nation-state. These experiences included a victory over Paraguay in the 1865–1870 War of the Triple Alliance (along with Brazil and Uruguay) and the Campaign of the Desert (1879–1883), in which the Army acquired considerable prestige and a sense of nation building as it cleared important sections of Pampa and southern Argentina of marauding bands of the last Indigenous groups in the area. As the century came to a close the conviction that the military had an important role was heightened by tensions with Chile and the real possibility of a conflict with that neighbor.

Twentieth Century Until 1930: Minimal Pressure Group Role

With these real missions and responsibilities absorbing most of the military's time and effort, it is understandable that its political role remained minimal through the first three decades of the twentieth century, despite occasional efforts by civilian politicians to involve it more deeply in their political struggles.

However, things were changing, and the military was becoming slowly drawn into the political battles between the long-ruling Conservative Party and the emerging middle-class Radical Party under the leadership of Hipólito Irigoyen (president 1916–1922 and 1928–1930). Both political parties appealed for support among sympathetic military officers, particularly during a series of violent political clashes. While in power Irigoyen compounded the problem by promoting and otherwise rewarding those officers who had supported him. He also used the Army in what were traditionally police functions to enforce some of his more blatantly political decisions involving the removal of Conservative governors and legislators (Manzetti 1993:chap. 5). In so doing, Irigoyen violated the military's principle of institutional autonomy and greatly accelerated the polarization and politicization process. One reaction was the creation of secret *logias* (lodges) among key officers who hoped to protect their autonomy and resist political involvement. Ironically, the end result of the *logias*, especial the main Logia San Martín, was to get the military even more involved in politics as it sought to isolate those officers perceived to be excessively political. One bizarre episode in this period occurred shortly after the Bolshevik Revolution, when Argentine army officers discovered that there was an attempt by some soldiers and sergeants to organized communist-type soviets among the ranks. In a grim and eerie foreshadowing of the "dirty war" of the 1970s, army officers perceived this as an ideological threat that had to be "extirpated."

Direct Rule, 1930–1932: General Uriburu

By 1930 the politicization of the military and the decay of the second Irigoyen administration had reached such a critical point that, supported by most Argentines, the military broke precedent and staged the first coup in modern Argentina. The September 1930 coup that removed the ineffective and senile President Irigoyen was a watershed moment for Argentine democracy and military politics. With the coup a tradition was broken and a precedent established; the next coup attempt would thus be easier to organize and carry out. The coup also revealed serious divisions within the military, another characteristic that was to plague Argentine democracy for decades. The navy stayed out of the coup process, and within the army there were two distinct currents, one that advocated a quick return of power to civilians, and the other that felt a prolonged period of military tutelage in power was necessary. This latter current held the upper hand for this first year-and-a-half of direct military rule under General José Uriburu, who was a fanatic nationalist and admirer of authoritarian corporatist models associated with Italian fascists such as Benito Mussolini (American University 1985:290). Uriburu and his supporters held most civilian politicians in contempt, believed that democracy was ineffective, and felt that the army was more truly representative of the Argentine nation and thus more fit to govern.

Fortunately for Argentina, this period of direct military rule was relatively brief, although what it revealed and portended was deeply troubling. In only eighteen months Uriburu's support from inside and outside the military slipped away, and he was forced to permit elections by another general, Agustín P. Justo, who had also been involved in the 1930 coup.

Pressure Group, 1932–1943: Presidents Justo, Ortiz, and Castillo

With the Radical Party prohibited from running, General Justo himself easily won the 1932 election as the candidate of the oligarchs, and by virtue of his personal prestige and his commitment to the electoral process he was able to persuade the military to remove itself from its "direct rule" role and revert to simply being a pressure group. Justo was not able to totally suppress army politics, however, and his period in office saw several coup attempts by the Uriburu authoritarian/corporatist wing of the military. The political divisions brought out by the 1930 coup were now leading to what has been called the *partido militar* (Wynia 1992:74).

For eleven years and under three presidents (Justo, Roberto Ortiz, and Ramón Castillo) under the so-called Concordancia, government was at the service of a conservative and oligarchic elite. The military's loyal support for this regime was rewarded with increases in size and pay raises. As fascism gained strength in Europe and World War II neared, the nationalist-authoritarian currents in the military began to grow stronger, and a significant number of officers, especially in the army, argued that Argentina should throw its lot in with the fascists and not support European democracies or the United States in the ensuing conflict. An important corollary in this process was a move to industrialize Argentina to make it independent of European or U.S. sources of arms and heavy industrial equipment. In this connection the military began to set up a network of state-run industrial enterprises ranging from the oil monopoly (Yacimientos Petrolíferos Fiscales—YPF, 1922) to an aircraft factory (1927) to a conglomerate of army-run enterprises, the Dirección General de Fabricaciones Militares (1941) (Manzetti 1993:170–171). Although still at the "pressure group" level, the military's role and size were dramatically expanding.

Divisions within the military and the onset of World War II led to the creation of new secret lodges that debated politics and whether Argentina should support the Allies or the Axis. One of the principal fascist-oriented lodges was the Grupo de Oficiales Unidos (GOU); a key member was Colonel Juan D. Perón.

Direct Rule, 1943–1946: Generals Ramírez, Farrell

In what seemed at first a replay of 1930, in 1943 the military deposed the unpopular and ineffective Castillo and assumed direct rule of Argentina. However, this time the military closed down the Congress and political parties, making it clear that they would be in control for an extended period. Furthermore, the struggle for power within the army involved a new factor: military populism, a startling development under which a charismatic officer, Juan Perón, would forge an unprecedented alliance with urban labor and permanently change the face of Argentine politics.

When the GOU emerged as the dominant faction within the military, President and General Pedro Ramírez was replaced by President and General Edelmiro Farrell, who was a supporter of Perón and his alliance with labor's "*descamisados*." The struggle for power within the military continued through October 1945, when for a brief period the more conservative faction seemed to hold the upper hand, removed Perón from his key post as secretary of labor, and put him in jail. But in a dramatic turnabout, on October 17 (a day enshrined in Peronista history) a massive labor demonstration in Buenos Aires forced the conservative wing of the military to release Perón, who was restored to his posts and easily won election to the presidency the following year.

Government Partner, 1946–1955: General Perón

In the ten years of the first Perón administration (1946–1955) the military's role was no longer that of "direct rule"; nor was the military simply a pressure group. Perón came out of the military, and important factions of the army strongly supported him throughout this period. But the military was forced to become the political partner (in a subordinate role) of a popular leader (and his also very popular wife, Evita) as well as with labor. Furthermore, there were important cleavages within the military: the navy was basically hostile to Perón for most of this period and played a key role in deposing him in 1955.

Among the sectors of the military favored by Perón were his own branch as well as the heavy industry activities of the Fabricaciones Militares. Those factions of the military that were loyal to Perón in this period were handsomely rewarded, whereas those who opposed him found their budgetary support and institutional roles diminished. In the short run this strengthened Perón, but in the long term this violated the notion of institutional autonomy just as it had under Irigoyen, and toward the end of the decade it provided the nucleus for several attempts to remove Perón from office.

Perón had been influenced by his assignment in Italy (1939–1940), where he had the opportunity to observe the Italian fascists and Mussolini. Although he never openly advocated Argentina's participation in the war on the side of the Axis, his proclivities in this direction were frequently obvious and gave rise to much suspicion in Washington that he was in effect a secret ally of the fascists.[2]

A number of different causes led to the decline of Perón's partnership with the military. For one, there was the old cleavage between those officers who had always advocated a quick return to civilian politicians and those who felt that Argentina needed a long period of military tutelage. The nature of the tutelage under Perón, however, was different from that favored by many hard-liners, who saw the alliance with labor as unnatural. The Argentine military is surprisingly puritanical in certain personal matters, and many officers never accepted Evita as a social equal and were shocked when Perón suggested she might be his running mate. After her death in 1952 the rumors regarding Perón's activities with teenage girls further offended these officers. His talk of arming labor supporters to form a worker's militia loyal to him was unacceptable to the professional military, as were the steps he took against the Catholic church.

When the end came in September 1955, many of these army officers did nothing during the navy's successful coup (after a failed one in July). The navy's action in the removal of Perón was something of an anomaly in this normally less-political service, but it can be explained in terms of the navy's traditionally close ties with upper levels of Argentine society, who never relented in their opposition to Perón.

Direct Rule, 1955–1958: Generals Lonardi, Aramburu

Like the coups of 1930 and 1943, the 1955 removal of Perón was justified by the military on the grounds that the interests of the Argentine *"patria"* required armed intervention to put an end to a corrupt and oppressive regime. However, a new factor in 1955 was to drive military politics for the next seventeen years: the obsession to keep Perón (and Peronistas) out of power.

Thus the military president for most of the 1955–1958 period of direct rule was a strong anti-Peronista, General Pedro Aramburu. But Aramburu faced what became known as the "impossible game" (Manzetti 1993:175): how to govern effectively while denying an active political role to important sectors of voters (mainly urban labor and the rural poor) who remained strongly supportive of Perón and favored his return. A failed revolt by Peronista elements within the military in 1956 was met with uncharacteristic harshness as twenty-seven of the plotters were executed, some with only the briefest of courts-martial.

In the post-Perón years the military had only limited and unattractive options. They could rule for whatever indefinite period would be long enough to eradicate Peronismo, but this might be decades. They could allow free elections, but this would be unacceptable because it would undoubtedly permit the return of Peronismo and perhaps even Perón himself. Finally, they could hold elections and exclude the Peronistas, which would create a weak minority regime. After considerable debate, and realizing that they had no stomach for indefinite rule, the military chose the last option, which led to the civilian presidency of the Radical Party's Arturo Frondizi in 1958.

Veto Power, 1958–1962: Frondizi

But Frondizi had a fatal weakness in the eyes of the military: He had made a deal with the Peronistas that got their votes in exchange for a promise to legalize their party. The military never fully trusted him and exercised a strong veto power role in his presidency, carefully scrutinizing all his important decisions to ensure that none of them favored the proscribed Peronistas. Ironically, the Peronistas did not trust Frondizi either and turned against him shortly after helping get him elected.

The factionalism within the military acquired new names, although not particularly new features, in the Frondizi years. The *colorados* (also known as *golpistas* or *gorilas*) were the most hard-line anti-Peronistas and argued for indefinite military rule based on the notion that this was required in order to wipe out not only Peronismo but also the conditions that led to it. With the triumph of the Castro Revolution in Cuba this group began to identify Peronistas as the local Argentine version of communist subversives (Snow 1993:105). Opposing the colorados were the *azules* (sometimes called *legalistas*), who felt that the 1955 Liberating Revolution had achieved its principal goal when it removed the dictator Perón and that it was now time to return the political process to the civilians and accept any result that emerged unless it degenerated into chaos or another dictatorship such as Perón's.

Unfortunately, Frondizi sometimes took actions that undercut the *azules* and validated the *colorado*'s worst fears. His Cuban policy, for example, was seen as excessively inclined towards Castro, and soft on the perceived communist threat posed by the example of his triumph. One incident that infuriated the *colorados* was the 1961 secret visit paid to Argentina (at Frondizi's invitation) by Ernesto "Che" Guevara, who at the time was attending a conference in neighboring

Uruguay in his capacity as Cuba's minister of industry (Potash 1980:338–341). A few months later Frondizi was forced by the military to resign and turn the presidency over to his constitutional successor, José Guido, president of the Senate, who served until the 1963 elections; the military's veto power role continued undiminished in the Guido transitional presidency.

Pressure Group, 1963–1966: Illia

Internal factional maneuvering and several armed confrontations led to control by the legalistic *azul* faction in 1963, and this permitted a new election. As in the Frondizi election, Peronistas were not allowed to run candidates in 1963, and the military was careful to ensure that there was no Frondizi-style deal with the Peronistas. The predictable result, given the rules of the "impossible game," was a weak Radical Party president (Arturo Illia) elected with only a quarter of the ballots and subject to constant battles with the Peronistas and their still-strong labor unions. The military pulled back to a pressure group role in the Illia administration, but this was also a period of watchful waiting and internal regrouping until a discredited and fatally weakened President Illia was removed by yet another coup in 1966.

Direct Rule, 1966–1973: Generals Onganía, Levingston, Lanusse

The military that replaced Illia in 1966 was, for a change, fairly united by the fear of leftist guerrillas and their reaction to it: the Doctrine of National Security. The unity and the doctrine had been carefully nurtured by General Juan Carlos Onganía during the Illia years as he prepared for what he saw as an eventual and long-term government by the armed forces.

The doctrine requires some explaining. Its point of departure is the old geopolitical concept of the nation-state as an organism that is subject to a variety of threats (Child 1985:chap. 4). A conventional military can deal with conventional external threats through traditional military means. But with the triumph of Castro's Marxist-Leninist revolution, and the attempt to export it to sympathizers within Argentina, the major threat was now internal, in the form of subversion, terrorism, and ideological warfare. This new danger was like a cancer from within the organism itself and included political, psychological, and economic facets that had to be countered by counterinsurgency techniques, including the linking of security and development. To President and General Onganía and his followers the two experiments with elected civilian regimes (Frondizi and Illia) had demonstrated the inability of civilians to adequately mount a defense against the new threat; what was required, and for an extended period of time, was a government of the armed forces that would install a National Security State (NSS) to defend Argentina. The nation was embarking on its longest period yet of direct military rule.

The type of direct rule regime installed in the 1967–1973 period can also be seen as a long-term authoritarian regime dedicated to overseeing Argentina's development via the NSS model. The Argentine case had a strong parallel in the 1964–1985 Brazilian military regime, which in effect changed the words in the Brazilian flag from the old positivist "order and progress" to the NSS's "security and development." The model was labeled "bureaucratic authoritarian" by the Argentine analyst Guillermo O'Donnell (1982), who also pointed out that in countries like Argentina and Brazil modernization was not necessarily associated with democracy but, rather more often, was associated with authoritarian regimes headed up by the military in an alliance with nonpolitical technocrats.

General Onganía lasted for most of this period of direct rule, in which he personally made many of the key decisions and was reasonably successful in keeping the military away from the minutiae of presidential actions. But by 1970 a deteriorating economic situation and increasing violence (especially in the interior province of Córdoba) caused the military to lose confidence in Onganía, who was first replaced by a figurehead military officer (General Roberto Levingston, military attaché in Washington at the time he was chosen president), and then finally by the commander in chief of the army, General Alejandro Lanusse.

It took seven years for the Argentine military to exhaust the possibilities of their bureaucratic authoritarian regime, admit defeat, and finally recognize the realities of the "impossible game": Argentina could not be governed without the cooperation of the Peronistas.

Pressure Group, 1973–1976: Peronismo Returns

And so, finally, and with reluctance, President and General Lanusse permitted the first steps toward allowing the Peronistas to run a candidate and eventually open the door for Perón's return from his long exile. Lanusse's actions were all the more remarkable in light of the fact that his anti-Peronista credentials were impeccable: He had served time in Perón's jails for involvement in a failed anti-Perón coup.[3] The military reverted back to the pressure group role and awaited developments from the final Perón administration.

Following a brief transitional presidency by a figurehead Peronista, the aging Juan D. Perón came back to Argentina and easily won election, with his wife Isabelita as vice president.

But Peronismo was by now deeply divided among several violent factions, whose surface unity evaporated when Perón died in 1974 after only a year in office. Isabelita Perón assumed the presidency, but the task was clearly beyond her abilities. Internal Peronista violence was matched by the violence of leftist guerrillas and the mysterious right-wing death squads associated with security forces. Economic instability and political uncertainty fueled the generalized chaos until many sectors came to the realization that only another period of military rule could restore order. The stage was set for the most protracted and violent period of military rule, which brought with it Argentina's own special dark night of its national soul.

Direct Rule, 1976–1983: The Proceso (Generals Videla, Viola, Galtieri

The coup of March 1976 was widely anticipated and indeed welcomed by broad sectors of the Argentine population, including even Peronistas and labor. Almost anything seemed better than the violence and chaos of the Isabel Perón period.

The military began this extended period of direct rule with strong popular backing, substantial institutional unity, a clear set of goals, and a firm determination to stay in power for the extended period of time necessary to change (or "reorganize") Argentina. The objectives of the "Process of National Reorganization" (or simply, "el Proceso") were in three broad categories: The military goals were focused on the need to wipe out internal subversion, although an external conflict was also possible (Chile was the obvious candidate, but it ended up being the United Kingdom); political goals included the need to reorganize the nation so as to eliminate the corruption and disorder of the Perón years; and finally the economic goals included the need to wipe out the debilitating inflation and install a strong free market–oriented system.

Unlike the previous Onganía period of direct rule, this time the military governed much more as an institution. The highest decisionmaking power lay in the Junta composed of the three service chiefs, and the president had to answer to them. In practice this system frequently led to paralysis, decentralization, and duplication of projects and initiatives by each service. There was a sort of "feudalization" of power as each of the three services carved out geographic and functional areas of interest for themselves. The bureaucratic authoritarian state described by O'Donnell multiplied itself and went wildly out of control, to the detriment of all Argentines, especially the victims of the military and ultimately the military itself.

The first priority of the Proceso was the elimination of subversion, which was seen as a major threat to the nation. The brutal excesses of the "dirty war" that ensued have been told elsewhere,[4] but some analysis of what happened and why is needed here. The first targets were the obvious ones: the armed guerrillas and terrorists of the left, mainly the Montoneros and the Ejército Revolucionario Popular (ERP). They were contained and finally defeated in the first three years or so of the Proceso by a mixture of counterinsurgency approaches and the use of paramilitary groups on the right. The most notorious of these, the Argentine Anticommunist Alliance (AAA) had been operating since the days of the second Perón period. But as the armed revolutionaries were being contained, a massive intelligence and security network was being established independently by each of the three services to "process" suspects, a euphemism for torturing prisoners to extract information, and then "disappearing" (that is, killing) them to cover up the evidence of mistreatment. As the repressive network began to run out of armed subversives to process, it turned to the unarmed "intellectual authors" of the subversion, and the distinction between armed subversives and political opponents of the military regime was blurred. The net was cast wide, to include labor leaders, students, psychiatrists, intellectuals, Jews, and political activists. No one knows the exact number tortured or killed, but the official account contained in the CONADEP Commission headed by the intellectual Ernesto Sábato documents almost 9,000 cases; the actual number is much higher, and may be two or three times that number.

How was this "dirty war" possible in a nation that considers itself civilized and by a military establishment that stressed professionalism and high institutional values? Part of the answer goes back to the geopolitical concept of the nation-state as an organic entity threatened by the internal "cancer of subversion." This cancer, in the eyes of the military, had not responded to the persuasive treatment of chemotherapy or radiation; thus the only way to protect the state now from the threat was to "extirpate" it by surgical means, by killing the subversives. And the extirpation that began with armed subversives had to logically be extended to those who gave the guerrillas their dangerous ideas. A second factor that explains the excesses of the dirty war is the decentralized nature of the repressive operations. The over-all directives to get rid of the subversives were given from the highest level, but the specifics of how to execute these orders were at the discretion of local commanders and frequently of the units and individuals who carried them out. There was little control over these individuals, some of whom were clearly sadists and thugs, motivated by their own inner pathologies and the drive to extract *revancha* (revenge) against those enemies of Argentina who had used violence against the state and the security apparatus.

The ideological underpinnings of the dirty war were at times bizarre. A popular explanation among the Argentine military at the time was that World War III had already begun and that Argentina was its first combat theater. The struggle was between violent Marxism-Leninism and Western Christian civilization (defended by the Argentine military). The enemies of Western Christian civilization included not only communist guerrillas but also a wide-ranging conspiracy of international financiers, Zionists, human rights organizations, and anyone else who did not appreciate the sacrifices that the Argentine military was making on behalf of the Western world. The historic close ties between the military and conservative elements of the Catholic church in Argentina gave the dirty war a crusading aspect, and military chaplains (all Catholic) told the perpetrators of abuses that the excesses were justified by the apocalyptic nature of the struggle and by the excesses of the other side.

As documented by several authors (Timmerman 1982; Partnoy 1986), anti-Semitism was an additional element that drove some segments of the Argentine military in the dirty war. Argentina's approximately 400,000 Jews (the largest number in any Latin American country) were a ready target for the military, who considered them "bad Argentines" because of their perceived loyalty to Zionism and Israel; they were also associated with three Jews who had done great damage to Western Christian civilization: Karl Marx because of his contribution to communism; Sigmund Freud because of his undermining of family values; and Albert

Einstein because of his challenge to traditional Catholic notions of space-time relationships. There is no suggestion here that all or most of the Argentine military believed these bizarre ideas, but enough who were involved in the repression did believe them and carried them to their logical and violent conclusion. The majority opinion in the Argentine military seemed to argue that the subversive enemy was ruthless, that extraordinary measures had to be taken to eliminate the enemy, and that the sacrifices the military made in this murky theater of war should be appreciated by civilians at the same time as they understood the need for "excesses" (Hang 1993:5).

Even if the military could in their own minds rationalize and justify their "victory" against subversion, it was harder for them to explain the failure to reach the Proceso's goals of economic stability or political reorganization. On the economic side the free-market ideas of Minister Martínez de Hoz led to bloated budgets, speculation, corruption, and a dramatic rise in the external debt. A significant portion of this debt and budget increase was represented by the growth in the military itself: The per capita share of the military side of the budget in 1980 was $125 for each Argentine, in comparison with about one-tenth that for each Brazilian; in that same year the Argentine armed forces reached a strength of 175,000 men (Manzetti 1993:186).

By early 1981 the failures of the Proceso were becoming more and more evident, and General Videla was replaced with the army's commander in chief, General Roberto Viola, who lasted only a few months before being pushed aside by General Leopoldo Galtieri, who led the military into the Proceso's last and fatal mistake: the South Atlantic War with Great Britain over the Falkland/Malvinas Islands. There are many accounts and analyses of that fiasco, but the extent of the military regime's incompetence can be illustrated by the simple fact that they apparently never seriously considered the possibility that Margaret Thatcher's government would be willing, or able, to mount an effort to retake the islands once the Argentines took them in April 1982.

And so the Proceso ended with humiliating failure and bitter memories of the disappeared of the dirty war and the incompetence and deceit of the regime in the 1982 conflict. Other than destroying the subversives (at a terrible Pyrrhic price), none of the major objectives of the Proceso were accomplished. The unity and prestige of the military in 1983 were at their lowest ebb. Cleavages in the military were deep and both horizontal and vertical: The old horizontal divisions between the three services were worse than ever, and now there were new vertical splits between the leadership and mid and lower-level officers who felt they had been betrayed by the generals.

A bitter joke making the rounds of Buenos Aires in late 1982 sums up the end of the Proceso: "First they messed up the economy, and we could understand that because they are not economists. Then they messed up the government, and we could even understand that because they are not politicians. But then they went and started an unnecessary war, lied to us about it, and then lost it."

Pressure Group, 1983–Present: Alfonsín, Menem

One silver lining in the Malvinas disaster and the other failures of the Proceso was that they had seemingly removed the military from politics, or had at least given civilian politicians an extended breathing space. Had Galtieri and his fellow Junta members been successful in their Malvinas adventure, Argentina might have had a military government for an extended period, and military adventurism might have extended to an attack on Chile over the Beagle Channel islands issue and to what General Galtieri called "full Argentine sovereignty over our other Southern territories" (that is, the Antarctic claim).

The two post-Proceso presidents (Radical Raúl Alfonsín and Peronist Carlos Saúl Menem) took different approaches to the military, although both were firmly committed to keeping the military's role at the "pressure group" level. In this they were aided immeasurably by the military's internal divisions and severe loss of prestige during the Proceso.

Alfonsín had campaigned on the promise of bringing military human rights violators to justice, and much of the tension he had with the military came from this commitment. From the military's perspective it might be acceptable to try a few individuals for excesses, but the institution as a whole should not be blamed. Rather, Argentina should be grateful for the way the military saved it from the leftist subversives and should not try to use the errors of the Proceso to back the military into a corner.[5]

Public opinion supported Alfonsín as he began the unprecedented effort to bring those most responsible for the dirty war and the excesses of the Proceso to trial. The first attempt at trying the nine generals and admirals who led the three juntas of the Proceso was left in hands of the military justice system, which delayed the proceedings and finally admitted it could not reach a verdict; Alfonsín's attempt to get the military to admit its own responsibility had failed. The judicial initiative then passed to the civilian federal court system, which did indeed impose long sentences (General Jorge R. Videla and Admiral Emilio Massera, the two architects of the bloodiest portion of the dirty war, were sentenced to life). Members of the last junta (including General Leopoldo Galtieri) were later tried by military courts for their conduct of the 1982 war and found guilty. Attempts by relatives of the disappeared and human rights groups to prosecute a much larger number of military men involved in the dirty war caused serious reaction among the military and led Alfonsín to attempt to put an end to the legal process by means of the so-called Punto Final law (Potash 1993:53–72).

Alfonsín took a number of other significant steps to place limits on the military: Their budget was cut by half from its historic 1981 high; a corresponding reduction in size and weapons procurement severely hampered operational capabilities; the massive Fabricaciones Militares were severely cut back in scope; and the upper levels of the military were reorganized, creating a civilian minister of defense and changing the top job in each service from "commander" to "chief of staff." In the international arena he concluded negotiations for a peaceful solution to the Beagle Channel controversy that had almost led Argentina to war with Chile. In so doing he eliminated the last serious external military threat to Argentina and used this as a justification for size and budget cuts.

These steps were not easily accepted by the military, especially midlevel officers who felt they had been twice betrayed: first by their senior commanders and now by their civilian president. Numerous indications of military discontent plagued the Alfonsín administration, and two serious attempts at revolt were launched by the so-called *carapintadas* (a reference to the combat camouflage favored by commando troops). Although none of these had much popular support and apparently were not aimed at deposing Alfonsín as president, they did succeed in removing certain senior generals not respected by the midlevel officers and placed restraints on some of the steps Alfonsín would have liked to take to limit the military.

In the Alfonsín years many in the military came to see the Radicals as their enemies because of their zeal for prosecuting them, and they began to leave aside their historic animosity towards Peronismo and its candidate in the 1989 elections, Carlos Saúl Menem. Menem's approach to the military was to continue many of the steps taken by his predecessor to limit the military, such as downsizing and privatizing the military-industrial complex, but with a much more conciliatory attitude to the military involved in the dirty war and the 1982 conflict. He began by pardoning most of the officers who had been tried under Alfonsín, despite widespread protests by those who had fought so hard to have them prosecuted. His personal relationship with senior officers and all ranks was much closer than Alfonsín's had been. He participated in a number of military ceremonies in an attempt to signal that the important thing was to put the past behind, to resolve differences, and to move ahead. His approach paid off in December 1990 when another *carapintada* revolt failed to obtain support among other sectors of the military and indeed was crushed violently (and unprecedentedly) by the army.

Menem differed from Alfonsín in another important aspect: He attempted to find meaningful roles for the diminished military and to try to incorporate them into Argentine society in ways they had historically resisted. The new mission was international peacekeeping under both U.S. and UN aegis. He sent forces to participate in the Gulf War and, later, a significant number of peacekeepers to Croatia. The Argentine UNPROFOR battalion in Croatia was unusual, being composed almost exclusively of officers and sergeants, and the six-month rotations in and out of the unit were intended to expose the maximum number of career soldiers to the benefits and significance of this new role,[6] which in 1993 was formally included in the army's mission statement (Child 1995:30–32). One basic assumption was that such UN service would help the military, and especially the army, recover some of the prestige it had lost in the dirty war and the 1982 conflict.

Also new was the concept of "cooperative security" pushed by civilians in the Menem administration. Significantly, in the past such definitions of strategic concepts and security arrangements had been a purely military province. But this new idea stressed preventative steps (such as confidence-building measures) that would make interstate conflict in Latin America less likely. By implication, this reduction of tensions could be used as a justification for further cuts in military budgets, manpower, and weapons acquisitions. Other steps taken by the Menem administration to reduce the historical isolation of the military were to encourage military officers to attend civilian higher education institutions and to get civilian functionaries and intellectuals more involved in the strategic planning process, which had historically been off limits to civilians.

At the time of this writing the indications are that most of the Argentine military is accepting the downsizing and redefinition of roles that has taken place under civilian presidents since 1983. Its status as a pressure group (and a diminished one at that) seems firmly established, and there seems little prospect of any increased political role in the near term. The old feeling among the military—that they are a special caste above civilians—has seemingly shrunk to the vanishing point, giving way to what one colonel has called a new trait among the Argentine military: humility (Hang 1993:9). There is also a greater willingness to accept more responsibility for the outrages of the dirty war: In early 1995 came the first admissions by navy and army officers of their direct involvement in the killings and disappearances of their fellow citizens, and shortly afterward the chief of staff of the army apologized to the nation, stating that "we must no longer deny the horror we lived through" (Escobar 1995:A13).

Analysis of the Military's Political Role and Democracy

This section will attempt to identify some of the factors noted and analyzed previously that explain the military's political activity (or lack thereof) beyond the acceptable minimal role of serving as a pressure group. The factors that tend to lead the military to take a more active political role can further be subdivided into those stemming from within the institution ("push" factors), and those coming from the broader political environment ("pull" factors).

"Push" Factors from Within Causing Greater Political Activity

Ideological: For many years the ideology was bitter anti-Peronism, to which was later added anticommunism. The ideological motivation can also be developmental, such as in the bureaucratic authoritarian period.

Basic needs or growth: Beyond the simple pressure group role, this category of motivation can stem from a feeling that civilian leadership does not understand the institution's basic needs or requirements for growth due to new circumstances.

Tutelage: This is the feeling that the military embodies the best civic (and sometimes moral) values of the nation and has the responsibility at times to teach these values to civilians.

Ambitions: These may be either personal (caudillismo) or small group elite (the *logias*).

Cleavages: These are splits within the military that spill over into the civilian political milieu.

"Pull" Factors from Without Causing Greater Political Activity

Invitation: This has occurred frequently in Argentine political history as one civilian political faction or another feels it is being unfairly denied power and seeks allies within the military in order to achieve it. It should be noted that frequently the civilian invitation to the military is for short-term purposes only and that often the military has stayed in power far longer than the civilians wanted it to.

Disorder, chaos, corruption, or perceived illegitimacy of the civilian regime: These are sometimes accompanied by the invitations described earlier.

Threats: These may be made by external or internal enemies (subversion) that the military feels are being inadequately dealt with.

Interference: The military may move in response to interference in internal matters such as promotions or assignments, or if used for blatant political purpose, such as attacking opponents of the civilian regime. The second Irigoyen administration (1928–1930) is illustrative here.

Need to change the system: The military may move against a civilian regime that it sees as detrimental to national interests and that it feels requires systemic change. The exclusion of large sectors of possible political participants may trigger such an intervention.

Self protection: If the military feels it is under attack, such as during the trials of the Alfonsín period, it may seek greater political activity.

Precedent: Sometimes the sheer weight of past political interventions seems to make the next one easier. Conversely, the lack of recent such interventions tends to make them less likely.

Factors That Tend to Keep Political Activity by the Military Low

- Rejection by civilians of such a role.
- Lessons learned from unhappy experiences in the past. The Proceso stands out as a major recent example.
- *Desgaste* (grinding down or decay) based on the erosion of military roles and values during an extended period of direct rule.
- A sense of a meaningful military mission, such as the current involvement in peacekeeping.
- Elimination of internal defense or police roles for the military. The Menem administration has done this, except for cases of obvious emergencies that civilian police forces cannot handle.
- Better links between civilians and military that tend to reduce the military's sense of isolation.

- International pressure, influence, or condemnation. These would make a coup more difficult, although not impossible. Backlash among more nationalistic sectors is also possible.

Prospects and Conclusions

In the past half-century the relationship between the military and democracy in Argentina has been an uneasy one. The military's political roles have ranged from extended periods of almost absolute and abusive direct rule (the Proceso) to the present period of almost minimalist pressure group. One can also see cycles of failed direct military rule followed by withdrawal followed by another period of direct rule when the necessary constellation of push-and-pull conditions are present. As we enter the last years of the century we are entitled to ask if we are merely seeing the pendulum swinging to the minimalist pole (only to return back to greater intervention in the future) or whether there has indeed been a sea change in the relationship between democracy and the military in Argentina.

The indications of a dramatic shift stemming from the disasters of the Proceso and political withdrawal under two civilian presidents since then are many and strong. There has been an extended period of civilian rule with the military's role held down at an acceptable pressure group level. In this period the military has been significantly downsized, and they have generally accepted this decline in size, budget, and importance. The military's stated roles have shifted, releasing it from the political dangers of internal policing and giving it an important (albeit secondary) international role in peacekeeping that has done much to restore some of its prestige. There continues to be a greater social and intellectual integration into civil society, with a number of bridges being built between civilian circles and the historically isolated military. The negative experiences in the Proceso that so discredited the military have presumably given them much reason to carefully think through the consequences of any future greater political role. Further, a number of the past reasons for intervening and limiting democracy are now gone or diminished: The Cold War is over, the Marxist guerrillas are no more, and the threat of war with neighbors is minimal. Finally, there has begun to emerge a willingness to accept responsibility for past mistakes, to learn from them, and to replace the old arrogant sense of having lessons to teach civilians with a more realistic sense of institutional limitations and even humility.

However, there are also negative signs. There is opposition within the military to many of the initiatives and changes noted earlier. International peacekeeping is not universally welcomed and in some sectors is seen as detrimental to the nobler mission of defending the nation; some warn that these international missions will lead to a "denaturing" and weakening of the military. While there is indeed a sense of lessons learned from the Proceso period, there is still a lingering resentment that civilians do not understand the sacrifices the military made to save the nation from the subversive left, and many of the human rights violators of the Proceso period remain on active duty, unrepentant about their past abuses. Furthermore, old habits and traditions die hard, and there is no guarantee that in the ranks of mid- and upper-level officers there might not be those who think, in the old style, that they have better answers than do the civilians. The old habits among civilian politicians may also have a long half-life, and the old "pull" factors of civilian invitation to a greater political role for the military may still emerge. Finally, the economic situation may worsen to a point where public discontent and the inability of politicians to deal with it may convince many inside and outside the military that they should replace the civilians, as they have done so often in the past.

On balance, there is reason for cautious optimism. The internal changes within the Argentine military are deep and very possibly irreversible. The longer the period of reasonably competent and legitimate civilian regimes lasts, the more irreversible the changes will be. If the Argentine military, its civilian leadership, and the population at large can work jointly to limit those factors that led the military to intervene politically, then it may someday be possible to look back on periods such as the Proceso years and view them as aberrations not to be repeated in Argentine political history.

Notes

1. The classification and time periods used in Figure 18.1 have been adapted from those used by several authors, including Snow 1993:91 and Manzetti 1993:chap. 5.

2. Messages and analyses by U.S. diplomats and intelligence personnel stressed this orientation; see, for example, OSS R&A report 2304, July 4, 1944, National Archives 097.3.

3. Lanusse had the door of his jail cell placed in his private office while president. He would joke that, for a good Catholic like himself, time in a Peronista jail was an excellent contraceptive method. Personal discussions with General Lanusse, Washington, 1969.

4. See Comisión Nacional Sobre la Desaparición de Personas 1984; Graziano 1992; Partnoy 1986; Timmerman 1982.

5. Discussion with an Argentine army colonel, Washington, D.C., 1987. The phrase the colonel used in Spanish was "no se nos debe acorralar."

6. Discussion with Argentine army chief of staff General Martín Balza, Washington, June 1994.

Bibliography

American University. 1985. Argentina: A Country Study. Washington, D.C.: GPO.

Child, Jack. 1995. Argentina: Guns and roses. Hemisphere 6:30–32.

_____. Geopolitics and Conflict in South America: Quarrels Among Neighbors. New York: Praeger.

Comisión Nacional Sobre la Desaparición de Personas. 1984. Nada Más. Buenos Aires: EUDEBA.

Escobar, G. 1995. Ex-sergeant details role in killings. Washington Post (April 25):A13.

Graziano, Frank. 1992. Divine Violence. Boulder: Westview Press.

Hang, Julio. 1993. *Las Fuerzas Armadas y la Estabilidad Político-Institucional en la República Argentina*. Washington, D.C.: Inter-American Defense College.

Manzetti, Luigi. 1993. *Institutions, Parties, and Coalitions in Argentine Politics*. Pittsburgh: University of Pittsburgh Press.

O'Donnell, Guillermo. 1982. *El Estado Burocrático Autoritario*. Buenos Aires: Editorial de Belgrano.

Partnoy, Alicia. 1986. *The Little Schoolhouse*. Pittsburgh: Cleis Press.

Potash, Robert A. 1993. The military under Alfonsín and Menem: The search for a new role. In *Argentina in the Crisis Years 1983–90* (Colin M. Lewis and Nissa Torrents, eds.), 53–72. London: Institute of Latin American Studies.

_____. 1980. *The Army and Politics in Argentina, 1945–62*. Stanford: Stanford University Press.

Snow, Peter G. 1993. *Political Forces in Argentina*. Westport, Conn.: Praeger.

Timmerman, Jacobo. 1982. *Prisoner Without a Name, Cell Without a Number*. New York: Vintage Press.

Whitaker, Arthur P. 1962. *Nationalism in Latin America*. Gainesville: University of Florida Press.

Wynia, Gary W. 1992. *Argentina: Illusions and Realities*. New York: Holmes and Meier.

Chapter Nineteen

Democracy in Bolivia and Paraguay: A Comparison

PHILIP KELLY AND THOMAS WHIGHAM

During the fifty-year period of the Fitzgibbon surveys, both Bolivia and Paraguay have taken paths very distant from the democratic ideal. In the combined rank totals of Table 1.2 in this volume, Bolivia places eighteenth, and Paraguay, nineteenth. Only Haiti, of the twenty republics, stands lower. Bolivia earned its highest response from panelists, fourteenth place in 1991 and 1995, during a time when civilian presidents came to office after relatively free elections. Paraguay, in last position until 1965 and in next to last from that year until 1985, has improved its survey image since the ouster of long-time dictator General Alfredo Stroessner, rising to fifteenth in the last poll following two internationally validated elections in 1989 and 1993.

As neighbors, the two nations' backgrounds coincide in as many areas as their traditions differ. Both exist as poor, isolated, landlocked, and often military dominated. Boom-and-bust cycles characterize their economies, derived largely from a dependence on the "white market" of exporting agricultural and mineral or energy products and the "black market" of smuggling cars, whiskey, and cigarettes in Paraguay and cocaine in Bolivia. Frequent manipulation by Brazil and Argentina along frontiers and in foreign policy likewise describe their common condition.

Unlike Paraguay, Bolivia in 1952 experienced a social revolution in which Indian miners and peasants entered the political arena for the first time and saw their popular aspirations lifted, although their new leaders failed to deliver on their initial promises. As a result, Bolivia has seen a paralyzing succession of coups, intrigue, corruption, failed reforms and elections, and short-lived dictators. Paraguay in contrast maintained governmental stability, albeit under the harsh dictatorship of Alfredo Stroessner for most of the period. The two elected presidencies since 1989 have, willy-nilly, established some sense of a sometimes unfathomable transition to respect for a democratic order. Unlike in Bolivia, however, one would have great difficulty locating revolutionary aspirations in Asunción during this century, with the possible exception of the Febrerista movement of the late 1930s and 1940s.

These basic differences between Paraguay and Bolivia contribute to other dimensions of variance as well. For example, more groups compete within the arena of Bolivian national politics, and the topography of the country presents exasperating challenges to any regime that might want to foment national integration. The military in Bolivia, although it is the dominant force in deciding policy and providing leadership, is divided, and regional rivalries appear among both civilian and military partisans, particularly between the Altiplano and the frontier lowlands around the regional centers of Santa Cruz and the Beni river valley. This complexity is largely absent in Paraguay, where the army and the Colorado Party command the nation.

In both countries democracy clearly has failed to establish itself, lacking a supportive culture and the resources that might nurture an open play of partisan competitiveness and a constitutional stability. We will describe, first for Bolivia, then for Paraguay, the important events and transitions that have led to this era of democratic uncertainty. In a final section, we define the major obstacles that we feel impede the rise of free systems.

Bolivia

Between 1945 and 1996, fully twenty-five chief executives held office in Bolivia, an average of one leader each two years. Two "democratic transition" periods emerged, the first from 1952 until 1964 in which far-reaching reforms were attempted, and the second from 1983, when economic collapse and popular anti-military sentiment stimulated a return to constitutional government. To date, four civilian presidents have brought the country's longest period of stable democratic rule. Military regimes characterized the eighteen years between, with fourteen different army officers taking charge of policy and patronage for varying lengths of time.

Historian James Cockcroft described the 1952 Bolivian upheaval as the first Latin American revolution after Mexico's "based on popular participation," adding that to "know Bolivia is to know the roots of that revolution; how it came about and was reversed" (1996:487). The sources to that event began to appear in 1941 at the formation of a new political party, the National Revolutionary Movement (MNR), destined to play a leading role in the politics of the coming half-century. Established by a group of urban middle-class lawyers with links to the army, peasants, and tin miners, who persistently lacked a coherent program, and who were themselves plagued by factions and breakaway dissidents, the party and its candidate, Víctor Paz Estenssoro, won the 1951 presidential elections. He was denied office by the army, and a successful MNR-led revolt in April 1952, backed by the national police, students, workers, and ultimately the tin miners, initiated a twelve-year epoch of reform ventures and later disillusionment and defeat.

As the revolution's first president (1952–1956), Paz Estenssoro administered a country with one of the world's most dismal living standards. Poverty and illiteracy were rampant; transportation, education, agriculture, industry, and mining had never developed beyond a near-feudal environment. Yet Paz succeeded in his first term in disbanding the military, replaced it with local militia (although these quickly transformed themselves back to a national army), mandated a widespread redistribution of land to peasants, nationalized the tin mines and unionized mine workers, started to modernize education as well as highway and aviation transportation, and attracted substantial financial and technical backing from the United States and from other foreign outlets. The United States at this time supported Bolivia's revolution because, unlike in the case of Guatemala, the Americans did not perceive Soviet influence. Discovery of large oil deposits further enhanced Paz's reform efforts. With the first free elections of the nation's history, and near universal suffrage, Paz turned over the presidency to his vice president, Hernán Siles Zuazo, who likewise completed an uninterrupted term of office and administered honest elections at the end of his tenure in 1960.

Paz's first term unfortunately proved to be the revolution's most successful, for division, disillusionment, and program failures plagued the next two administrations, encouraging the military coup that ended the revolutionary period in 1964. (One could argue, nonetheless, that some of the military officers, especially René Barientos, were at times more revolutionary than the MNR.) In particular, Siles Zuazo's tenure in office faced serious defections of major MNR factions, in addition to falling world prices for tin that caused serious cuts in government revenue and an inflation that rose precipitously. Reforms aiming to make the mines more efficient faltered, and agrarian land distributions failed to improve agriculture. In brief, improvements faltered or came too slowly to please the destitute and frustrated, and they came too quickly to establish foundations for lasting renovation. Bolivia proved too unstable to carry forward the aspirations of the MNR revolution.

For the next eighteen years, until 1982, a parade of military officers assumed the presidential sash. None ruled effectively. Air force general René Barrientos Ortuño, although popular among peasants because he spoke Quechua fluently and showed concern for their interests, repressed the miners, the MNR, and other groups bent on democratic government. Following his 1968 death in a helicopter crash, brief and unsuccessful attempts at reestablishing a leftist line by Generals Alfredo Ovando and Juan José Torres ensued, succeeded in the 1970s by the eight-year regime of General Hugo Banzer.

Banzer repressed and exiled his most important opponents; rewarded his major supporters; forced a political balance among military contingents, foreign interests, and regional economic centers; fractionalized political parties; and benefited from an economic upturn that derived from international factors and not from Banzer's own initiatives (Whitehead 1976). The general consequently capitalized on good fortune, on rivals' weaknesses, and on his selection of policies that would win public approval; one case in point is his seeking of the "*salida al mar*" access to the Pacific coast, lost to Chile during the past century's War of the Pacific.

The infamous "cocaine coup" in 1980 gave power to the notorious General Luis García Meza—who openly collaborated with narcotics traffickers—and instigated fourteen months of violence; harassment of parties, trade unions, and universities; wildly expanded corruption; doubling of the cocaine export; and an international pariah status. Indeed, the García Meza regime became one of the most repressive Bolivian regimes of this century.

García Meza took over during a time of governmental and economic collapse. Political parties continued to be divided and without popular leaders who could unify civilian groups; the MNR, as probably the best-known national bloc, remained discredited; and the Congress and bureaucracy proved to be unable to govern effectively. Although disliked by most civilian groups, military rule continued its domination of the presidency despite the infighting among army factions. In this respect, the armed forces themselves were sufficiently fractionalized that an autocrat could manipulate, and thus neutralize, the officer corps. For an initial period, the violence of García Meza stunned the opposition, and the regime received substantial financing from the narcotics cartels and from Italian mafia mercenaries as well as intelligence and training assistance of such Southern Cone tyrants as Argentina's Jorge Videla.

Yet after a year the regime fell, from reaction to its arbitrary rule, from international pressures that reflected a trend toward democracy in the Southern Cone, and from widespread popular demands to remove the army from direct political involvement. The military era came to an end. Four civilian presidents have followed, gradually introducing a second democratic transition that appears more stable with each successive administration.

Three major factions vied for control in the new era (Klein 1992:269–286), a progressive sector led by Hernán Siles Suazo and Jaime Paz Zamora as supported by most miners, peasants, and middle-class intellectuals; a centrist segment formed primarily of moderate groups within the MNR and led by Víctor Paz Estenssoro; and an assembly of conservative technocrats and newer economic elites, headed by former dictator Hugo Banzer and his National Democratic Action (ADN) coalition. Despite periodic rumblings from the officer corps, the military remained tolerant of all three alignments, a vital contributor to stability.

Hernán Siles Suazo, who governed until 1985, moved quickly to purge the armed forces of its left and right extremists and to exile foreigners, such as Klaus Barbie, who had aided the previous military regimes. Yet his inability to stabilize the national economy, in its worst condition in decades because of falling world prices for tin, high debt repayment, and inflation rates of 30,000 percent, in addition to his ineptitude in maintaining a ruling coalition, weakened progress toward democracy.

Filling the presidency next, Paz Estenssoro attained his third term as chief executive by way of Congress, the popular elections failing to render the necessary majority to any candidate. This characteristic appeared again in the next two presidential selections. In a New Economic Plan he adroitly instituted a drastic austerity policy against inflation and debt, following the plans of Harvard's Jeffrey Sachs that divested major public ventures, including the tin mines, and sought to focus the economy according to "market forces." In alliance with Banzer's ADN, Paz Estenssoro aspired to break the tin miners' power to disrupt austerity measures, and lengthy periods of martial law discouraged the most assertive opposition. The illegal trade in cocaine persisted during this term also, controlling a quarter of Bolivia's gross national product and causing Paz to agree to a U.S. Drug Enforcement Agency presence aimed at stemming this traffic (Burke 1991).

Receiving just 19 percent of the national vote, Paz Zamora and his Left Revolutionary Movement (MIR) nonetheless gained the presidency in 1989 by acquiring the votes of General Banzer's ADN faction in Congress. The new leadership continued the austerity and privatization policies of the New Economic Plan. This contributed to a drop in inflation to 10 percent and an impressive economic upsurge in 1991, in which inflation dropped to 4 percent. The government implemented a variety of political reforms, with more widespread suffrage, additional Indian rights, concern for the environment, and new groups mobilized. As always, the armed forces continued watching from the sidelines. The 1989 elections also witnessed the passing of the former generation of leaders, a clear-cut break with the revolution of 1952 and its unfulfilled promises.

Gonzalo Sánchez de Lozada, a millionaire mining entrepreneur and former planning minister under the last Paz Estenssoro government, won the presidency in 1993. He had a clear mandate to continue privatization and other reform policies. His vice president, Víctor Hugo Cárdenas, an Aymara Indian from the highlands around Lake Titicaca, has drawn international attention as one of the first modern Indigenous Americans (others would include Peru's Sánchez Cerro) to hold high office in postdiscovery Latin America (Nash 1993). At present, the economy appears stable and growing and the political system increasingly open to minority protest. There has been a greater scrutiny in an attempt to stop corruption and cocaine trafficking, and the system has grown more resistant to military involvement and more comfortable in the democratic model. In sum, a new generation of leaders and policies has risen in Bolivia, apparently boasting a greater clarity in political direction that has created the current momentum toward constitutionalism.

Paraguay

Until this decade, one can glean few, if any, positive examples of democratic conduct in Paraguay (Lewis 1993). A first glimmer of political opening, although short-lived, came to Paraguay in 1936 following the brutal Chaco War (1932–1935). Army veterans and civilian intellectuals established the Revolutionary Febrerista Party that attempted a variety of changes, although few specifically in the democratic mode. The party soon fell from power, however, and dictatorship continued in a series of repressive regimes, that of General Higinio Morínigo (1940–1947) being one of the most noteworthy.

Out of the watershed 1947 civil war and the resulting political vacuum arose General Alfredo Stroessner, a thirty-five-year-old Chaco War veteran, who led a 1954 coup and soon established a system of subjugation and manipulation that would endure until his ouster in 1989 (Lewis 1980). Unlike other Latin American dictators, Stroessner maintained a close alliance with civilian politicians, in this case, in the majority faction of the Colorado Party. He also kept a not-so-tight rein on the army but rewarded the officers generously to maintain their backing. By the end of his first decade as president, the general had purged opponents from Colorado Party ranks. Henceforth, all public employees, teachers, and army and police officers were required to affiliate with the party. During the thirty-five-year "Stronato," opposition groups remained splintered and ineffective, and, despite ample evidence of heavy-handedness, the general could probably have won a succession of free elections in a situation that John Hoyt Williams describes as "authoritarianism swept into office by the electorate" (1983:66).

State clientelism, used effectively by the dictator, favored friendly local and foreign business interests with profitable contracts and inoperative taxes and regulations. Commonplace were interventions against universities, newspapers and radio stations, unions, and peasant groups. Party toughs bullied opposition party members, and the infamous *pyragües* ("soft-footed ones"—informants or spies who worked with the police but were not police themselves) terrorized and tortured dissidents.

Under such pressure, exile, imprisonment, and assassination were common. Cockcroft describes a "preventive repression" and "culture of fear" where government partisans sought "to nip in the bud every sign of unrest by any conceivable means," although a controlled "loyal" opposition was permitted for foreign consumption (1996:521). Ultimately, Stroessner's dominance rested on the principal groups within the military, and accordingly, important officers drew high salaries and benefits, enjoyed professional resources and status, and pursued lucrative and illegal business smuggling ventures without state oversight, in return for their loyalty to the system.

Other factors contributed to General Stroessner's lengthy tenure. Since Paraguay lacked experience in constitutional rule, its affluent sectors preferred political stability to the social risks inherent in reform. Paraguay's neighbors, especially Brazil, also encouraged this status quo stability and broadly supported the Stroessner peace. Probably most of the Paraguayan peasants of the rural areas favored the dictatorship, and especially the Colorado Party, as the best of the series of bad options available to them. Finally, the Stronato benefited from significant economic growth and status, particularly during the "Itaipú years" of 1977–1983, when the gigantic hydroelectric project on the Paraná River brought tremendous profits (and corruption) to local and international groups who could take advantage of Stroessner's blessing. Specifically, construction at Itaipú employed many poor Paraguayans and gave middle-level jobs to the nascent middle class.

The crisis over the succession issue of the Stronato ended predictably but abruptly in February 1989 when General Andrés Rodríguez and the military successfully toppled Stroessner, sending the old dictator into exile in Brazil. During the middle part of the decade, inflation came with the completion of the main part of the work on the Itaipú dam, and strikes and protests by peasant, labor, church, student, housewives, and business groups became increasingly commonplace.

The Paraguayan elite felt that Stroessner himself was losing his grip on power, and this produced the greatest immediate impetus for change. Visualizing an eventual end to the dictatorship, several Colorado Party factions competed for control of the party, and the *militantes* bloc gained an ascendancy by 1987. The *militantes* might best be described as corrupt Colorados masquerading as ultra-Stroessner loyalists to feather their own nests. But Stroessner committed his most fatal error by trying to demote Rodríguez, his son-in-law, and the dictator suffered banishment in consequence.

Rodríguez promised open elections for May, and with international observers' validation, was chosen president as a Colorado. His party won two-thirds of the seats in Congress. The general pledged not to seek reelection, and he enacted a variety of electoral reforms, although the lack of serious enforcement remained a problem. Rodríguez himself had been one of the more infamous smugglers during Stroessner's time and could hardly be expected to set a good example. A jolt to Colorado confidence came in the 1991 election of Dr. Carlos Filizzola, an independent candidate, to the Asunción intendant's office, although the Colorado's carried the countryside (Brooke 1991). The establishment of a new constitution in 1992 prohibited party membership for military officers (present members exempted) and stipulated no immediate reelection for officeholders but shielded the armed forces from governmental oversight. Entry of Paraguay into the MERCOSUR common market of the Southern Cone nations, some U.S. economic assistance, and privatization of the state sector could stabilize the regime and provide some momentum for more democratic openings of the political system.

Colorado divisions continued into the 1993 presidential elections. In the end, after much back room maneuvering, the party nominated the politically moderate and wealthy businessman Juan Carlos Wasmosy over Luis María Argaña, a traditional Colorado with strong support from the countryside who had cut deals with former Stroessner loyalists. General Lino Oviedo, the leading army commander, also backed the Colorados and Wasmosy, but he vowed the military would remain a force in national affairs. Despite some electoral fraud in the countryside, most observers concede that Wasmosy's victory in the general election appeared to be legitimate.

The apparent transition to democracy continues in Paraguay, albeit with dissension. Military involvement in corruption and smuggling persists, and officers occasionally threaten civilians who seek to cancel their long-held privileges. One telling example of this is that of army Colonel Luis Catalino González Rojas, who attempted to publicize a stolen-car ring (Brooke 1992), only to be punished by his superior officers who themselves were sponsoring these crimes. Public and media protest caused Colonel Rojas's exoneration, and four generals ultimately faced jail sentences. Another example was a 1996 coup attempt against Wasmosy by General Oviedo, in which public outcry and international pressure prevented the general from coming out on top.

Serious anticorruption investigations from Congress, from the Supreme Court, and from the Comptroller's Office, all newly constituted in reform efforts, have furthered public demands for cleaning up the political system, although significant public pilfering yet continues. In some instances, such as the 1996 scandal in the Central Bank, the corruption may have reached higher levels than under Stroessner. A new constitution and electoral reforms likewise have been legislated, and a broader interest and participation in public affairs are reflected in recent general strikes and in the numerous protest marches in Asunción by students, workers, peasants, and government employees. Nonetheless, there seems to be little commitment to democracy as a system within the higher echelons of government. For many at the top of society, democracy is most often merely expedient.

Much maneuvering went on among the leading political groups in preparation for the 1997 elections. Still seriously split, the Colorados had difficulty reaching a consensus for presidential candidate. Three factions existed, and their nominees, Luis María Argaña, General Lino Oviedo (then in jail), and the current vice president, Angel Roberto Seifart, vied for endorsement. Leading opposition contenders were the Liberal Party's Domingo Laíno and the Encuentro Nacional's Guillermo Caballero Vargas, both unsuccessful 1993 election candidates. Perhaps out of this ongoing process, Paraguay will finally cross the threshold of democracy away from its repressive past.

Obstacles to Democracy in Bolivia and Paraguay

In this section, we pose the query: What chance exists of a solid and permanent democracy eventually forming in Bolivia and in Paraguay? Expressed differently: Which advantages and which obstacles appear most salient, and what side of this dichotomy, whether democracy or dictatorship, may attain the highest measure of success? Or will some type of combination of the two systems transpire, a "repressive democracy" or a "democratic autocracy"?

Some level of democracy is conceivable in both countries, although unlikely in the short term. An image of democracy remains a popular aspiration among a majority of both peoples, and progress toward this ideal has occasionally taken place. Dictators eventually fall, even Stroessner and Banzer, and more than occasionally their replacements at least voice support for reforms that may prevent the rise of new dictatorships. Voters normally oppose a high occurrence of corruption and blatantly fraudulent elections, although apathy and disillusionment usually result when their protests go unheard. Also, the perceived growth in common crimes, such as smuggling and car theft, has resulted in many middle-class people in both countries pining for the "security" of the past. Nonetheless, at least for the time being, the factors favoring democracy leave us with some optimism for the future.

Both political systems look simple compared to those of Brazil, Mexico, or Argentina: They are not overloaded with unintegrated immigration, excessive urbanization, scarcity of land, and guerrilla revolts. Instead, their lack of complexity may actually assist the staying power of democracy, as it has in Costa Rica.

Furthermore, democracy in Bolivia and Paraguay benefits from the current support for democracy worldwide, and particularly within Latin America. Studies have shown a contagion effect in political affairs (Govea and West 1981; Most and Starr 1980), where outbreaks of violence in one nation may encourage similar outbreaks in adjoining states. The same phenomenon seems logical for democracy as well. The repression in Bolivia and Paraguay in the 1970s and early 1980s almost certainly received assistance from the military regimes of Brazil, Argentina, and Chile (for instance, the 1970s subjugation, the Letelier affair, the neutralization by the Colorado Popular Movement (MOPOCO) exiles in Buenos Aires by the Argentine police, Operation Condor). With Argentina, Brazil, and Chile (the ABCs) no longer under military control, such regional intervention against democracy has evaporated, stabilizing domestic affairs in Bolivia and Paraguay. In fact, in the latest threat by General Oviedo, the ABC countries, the Organization of American States, and the U.S. ambassador immediately came to Wasmosy's aid. Furthermore, the armed forces of both countries continue to be divided and discredited, and neither currently holds sufficient power to topple the civilian governments.

This does not change the fact that both nations have experienced and continue to suffer serious problems. Remaining are entrenched militarism, depressed social and economic conditions, inexperience in operating democratic elections, deficiencies in national leadership, abundance of corruption and frail public administration, lack of popular consensus toward policies and goals, regional and international isolation, scarcity of natural and technological resources and sluggish or nonexistent industrial development, and exploitation and territorial dismemberment at the hands of larger neighbors. Obviously, such features seriously affect the development of progressive government, in large part explaining why Bolivia and Paraguay have ranked so low on the Fitzgibbon surveys and why democracy in Bolivia and Paraguay faces such a difficult future.

If one compares advantages and obstacles, the authors would rate the potential for growth in democracy to be about even in Paraguay and in Bolivia. At this time, neither republic would probably show substantial improvement if new Fitzgibbon polls were again tabulated. Bolivia's problems are complex. Corruption, particularly in cocaine trafficking, appears entrenched in the country's infrastructure, and this separates voters from elected officials and defiles the democratic process. In contrast to Paraguay, a higher portion of the population remains illiterate, marginal, undernourished, and with little hope of advancement. Concomitantly, a strong middle class has yet to develop that might guide the nation to a better balance between growth and distribution of resources.

In addition, the major groups and regions in Bolivia are not well integrated nationwide. Its revolution, such as it was, has yet to bring a consensus to policies and goals. The question of whether to maintain an economic austerity that tends to favor the affluent or to support social programs that may assist the poor still seriously divides Bolivia, and a solution continues to be elusive. Accordingly, the political system's steadiness remains questionable, although the past decade of civilian governments carries promise.

Clearly, Paraguay shares these liabilities with Bolivia. Corruption comes primarily in thefts of government moneys and in smuggling, not in the growth and production of narcotics as in the Altiplano. Smuggling may have become somewhat less extensive because of increasing public condemnation and because MERCOSUR has mandated the elimination of trade tariffs, thus removing the profit from smuggling. Yet the black market continues to run deep in Paraguayan society.

Paraguayan social conditions for the marginal classes, though not praiseworthy, have never approximated the depths of those in Bolivia. For example, World Bank figures for 1992 show per-capita gross national product for Paraguay at $1,380 and for Bolivia at $680 (Kryzanek 1996:8). Also, Paraguay rates far in advance of Bolivia in mechanized agriculture, revealing 2.95 tractors per 1,000 hectares to 0.24 tractors per 1,000 hectares in Bolivia (Kurian 1979:139). That Paraguay may perhaps rank somewhat ahead of Bolivia in Fitzgibbon's next surveys may stem from Paraguay's higher marks in Philip Kelly's key indicators for Latin American democracy (that is, tractors per hectare and newspaper circulation per capita) as he described in Chapter 1 of this book.

Furthermore, Paraguay suffers less than Bolivia from disunity. The country is more compact and more uniform geographically; Asunción holds more sway over national politics than do the outlying regions; and in ethnic homogeneity Paraguay ranks somewhat above Bolivia (Kurian 1979:45).

Although Paraguay and Bolivia have yet to determine clear national directions, and political instability in both countries persists, progress is amply shown in the tenures of recent civilian presidents, in better adherence to constitutions, in the reining in of the armed forces, in increased civic participation, in regional and international pressures favoring progressive government, and in like examples, attainments that could eventually encourage stronger institutions of democracy and contribute to possible improvement in their Fitzgibbon index standings.

Bibliography

Brooke, James. 1992. Asunción journal: Remember Paraguay? It is rejoining the world. *New York Times* (December 24):4.

_____. 1991. Opposition "new face" in Paraguay city hall. *New York Times* (August 26):7.

Burke, Melvin. 1991. Bolivia: The politics of cocaine. *Current History* 90:65–68, 90.

Cockcroft, James D. 1996. *Latin America: History, Politics, and U.S. Policy.* 2nd ed. Chicago: Nelson-Hall.

Govea, Rodger M., and Gerald T. West. 1981. Riot contagion in Latin America, 1949–1963. *Journal of Conflict Resolution* 25:239–368.

Klein, Herbert S. 1992. *Bolivia: The Evolution of a Multi-Ethnic Society.* New York and Oxford: Oxford University Press.

Kryzanek, Michael J. 1996. *U.S.-Latin American Relations.* 3rd ed. Westport, Conn., and London: Praeger.

Kurian, George Thomas. 1979. *The Book of World Rankings.* New York: Facts on File.

Lewis, Paul H. 1993. *Political Parties and Generations in Paraguay's Liberal Era, 1869–1940.* Chapel Hill: University of North Carolina Press.

_____. 1980. *Paraguay Under Stroessner.* Chapel Hill: University of North Carolina Press.

Most, Benjamin, and Harvey Starr. 1980. Diffusion, reinforcement, geopolitics, and the spread of war. *American Political Science Review* 74:932–946.

Nash, Nathaniel C. 1993. Conversations/Victor Hugo Cárdenas: Bolivia's vice president, first Indian in high office, waits for change. *New York Times* (September 19):9.

Whitehead, Laurence. 1976. Banzer's Bolivia. *Current History* 70:61–64, 80.

Williams, John Hoyt. 1983. Stroessner's Paraguay. *Current History* 82:66–68, 82–83.

Chapter Twenty

Democracy and Development in Brazil: Cardoso's Catch-22

JAN KNIPPERS BLACK

In Brazil, on October 3, 1994, a popular labor leader, running for the presidency on an economically nationalistic platform—one that might have been constructed in the 1960s by renowned dependency theorist Fernando Henrique Cardoso—was decisively defeated. The upset victory went to a neoliberal candidate supported by the center right: the same Fernando Henrique Cardoso. For Cardoso it was perhaps less a political victory than an intellectual one. In achieving "power" essentially by running against himself, he served to validate his own theories.

What happened in the last three decades that might explain such an ironic turn of events? One of the problems for the analyst, as for the Brazilian voter, is that of confusion between the old and what is new in the post–Cold War order. Much of what seems to be new, including the rationales underlying neoliberal economic policy, is as new as the nineteenth century, or perhaps as the sixteenth century, when the externally driven boom and bust pattern of the Brazilian development was established. But the technologies and the global concentrations of economic power serving and served by such a policy agenda are new.

The democracy of the new order has in common with that of the previous democratic era (1945–1964) a legitimation based on elections and civilian-dominant institutions. And as before there is less to such democracy than meets the eye. Whereas parties of the Left in the early 1960s rejected liberal electoral democracy in principle but accepted it in practice, parties of the Right did the opposite: They embraced electoral democracy in principle but rejected it in practice, leaving the democracy of that era to be discredited by fraud and by vulnerability to military reprisal.

The "haves," domestic and foreign, of the early 1960s rejected political democracy in fear that it might lead to economic democracy. Such fears appear to have been tempered in the 1990s by the restriction of the economic policy options available to national leaders—and thus the seeming irrelevance or frivolity of elections.

Though the fears of the "haves" are tempered, can the hopes of "have-nots" be sustained? In economic terms, the democracy of the last decade has been no kinder to the majority of Brazilians than were the preceding two decades of militocracy. Remarkably, however, nonaffluent Brazilians appear to maintain hope—a hope perhaps more resolute than ingenuous—in the fruits of popular participation. Such hope is suggested in high levels of voter turnout, in quirky and exuberant forms of grassroots mobilization, and in the strongest voice for a working class in partisan politics in the hemisphere.[1]

The Politics of Plunder

Since the beginning of European colonization Brazil has been subject to an exaggerated version of boom-and-bust development, the booms fleetingly enriching mostly nonnationals, or at least nonlocals, the busts impacting enduringly on plundered regions and communities. The dependence on fickle export and capital markets that has dictated periodic shifts in the country's geographical and sectoral centers of gravity has shaped the nature of political competition as well.

Among the resources to be nearly depleted early on, along with the turtles and manatees of the Amazon, were the indigenous peoples, enslaved to stoke the sugar boom in the northeast. Subsequent boom-and-bust cycles drew population, resources, and political intrigue to the mines and the dairy farms of Minas Gerais and then farther south, to São Paulo, where coffee was competing with sugar for the first place among export earners.

As colony gave way to empire in 1822 in an independent Brazil coffee continued to grow in importance, and at the end of the century planters and dairy ranchers in the south needed the labor, by then largely of African descent, that continued literally to be held captive in the northeast on the sugar plantations. Therefore, together with abolitionists of more idealistic bent, coffee and milk teamed up against sugar to press for an end to slavery. Abolition was finally declared in 1888; irritated sugar planters then made common cause with ambitious military officers and ideological republicans to topple the empire a year later.

The establishment in 1894 of Brazil's First Republic coincided with another boomlet in the Amazon, based this time on rubber; but after the rubber tree had been transplanted to Malaysia and after an interregnum of military rule in Brazil had given way to limited democracy, the politics of *café com leite* (coffee and milk) once again assumed ascendance. Control of the presidency alternated between the coffee-producing state of São Paulo and the dairy-producing state of Minas Gerais. It was a agriculture-based patrimonial system that was to last until 1930, but the seeds of the system that was to uproot it had already been sown.

With the disruption of World War I, followed in short order by global depression, markets and credits were lost, and the country had little choice but to begin to manufacture some of the products previously imported. Not until the 1970s did manufacturing overtake coffee as the major export earner, but industrial production doubled during World War I and had tripled by 1923.

The new boom accelerated urbanization and in turn generated in classes and pitted the coastal cities against the interior, linking in some limited contexts the interests of industrialists and their workforces. In other contexts, however, the interests of those groups appeared sharply divergent. The political fluidity and shifting alliances so generated finally settled into a new set of strange bedfellows that underwrote the long dominance of Getulio Vargas.

Vargas was, in turn, democrat and dictator, leftist and rightist and leftist again; he was above all an opportunist and a consummate politician. Like so much else about his person and his politics, the question of whether his overthrow by the military in 1945, after elections had been scheduled, came about because he had been a dictator or because he was likely to be elected continues to be debated.

By the end of the Vargas era, the country's center of gravity had definitively moved into town (70 percent rural as late as the 1920s, Brazil is now more than 70 percent urban). The import-substitution model of industrialization, begun for lack of options, had become by midcentury a carefully elaborated development strategy involving government planning, investment in infrastructure, tariff protection of domestic industry, and regulation of foreign investment. But the situational perception of common cause between industrialists and labor that had allowed urban forces to break the stranglehold of landed interests dissolved as industry grew.

The coalition pieced together by Vargas that prevailed during the Second Republic, or "democratic era" (1945–1964), was an upside-down version of the Roosevelt-legacy Democratic Party in the United States. It linked old-fashioned landholding party bosses in the northeast and urban organized labor in the southeast against an industrial nouveau riche class. Meanwhile, the legacy of corporatism (or top-down control through coaptation) that had held new popular forces in check was fast eroding.

In the early 1960s, with debt and inflation on the rise, it became clear that further industrialization in accordance with the import-substitution model would require broader redistribution in order to expand the domestic market, but economic elites—domestic and foreign—were alarmed rather than persuaded by the rising demands of the working classes, and political stalemate gave way in 1964 to military counterrevolution. Political crisis was resolved through the abrupt demobilization of popular forces, that is, the dissolution of parties, unions, and other organizations that had given voice to lower-class demands, and economic crisis gave rise to a different approach to industrial development. The latter featured "constructive bankruptcy" for unprotected domestic firms, new incentives for foreign investors, and emphasis on export promotion, a strategy compatible with bottom-up rather than top-down redistribution of income.

Commenting in 1970 on Brazil's so-called economic miracle of rapid growth in the gross national product, President-General Emilio Garastazú Médici observed: "The economy is doing fine, but the people aren't" (quoted in Griffin 1993:C5). The energy crisis, beginning in 1973–1974, exacerbated economic problems that, in concert with military factionalism and international pressures to end human rights abuses, led to the *distensao* (decompression) of the late 1970s and the *apertura* (political opening) of the early 1980s. But redemocratization has been too incomplete, too fragile, too frivolous, and perhaps too fraudulent to bring the benefits of Brazilian resources and labor back home to the Brazilian peoples.

Redemocratization Brazilian Style

Little by little the facade of an electoral and parliamentary system that earlier served to legitimize the dictatorship attained reality. The elections of November 1982 produced stunning victories for the opposition, and in 1984, for the first time in more than twenty years, the Electoral College chose a civilian president, Tancredo Neves of the opposition party, the Party of the Brazilian Democratic Movement (Partido do Movimento Democrático Brasileiro—PMDB). Undergoing surgery, however, Neves missed his scheduled inauguration in March 1985; he died on April 21. Vice President José Sarney, who then assumed the presidency, had been a late defector from the military government's Social Democratic Party (Partido Democrático Social—PDS).

The Congress elected in 1986 also served as a constituent assembly for the purpose of drawing up a new constitution. That constitution, promulgated in 1988, was expected to resolve issues of economic decisionmaking and to guarantee redistribution of land and income and effective protection of civil and human rights.

The new document, unfortunately, has failed to live up to those expectations. It is full of contradiction, reflecting social conflict rather than resolving it. Even the very fundamental choice between the preexisting presidential system and a proposed parliamentary one was put on hold for a 1993 plebiscite, which opted for retaining the presidential system. The new constitution did, however, extend the vote to all citizens over the age of sixteen, including illiterates, and it dictated the restoration of direct elections for president and vice president, elections that Sarney had managed to postpone until 1989. The presidential election—to a five-year term with reelection precluded—allows for a runoff if no candidate receives an absolute majority in the first round.

In an electoral system modeled in part after that of the German Federal Republic, three members from each state and the federal district (Brasilia) are elected to the Senate by majority vote for staggered eight-year terms. Deputies, whose representation corresponds more nearly to population, are elected by proportional representation for four-year terms. Rural areas, still dominated to some extent by patron-client networks of the traditional "colonels" system, remain overrepresented in the Congress.

Over the past decade state and local governments have retrieved a considerable measure of the independence lost to an extremely centralized military government. Direct election of governors and mayors, suppressed under military rule, was reinstated in 1982. State legislatures and municipal councils are also elected directly for four-year terms.

The federal government, however, has exclusive access to the major sources of revenue. Despite a constitutional obligation to pass half of the federal revenues on to states and localities, executives manage to reward political allies, to punish adversaries, and in general to leverage compliance with their wishes through generosity or parsimony in the extension of federal aid and the provision of public services. Rio de Janeiro, for example, under the governorship of Leonel Brizola in the 1980s, was starved by the governments of João Baptista de Oliveira Figueiredo and Sarney; it fared better after Brizola, who was elected governor again in 1990, came to terms, politically, with the government of Fernando Collor de Mello.

Free Enterprise and Costly Elections

The party system that prevailed during the Second Republic was a legacy of the Vargas era. During most of that period the government rested on a tenuous coalition between the conservative pro-Vargas PDS and the Brazilian Workers' Party (PTB). The National Democratic Union (União Democrática Nacional—UDN), conservative and anti-Vargas, was the strongest opponent of the coalition. After purging the Congress and the parties, along with other institutions, the military dictatorship abolished all existing parties in 1965; in their place it established a controlled two-party system, comprising a government party, the National Renovating Alliance (Alianza Renovadora Nacional—ARENA) and a "loyal opposition," the Brazilian Democratic Movement (Movimento Democrático Brasileiro—MDB). This system was intended to provide a facade of continuity in democratic institutions, but the Brazilian polity, not easily taken in, labeled them the parties of "yes" and "yes, sir."

Party and electoral rules were changed regularly between 1964 and 1985 to ensure the continued dominance of pro-military legislators. When it appeared, in 1979, that the MDB was beginning to take itself seriously and to gather momentum as an opposition movement, President Figueiredo, the fifth and last general to hold that post, demolished the two-party system in favor of a multiparty one. A reorganized ARENA became the PDS and the MDB became the PMDB.

Several parties of the previous democratic era were revived, but none acquired major followings. These included the Brazilian Socialist Party (PSB), the Christian Democratic Party (PDC), and the two communist parties. The PTB also reemerged, but under new and far more conservative leadership.

Opposition victories in the largest states in 1982 began to shake the confidence of the pro-military PDS, and a faction favoring direct presidential elections spun off in 1984 to form the Liberal Front (FL, or subsequently, as a party, the PFL). José Sarney defected from the PDS to the FL before joining Tancredo Neves on the PMDB ticket in 1984.

Sarney thus assumed the presidency, vacated by Tancredo Neves's death, with a twofold problem: His colleagues in the party he had left looked upon him as a traitor, and those of the party he had joined regarded him as an opportunist. Lacking a popular base, he nevertheless benefited from a remarkable rebounding of the economy in 1985. That, together with his 1986 Cruzado Plan freezing prices and wages, served to break the momentum of a new leftist-populist movement that had been coalescing around Leonel Brizola, governor of the state of Rio de Janeiro.

Having launched his own party, the Democratic Labor Party (Partido Democrático dos Trabalhadores—PDT), in 1982, Brizola, a leading figure on the left in the early 1960s, was making a spectacular comeback as a moderate European-style social democrat. He was soon to be overtaken, however, by a relative newcomer. Luis Inácio "Lula" da Silva, a labor leader propelled to prominence by his staging of successful wildcat strikes in the late 1970s, had also organized a party, the Workers' Party (Partido dos Trabalhadores—PT), in 1980 and was threatening to pass Brizola on the left.

Brazilians approached the national and state elections of November 1986 in a spirit of revelry. The campaign clichés that would sell candidates as blithely as soaps offered no clues as to what the country had so recently endured or what was now at stake. The tortured generation could only look on in anguish as their compatriots seemed to disregard their recent history and to treat politics as the moral equivalent of sport.

The election of 1986, featuring some 45,000 candidates representing thirty parties, resulted in a sweeping victory for the ruling PMDB; it took all but one of the then twenty-three governorships and won absolute majorities in both houses of Congress. Between them, the PMDB and its coalition partner, the Liberal Front Party (PFL), won 90 percent of the contested offices. Such a sweep, however, did not suggest that Brazil was en route to the kind of monopolistic one-party system so common in the Third World. Personalism continued to reign supreme. One found little trace of party loyalty or discipline; thus the PMDB victory, impressive as it was, suggested neither a high level of consensus within the polity nor predictability in the policymaking process. Then PMDB senator Fernando Henrique Cardoso, of the state of São Paulo, compared the party to a bus in which all of the passengers wanted to go in different directions.

Indeed, many who had supported the PMDB on the strength of its economic politics were stunned when, only days after the election, President Sarney lifted price controls. Workers accused the government of betrayal. Rioting broke out in Brasilia, and strikes began to unsettle the industrial heartland, contributing to impressive victories for Brizola's PDT and Lula's PT in major metropolitan areas in the municipal elections of 1988.

Meanwhile, for winners and losers alike, free elections had become increasingly costly. In 1986 Paulo Maluf spent the equivalent of about $70 million, and Antonio Ermirio de Morasis $50 million in unsuccessful campaigns for the governorship of the state of São Paulo. In a sense, the United States had finally succeeded in exporting to Latin America its own version of democratic process. Consultants, pollsters, fund-raisers, communications advisers, and media campaigns were replacing platforms, party organizations, and political rallies in elections with soaring costs and sinking value. The fact that ballots had edged out bullets in Brazil as elsewhere was a reflection in part of the extent to which elite interests were shielded from the consequences of popular participation by the "outsourcing" of economic policymaking.

A Balance Sheet for the 1980s

As the *apertura* got underway at the beginning of the 1980s, a Brazilian social worker commented that military rule had "democratized" the violation of human rights in that the rich had also been victimized. Redemocratization, she said, would mean that violations would be restricted once again to the poor, who had always been vulnerable. That prediction has been borne out in full in the 1980s and early 1990s.

Land reform legislation has produced very little redistribution, in part because peasant leaders who have sought to present claims have so often paid with their lives. The Brazilian Pastoral Commission for Land documented more than 1,200 murders of activist peasants, union leaders, priests, and lawyers in connection with land disputes in the 1980s. Human rights organizations attribute such casualties to death squads in the hire of landlords who operate with the support, or at least the tolerance, of local authorities. Similar death squads, apparently serving business interests, operate with seeming impunity in urban areas and are believed to be responsible for the murder of several thousand street children each year.

Brazil's prospects of gaining a measure of sovereignty and of making "democracy" something more than a charade should be much greater than those of most Latin American countries. Its political and intellectual leadership is highly sophisticated and creative. More important, it has a network of grassroots organizations and political parties that, despite its weaknesses, is more vibrant than that of most countries in the Third World and some in the First.

Brazil has half of the territory and population of Latin America and commands the world's ninth largest economy. Over the course of the 1980s, the country expanded and diversified its economic and political relationships. Its exports quadrupled. It became a major exporter of weapons. It even became one of the world's top producers of petroleum. By the end of the decade, however, Brazilian independence had been tempered by debt and hyperinflation. Consequently, it also suffered from increasing denationalization of decisionmaking on the most essential elements of economic policy as creditors, multilateral financial institutions, aid donors, and investors gained ever greater leverage.

Even after the country recorded a 4.6 percent economic decline in 1990 (the largest drop since such figures were first recorded in 1947), even after a decade of three-to-four-digit inflation (a record 1,795 percent for 1990), and even after running up the Third World's largest foreign debt ($120 billion in 1991), the boom of export-oriented industrialization could not be said definitively to have gone bust. It continued to enrich a small elite of Brazilians along with a great many multinational concerns and, above all, foreign creditors. But for most Brazilians it has been disastrous. By 1990, according to a World Bank report, only in Honduras and Sierra Leone was income distribution more unequal than in Brazil (Schneider 1991:321–347).

Meanwhile, Brazil's boom fever was zeroing in once again on the Amazon, the country's mineral-rich heartland and its last frontier. The feeding frenzy over resources gaining appetite in the 1980s was a global phenomenon, prompted in large measure by the combination of flush capital markets and debtor-state vulnerability. In Brazil it was also driven by the fears of military nationalists, who predicted that if Brazilians did not explore, develop, and settle the region, they would lose it to their neighbors.

During the mid-1970s the government had begun to offer incentives for clearance of the rain forest, a ploy that simultaneously offered tax shelters to major corporations and appeared to constitute an alternative to desperately needed and fiercely resisted land reform. The offers drew large numbers of peasants displaced by drought in the northeast and mechanization in the southeast. Most have found, after inordinate investment of time and labor, that the leached soils respond very poorly to farming and not much better to grazing. Worse still, land titles have been drawn poorly, with outright fraud making it easier for landholders or speculators to push peasants off the lands they had cleared.

This frontier free-for-all had produced hundreds of deaths and a land ownership pattern comparable to that of parts of the country settled centuries earlier. By 1985 the largest 152 Amazonian estates occupied 40 million hectares, an area equal to the rest of Brazil's cultivated land (Maxwell 1991:24–29). The ejected peasants, lacking options, have become an itinerant labor force living in instant slum towns on the margins of the land they had cleared. Reconcentration has also meant food shortages, since 80 percent of the crops had been produced by holders of small plots. Major landholders were more likely to be engaged in export agribusiness. Even so, since the soil is so infertile, they have often earned more from tax write-offs than from anything cultivated. Forest clearance incentives were revoked in 1987, in response to international pressures, but speculation in land continues to be fueled by hyperinflation.

Adding to the Wild West ambiance of the Amazon Basin has been a gold rush that began in 1980 and that before the end of the decade had made Brazil the world's third-largest producer of the precious mineral. Mercury used to process the ores has contaminated the water and lowered the fish catch over a large portion of the basin.

Once again the plant and animal species endangered by a multifaceted boom in the Amazon include its people. It is estimated that only about 200,000 of Brazil's indigenous tribal peoples have survived, with perhaps 50,000 of them still living deep in the rain forest. Some 20 percent of the 10,000 remaining Yanomami died between 1987 and 1991; the miners had polluted their water and scared away game, prompting the government to establish rain forest reserves, or protected homelands, for the Yanomami and other indigenous groups. The mid-1990s was seeing a tragic depletion of a different sort among indigenous groups, particularly the Guarani-Kaiowa of Mato Grosso do Sul: a rash of youth suicides.

The 1990s: A New Beginning or Just Another Old One?

For most Brazilians, the elections of 1989 represented the first opportunity to cast a vote, directly, for a presidential candidate. This electorate, 85.6 percent of whom turned out for the runoff, numbered more than 82 million, compared to an electorate of 15.5 million at the time of the last direct presidential election in 1960. The electorate in 1989 was young, about half of them under thirty, and almost three-fourths urban, whereas that of 1960 had been predominantly rural. Young, urban voters might be expected, on balance, to favor the more leftist candidate; but they are also more heavily exposed to television, and the conservative former governor of Alagoas, young and attractive, with a populist appeal, had mastered the medium. With seemingly limitless funds, he rose from obscurity to surprise the oddsmakers and edge out the early favorites, Lula and Brizola.

Collor's Ill-Fated Rule

The December runoff pitted Collor's personalist vehicle, the Party for National Reconstruction (Partido de Reconstrução Nacional—PRN), in concert with the PFL, PDS, and PTB, against a coalition, known as the Brazilian Popular Front, of Lula's PT, the PSB, the Green Party (Partido Verde—PV), and the Communist Party of Brazil (Partido Communista do Brasil—PC do B). Lula also enjoyed the crucial support of Brizola's PDT. The PMDB, now occupying the center, proved characteristically ambivalent about the runoff, but its breakaway faction, the Party of Brazilian Social Democracy (Partido da Social Democrácia Brasileira—PSDB), or *Tucanos*, supported Lula.

Collor's 4-million-vote margin of victory represented slightly fewer votes than those that were blank or for other reasons discarded. Along with more traditional election day *jeitões* (bribes), the conservative coalition on that day made good use of public opinion polls, pinpointing the constituencies of the two candidates to rearrange the public transportation system in key districts, shifting buses, most of which are privately owned, from major urban concentrations, for example, to more rural and provincial areas.[2]

The gubernatorial and legislative elections of October 1990 featured some 70,000 candidates vying for more than 1,500 offices. Almost two-thirds of the winners in congressional races were newcomers. Otherwise, the elections followed a now familiar pattern: While results in the predominately rural congressional races favored parties of center and right, giving Collor the potential of a working majority, governorships and mayoralties in the most populous and most industrialized areas went to candidates of center to left.

After some two years in the presidency, years of economic decline and allegations of corruption, Collor lost much of the public support that had propelled him to that office. Attempting to court the relatively progressive PSDB, he was nevertheless becoming increasingly dependent on the far more conservative PFL. By mid-1992 he had found it necessary to replace his entire cabinet, with the exception of those members representing the military.

With both inflation and unemployment climbing, Collor found that his lack of political definition and the low profile of his own party, which had served him well initially, allowing him to shift alliances as he changed policy course, had become liabilities. They served to underline his isolation when polls suggested that his fortunes were sinking.

The coup de grâce for this beleaguered government came with revelations of Collor's complicity in an elaborate bribery and influence-peddling scheme. Demonstrations involving millions of Brazilians, particularly students, reinforced the resolve of legislators, who launched an impeachment campaign.

On September 19, 1992, the Federal Chamber of Deputies voted 441 to 38 in favor of impeachment. Vice President Itamar Franco of the PMDB became acting president while Collor awaited trial by the Senate; following Collor's conviction, Franco became president to serve out the remaining two years of Collor's term.

An Interim of Shared Leadership

The government of Itamar Franco, a little-known provincial politician, inherited most of the problems that had bedeviled its predecessor. The corruption scandals that had previously centered on the presidency now moved into the Congress, felling members in virtually wholesale fashion. The shadow of kickback schemes and other financial shenanigans that so sullied the body politic did not touch Itamar Franco personally; a man of modest tastes, he seemed indifferent to the perks and temptations of office. But he fell victim to the sort of sex scandal to which Brazil's "telenovelas" had so addicted the TV-viewing public. A very public romp with a less-than-fully-clad showgirl at the 1994 Rio carnival, allegedly set up by the media, made him a figure of ridicule.

Itamar's low-key and weakly undergirded government seemed at first ill prepared to deal with any of the country's deepening problems, least of all the juggernaut of three-to-four-digit inflation. The parliamentary style of governing, leaving considerable latitude to cabinet members, was perhaps the only one available to a regime whose political support was broad but shallow. But such an approach, deriving initially from weakness, was ultimately judged a strength, as initiatives fell more and more to the very able former senator from São Paulo, Fernando Henrique Cardoso. Cardoso served first as foreign minister, but it was as finance minister after mid-1993 that he made his mark.

In June 1994 Cardoso launched his *plano real* introducing and defending a new currency. There was nothing new about new currencies in Brazil at this juncture, but this one, pegged loosely to the U.S. dollar, was underwritten by a mountain of reserves in hard currency. It was no doubt protected as well by the anxieties of foreign and would-be investors about the popularity of Lula and the PT and their hesitance to undermine the most promising alternative to a labor-based government.

When the *real* was introduced, prices for most goods quadrupled almost overnight; but in the months that followed prices held more or less steady as the *real* fluctuated within a narrow band, even at times increasing somewhat in value vis-à-vis the dollar. Thus the initial price shock to consumers accustomed to living on the rack was ameliorated over time by the hope that they were indeed witnessing the miracle of price stabilization.

Though Cardoso's political skills should not be underrated (one of his nicknames is "Fernando Henrique Charmoso"), the effectiveness of the *plano real* proved the most decisive factor in the elections of 1994. It convinced the middle classes that Cardoso was the only one who could defeat inflation and thus convinced the upper classes that he was the only one who could defeat Lula. It should also be noted that there were opinion leaders (perhaps including Cardoso himself?) who were more comfortable with Lula's platform and his constituency but who feared that Brazil under a labor-left government would be devastated by capital flight and credit freezes.

Four public opinion polls published in May 1994, just before the unveiling of the *plano real*, showed Lula leading in the presidential contest with the support of 36 percent to 42 percent of the electorate. Cardoso was running a distant second, with a following of 15 percent to 23 percent.[3]

Five months later, in the poll that mattered, Cardoso won in the first round with about 54 percent of the vote to 22 percent for Lula. Cardoso's victory was broadly based geographically. He defeated Lula in all of the twenty-seven states except Rio Grande do Sul and the Federal District.

Runoff elections in November gave the largest number of governorships, nine, to the PMDB. Cardoso's PSDB followed with six. The Progressive Renewal Party (PPR), a São Paulo–based center-right party, largely a vehicle for Paulo Maluf, took three states, while the PT, the PSB, PDT, and PFL took two each, and the PTB took one.

The coalition backing Cardoso (PSDB, PTB, and PFL) won only 210 of the 514 seats in the Chamber of Deputies, but an accord reached in December with the PMDB, holding 107 seats, gave Cardoso what he called "unorganized majority support" going into his inauguration on January 1, 1995. In the eighty-one-member Senate, Cardoso could count on support, at least for some measures, from the PMDB's twenty-two members, along with the PSDB's ten and the PFL's nineteen. The PT increased its representation in that body, but only from one member to five. The National Congress saw very considerable turnover of membership in the 1994 election: 70 percent of its members were new (Hoge 1995:62–75).

Cardoso's Pyrrhic Victory

At his inauguration, Cardoso pledged that social justice was to be his top priority, and some who spoke for the nonaffluent dared to believe. They found grounds for optimism in the fact that as a candidate he had already sold out his friends in order to appeal to his enemies. They reasoned that as president he could only sell out his enemies. Over the course of his first year in office, however, that turned out to be wishful thinking.

Cardoso's legislative agenda catered to his neoliberal allies, who dominated the Congress. Price stabilization and economic growth appeared to call for the acceleration of privatization, the proceeds of which were to cover the federal government's deficit. Many of the state-owned enterprises were put up for sale. Though the sacrosanct state-owned petroleum production agency Petrobras would remain in public hands, it would be forced to compete with foreign investors, as the state's monopoly in the oil sector was to be ended. (A strike by oil workers in opposition to this move was contained by the dispatch of troops.)

State monopolies in telecommunications and shipping were to be ended as well, and national companies were to be stripped of any advantages that they held over foreign ones. Tax reforms were intended to enhance revenue collection and to force states to assume responsibility for their own debts. Another reform in the works, though Cardoso claims no authorship of it, would permit presidential reelection.[4]

A report in late 1995 by the UN Economic Commission for Latin America and the Caribbean called Brazil's *plano real* "the most successful stabilization plan attempted in the past 10 years" (*UNECLAC Review* 1995). Highlights included: (1) reduction in inflation from an annual rate of 5,000 percent in June 1994 to 26 percent in August 1995; (2) growth in the gross domestic product expected to exceed 5 percent for 1995; (3) unemployment shrinkage to 4.4 percent, the lowest rate in five years;[5] (4) a reported increase in real wages; they were 12 percent higher in São Paulo during the first half of 1995 than during the same period of 1994; and (5) gross capital formation up to 18 percent, the highest rate so far of the decade.

Such achievements were not to be taken lightly, and indeed, opposition forces appeared to have given Cardoso a lengthy honeymoon. But by midyear frustration was mounting, even among some groups, such as progressive bishops and nongovernmental organizations, that had been supportive initially. A new development initiative, Comunidade Solidária, under the direction of the president's wife, Ruth Cardoso, a highly respected anthropologist, aroused some hopes, as did a new program to deal with human rights abuses and a commitment to compensate some families victimized by the military regime. But Cardoso's land reform proposal was generally viewed by progressive groups as woefully inadequate. Salaried workers were perturbed by proposals to shrink social security benefits and privatize portions of the program and to terminate job security in the public sector. Environmentalists and defenders of the rights of indigenous peoples were stunned by the issuance of a presidential decree on January 9, 1996, allowing loggers, miners, farmers, and businessmen to contest in court the boundaries of areas set aside as nature and indigenous reserves (Goering 1996:A10).

To those who have fought long and hard for the resurrection of democracy, Brazil's party and electoral system still represents unfinished business, and in many ways even a project derailed. The kind of democracy that is compatible with the new version of free enterprise may be the best that money can buy. Brazil has avoided some of the worse abuses of the process seen in the United States by requiring that television stations offer free time for live appearances by major candidates. But candidates may purchase additional TV advertisements. With campaign contributions reaching into the millions of dollars, corruption becomes institutionalized, and virtually all politicians are to some degree vulnerable.

Cardoso notes that Brazil's parties (numbering eighteen in 1996) are not ideologically but, rather, interest oriented (Hoge 1995:74). The combination of intraparty and interparty contests in a single "open list" for congressional offices reinforces the tendency to personalism and party fragmentation and leaves an electorate that is largely semiliterate with the overly challenging task of selecting a preferred candidate from a remarkably lengthy menu (As lições da eleição 1995:8). Party stability is further challenged by the ease with which elected officials change from one party to another. It was reported in October 1995 that forty-three members of the National Congress had switched parties in the previous eight months (*Brazil Report* 1995).

The strengths of Brazilian democracy are manifest in the fact that both the major contenders in the last presidential election—Fernando Henrique, the extraordinarily sophisticated and insightful social scientist, and Lula, the skillful community organizer and eloquent spokesman of popular interests—are a cut above the best in the political stables of most countries of north or south.

The weaknesses of the system are set in relief by the enormity of the challenges they face. These two remarkable men have in general continued to treat each other with respect and to keep the crucial channels of communication open. But it is not clear that the best of their efforts will suffice to bridge the country's ever growing gap between rich and poor.[6] The fact remains that any upward shift in burden bearing would threaten to dry up credit and set off a stampede of fleeing capital, a problem understood and underscored three decades ago by Cardoso the theorist.

Cardoso once noted that the great merit of dependency theory was that there was no presumption of scientific neutrality, that it proceeded from a radically critical viewpoint (1977:16). In other words, its adherents actively sought to transform a social system that exacerbates poverty and inequality. Addressing friends and former colleagues at the headquarters of UNECLAC in Santiago, Chile, on March 3, 1995, Cardoso referred to his own dependency theory as a monster like Frankenstein's. But he also spoke of the arrogance of the Bretton Woods institutions and of the problem of elites who live in Latin America as if they were foreigners, looking once to Europe, now to the United States, and perhaps in the future to Japan for their identities. And he spoke of the challenge of maintaining growth and democracy in the midst of such great poverty and inequality (1995:7–12). Little wonder then that Cardoso's monster returns to him from time to time like Dickens's ghosts of Christmas past and future.

Notes

1. Results of the 1991 and 1995 Fitzgibbon-Johnson Image-Index of Latin American Democracy suggest that analysts of Latin American politics share this faith in participation and in the Brazilian polity. From a low of twelfth place in the index in 1980, Brazil had moved back up to sixth among the twenty countries considered, its highest ranking since it placed fifth on that index in the 1950s.

2. This tactic was explained to the author by political scientist Maria Helena Moreira Alves of the Universidade Federal do Rio de Janeiro and by others supporting the candidacy of Lula.

3. *Facts on File*, June 16, 1994.

4. Latin American Regional Reports. *Brazil Report* (London), June through October 1995.

5. It should be noted, however, that a recent study by economist Edward Amdadeo of Rio's Catholic University indicates that the total number of unemployed, self-employed, and informal-sector workers about equals the number of workers in the formal sector.

6. Brazil's richest 20 percent earn twenty-six times the income of its poorest 20 percent.

Bibliography

As Lições da eleição. 1995. *Cadernos do Terceiro Mundo* (November):8.
Brazil Report (London). October 26.
Cardoso, Fernando Cardoso. 1995. Democracy and development. *UNECLAC Review* (Santiago, Chile):7–12.
_____. 1977. The consumption of dependency theory in the United States. *Latin American Research Review* 12:7–24.
Goering, Laurie. 1996. Brazil changes direction on Amazon development. *San Francisco Examiner* (February 4):A10.

Griffin, Dan. 1993. The boom in Brazil: An awful lot of everything. *Washington Post* (May 27):C5.

Hoge, James F., Jr. 1995. Fulfilling Brazil's promise: A conversation with President Cardoso. *Foreign Affairs* 74:62–75.

Maxwell, Kenneth. 1991. The tragedy of the Amazon. *The New York Review of Books* 38:24–29.

Schneider, Ben Ross. 1991. Brazil Under Collor: Anatomy of a crisis. *World Policy Journal* 8:321–347.

UNECLAC Review. 1995. Santiago, Chile, August.

About the Editor
and Contributors

Robert E. Biles is Professor of Political Science at Sam Houston State University. A Fulbright Scholar and Visiting Professor at the Universidad de los Andes in Bogotá, Colombia, and the Pontificia Universidad Católica del Ecuador in Quito, he has published *Inter-American Relations: The Latin American Perspective* and articles and chapters on Ecuador and Colombia in both English and Spanish.

Jan Knippers Black is a professor in the Graduate School of International Policy Studies at the Monterey Institute of International Studies in California and a Senior Associate member at Saint Antony's College, Oxford. Previously she has served as Research Professor of Public Administration at the University of New Mexico and as Senior Research Scientist and Chair of the Latin American research team in the Foreign Area Studies Division of American University. She has authored, coauthored, or edited ten books and has three forthcoming: *Latin America, Its Problems and Its Promise*, 3rd rev. ed.; *Recycled Rhetoric and Disposable People;* and *Bridging the Gap*, 2nd rev. ed.

Roderic Ai Camp is Professor of Political Science at Tulane University and has taught also at the Colegio de México and the Foreign Service Institute. He has received a Fulbright Fellowship on three occasions, as well as a Howard Heinz Foundation fellowship for research on Mexico. The author of numerous articles and books on Mexico, his most recent publications include *Crossing Swords, Politics and Religion in Mexico, Politics in Mexico, Political Recruitment Across Two Centuries, Mexico,* and *Democracy in Latin America: Patterns and Cycles.*

Jack Child is Professor of Spanish and Latin American Studies, American University, Washington, D.C. Dr. Child was born in Buenos Aires and lived there for eighteen years before coming to the United States (and thus dodging the Argentine army draft). Following graduation from Yale, he entered the U.S. Army and served for twenty years as an Army Latin American Specialist until his retirement as a lieutenant colonel. His publications include *The Central American Peace Process, 1983–1991; Antarctica and South American Geopolitics: Frozen Lebensraum;* and *Quarrels Among Neighbors: Geopolitics and Conflict in South America.*

Damián J. Fernández is Associate Professor and Chair of the Department of International Relations at Florida International University. He is the editor of *Cuban Studies Since the Revolution* and the author of chapters and articles on Cuban politics and foreign policy. At present he is completing a book-length manuscript tentatively titled *Cuba and the Politics of Passion* and is coediting a volume titled *The Elusive Nation: Rethinking Cuban National Identity.*

Kathryn Hochstetler is Assistant Professor of Comparative Environmental Politics at Colorado State University. She is the author of several articles on social movements, political participation, and environmental politics in Brazil and Venezuela.

Philip Kelly, editor of this volume, is Professor of Political Science and Chair of Social Sciences, Emporia (Kansas) State University. A Fulbright Scholar in Paraguay and former president and present secretary-treasurer of the Midwest Association of Latin American Studies, he has administered in part or entirely the Fitzgibbon democracy survey since 1985. His books include *Checkerboards and Shatterbelts: Geopolitics of South America* and *Geopolitics of the Southern Cone and Antarctica* (with Jack Child), in addition to chapters and articles on democracy and geopolitics in English, Spanish, and Portuguese.

Thomas M. Leonard is Distinguished Professor and Director of the International Studies Program at the University of North Florida. He has authored seven books, the most recent being *Guide to Archival Material in the United States on Central America.* He served as a Fulbright lecturer at the Instituto Juan XXIII in Bahía Blanca, Argentina, and at the Institute for Advanced Studies in Guadalajara, Mexico.

John D. Martz is Distinguished Professor of Political Science at the Pennsylvania State University. The most recent of his many books is *The Politics of Clientelism in Colombia.* Since 1989 he has been editor of *Studies in Comparative International Development*, and in earlier years was editor of *Latin American Research Review.*

Ronald H. McDonald is Professor of Political Science at the Maxwell School, Syracuse University, and former chair of the department. He is the author of *Party Systems and Elections in Latin America* and coauthor of *Party Politics and Elections in Latin America* (Westview Press, 1989).

Richard L. Millett is Professor of History at Southern Illinois University at Edwardsville and Senior Advisor for Latin America to Political Risk Services. He has over 100 publications, including *The Restless Caribbean* (coedited with W. Marvin Will) and *Is Latin American Democracy Sustainable?* A Senior Research Associate at the North-South Center, University of Miami, he has testified before Congress on Latin America nineteen times and has made over twenty national television appearances.

Stephen Mumme, Professor of Political Science at Colorado State University since 1983, is a graduate of Arizona State University and the University of Arizona. His current research interests center on environmental politics and policy in Mexico and the Americas. His published work appears in the *Journal of Inter-American Studies and World Affairs, Latin American Research Review, Latin American Perspectives, Journal of Environment and Development, Natural Resources Journal, Environment,* and *Environmental Management,* among other sources.

David J. Myers, with a Ph.D. at UCLA with Russell Fitzgibbon, is Associate Professor of Political Science at the Pennsylvania State University. He has published numerous books and articles, the most recent of which—"Support for Coups in Democratic Political Culture: A Venezuelan Exploration"(1997)—appeared in *Comparative Politics.* He currently is finishing a book on policymaking in Caracas and democratic consolidation.

Martin Needler is Dean of the School of International Studies at the University of the Pacific. He has held teaching positions at Dartmouth, the University of Michigan, and the University of New Mexico and research appointments at Harvard and St. Antony's College, Oxford. His best-known books are *Political Development in Latin America, Understanding Foreign Policy,* and *Politics and Society in Mexico*; most recently he has published *The Concepts of Comparative Politics, Mexican Politics,* 3rd ed., and *Identity, Interest, and Ideology: An Introduction to Politics* (1996).

David Scott Palmer is Professor of Political Science, Professor of International Relations, and Founding Director of the Latin American Studies Program at Boston University. From 1976 to 1988 he served at the Foreign Service Institute of the Department of State as Chairman of Latin American and Caribbean Studies. His published work includes studies of Peruvian politics, military regimes and redemocratization in Latin America, and U.S.-Latin American relations. His most recent book is *Shining Path of Peru*, of which he is editor and contributor.

Robert L. Peterson is Associate Professor of Political Science at the University of Texas at El Paso. He founded and was the first director of the Center for Latin American Studies at that institution. He has also written extensively on Central American political systems, especially those of Guatemala and Honduras, and is currently preparing an extensive survey of social democratic movements in Latin America.

Guy Poitras is Professor of Political Science at Trinity University in San Antonio. He has authored three books on Latin American politics and international relations in Latin America. He has published more than two dozen chapters and articles on Mexico, Central America, and U.S.-Latin American relations.

Charles L. Stansifer has taught Central American history at the University of Kansas since 1964 and has done research in the archives of Nicaragua and Costa Rica. He is author of articles on José Santos Selaya of Nicaragua, the Washington conferences on Central America, U.S.–Central American relations in the nineteenth century, Nicaraguan culture policy, and the Contra War. His annotated bibliography of Costa Rica was published in 1991 in the World Bibliographical Series by ABC-Clio Press.

Thomas Whigham is Associate Professor of History, University of Georgia. He is an exponent of Paraguayan and La Plata history and has published various articles including "The Iron-Works of Ybycui: Paraguayan Industrial Development in the Mid-Nineteenth Century," "Agriculture and the Upper Plata: The Tobacco Trade, 1780–1865" "Cattle Raising in the Argentine Northeast, c. 1750–1870," and "Geopolítica del Paraguay: Vulnerabilidades regionales and propuestas nacionales." His most recent work is *The Politics of River Trade: Tradition and Development in the Upper Plata, 1780–1870*.

Howard J. Wiarda is Professor of Political Science and the Leonard J. Horwitz Professor of Iberian and Latin American Studies at the University of Massachusetts/Amherst. He is also a Senior Associate of the Center for Strategic and International Studies in Washington, D.C., and editor of the Harcourt Brace series New Horizons in Comparative Politics. Professor Wiarda is the author of *Introduction to Comparative Politics, American Foreign Policy, Latin American Politics and Development, Corporatism and Comparative Politics, Politics in Iberia, New Directions in Comparative Politics*, and *Ethnocentrism in Foreign Policy: Can We Understand the Third World?*

W. Marvin Will, Professor of Politics of Latin America and the Caribbean, is past president of the Midwest Association of Latin American Studies. He is a founding member of the Caribbean Studies Association, has authored numerous articles and book chapters, has coedited *The Restless Caribbean: Changing Patterns of International Relations,* and co-contributed (with Jacqueline Braveboy Wagner et al.) to *The Caribbean in the Pacific Century: Prospects for the Caribbean-Pacific Cooperation* (1993). He was awarded a 1991–1992 Fulbright Award to the insular Caribbean and was voted the Political Science Scholar of the Year by the Oklahoma Political Science Association. He has monitored or supervised elections in Grenada, Nicaragua, Guyana, Cambodia, and Bosnia.

Index